Make Money
Selling
Your Shareware

Steven C. Hudgik

Windcrest®/McGraw-Hill

New York San Francisco Washington, D.C. Auckland Bogotá
Caracas Lisbon London Madrid Mexico City Milan
Montreal New Delhi San Juan Singapore
Sydney Tokyo Toronto

NOTICES

ASP	Association of Shareware Professionals
AutoMenu	Magee Enterprises, Inc.
CompuServe	CompuServe, Inc.
dBASE	Ashton-Tate
Fastback	Fifth Generation Systems
Finance Manager II	Hooper International
GEnie	General Electric
GoScript	LaserGo, Inc.
Grab Plus and **ZPay 3**	ZPAY Payroll Systems, Inc.
IBM	International Business Machines Corp.
Lotus and **1-2-3**	Lotus Development Corp.
Norton Utilities	Peter Norton Computing
PC Tools	Central Point Software
PC-File	Jim Button
PC-Write	QuickSoft, Inc.
Pizazz Plus	Application Technologies, Inc.
Play 'n' Learn	H.C.P. Services, Inc.
Book Minder	
Home Insurance	
For Record Collectors	
ORGANIZE! Your Collection	
ProComm	Datastorm Technology
Prodigy	Prodigy Services Co.
ProPak 2.0	
EasyFormat	Falk Data Systems
Quattro	
Quattro Pro	Borland International
Windows	
MS-DOS	Microsoft Corp.
QuickBASIC	
GW-BASIC	
STAR	Shareware Trade Association & Resources
XTree	Executive Systems, Inc.

THIRD EDITION
FIRST PRINTING

Library of Congress Cataloging-in-Publication Data
Hudgik, Steve.
    Make money selling your shareware / by Steve Hudgik.—3rd ed.
      p.   cm.
    Includes index.
    ISBN 0-07-030865-9
    1. Shareware (Computer software)   I. Title.
    QA76.76.S46H82   1994
    005.36'068'8—dc20   93-21367
                                   CIP

The title of the second edition of this book was *Writing and Marketing Shareware*.

Acquisitions Editor: Brad Schepp
Book Editor: Kellie Hagan
Designer: Jaclyn J. Boone
Associate Designer: Brian Allison
Cover Design: Lori E. Schlosser   WP1
Textured paper: Douglas M. Parks, Blue Ridge Summit, Pa.   0308659

Contents

To my family, who has been patient and understanding as I've spent 18 hours a day writing this book and running my shareware business.

Acknowledgments

I've had a lot of help in writing this book, and I appreciate that help very much. This book could not have been completed without the support, cooperation, and assistance of many people.

I want to express my sincere thanks to the over 1,200 shareware authors, distributors, users, BBSs, and magazine editors in five countries who responded to the various surveys I've conducted over the past four years. I would also like to thank the five shareware authors and dealers who allowed me to interview them on the phone for chapter 16 of this book.

Many thanks go to the ASP for establishing a forum on CompuServe where even nonmembers can drop in, "listen" to conversations, ask questions, and learn how to become successful shareware authors.

I would also like to say "thank you" to the shareware dealers and many unknown users who have put up with my experiments with various methods of encouraging the registration of shareware.

Finally, I must thank Jeannine M. E. Klein, who edited the first version of this book and, in the process, taught me a lot about writing. And my thanks to Michelle Gaudreau, who edited this new version and continued to help me improve my writing.

Preface

This is a marketing book. It's a book for Macintosh shareware authors as well as MS-DOS and Windows shareware authors. This book is not about any specific type of programming language or computer platform; it's a business book that will show you how to run a successful shareware business and use shareware to reach your financial goals.

I wrote this book because I believe in shareware. Shareware is the only risk-free way for users to find the software they need. Shareware brings fresh ideas, new approaches, and innovation to software—forcing all software publishers to be more responsive to users' needs. I believe in shareware as a way for small software publishers to get started. In fact, shareware is the only business I know that you can start with very little money and grow into a million-dollar business—sometimes within just a couple of years!

I started writing the first version of this book shortly after I left my job as a client manager for ABB Combustion Engineering in 1990 to become a full-time shareware author. I self-published that version in the spring of 1992. By the fall of that same year, it had expanded by over 50%. Windcrest books published the second edition, which went through two printings, and this newly updated version is the third edition.

In writing this new version, I've updated each chapter where necessary. In general, though, I found most of the information to be good, sound, business advice that hasn't changed with time. I've also added several new chapters including a discussion of selling shareware in retail stores; the results of shareware users surveys I conducted in 1993; and a chapter that profiles five successful shareware companies, including one that sold over a 600,000 dollars of software—based solely on shareware registrations—in their first ten months.

I've tried to provide all the information you need to start a software publishing business. As a result, this book covers a broad range of topics. It's also an excellent summary of how to run a direct marketing business. (Yes, shareware is direct marketing.) But there is more to each topic than I can include here. There are books devoted solely to each of the individual topics: goal setting, advertising, marketing, running a mail-order business, writing software documentation, etc. I hope you keep reading and learning. In running a business, there is always more to learn.

Please don't take what I write here as an absolute set of rules, or even limit yourself to the suggestions I've offered. Business is a dynamic, changing environment. The software business can be even more dynamic than other businesses, and changes happen almost every day. Pay attention to what's happening in your targeted market. Take any software ideas you have and experiment with them. Then build your business around the ideas that best fit your market.

I repeat, this is a marketing book. It covers a wide range of activities that are necessary to get any product or service to the consumer: product design, packaging, advertising, publicity, customer support, telephone etiquette, and much more. Specifically, it covers software marketing.

Marketing rule #1 is "know your market"—because that is where your customers are. Your target market is a specific group of people who need your product or might need it in the future. For example, the target market for tennis balls is people who play tennis. You don't try to sell tennis balls to golfers. For software, the target market for DOS utilities is everyone who has an IBM-compatible computer. The target market for Loran locator software is much smaller—primarily airplane pilots. So remember: know your customers and target them.

What are my qualifications for writing this book? To start, I am a successful full-time shareware author. I have been writing public-domain software since 1983. I have been marketing my software using shareware since 1985. I've written over 45 shareware programs, and the list of software I currently have in circulation includes:

MS-DOS shareware

ORGANIZE! Your Books
ORGANIZE! Your CDs, Albums & Tapes
ORGANIZE! Your Video Tapes
ORGANIZE! Your Stamp Collection
ORGANIZE! Your Sports Cards
ORGANIZE! Your Coin Collection
ORGANIZE! Your Art
ORGANIZE! Your Comic Book Collection
ORGANIZE! Your Home
ORGANIZE! Your Classical Music
ORGANIZE! Your Jazz
ORGANIZE! Your Memorabilia

ORGANIZE! Your Photographs
ORGANIZE! Your Model Railroad
ORGANIZE! Your Gun Collection
ORGANIZE! Your Fabrics & Notions
ORGANIZE! Your Business
ORGANIZE! Your Business - Industrial Version
ORGANIZE! - The Sportman's Pak
ORGANIZE! - Home Improvement Pak
Your Financial Advisor
PC Bartender
Play 'n' Learn
HomeCraft Small Business Journal
HomeCraft's Personal Journal

CP/M public domain

Personal Asset Manager
Home Loan
Holiday Manager
Home Money Manager I and II
Home Insurance

Commercial packages

The Complete Catalog of 45s
The Complete Catalog of U.S. Stamps
The Complete Catalog of Canadian Stamps
ORGANIZE! Your Sports Cards - lite version
ORGANIZE! Your Stamp Collection - lite version
ORGANIZE! Your Home - lite version
ORGANIZE! Your Music - lite version

Although I've written a lot of code, my true strength is in marketing. I read and study business and marketing books. I have been a marketing consultant for the past eight years and have helped several small businesses get their start. I have a Master of Business Administration and a Bachelor of Science in Electrical Engineering, but, more importantly, I have real-life experience—including over 10 years as a Senior Client Manager (sales and marketing) with a Fortune 500 company. I was the top salesman in 1988 with over $20 million in sales, and I received their Flame of Excellence award in 1989.

I have run my own business since I was 12 years old. In high school, while other kids went to parties, I formed a company to provide the music for those parties. I paid for my college education by running several businesses. I can't help it—it's in my blood! I love running a business and making it a success. And although I've made a lot of mistakes along the way, I've learned from them.

Do my qualifications mean this has to be a good book? No. I've read many poorly written and useless books by highly qualified authors. You're the one who will decide whether this book is worthwhile. So I leave it in your hands. You decide. If you don't feel the information in this book is of value to you or if you find some parts useful but disagree with others, please write and tell me what you think. If you feel I've missed important points or if you have a question, please write. If this book gives you the start you need to form a multimillion-dollar corporation—please write. Whatever the situation, I would like to read your comments. My address is:

Steve Hudgik
c/o HCP Services, Inc.
P.O. Box 974
Tualatin, OR 97062

Thank you, and I wish you success!

Introduction

Shareware is exploding. Over 27,000 shareware authors have written more than 100,000 programs. Major software publishers, such as Microsoft and Lotus Corporation, are moving toward the shareware concept by providing copies of their software on the hard disks of new computers and allowing users to try it before they buy it. Users purchase over 40,000 shareware disks every day, and over 20 shareware publishers sell over $1,000,000 of software a year. In 1992, the overall size of the shareware industry exceeded $233,000,000. Shareware, with roots in thousands of companies started around kitchen tables, has become big business. But it remains one of the few businesses you can still start around a kitchen table.

This book will show you how to become a successful shareware author. If you're just starting out and have no business or marketing skills, you'll learn everything you need to know to get started. If you're already running a successful shareware business, you'll find tips and suggestions to help you improve your business.

This is the only book that includes everything you need to know to market software using the shareware method. You'll learn what shareware is, why it works, and how to develop marketable software ideas. On the business side, you'll learn how to price your software, get free publicity, run a home business, handle legal concerns, and get the equipment and supplies you need. You'll find software reviews that might help you select programs useful for running your business. You'll also read the comments and suggestions of shareware authors, disk distributors, shareware users, and magazine editors. Their experiences could reveal proven ways to effectively promote your software using the shareware method.

In every chapter of this book you'll find practical information and real-life examples. This isn't a book filled with theory. It will show you how to combine your programming skills with solid business practices and proven marketing techniques to run a successful software publishing company. It's a step-by-step guide to success.

How this book is organized

This book has eighteen chapters, an appendix, and an included disk. The first four chapters cover the shareware marketing concept and how you can use shareware to sell your software. They include a brief history of shareware, a description of how shareware works, and some suggestions to help you develop ideas for new software. You'll also find out how to set a price for your software and how to encourage users to pay the registration fee.

The next five chapters are about selling and promoting your software. You'll learn that the primary method of promoting shareware is through shareware disk distributors and BBSs, and that retail sales of shareware is rapidly growing. Chapter 5 provides guidelines for sending your software to shareware vendors and BBSs. You'll also learn about advertising, free publicity, and trade shows.

Chapters 10 through 12 provide help with running a home business. These chapters cover everything from postage machines to writing a business plan. You'll learn how to copyright your software, how to protect your trademarks, and what to do about the copyright office's shareware registry.

The next chapter examines techniques for writing good software. You'll find out what users most want in software and determine whether your software is what they want. This chapter provides recommendations for testing your software and designing your distribution disk.

The final four chapters cover a variety of topics that will help you become a successful shareware author. Chapter 15 profiles five successful shareware companies. It describes how they got started and what they did to become successful. An important tool to ensure your success is to be part of a network of shareware authors that can provide support and guidance. Professional associations such as the Shareware Trade Association & Resources (STAR) and the Association of Shareware Professionals provide this network, and are discussed in chapter 14. Chapter 16 presents the results of the most recent shareware industry surveys on which parts of this book are based. Chapter 17 lists other sources of information about running a shareware business, including a directory of suppliers and services.

The included disk provides mailing lists and transcripts from the 1992 Summer Shareware Seminar. The mailing list and transcript files are contained in the self-extracting files MAILLIST.EXE and HSBJSP1.EXE and, when uncompressed, take up a total of 1.5 megabytes of space. Type GO and press Enter to display the information contained in the README.TXT file. If you're using a Macintosh, see the file MAC.TXT.

Becoming a successful shareware author is what this book is about. I hope you enjoy it and I wish you good luck in running your business!

1
Introduction to shareware

When I told my family I was leaving a high-paying job as a senior client manager for a major international corporation to run a computer software company, they looked proud. Then I explained I would be giving my software away to anyone who wanted a copy and relying on their honesty to pay for it. My family clearly thought I was crazy. They didn't say anything, but the looks on their faces said "The crazy fool is putting our grandchildren's future in jeopardy by trusting people to send him money."

What is shareware?

What shareware is all about is letting people try your software before they pay for it and trusting that they will pay for it if they use it.

Shareware is not a type of software; it's a marketing method, a way to let people know about your software. The idea originated with the late Andrew Fluegelman, the founding editor of *PC World* and creator of PC-Talk software.

As a user, you obtain a copy of a program from a shareware dealer for a small copying or handling fee, usually around $3 or $4. Or you might get a copy from a friend or user group, in a retail store, or from an electronic bulletin board. The software you get is fully functional, allowing you to try it, see how well it works, and decide whether it's useful to you. If you continue to use it, you're required to purchase the software by paying a registration fee. Registration fees can be anywhere from a few dollars to several thousand dollars. When you register the software, you usually receive a disk with the most recent version, a printed manual, information about upgrades, access to telephone support, and information about future updates. You might also receive discounts on other software published by the same author, additional utilities, or additional data files for use with the software. This procedure varies with the author and depends on the type of program, purchase price, and other factors.

Shareware is a great deal! I have an eight-foot shelf full of commercial software I purchased in retail stores, half of which I don't use because the programs didn't work correctly or weren't what I needed. For less money than you would spend on gas to drive to a software store, you can "test drive" software programs you think might be useful. You pay for them only if you continue to use them.

Before I go too far, let me define two terms. Software that has a user license that prohibits its copying and sharing is called *retail software*. This terminology is not entirely accurate, as the word *retail* means the sale of goods directly to the ultimate user. However, because most of this type of software is sold through retail stores or mail-order houses, it will do for our purposes. *Shareware* refers to software that can be freely shared among users. Shareware is copyrighted, and the author retains ownership of that copyright. Anyone who continues to use shareware is obligated to purchase the program by paying the registration fee. Remember, shareware is just a marketing method that makes people aware of your software and gives them the opportunity to try it before they buy it. Some better-known programs marketed using the shareware methods include Automenu (Marshall Magee), PC-Write (Bob Wallace), and PC-File (Jim Button).

The following types of software are sometimes distributed along with shareware and sometimes confused with it:

Public-domain software   Some software has been released into the public domain. This means it is not copyrighted and is available for anyone to use without obligation or limits. As an author, if you release software into the public domain, you lose all rights to control the use of that software. To do so, include a statement in your documentation that says "I donate this program to the public domain" and don't include a copyright notice. If you want to give away your software for free, but have any thoughts about possibly converting your software to shareware or retail software in the future, then you should release it as freeware.

Freeware   Freeware programs are copyrighted programs you can use without compensating the author. Like public-domain software, freeware has no registration requirements. However, by copyrighting freeware, the author retains all rights to the program. This allows the author to control distribution and to release new versions in the future that might require a registration payment or even be released as retail software. With freeware, the author generally does not provide support or help.

There used to be significant confusion with the terms *shareware, freeware*, and *public-domain software*. For a time some shareware dealers mixed shareware, freeware, and public-domain software in their libraries and implied that users could "buy" complete programs for from $3 to $6. This problem has almost been eliminated (it still exists in many foreign countries) as a result of user complaints and the efforts of the Association of Shareware Professionals (for more about ASP, see chapter 14).

Demoware   Some shareware dealers and BBSs (bulletin board systems) carry programs that have been written to show the features of a retail software package. These types of programs demonstrate a program without letting you try it yourself. They might also include advertising and are really nothing more than disk-based advertising for software.

Crippleware   This is software with one or more major functions disabled, or software with incomplete documentation. Based on a survey I did of shareware authors, more than 25% of them had crippled their shareware version in some way. This is usually done as an incentive to encourage users to register and get a fully functional program. These authors feel they'll get more registrations this way. Experience has shown me, however, that the opposite is true. I discuss this in detail later in the book.

Olderware   Another approach to shareware is to release an older version of a program and call it shareware. This is not shareware. Shareware should be the most current and fully documented version of the software. You want users to see how good you are, not how good you were.

Does shareware work?

According to a November 1988 *Forbes* magazine article, Bob Wallace of Quicksoft had $2 million in sales and a 5% before-tax profit. But that was a long time ago—what about now? At the end of September 1992, Software Vision Corporation released EnVision Publisher as shareware. By July of 1993, ten months later, they had received more than $600,000 in shareware registrations. Yes, I would say shareware works.

"Our business has enjoyed a tremendous amount of growth over the last year. As a matter of fact, our business sells products other than shareware. For example, we're very heavily involved in commercial software distribution. But I see the shareware as, by far, the highest growth products we have in our line."

— Roger Jones, president of Shareware To-Go

Take a look at the results of the shareware author survey in chapter 16. Survey responses from 18 authors showed sales in excess of $50,000 per year. Yes, shareware works. The example I know the most about, however, is my own. I am a full-time shareware author. I have no other job. Next week's groceries and my children's college education depends on shareware working for me. And it does!

"I think shareware is in an excellent position. More people are standing up and taking notice. If you look in the general PC press you'll see more and more mentions of shareware as people realize how professional the shareware market is. I think shareware is going to take off."

— Marilyn Young, editor of *Shareware Magazine*

Look at this from the other side. Maybe these shareware successes happened because the authors were lucky. They were in the right place at the right time. Maybe EnVision Publisher made it big because it came out at the right time, before anyone else had a shareware desktop publishing program.

I've heard these arguments many times in many different industries. The answer is always the same—luck has nothing to do with it. You make your own luck. Being in the right place at the right time is nothing more than putting yourself in a position where you can take advantage of opportunities as they present themselves. Luck has nothing to do with being successful. Preparation, market research, hard work, and learning everything you can about your industry and target market are the ingredients of success. Add to that the initiative and courage required to start your own business, and you're on the way to the top.

Shareware works, but just like any other business it takes years of hard work. In almost any industry, you'll find that "overnight successes" are actually built on a lot of work, past failures, and a strong background of knowledge.

As I first looked over the shareware author surveys, one characteristic was immediately apparent. The shareware authors getting the most registrations seem to be doing business in a professional manner. On the other hand, many of those getting few registrations seemed to have poor business skills. This is not a quantifiable result because the survey wasn't designed to measure business skills. I offer this only as a personal observation. I saw the distinction most clearly in how the survey questions were answered and in the letters, brochures, and shareware disks some authors included with their survey responses. This book is designed to solve this problem by providing a complete shareware publishing guide in a single volume.

An important point to remember is that shareware is not a way to get rich off of trivial or unprofessional software. Your software must be as good or better than retail software. People won't pay a registration fee because you put a lot of work into your software or because you're a nice person. Your software must be useful and provide value. You don't buy a new car because GM spent a lot of time designing it and would really like you to buy it so they can make some money. You buy a car because you feel it provides you with something (transportation, image, or whatever) that has value equal to or greater than what you pay for that car. It's no different for software, but it's tougher for shareware authors than for car dealers or retail software publishers.

I say it's tougher for shareware authors because potential customers get to see and use what they're buying before they pay for it. The software has to be good. Much retail software is sold based on advertising claims and packaging. Only after you purchase the software do you find out about limits on certain functions, incompatibilities with other hardware and software, and other disappointments. As I've already mentioned, I have a shelf of retail software and use less than half of it because of these reasons. That is a lot of wasted money.

Shareware can provide you with what you want to achieve—if you create a quality program that people want and if you're willing to put the necessary effort into your software and your business. Many shareware authors run their business as a hobby and don't expect big returns. That's fine and that person is a great success if he or she receives 10 registrations a year. Success lies in achieving the goals you've set for yourself, not in how much money you make.

"Love, not money, drives the industry" is a quotation from an article called "Cheap Software" in the September 1989 issue of *Compute!* magazine. If you write software and market it using shareware just for pure enjoyment—go ahead, have fun! Enjoy yourself. If you want a good income from shareware, however, expect to put in a lot of hard work. Some programs are so well written and so useful that they sell with little marketing effort, but these are the exceptions. Don't count on this happening with your software.

Why publish your software as shareware?

What are the advantages of shareware for a small software publisher/ author? Shareware is not a small industry. Over 100,000 shareware programs are in circulation, and more are released every day. I have over 3,000 authors on my mailing list. They range from corporations with 60 employees to people working by themselves in an upstairs bedroom. Most shareware is written and published by individuals working alone in their homes, part time. They have no advertising budget, marketing staff, or fancy packaging. For these authors, shareware is the only option they have for selling their software. They might have a good product, but the cost of selling it through traditional retail channels is prohibitive.

To understand how prohibitive it can be, look at what's involved in selling retail software. It has to have packaging that looks sharp to catch a shopper's eye and a distributor's interest. Retail software needs advertising to make dealers and users aware that it's available. Retail software needs to get onto dealers' shelves and be accepted by distributors. All of this is called *marketing*, and it's very expensive. With advertising costs running over $25,000 per page in some cases, even a limited marketing effort can cost a lot. Plus, distributors won't touch a product unless it already has a large demand and is backed by a strong advertising campaign. Consider the following advantages to publishing your own shareware:

Cost

Shareware can cost as little or as much to market as you want to spend. Some authors just upload their program to one or two bulletin board services (BBSs) or send copies to five or six mail-order shareware dealers. The total marketing cost is $9 or $10. This is a marketing budget anyone can afford. If you're serious about making a profit, I don't recommend such a limited marketing effort, but with shareware you can get started by spending almost nothing.

Specialized products

Shareware is the perfect way to sell specialized, hard-to-find products. My user surveys found that one of the aspects of shareware that users like is that they can find specialized software available nowhere else.

Many shareware programs have a very limited market. One of my shareware programs is a good example of this. I offer a specialized database for cataloging tokens. Not many people collect tokens, and there's no way a retail store can carry a program like this. However, in a shareware catalog, this program might take just one additional line to list it, allowing shareware dealers to carry it and make a profit selling it.

Control

With shareware, you have control of your product. No one else can tell you to make changes. No banks or investors (who usually supply the marketing money) are putting conditions on your product. You make your software as you like it, package it the way you like, and take orders from no one. Of course, if you want to be successful and make shareware more than a hobby, you had better listen to your customers and your market. They will always be your boss and will ultimately determine the extent of your success.

No fuss

Shareware makes life easier. I first started writing and selling software in the days of CP/M machines. I didn't know about shareware, and I sold my software through small ads in magazines. My software received good reviews, and I sold enough to pay for my computer, which was the extent of my goals at that time. But I was always worried about people making unauthorized copies of my software. I knew it was happening because I would get calls from users whose names I didn't recognize. (I knew nearly all my users by name back then.) They were stealing my software and I felt victimized.

Releasing your software as shareware immediately eliminates that problem. Anyone can get a copy essentially for free. No one can steal something from you that you're willing to give them. It's great—no more worries about piracy! Of course, if you need something to worry about, you can worry about all those people using your shareware who haven't paid the registration fee.

Some people will use software without paying for it. They "borrow" it from friends or get it from dealers who put "free" copies on a hard disk when they sell a computer. If people are going to use software without paying for it, either intentionally or because they don't know they should be buying their own copy, there's nothing you can do to stop them. Based on my experience, however, most people are honest and want to do the right thing. By most people, I mean over 90%. If you provide software with value and make the user aware that your software is shareware that must be paid for, they will eventually pay for it.

Small scale

As a small company just getting started, you don't have the money to create a national marketing campaign that'll make large numbers of people aware of your product. With shareware, however, if you've created a good program, disk distributors and BBSs will make your software known around the world. Why is this important? Because many publishers now look to the shareware industry for new software products. By finding products in shareware that they can convert to retail packages, they're getting market-tested and proven software that they can quickly turn into a retail product. If they had to develop the software themselves, it might take a year or more. By licensing existing shareware, they can have a new product out in just a couple of months.

Eliminating bad sales

With any type of product, there are good sales and bad sales. Good sales are made to customers who buy, like, and use your product. It's what they need, and if they're pleased they'll spread the good word.

A bad sale is when you sell to customers who don't fit your application. If they buy your product, you might have to take it back or else they'll be unhappy and will tell other people. It's like fitting a square peg in a round hole.

Bad sales can waste a lot of your time. You can spend time on product support trying to help a user get your software to do something it wasn't designed to do. You can spend time answering questions, maybe doing some custom programming to try to keep a user happy. Sometimes the user will call or write and verbally abuse you. (I've been through it all.) You don't need bad sales. No software is perfect for everyone, and with shareware you eliminate users who aren't a good fit for your product before you get mired in problems and complaints.

Shareware vs. retail software

Yes, shareware has many advantages over retail software—so many advantages that many retail software publishers are starting to market their software using shareware. VP-Info, which has sold over 50,000 copies worldwide as retail software, has been upgraded and released as shareware. Some software publishers are taking a slightly different approach: the June 21, 1993 issue of *U.S. News & World Report* included an announcement about Computer Associates' new home-accounting software. The first 1,000,000 people who called their 800 number would receive a free copy of the software. Callers had to pay only a $6.95 shipping fee. Computer Associates has gone one step beyond shareware. They're not interested in selling the program; they want build their user base and sell updates. And users want to buy updates, as you'll see in chapter 4.

IBM is even becoming a shareware-like company, The July 26, 1993 issue of *Information Week* announced that IBM will be producing a CD-ROM called the CD-ROM Showcase. Quoting from the article, the CD-ROM Showcase will contain "copies of popular desktop applications that customers can evaluate in their home or office." If a customer likes a program and decides to purchase it, he just calls the publisher and purchases a copy. Software publishers such as Borland, Lotus Development, and Knowledgware have software on the CD-ROM Showcase. Although I haven't seen a copy of it, it sounds a lot like shareware to me.

So big companies are starting to discover that shareware works. It's the one method of software marketing that provides opportunities for both small and large companies to become successful. Over 20 individuals have started shareware companies that now have over one million dollars in sales. I know shareware authors who have used their shareware profits to pay for a beach house—with cash. There's no better way for you to get started as a software publisher.

Macintosh authors

This is a business book. It doesn't matter what computer platform you work on; the same key principles of success apply. Although this book is written from the point of view of the majority of shareware authors, everything I discuss also applies to Macintosh shareware. All the reasons for using shareware to market your software apply in the Mac market. Although the market is smaller and Macintosh shareware authors currently have only about 15% of the sales of comparable MS-DOS shareware authors (about the same ratio as the number of Macs to the number of IBM-compatible computers), Mac software is one of the fastest growing areas in the software industry.

2
Making money with shareware

What does it take to be successful with shareware? First you have to define what you mean by successful. What are your goals? Do you want to get rich? Do you want to write programs and play with your computer? Do you want to help people? Do you want just enough extra money to buy a new computer or maybe a big-screen TV? Do you want to learn more about computers? Do you want to learn more about business? Do you want recognition? Do you want to run your own business?

Or possibly you aren't sure what your goals are. These are all acceptable questions, and I'm sure there are many more. All of them can be answered using the shareware method of marketing software. But first you have to decide what you want and the direction you want your shareware business to go.

What type of business do you want?

Some shareware authors feel they have a good idea and they put all they have into it. They quit their job, do market research, create a program, buy advertising, and design a great looking four-color package. They blanket BBSs, user groups, and distributors with copies of their program. They travel the country visiting magazine editors, talking at user-group meetings, and attending trade shows. Several shareware companies have done this, but it's a tough way to start.

Other authors, taking a more conservative approach, write a good program in their spare time and upload it to one or two bulletin boards. They might have photocopied manuals and technical support only by mail because they still need to spend most of their time working at a "regular" job. A couple of years ago, I read a review in *PC Magazine* that highly recommended a shareware utility program. It also mentioned that this shareware program's author didn't take phone calls or answer mail. He shipped registered copies of his software only once a month. If you wanted to buy a copy, you had to be patient. How you run your business depends on what you want to get out of it.

If you're going to approach writing software as a hobby, you still need to release only quality software. Even though you might not be trying to make money, your reputation will be based on the quality of your software and documentation. Releasing a poor-quality program does nothing to help users; all it does is hurt you. In the end, all that you accomplish is to ruin your future as a software author. Although this book is for authors who want to make money marketing their software as shareware, beginners should follow the same guidelines for producing quality, nontrivial, and thoroughly tested software.

Marketing versus programming

The more financially successful you want to be, the more time, effort, and money you'll have to put into marketing. Shareware is one of the few businesses that allow you to put your time into whatever aspect of your business you want. You can put as much or as little effort into it as you like. However, don't expect big dollar returns for a little effort.

Goals

A common approach is to start with only a few goals in mind. Most books on business say you must have clear goals in your mind and a business plan in your hand. This is great and is the theoretical ideal. However, most people don't know *exactly* what they want until they've gained some experience. With shareware, you can start small and build your business along the direction you would like it to take.

I'm not saying you should start with no goals in mind. What I *am* saying is that your first goal can be to just get your business started. I've met many people who have had great ideas that someone else turned into a money-making venture. These people never got started.

"The best way to learn how to run a software company is to do it."
— Bob Wallace

One possible sequence of goals and actions for a shareware company might be as follows:

1. Write a quality, useful program that is not trivial. (This is your first goal.) For your first program, this could be something for your own personal use. Some people start writing software with no intent of

publishing. Others start with the intention of eventually selling copies of their software and making money from it. By starting with a program you need, you're writing software in which you have some background and that you use every day. If you don't get user registrations, you still have a useful program for yourself.

2. Now that you have a program, your next goal is to have different kinds of people use your program and give you feedback. Show the program to some friends who also need this type of software or upload it to a few local BBSs and ask for people's opinions. Change the program to take into account a wider range of requirements. Fix bugs, make the program easier to use, and add useful features you didn't originally think of.

3. At step three, there are two possible directions you can choose. One is to write software as a hobby. The other is to run a business and make money with the software you've written.

   3A. If you choose to write software as a hobby, your goal is to enjoy using your computer and writing software. This goal requires no further marketing efforts to distribute your software. Just enjoy using and refining it, and any registration payments are an added bonus. (Note that, regardless of the amount of time you put into your shareware, you should always acknowledge registration payments. It's rude not to send, at least, a thank-you note.) The process stops here for you.

   3B. If you choose to run a business, you need to test-market your software. Find out whether or not people will pay money for your program. Do this by further improving your program and sending copies to a few shareware distributors and user groups. You should continue to work to identify bugs and make improvements before your program is widely distributed.

4. You again have two possible directions you can take. One direction is a casual approach to marketing software that involves essentially no marketing efforts. The other direction is to run a serious business and work to make a profit from your software.

   4A. For the casual approach, make no further marketing efforts and enjoy a small part-time income. Continue to improve your software (the improvement process never stops). Your goal is to supplement your regular income with a few dollars each year without interfering with your family life or Monday-night football.

   4B. If you intend to start a serious business, improve your program and send copies to as many shareware distributors and bulletin boards as you can find. Start writing a second program. Your goal is to start building a revenue stream that can be used to fund further expansion.

Figure 2-1 summarizes these steps. As you can see, your business can

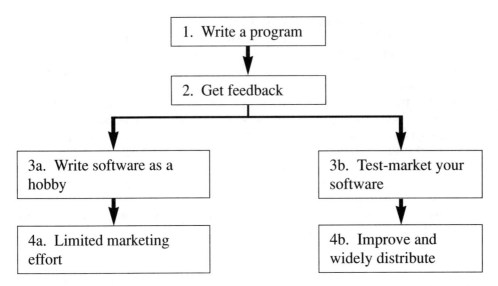

2-1 Shareware can develop into a hobby or a professional business, depending on the direction you want it to take.

go in the direction you want, moving one small step at a time. You can change your goals as you progress. At each step, you'll learn more about the direction toward which you're moving and whether or not you'll want to continue or get out of the software business.

Success requires marketing

If you're working toward expanding your business, increasing your sales (registrations), and increasing your income, you'll find that most of your efforts will go into marketing. As the author of 45 shareware programs, I've written a lot of code, yet I spend only about 10% of my time writing programs. I spend the rest of my time on marketing. This includes writing press releases, designing promotional material, taking orders, answering technical questions, and updating mailing lists. An interview with *Shooting Industry Magazine* (about my software called ORGANIZE! Your Gun Collection) was conducted in the middle of writing this paragraph—more marketing.

If you want a successful shareware business and you like writing code but have little interest in the marketing side, you might want to form a partnership with someone who knows marketing. However, be sure you put together a written agreement stating what each party will contribute and how earnings will be split. Even between friends, a business relationship should always be established in writing. It has nothing to do with trust. It's simply a good business practice. At a minimum, the agreement should cover how profits and losses will be split, what happens if one partner leaves the business, and what each partner will contribute (e.g., program code, writing a manual, graphic design, advertising). Although most people don't want to spend the money, if you're serious about your business you should have a lawyer write the agreement.

Using distributors

Another approach is to find a distributor who will do the marketing for you. For example, some shareware distributors will sell registered copies for you. If you feel you have enough volume to support it, you can even hire an outside service to handle printing and packaging, allowing you to also avoid this aspect of marketing. However, paying other people to handle marketing for you will cut your profits significantly. For example, a shareware distributor might require a 60% or higher discount off the selling price of your software. If this is what you want, it will free you to do what you enjoy—programming.

Maybe you think that all you need to do is sell your program to one of the major retail software publishers and then sit back and watch the royalty payments come in. They handle the publishing and marketing; all you have to do is write the code! I'm sorry, but until you've created a program with an established sales record in shareware, this is probably just a dream. It doesn't happen. Most software released by major publishers is written by their in-house staff. If a software publisher buys a program from the outside, it will either be an established product from another publisher or a successful shareware program that already has a proven sales record. Although shareware has become a route you can take to get your software published, publishers are generally not interested in taking a chance on an unproven product.

Time

The steps I previously outlined as a possible way to get started in shareware take time. The length of time depends on how much effort you put into each step.

Step 1 is getting your program and documentation written. How long this step takes depends on the size of your program and how fast you write code.

For step 2, testing and getting feedback, you could spend six months to a year from when you first issue your software until you work out all the bugs. On a small- or no-budget basis, it also takes six months to a year to evaluate the market, get feedback on your software, and make changes in response to that feedback.

Steps three and four depend on the direction you set for your business. You might spend anywhere from a few days to several years working at these steps.

The difference between shareware and retail software

I briefly discussed the retail channel for selling software in the previous chapter. Now I'll go into more detail about marketing software through the retail channel and how it compares to shareware as a primary marketing tool.

The retail channel introduces several steps between you and the final user. For example, you might sell your software to a distributor. The distributor sells it to a retailer. The retailer sells it to the end user. Each person in this chain needs to make a profit, so they all have to add a markup sufficient to pay their costs and generate a profit. Few businesses can operate with markups less than 40%, and markups of 100% or more are common. Although the next chapter deals with pricing, let's quickly look at an example.

Dealer/distributor discounts

Assume you have a program you sell at a list price of $100. A typical dealer discount would be 40%. Thus, you would sell this program to a dealer for $60. The dealer sells the software for $100, which is a 67% markup on the $60 price paid to you (the dealer's $40 markup divided by the $60 dealer cost). If you sell your software through a distributor, you need to discount it further to allow the distributor to make a profit. A 60% to 80% discount is typical. You might sell your software to the distributor for $30. The distributor sells it to the dealer for $60, a 100% markup. The dealer then gets a 67% markup when the software sells to the end user for $100.

Please note that discount percentages will vary depending on factors such as type of software, price, and volume. The point is that your returns are much lower because of the middlemen. The benefits of middlemen are that you can have dramatically greater sales with less effort.

Regardless of how you distribute your software, you have to find a way to make potential users aware of it. If they don't know about your software, they can't buy it. With shareware, you make people aware of your product by sharing copies. With retail software, you have to advertise.

Advertising

Advertising is very expensive. You can spend a lot of money quickly. Even the small ads in the back of a computer magazine can cost $400 to $500 per column inch. Small ads are usually measured in column inches. A column inch is a space the width of one column that's one inch high. To be effective, you need to run an ad for at least three consecutive months. With most magazine's two-inch minimum size requirement, you're looking at spending at least $2400 to $3000. This is the lowest cost for you to get started using a classified ad in a major computer publication such as *PC Magazine*. Using the shareware approach, you can start with any level of financial commitment. For the cost of running one small ad for one month, you can send your disk to over 250 shareware dealers.

Inventory

Another big disadvantage of the retail software method is that you must manufacture and deliver a significant quantity of software to distributors before you get paid. And you still might not get paid until they sell it. You could find yourself making several thousand copies of your software and having it sit on distributor's shelves. And the scenario could get worse— you might find a major bug. Now you have several thousand copies of your software somewhere in the retail channel, all with a bug that will create bad feelings among your users and tie up your phone with product support calls.

With shareware, you can produce what you need as you need it. If you want to start on a small scale, you can photocopy your manual as you receive registration payments. It's the ideal system of just-in-time inventory management. Shareware also has another advantage. It allows you to be much more responsive to the market.

Niche markets

With shareware, you can identify niche markets or market trends and respond to them faster than retail software companies. Big retail companies take time to make decisions, both on what to do and how to do it. With the large dollar commitment they must make to advertising, inventory, and other marketing costs, a mistake would be expensive. As a shareware author, your risk is less and you can move faster. For example, I can come up with an idea to improve my software this morning, write the code by 10 A.M., test and debug it by 1 P.M., write an addendum to the manual, and have the upgraded version ready for my 3:30 P.M. UPS pickup.

Some people have identified Windows, OS/2, and Macintosh as big potential markets into which shareware can explode. While the sales of retail DOS programs have been steadily declining, the sales of Windows and Macintosh software are rapidly increasing. In shareware, these are areas in which there are still many opportunities for new programs and conversions of existing DOS applications.

A good example of a niche market that shareware authors recently filled is virus checkers. Virus checkers first came out as shareware, with several achieving significant financial success. Now, as viruses have gained widespread publicity, the demand for virus checkers is growing. As the market grows, it attracts the attention of retail software publishers. In this case, shareware publishers are already established with both brand-name recognition and a quality reputation. A rule of business that Lotus, Microsoft, WordPerfect, and their competitors all know is that it's almost impossible to dislodge a company that has the top position. Thus, if you can find a niche, establish yourself, and gain significant market share, you have a tremendous advantage.

Shareware is also ideal for niche markets that are too small to attract the attention of retail companies. Retailers can offer only software that sells in volume. The typical examples are word processing, spreadsheets, utilities, and games. To stay profitable, they must turn over their inventory, meaning they cannot have software sitting on the shelf—it must sell and be replaced by new inventory. For example, the software I market as shareware is specialized database software for cataloging collections. There aren't enough serious collectors in any one area to provide a large enough volume to make it worthwhile for a dealer to stock my software (although I do get a lot of special orders from dealers).

Dealers can't afford to carry a program that isn't well known and already a big seller. You might write the best word-processing program that has even been written. But if you don't have a recognizable brand name and if no one knows who you are, dealers won't touch your program. Shareware provides an opportunity for good programs to sell without having big marketing budgets behind them. It gives you the opportunity to build your brand-name recognition, and a reputation for quality and service.

Marketing your software using the shareware method doesn't mean you should avoid the retail channel. As shareware becomes more successful, programs such as Automenu, By Design, Procomm, and PC-Write have made it onto retail shelves. Many others are being released as *low-cost retail* (LCR) software sold on racks through mass-merchandising stores such as K-Mart. And major shareware companies such as OSCS (QuikMenu) and Hooper International, Inc. (Finance Manager II) continue to expand as they aggressively move into the retail channel. On the other hand, XTree is one of the companies that includes shareware as a part of their marketing mix, in addition to retail.

Shareware profitability

"My personal opinion is that about 85% of U.S. users won't register."
— Jim Hood, author of PC-LEARN and The $hareware Marketing $ystem

"Probably only 1 in 10 people using the software will register it."
— Shareware author survey response

According to several magazine articles I've read, some shareware authors estimate that more than 80% of the people using their programs have not paid the registration fee. Some responses from my shareware author survey also state the same thing. Although there's no way to quantitatively test the validity of these statements, the recent success of some shareware authors shows that you can make a lot of money selling shareware. In chapter 16 you'll read about three shareware companies—all with sales in the six- or seven-figure range, and one that had over $600,000 in sales during just its first ten months. The success of these companies and their shareware shows that people *do* register shareware.

My survey of users showed that if you create a quality product people want to use, they will pay to register it. However, the users that responded to my survey might not be typical. My user mailing list was based on people who had requested shareware versions of my software and the software published by another author, and a list of shareware users provided by a shareware disk vendor, user-group memberships, people who responded to my ads in magazines such as *PC Computing* and *PC World*, and a list of names purchased from a shareware dealer. Almost of these users are shareware customers who have already registered at least one shareware program. I wonder whether or not someone would respond to a survey and say "Yes, I use shareware all the time and I don't pay for it."

An interesting result of my user survey is that some users reported it might take up to two years from when they obtain shareware until when they pay the registration fee. Many people pick up shareware disks that appear interesting and then let them sit until they have time to look at them. With disks selling for as low as 99 cents from some shareware distributors, users feel it's worth a few bucks to buy disks that look interesting.

My opinion on user registrations

My personal opinion, based on my experience as a shareware author, is that users do pay the registration fee. Let's look at an example of a program marketed as shareware that might be expected to get few registrations. My surveys show that shareware dealers and authors feel that business programs get the most registrations and games the fewest, unless the game is published as a part of a trilogy. I publish a disk of games for very young children (Play 'n' Learn) that isn't part of a trilogy. Based on conventional wisdom, I should expect few people to purchase this software, yet I received over $7,000 in registrations in 1992. People *do* pay for software they use. One of the biggest shareware authors publishes games exclusively and is very successful.

"I see why most people don't make money from games. They don't put the effort into marketing or into making a quality game."
— Scott Miller, President of Apogee Software

"Make sure you have a good, solid, *useful* program."
— Shareware author survey response

Users will pay for quality software that's useful and provides value to them. Keep in mind that what you think provides value and is useful might not be valuable and useful for most people. Don't overestimate the value and quality of your software. Another possibility is that your shareware might not reach the right people, or there might not be as many people as you think in need of the software you write. Don't overestimate the number of potential users.

As a consultant, I've talked with many authors who have overestimated the quality of their software and the number of potential users. For example, here's a quote from a shareware author with this problem: "I've seen my software on BBSs all over the country, but I've gotten only 18 registrations." If you find yourself in this situation, take some time to find out why you aren't receiving registrations. Check with the BBS operators (or disk distributors) to find out how often your software is downloaded. This will give you a feel for the potential market. If your software is being downloaded frequently, then work to improve it and add features users need.

"Writing a program that meets the needs of a significant number of computer users is not easy."
— Shareware author survey response

Users don't want to buy a dead-end program. It's important to continue to improve. Don't wait to fix bugs. Add new features as users tell you about their needs. One question people frequently ask when they call to buy my software is "Do you issue upgrades, and how do you let users know about them?" Users want software that's kept current, that takes advantage of the features of current hardware, and that grows with them as their needs grow.

Users also need to understand how shareware works. One of the major problems with shareware is that some people mistakenly feel they purchased the software when they purchased a shareware copy. This can be a problem, in particular, when the user has purchased the shareware disk in a retail store. People don't expect to buy something in a store and then have to "pay for it again." Don't get mad at these people. Do your best to help them. Explain how shareware works. You can also help eliminate this problem by joining the Association of Shareware Professionals (ASP). ASP has been very effective in publicizing the shareware concept and in making users aware of how shareware works. (Information on joining ASP is available in chapter 15.)

Two key factors that will affect the number of registrations you receive are your professionalism and your trust in the user. When I talk with other ASP members, they often say that the most important thing they've learned is how to be professional. Being professional means having a quality product, having someone available to answer the phone (or at least having an answering machine), answering your mail in a timely manner, using printed stationery, and never sending out anything printed on a dot-matrix printer.

Trusting your users is important. People like dealing with people they feel they can trust. If you feel that someone doesn't trust you, then you tend not to trust that person. The entire shareware concept is based on trusting users to pay a registration fee. When you cripple or limit your software, you demonstrate that you don't trust users. Your users will then tend not to trust you and you'll get fewer registrations.

"I'm comparing two shareware programs to see which one I should buy and had some questions. When I read the documentation with the program by (name withheld), he sounded very uptight and I didn't want to call him. Your documentation sounded like you'd be someone who'd answer my questions, so I called you."
— Comment made during a phone call to HomeCraft's technical support. The phone call resulted in a sale.

Some people will use your software without paying for it. There's nothing you can do about it. Adding code to restrict your software will only hurt the majority, the ones who pay for software they use. Don't hurt the majority of users in an attempt to block a small minority.

"Perseverance! It takes years to become known and for your product to spread."
— Shareware author survey response

"Don't expect much during the first 9 months to 1 year."
— Shareware author survey response

Typically, the two biggest problems authors have concerning registration payments are a lack of patience and a lack of marketing. Shareware takes patience. It can take a year for a program to get into circulation. While some distributors will add your program to their catalog as soon as they receive it, others might take 6 to 8 months to evaluate it. Once users have your program, they might take anywhere from a week to two years before they look at it. Yes, there have been some programs that have become big hits just a few weeks after they were released. But in most cases it takes much longer. I know it's difficult to hear shareware distributors say they're selling lots of your software when you aren't getting registrations. Give it time. Get all the feedback you can and keep improving your software. When I first released my Book Minder software, I would get reports from PC-SIG showing they were selling 600+ copies every quarter. Yet I was getting only one or two registrations a week and only a few of those were from PC-SIG customers. It took over a year until new registrations were coming in daily, many from PC-SIG customers.

"Marketing is as important as having a good product."
— Shareware author survey response

Not working at marketing is the other major difficulty shareware authors have. My guess is that most shareware authors are typical programmers who know computers, but have no experience in marketing or sales. They don't realize the importance of marketing and don't have the skills needed to properly market their software. Because there have been no resources available, except for the ASP, to show shareware authors the importance of marketing and how to do it, most have not realized how important it is. And, without marketing, the success of any program will be limited.

In this book I provide you with the information you need to successfully market your software using the shareware method and make a profit. The key marketing point to remember from this chapter is that if you're serious about making a profit, you need to put a lot of time into getting your program exposed. Get it reviewed by magazines. Talk about it in front of user groups. Most importantly, get feedback so you can continue to improve it. This is marketing and it's what this book is about.

3
Shareware design

I've used the term *marketing* many times so far. Marketing encompasses a range of functions, including determining what product you want to produce, promoting that product, and getting customer feedback. Marketing is essential to your software's success.

"Programming is only 25%; marketing is the other 75%!"
— Scott Miller, president of Apogee Software

Developing ideas for new software

To start, you need a product—a software program you want to market and sell using shareware as one of your marketing tools. There are several ways to come up with ideas for good, marketable programs. These range from intuition to extensive market research. Although intuition works for some people, it's a poor basis for developing a program you might spend several thousand hours and many late nights working on. If you're going to put that kind of effort into a program, you might want to see whether or not there's a market for it before you start.

Although there are many approaches for identifying good potential products, for shareware authors two stand out. The first approach is one I suggested earlier. Write a program you need or want for yourself. The second approach is to conduct market research to find out what type of software and features other people need.

Write software you need

"Write what you need—make it a labor of love—but listen to users and exchange ideas."
— Shareware author survey response

Write software you need and want. To be successful, it also should be a program with unique features not already available in other software. If you need simple word-processing software, don't write it yourself. Unless you value your time at about ten cents an hour, you're better off buying an existing word-processing package. However, if you need a word processing feature not available in any other software, write the program! This is called *market positioning.*

"Before entering the market, make sure you have a good, solid, useful program."
— Survey response from a shareware author with $50,000 in sales.

Positioning is what makes your product unique and creates its special "personality." It's the reason people will buy your software instead of another program. You could position your product based on its unique features, or as the low price alternative in a market that's served only by high-priced software. Your software might be the only one available in a niche market. A market position I often use is to publish a program that's the only one of its type available as shareware (although competition exists in the retail channel).

Your software is not limited to one position. Look for new opportunities to extend the market for your software, find new niches, take advantage of pricing opportunities, and add new features. You can also do this for software published by others, creating add-on utilities that provide additional functions or make other software easier to use.

Here are some responses from my survey of shareware disk vendors in response to the question "What new software would you like to see available as shareware?"

"More educational software—especially for in-school use."
— Shareware dealer who sells 250 disks per month
"Desktop publishing and more LAN (local-area network) software."
— Shareware dealer who sells 4000 disks per month. This was the most common response to this question.

"GUI (graphical user interface) applications."
— Australian dealer who sells 200 disks per month. Many dealers said Windows applications are needed.

"Point-of-sale inventory programs."

— Shareware dealer who sells over 10,000 disks per month

By the way, these answers are from my 1989 survey of shareware vendors. I did not update these for this new edition because the answers I got to my 1993 shareware vendor survey were the same. The details of the 1993 survey are in chapter 17.

Market research

In lieu of writing software for your own needs and then positioning it in the market, you could hire a market research firm to do the market research for you. Expect the cost to be $30,000 to $50,000. For most shareware companies, however, a more modest, do-it-yourself approach is needed. Actually, you're probably conducting market research continuously and might not know it. It mostly involves paying attention to what other people do and say. Market research involves answering five essential questions:

- Who/what is your market?
- How big is the potential market?
- Is the market computerized and to what degree?
- How many competitors are already in the market?
- How does the competition measure up in price/performance?

I'll cover these market research questions one at a time. Typically, you'll get answers to many of them simultaneously. This is not a step-by-step process.

First identify and describe the market you want to serve. For example, lawyers need to deal with large amounts of information, so a possible new software program might be a database for cataloging case histories and law references. If the author is attending law school and wants to earn a little extra money, this is a good market for him to work in. It's also a good market because it is one with which he is somewhat familiar.

This brings up another important guideline. Don't start by getting into a market you know nothing about. It's not that you can't be successful. The problem is that you'll spend a lot of time learning about the market, the language of the market, and the needs and requirements of the market. Start with a market in which you have some experience.

A good way to identify a target market is to talk with people you know. For example, pay attention to what's going on around you at work and in any groups you're a part of. Talk to as many people as you can, but do more listening than talking. This includes BBSs, as well as face-to-face conversations. Go to user-group meetings. Attend COMDEX or other computer shows to see what other products are available and identify areas other software publishers are missing (see chapter 9). Read a variety of magazines, not just computer magazines. Read newspapers, the *Wall Street Journal*, *U.S. News & World Report*, *Business Week*, trade industry publications, and anything that discusses what people and business are doing.

Look at the industry where you now work. What software would help you and your co-workers? What problems do you have with the software you currently use? Problems are opportunities. Find areas in which people have a problem and solve that problem. This is how the legal student in the previous example probably became aware of the need for case note software.

Sizing the potential market

Once you've identified a market, find out how big that market is. You need to know the market size to decide if it's big enough to support your software and to help determine the price you'll charge. Again, a good way to start is to talk to people. For example, ask them about the size of their user group or special interest group (SIG). Check the circulation figures of specialty magazines that serve the market you're targeting. Talk to representatives from industry trade associations. Don't be afraid to call trade associations (or any other group) and ask for help. Tell them what you're doing and what type of information you need. In nearly every case, they'll be happy to help you.

Continuing with the legal software example, the first step would be to find out how many lawyers there are. An excellent research tool is the Yellow Pages. How many lawyers are listed versus the population covered by that phone book? Then extrapolate from the local numbers to determine the size of the national market. The same approach works for plumbing, real estate, or any other industry.

Computerized markets

For business software, you can find out how computerized your target market is by reading computer publications directed at business users. They sometimes publish statistical information on how many people in a specific industry have computers and how they use them. For a specific industry, telephone editors of industry-specific publications or send them a survey. Not only will it help you research the market, but you'll make contacts that could be useful in publicizing your software in the future.

Talk directly with people in your target market or with other companies that serve it. For example, before I wrote my software For Baseball Card Collectors, I stopped in to visit about half a dozen baseball card shops. I talked with both the owners and customers, and learned a lot about what they needed. If you want to talk to professional people such as managers, make an appointment. You can also use a written survey and send it to all managers of specific companies in your area. How do you find their names? Call and ask for the name of the manager in charge of the area you're targeting.

For software aimed at the home market, talk to people in organizations you participate in such as church, clubs, and especially user groups. Ask people whether or not they find your idea useful. Don't be worried about giving away your ideas. Most people don't have the interest, initiative, or skills to do anything with it. If you're concerned that people might take your idea, ask them to sign a nondisclosure agreement. A nondisclosure agreement is a contract that prevents the signer from using your idea or discussing it with others. Don't expect people with whom you have casual conversations to sign a nondisclosure agreement. It's generally used only for people with whom you have a formal business relationship, such as a marketing consultant or beta testers.

Competitors

Next, learn about your competitors. How many are there? This is fairly easy to determine. Check retail software stores. You'll be competing directly with retail software. You need to study, in detail, the retail software with which you'll be competing. Get demo disks or buy copies of your competition's software. A good, low-cost way to purchase competitor's software is to use a competitive upgrade offer, if there's one available. (Upgrade from your software to your competitor's.) Then study the shareware market. Look through shareware catalogs to find similar programs. If you find software that might compete with yours, buy copies. Also read directories such as *Bowker's Software Encyclopedia* and *Dr. File Finder's Guide To Shareware*. Read computer industry publications.

Find out how your competition measures up in price and performance. To do this, talk to people who use your competitor's software. Ask about it on BBSs and CompuServe or GEnie. If you find people using a competitor's program, ask them how they like it, what good features it has, what problems they've had in trying to use it, what they don't like about it, and what they'd like to change.

"I advise new shareware authors to be very modest in their expectations. Check the competition and market need before beginning."
— Shareware author survey comment

Market research summary

When you're finished asking all these questions and have the answers, comments, and whatever else people have to say, you should have a good idea of what your market is, what its needs are, and whether or not this is a good market for your software. Pay attention to what people say and you'll learn a lot more about the market than just the answers to the questions I have outlined. People like to talk about themselves and what they do. Just give them a chance. Get them started with a few questions and you'll soon be an expert on your targeted market.

Other marketing questions

Based on your market research, you can now design and write your software. As you're doing this, there are additional marketing questions to be answered. What price should you charge? How do you promote your software? Do you want to restrict sales to one country or sell it internationally? The answers to these questions will affect how you design your software.

While writing your software, keep in mind that you should leave open opportunities for multiple marketing approaches to your market. Don't limit yourself just to shareware. Even if you don't intend to use other marketing methods now, leave your options open for the future. For example, many people are reluctant to put an unknown disk into their computers. Especially among novice users, there's a fear that the disk will somehow interfere with the data or programs already on the computer. Some dealers actively recommend that their customers not use shareware because of the virus scare.

There's also a large group of people who don't know that shareware exists. Don't eliminate these people as potential users by limiting your marketing efforts to shareware only.

The early promotion of your software starts with the five marketing questions, listed previously in this chapter, even before you decide what your market is and what software you want to publish. I don't mean you should buy ads or send out press releases before you know what your product is. The process of answering the five marketing questions begins to develop name recognition for yourself and a demand for your software. Anytime you talk about your software, you promote it.

"Create the first version of a product yourself before starting the business, distribution, or financing. Then grow the product, business, and distribution."
— Bob Wallace, author of PC-Write:

Once you have a product and are ready to offer it for sale to the public, you need to decide what price to set.

Pricing your software

"Shareware authors can increase registrations by offering quality software at low prices."
— Shareware dealer

"There's a large market out there. Low price encourages volume."
— Survey response from a shareware author

Shareware dealers want shareware registration prices to be low. Magazines tout shareware as a way to get low-cost software. Some authors say you have to have a low price to get registrations. Does this mean you should price your software at as low a price as possible? No!

These people have different perspectives and reasons for wanting registration fees to be low. Low prices get people's attention. Disk distributors and magazines like to see low registration prices because it helps sell more disks and magazines. But why would an author say that low registration prices are the way to go?

Many people believe that the lower they price something, the more of it they'll sell and the more money they'll make. In fact, many times the opposite is true for software. Sometimes the sales volume goes up when you increase your price. Yet, if you set too high a price, you could see your sales go to zero. Finding the right price is one of the most difficult problems facing anyone who has a product to sell.

"Don't underprice."
— Common survey response from successful shareware authors

The price you set depends on the type of software, who your market is, the quantity you expect to sell, your product's reputation and image, and the competition. The price you set also depends on how you want to run your business. Is it a hobby or does it need to make enough to pay the mortgage? Notice that I didn't include product manufacturing costs as a component in developing the price. The correct price for your software has nothing to do with what it costs you to make it. Users don't buy software based on the costs to make it; they buy software based on the value it provides them.

Before you start to think about what price to charge for your software, keep one important rule in mind: It's easier to introduce a program at a higher price and come down if necessary than to start at a low price and move up. If you introduce a product at a low price and later increase the price with no change in features, people will think you're taking advantage of them. If you introduce a product at a high price and then reduce it, people will feel like they're getting a bargain. Keep in mind that shareware stays in circulation forever. If you start with a low price, you'll be dealing with people who want to register at that low price for the next ten years. The best approach is to thoroughly study the market. Find out how your competition has priced its software and set your price based on how you feel your software compares with the competition. Try to provide a better quality program at a slightly lower price than the competition.

If you feel you must have a low price to enter the market, identify the price as introductory and available for a limited time. The time period can be anywhere from a few months to a year. For shareware, because it takes a long time to get to users, I would recommend a year. At the end of the year you can reevaluate your price and make changes without damage to your product's image.

Look at prices of other software

Some authors purposely underprice their applications in an effort to lure customers away from established competitors. It doesn't always work. Knowledgeable users might notice the small registration fee and dismiss your program without first testing it. Consider the following advice, given by Rob Rosenberger of Barn Owl Software, regarding pricing a shareware program:

- If your product performs *better than* the competition, consider charging two-thirds of the general retail list price;
- If it performs *as well as* its rivals, you probably want to offer it at half the going rate;
- If *slightly less powerful*, consider charging a third of the retail price for similar applications.

To set a price for your software, first look at your market and the pricing of other software in that market. If you're publishing business software, a price in the $60+ range is reasonable. Business software priced under $25 will typically be ignored as too cheap to be useful in business. It has nothing to do with quality of your software. This image is created because business users are used to paying $60 or more to get software that provides the functions and power they need. In a different market, such as educational games, $35 might be the top price you can get, and $15–$25 is a good average price range.

How do you determine the price range your target market finds acceptable? First look at the prices of other software that your targeted market purchases. Browse the shelves of retail software stores. Find out what competitive upgrades cost, because many times that sets the real price of the software. Read catalogs and mail-order advertisements in magazines. Check the registration prices of other shareware. Join STAR and ASP and talk with other authors who publish software for the same market. You want to determine both their registration prices and whether or not they're getting any registrations. Don't price your software based on programs that aren't selling! (For more information on pricing, see chapter 17.)

When discussing your software, ask questions of STAR or ASP members and other software publishers. Be honest about what you're doing and the type of software you're publishing. If you're planning to publish a spelling checker, don't go to authors of other spelling checkers and tell them you're writing a word processor. When you're eventually found out, your access to feedback and help will be cut off as your reputation in the industry drops below sea level. Be honest and complete in the description of your software. Give other authors and publishers the option of deciding for themselves whether or not to help you, especially if you're a direct competitor. Try to find software authors who serve the same market you're targeting but who have different products.

Estimate annual sales

Once you know the price range that's typical for your target market, estimate the volume you expect to sell in your first year. This can be tough to determine. Many people overestimate sales for the first year. It's easy to feel that, because you need the software you've created, everyone will need your software. Base the estimate on your market research, as discussed earlier.

As an example, my first big-selling program was software for cataloging record collections (LPs, CDs, cassettes, etc.). I looked at the subscriber base of the largest publication for collectors at the time, *Goldmine Magazine*, and came up with 7,000 record collectors as a starting number. At the time, 10% of the homes in the U.S. had computers, so this gave me an estimated starting base of 700 record collectors with computers. I also added to my figures 7,000 radio stations with record libraries, about half of which were computerized. Having talked with many collectors at record conventions, I estimated that about 10% of the record collectors with computers would be interested in my software. This gave me an estimated first year sales of 70 programs, plus whatever I could sell to radio stations.

At the time, the only way you could get software comparable to what I offered was to buy dBASE, or a similar program, for about $400 and write it yourself. There was no established software serving this market that I could use for comparison. Figuring I needed about $7,000 in sales the first year, I set my original price at $129.95.

After I sold a few copies and talked with more potential users, I discovered I had defined my market incorrectly. My market was the home user. Software costing more than $100 was too expensive for general home use. The $30–$70 range was typical for home-use software. Within three months I reduced the price to $59.95, where it remained for four years. To be fair to the users who had purchased the software for $129.95, I gave refunds for the $70 difference. At the end of my first year, I had total sales of over $16,000—exceeding my $7,000 goal by $9,000.

Leave yourself a way out

This example illustrates several important points about pricing. First, don't make fixed pricing or marketing decisions. Remain flexible and make adjustments as you learn more about your market. Second, in many cases setting a price is based on trial and error. Always leave yourself a way out of a pricing decision. You can always justify a price reduction by saying a higher-than-expected volume allowed you to decrease the price. It's almost impossible to increase your price without releasing a completely new version of your software.

Notice that, in the earlier example, I set my price at the higher end of the home market price range. If you think there's a chance you might want to sell your software through dealers and distributors, remember that they require discounts of 40–60%, and sometimes higher. If you price your software too low, neither you nor the dealer can make enough money for it to be worthwhile to sell through the retail channel. And you'll be passing up the high-volume benefits of this marketing channel.

Look at software prices in your market

Base your pricing structure on the type of software you're selling, as well as the type of market to which you're selling. You can't sell a small utility for $100 nor a spreadsheet for $10. Both will be ignored. Conduct a pricing survey. Check retail stores, catalogs, advertisements, and other shareware to determine the price range of your software. There should be an overlap between the price range determined from your market survey and the price range based on the type of software you're selling. If there isn't an overlap, you've either found a marketing opportunity or are trying to sell software in the wrong market.

Reputation has value

Another factor that effects price is reputation and brand-name recognition. WordPerfect Corporation can charge a high price for a software product because of its reputation for a quality product and customer support. In most cases, brand-name recognition won't be a factor in the pricing of shareware, except for the larger shareware publishers.

Competition

If no competition exists, you can charge a higher price. Having no competition allowed me to go to the upper-half of the home software price range for my record collecting software. At the time, I effectively had no competition.

Can you make a profit?

You should now have a rough idea of the price range your market supports. Can you make a profit at this price? Look at your costs. If you're publishing a small utility that sells for $20 and had planned to use a $22 package, you'll soon be out of business. How much profit do you need to make? That depends on your goals. Here is a typical breakdown of software publishing costs:

Product manufacturing costs (disk copying, manuals, etc.)	5–15%
Advertising and promotion	25–50%
Overhead and product development (office supplies, phone, electricity, etc.)	10–20%
Product support	5–15%
Cost of sales	5–20%
Profit	5–25%

Some of the items listed are direct cash expenses, such as product manufacturing costs and advertising. Others, such as product support and possibly cost of sales, require no cash, but use your time. What is your time worth? How much time are you willing to spend on the phone explaining your software to a potential customer? If you charge $10 for your software, you might not want to spend much time with potential customers. If you charge $500, a couple of hours on the phone per sale isn't too bad. Estimate both your direct cash expenses and the amount of time you need to put into your software. Then determine whether or not the price range, market, and type of software will provide you with an acceptable profit.

Many people expect shareware to be inexpensive. It's true that if you market your software from your home using just the shareware method, your overhead costs will be less than a retail software publisher's. You won't have big marketing expenses or the costs of maintaining an office. However, 87% of shareware authors sell less than $20,000 of software per year. On such a low volume, production and support costs per unit are very high. Don't be fooled into thinking that using shareware for marketing means you must charge a low price. By the time you run down to the print shop to photocopy your manual, copy disks one at time on your computer, and then hand-package and ship each program, it might cost you more per unit for a small utility than it costs Lotus to ship 1-2-3.

The main advantage of shareware's low overhead is that it allows you to start without a lot of cash. If you have a computer, you can start a serious shareware business with less than $1000. Thus, your financial risk in starting a shareware business is very low.

How do other shareware authors price their software?

My survey of shareware authors asked about the registration fees they charged for their software. Table 3-1 provides a summary of the results. I've divided these results into five sections, based on the annual sales reported by each author. Notice that the higher the registration fee, the more successful the author is. A few authors do sell several hundred thousand dollars of software per year and charge less than $25 per program, but they're the exception.

Table 3-1 The results of a 1990 survey of shareware authors show the average registration fees shareware authors charged. Notice that the more successful authors tend to charge more for their software.

Annual sales category	# of authors responding	Avg. annual sales per author	Avg. reg. fee per program
$50,000+	18	$447,920	$58.50
$10,000–$49,999	19	$23,412	$57.50
$2,000–$9,999	67	$4,965	$40.50
$0–$1,999	56	$300	$26.20
Not reported	25	n/a	$59.40

Shipping and handling charges

You should charge extra for shipping and handling. It's considered a normal part of doing business by mail. Because nearly all mail-order purchases require an additional shipping and handling charge, people expect to pay it. When most people look at your price, they won't include the cost of shipping and handling. Thus, a product that sells for $49.95 plus $5 shipping and handling will be seen as less expensive than one selling for $54.95.

When including shipping and handling charges in your documentation, keep it simple. For example, you might say the registration fee is "$49.95 plus $3.00 S&H, $8.00 for air mail outside the U.S." Your order form can then provide additional details such as the costs for expedited next-day air service or second-day air delivery. You might also want to have a lower shipping and handling fee for Canada and Mexico, as air mail within North America is less expensive than shipping a package overseas.

Some authors also charge extra for shipment to post office boxes. I suggest, however, that if you do this you make an exception for APO and FPO addresses. Military personnel don't have the option of using UPS. Since they must use the U.S. mail and an APO or FPO box, I don't feel they should be penalized by paying extra. I favor using the post office over UPS, so this is easy for me to do. I charge $6.00 for UPS ground shipment and $4.00 for shipment via priority mail. The reason is that UPS requires a lot of extra paperwork, the actual shipping cost is higher, and I have to supply a shipping box. With the post office, I can use priority mail and get two-day delivery at a lower cost than UPS ground delivery, and the post office gives me free shipping cartons. UPS does provide free insurance coverage, but I have lost only one priority mail package in the past year. And with the post office, the same $4.00 shipping and handling charge covers my cost of mailing my software to Canada or Mexico.

Tiered pricing

Tiered pricing is when you offer the user several levels of registration. For example, you might charge a base price of $20 to register as a user. Then if the user wants a printed manual, there's an extra $15 charge ($35 total). If the user wants to become registered, get a printed manual, gain access to telephone support, and get the next two updates at no charge, it costs $45. This is three-level, or three-tiered, pricing.

Some authors use a tiered pricing approach because they assume users who might not be able to afford the cost of a manual will still pay the minimum registration fee. My experience has shown, however, that when an author switches from a tiered pricing approach to a single registration fee that includes a manual and support, registrations increase. To maximize your sales, you need to make registration as simple as possible. A tiered pricing approach is complex, and the result is that users procrastinate because they have to make a decision.

Updates and upgrades

What is the difference between an update and an upgrade? An *update* provides a minor modification to a program, generally to fix a bug or provide an enhancement that's necessary for the program to function. An *upgrade* provides major modifications such as new features, expanded capabilities, an improved user interface, or greater speed. The documentation for an upgrade often requires a new manual. Updates might require no documentation changes or be discussed in a READ.ME file.

Updates are usually provided free to users who recently purchased the software. The definition of *recently* can vary from three months to twelve months. (The ASP requires members to fix serious bugs at no charge during at least the first three months after a user pays the registration fee. I recommend having this policy for your software regardless of whether or not you're a member of the ASP.)

My shareware author survey showed that most shareware authors give away upgrades at no charge. However, those who sell their upgrades are finding that they can increase their sales by 10% to 30% as a result. The typical upgrade price varies with the type of software, but it's usually about 15% to 25% of the original cost of the software. One good strategy is to price upgrades high enough to cover your costs plus a small markup, but low enough that the upgrades will be purchased by most of your users. You want most users to purchase the upgrade because it's a pain to support two software versions. You should have some markup in your upgrade price to cover the costs of supporting the installation of those upgrades. Upgrades always cause a surge of product support calls. Whether or not you include a significant profit in your upgrade price depends on your objectives.

From my survey, it appears that most shareware authors are working to build market share and user loyalty. A minimum or no markup on updates is appropriate in this situation. However, I don't recommend that you officially give away free updates. In most cases, the perceived value of a product is based on the price of that product. An update that's free has a low perceived value. An update that costs $10.00, but which people who have registered the shareware version can get free, has a higher perceived value. It's not free, it's worth $10.00.

If you offer free updates as an incentive for people to register, be sure to mention that updates normally cost a certain price. When you mail their update, include a flyer or letter that tells them that the update, which normally costs whatever amount you decided on, is free to say thank you for registering the shareware.

Site licenses

Your software should always include a license that permits the use of your software on only one computer at a time. (I cover user licenses in the legal section of this book.) A site license grants permission to use your software on more than one computer or on a network. With the growing number of networked computers, site licenses are becoming more important. The price of a site license usually varies depending on the number of computers the software will be used on and the terms of the license.

Site license sales are good for you because they bring a high volume of sales with little effort. Site licenses are good for the purchaser because they provide a means to use software on many machines without worrying about copyright infringement. It's also to your benefit to offer a reduced price per copy to encourage users to purchase site licenses and not use your software on multiple machines without your permission.

You can structure a site license so that the purchaser does all disk and manual duplication and provides support. This would be appropriate for an unlimited site license in which the purchaser can use your software on as many computers as desired. Another approach is to sell the purchaser a copy of your manual for each computer on which your software is used. In this case, the purchaser does all disk duplication and product support. A third approach is to provide a complete registered copy of your software at a reduced price for each computer. Each approach requires a different price structure in which you balance your cost of sales with your time requirements.

Pricing site licenses can be difficult because there are many different types of contracts that can be set up. Some of the responses to the site license question on the shareware author survey included:

"I usually charge about $20 per computer."
— Author who publishes a utility with a registration price of $35

"$500 per site, which can be applied as a credit toward other goods and services we offer. Mostly we sell manuals."
— Author with a $130 program

"Site licenses are 50% off per user."
— Author of business software with a registration price of $50

"Same as regular user."
— Author of a $25 utility with $50 of sales in 1989

"Site license fees vary depending on the negotiated contract."
— The most common survey response

A suggestion I can offer as a starting point for site license negotiations is a sliding scale. Start by offering software at your dealer price for the first few copies (1–10 machines), your distributor price for 10–20 additional computers, and then reduce the cost per copy incrementally until you reach 500 copies. Above 500 copies, you might want to charge a flat fee of $3000 or $4000. There are no hard rules for site license pricing. It will vary depending on the type of software, the market, and how badly the customer wants to use your software.

In a competitive bidding situation, you can lose a site license sale if you're priced too high or too low (a price that's too low makes it look like you don't know what you're doing). If you don't know what a good price for a site license should be, go for a higher price. If customers like your software but don't want to pay the price you've set, they'll generally negotiate with you. If a customer tells you that pricing was the reason for not purchasing your site license, while in some cases that might be true, most likely they preferred to purchase another program based on the qualities of that program.

Most of us want to believe that price is the key ingredient in making a sale. In reality, price is secondary. From the buyer's perspective, telling a vendor that he lost the sale because of price is the easy way out for everyone. It's also easier for the vendor to blame the loss of a sale on price (rather than having to face deficiencies or problems with the software). Sometimes sales are lost strictly due to high price, but in most cases businesses buy what they want, not what's cheapest. Here is an example of site licensing pricing, with the program list price being $100:

# of copies	Price level	Total price
1	$100	$100
2–10	$70	$730
11–20	$60	$1330
21–50	$50	$2830
51–200	$40	$8830
201–500	$20	$14,830
501+	$4000 one-time fee	$18,830+

Based on this example, the total price of the site license fees is calculated by totaling the number of copies ordered and filling up each cost level.

Thus, if someone ordered 12 copies of your program, the first copy would be priced at $100 (level 1), the next 9 copies (2–10) would be priced at $70 (level 2), and the last 2 copies (falling in the 11–20 copies range) would be priced at $60 (level 3). So the total cost of a site license fee for 12 copies of your program would be $850:

1 copy at $100 (level 1, 1 copy)	$100
9 copies at $70 each (level 2, 2–10 copies)	$630
2 copies at $60 each (level 3, 11–20 copies)	$120
Total of 12 copies	$850

The total site license cost for 501 copies would be $18,830, as follows:

1 copy at $100 (level 1, 1 copy)	$100
9 copies at $70 each (level 2, 2–10 copies)	$630
10 copies at $60 each (level 3, 11–20 copies)	$600
30 copies at $50 each (level 4, 21–50 copies)	$1500
150 copies at $40 each (level 5, 51–200 copies)	$6000
300 copies at $20 each (level 6, 201–500 copies)	$6000
1 copy at $4000 (level 7, 501+ copies)	$4000
Total of 501 copies	$18,830

Depending on the type of software you sell, the market, the competition, the type of customer, your objectives, and the general economic conditions, the numbers stated in the previous examples can dramatically change. I have shown them only as a typical example. As you gain experience, apply what you learn to improve your pricing of site licenses.

Even a lost sale can be valuable if you learn from it. The most important factor is that you price your software at a level you feel comfortable with. Don't underprice your software to make a sale—you might find that you're unhappy with the sale at a lower price.

Whether or not you provide support for software sold under a site license is a key negotiating point. For example, you don't want to sell an unlimited site license for $500 and then have 2,000 people call you for support. Your initial site license offer should include a contract in which you provide support only for one key contact at the site. That person then supports all the users at the site (see chapter 9 for a sample site license agreement). If a customer demands that you support individual users, I suggest you propose an hourly rate for that support.

OEM pricing

The final pricing topic I want to cover is OEM pricing. OEM is an abbreviation for *original equipment manufacturer*. These are computer manufacturers, many of whom bundle software with their computers. Typically, the computer manufacturer provides disk duplication and manuals and pays a small royalty to the publisher. Manufacturers might even write their own manuals to go with the software they bundle with their computers. The royalty payment will typically be about .5% to 2% of the list price of the software. For you, it's a good deal (pure profit with no effort), but watch out for one hidden danger—product support. Can you afford to support your $50 software package on a $2 royalty payment? Be sure your OEM agreement spells out who's responsible for support. If you are, make your royalty payment sufficient to cover support costs.

Encouraging users to register

"Shareware authors should not put threatening messages on disks regarding registration obligations of the user. Don't insult and alienate your customers."
— Survey response from a shareware dealer who sells 1,500 disks per month.

"Don't expect registration dollars unless you limit your program. You won't hear from users unless your program has a bug or is limited."
— Survey response from a shareware author with $800 in sales for 1989.

As an author, I know the feeling of having people use my software and not pay for it. I know they're using it because they call for help. I know how it feels when it appears that distributors are getting rich selling my software while I don't make a cent. Sometimes it seems that the days when you could make a lot of money as a shareware author are long gone. It was easier when the big names in shareware, Jim Button and Bob Wallace, first started. It worked backed then and it doesn't seem to work anymore. I want to do something to stop unregistered users from using my software. I would like to teach them a lesson!

I know many authors who have expressed feelings similar to these statements. I hope, with the help of this book, you can avoid these types of feelings—they have no basis in fact and result only in setting up an adversarial relationship with the people who can best make your software a success. These are thoughts that lead authors to cripple their shareware, and you'll find that none of the most successful shareware authors use any form of crippling or limitations.

Shareware-registered version

An equation you need to be familiar with is S = R, which stands for the shareware version equals the registered version. It means that that shareware version is exactly the same as the registered version. In theory, that's the best way to design your shareware. You want the user to be able to try every feature and fully evaluate your software. In reality, however, none of the successful shareware programs are fully S = R. In some cases the registered version includes additional utilities, or it might have additional COM port support, for example.

There can be any of hundreds of other possible small differences. The important point, however, is that any differences between the shareware and registered versions are small and not significant to the overall operation of the software. If users feel the software is missing an important feature, they're unlikely to continue using the shareware version and that means they won't register.

There's a fine line between software that's S = R and software that's crippled. Crippling is not something that can be precisely defined. What one person sees as crippled software another has no problem with. For example, in my survey of shareware vendors I asked them to give a percentage for the number of crippled programs they receive each month. The answers ranged from 1% to 50%. These vendors are all looking at the same shareware programs, mostly disks they receive from the ASP. Yet they have widely varying opinions about how many shareware programs are crippled.

Whether a program is crippled or not is in the eye of the beholder—which in this case is the user. A shareware program cannot have any visible limits, or it will appear to be crippled, and this generally means you'll get fewer registrations. However, you can offer users an enhanced version as an incentive to register.

A good example is the ZipKey program published by Eric Isaacson. ZipKey is a zip code directory that includes a database of over 42,000 zip codes. However, the shareware version includes a database that's at least six months old. To get a current, up-to-date zip code listing, the user has to register. This is a powerful registration incentive! Users realize that it takes a while for shareware disks to get distributed, so a database that's six months out-of-date doesn't appear to them to be crippled (it would if the data was two years old). Yet the shareware and registered versions are not exactly the same, so there's an incentive to register the shareware. Chapter 17 profiles several other authors and describes how they've done the same thing as Eric, but with a variety of other types of software.

Designing software that isn't crippled yet also not fully S = R is very difficult. I suggest you look at how other authors have done this by trying shareware programs. I'm doing that all the time and I get new ideas from what I see in other people's programs. However, I also see a lot of shareware that I find frustrating to use because of the "incentives" the author has used. For example, here is how I reacted to the following situations:

- Programs with delay screens that can't be bypassed get tossed in the trash after a few uses.
- Programs with limited features or limited documentation don't get tested. I don't have time to figure out what works and doesn't work. Besides, many other programs do the same thing, so why spend time fiddling with limited software?
- Programs with poor error-message reporting are frustrating to use, and I quickly delete them from my hard disk, especially if the author

didn't provide a phone number I could call to get the problem resolved.

- Programs that immediately run smoothly and have a simple installation procedure are tested, used, and then—if I find them useful and continue to use them—they get registered.

Test a few shareware programs you might find useful. Pay attention to how you feel as you use or try to use them. What programs do you quickly throw out and why? What programs do you take the time to look at in more detail and why? In the end, you'll learn how you feel about various registration encouragements, and you might find a few good programs you can use.

"Have you seen the shareware fonts that leave out the vowels? Talk about a useless package! Even worse are the ones that work only in obscure sizes in landscape orientation."
— A comment by a user

The best way to design a program is to make it such a good, high-quality, useful program that it doesn't need a registration screen to get people to register. However, the registration screen does more than just sell your software by encouraging them to register. It lets people know that the software is shareware—that they have to pay for the software if they are using it. It also tells them how to contact you to purchase a copy.

Introductory screen

All shareware should have an introductory screen that identifies the software as shareware, explains the shareware concept, and explains how to register as a user. One of the most common mistakes authors make is to not thoroughly identify their software as shareware. If the user doesn't know the program is shareware and needs to be registered, they'll never register. If the user doesn't know how to contact you, they won't register. If the user doesn't know how shareware works, they won't register. Even the most honest person can't register your software if he don't have this information.

The best place to provide this information is on the first screen that's displayed as the program starts.

Delay screens

In the past, a common way to encourage users to register was to include a delay screen. The purpose of a delay screen is to make daily use of a program annoying. There are several ways to do this, some better than others.

You can a shareware message screen that won't go away until a preset amount of time has passed. This approach is often too annoying and users stop using the software before doing a complete evaluation. A variation puts a timer on the screen that displays the time remaining until the program runs. This is slightly better because it lets the user know how long the delay is, but it's still too annoying to be effective.

You can use an introductory delay screen that the user can bypass by pushing any key (see FIG. 3-1). This is a good approach as it allows users to get to the program quickly, yet still notifies them that they're using shareware. Some shareware authors don't like this approach because they feel it's too easy to bypass the shareware notice screen. However, must users will read all screens the first time they boot a program and the main purpose of this screen is to make them aware they're using shareware.

You can display a delay screen that can be bypassed by entering a random number included in the screen display. This forces people to read the screen because they need to look for the random number. You could also display the delay screen only a few times, such as once every 20 times the software is booted. If you want to use a delay screen, this approach creates the least interference to the user running the software, but it also provides the fewest reminders that the program is shareware. Also, if one person tries your software and then passes the disk on to someone else, the second person might never know they're using shareware.

```
                    YOUR PERSONAL LEGAL GUIDE
                 Copyright 1993 BBS LEGAL GUIDE, INC.

 ┌─────────────────────────────────────────────────────────────┐
 │  This software is provided as shareware giving │ Registering is easy. │
 │  you a chance to try it before you buy it. It  │ Just send your name, │
 │  works like taking a test drive in a car, and  │ address, and $59.95  │
 │  just like taking a test drive, you need to buy │ plus $4 s&h to:     │
 │  (register) this software, if you keep it and   │                     │
 │  are using, or planning to use it.              │   Homecraft          │
 │                                                 │   P.O. Box 9742      │
 │                                                 │   Tualatin, OR 97062 │
 │  When you register you get:                     │                     │
 │                                                 │ or use your Visa,    │
 │  [] The current version                         │ Master Card, or      │
 │  [] Additional forms and tutorials              │ American Express and │
 │  [] Notification of updates                     │ call:                │
 │          ... and more                           │                     │
 │                                                 │ (503) 692-3732 (voice)│
 │                                                 │ (503) 692-0382 (fax) │
 │                                                 │ Please specify either a│
 │                                                 │ 3.5 or 5.25 size disk.│
 │════════════<< PRESS ANY KEY TO CONTINUE >>════════════│
 └─────────────────────────────────────────────────────────────┘
```

3-1 Introductory screens, such as this one for Your Personal Legal Guide, are the most common method of encouraging users to register.

You can also use a combination of approaches. One possible combination would be an introductory screen that can easily be bypassed, and a delay screen that can't be bypassed that comes up every 30 to 40 times the software is booted. Note that standards established by the Association of Shareware Professionals state that a shareware program can have only one promotional screen. This screen can appear just once each time the program is booted.

Other types of promotional screens

The best way to make people aware that they're using shareware and that they need to register if they continue to use the software is to use a variety of approaches that serve as constant reminders. If you get a chance, listen to the nationally syndicated Rush Limbaugh radio talk show. It doesn't matter whether you agree with his politics, pay attention to how he promotes himself. He never stops. He's almost constantly promoting himself or one of his products—and he's become a millionaire. You need to treat your shareware the same way. It needs to constantly promote itself and remind users that they need to register.

For example, in addition to having an information screen at the beginning of your program, you can also leave a message on the screen when the user exits the software. The message provides a reminder that this is shareware, encourages the user to register, and tells them how to register. Don't, however, use a closing screen as your main registration reminder screen. If the user has a DOS shell program or Windows, the last screen will appear for only a fraction of a second before the computer returns to the DOS shell or Windows.

An excellent way to remind users that they're using shareware is to include a small message in the border of every screen. For example, you could put "unregistered" or "shareware evaluation copy" at the bottom of each screen. This reminds users they're using shareware, yet in no way interferes with their use of the software.

Evaluation periods

Some shareware includes a built-in evaluation period. Each time the software boots, a message is displayed stating "This is the n day of a 30-day evaluation period." At the end of the evaluation period, there are various approaches you can take. One author I know switches to a different introductory screen that informs users that the evaluation period has expired and they need to register. Another switches to a delay screen requesting registration. Each month the introductory delay screen locks up the user's computer for a slighter longer time. (The author in the first example gets more registrations.)

Including a preset evaluation period can result in some problems. For example, let's say one person starts to use the shareware and finds it isn't the type of program he needs. If he passes it on to a friend who tries the software a month later, that second person will find that the evaluation period has expired before he can even try the software. You can avoid this problem by having the evaluation period reset itself if the software isn't used for two weeks. Or some authors have their software check the hardware configuration of the computer. If a different configuration is detected, the software resets itself.

Limited (crippled) software

My surveys of shareware authors continue to find that some authors feel that the best way to encourage users to register is to provide a limited program or omit part of the documentation. As an incentive to register, users get the complete program and/or documentation when they register. It's tempting to do this. Why should people who didn't pay for the program get all of it free? My experience has shown that this isn't an effective way to encourage registrations.

One negative approach for encouraging registration is to create memory-resident software that uses a lot of memory. The ASP calls this *hogware*. When users register, they get a version that uses a much smaller amount of memory. The general result is that users delete the hogware.

Whatever negative approach you can think of has probably already been tried. Look at the results. Authors who cripple their software are obscure or no longer marketing their software as shareware. Successful authors use positive incentives to achieve success.

As a user, I wanted educational games for my young children. I wrote one program, Play 'n' Learn, but needed more. I noticed an alphabet game that was consistently on shareware best-seller lists, so I bought a copy. When I tried to use it, I found that only a dozen letters worked. I needed to register to make all the letters functional. My kids never used it because it didn't do much. On the other hand, I also got a shareware copy of Amy's First Primer. It was fully functional, and when I saw my kids having a great time with it, I bought a copy by sending the author the registration fee.

As an author, I spent several years experimenting with different registration incentives. I would use several different approaches in different versions of the same program and send copies to various distributors. All of my shareware is marked with the dealer's name, so I can keep track of which dealer sold the program when I get the registration form. I tried fully functional programs, versions with limited features, delay screens that couldn't be bypassed, delay screens that could be bypassed, limited documentation, and several other incentives. I found that although the crippled versions created frantic calls from people who desperately needed to use the software, the greatest number of registrations came from software versions that were unlimited and easy to use. I got the fewest registration payments from crippled software.

Using positive incentives

One author responding to my survey said that to encourage registrations he included a message that comes up each time the program is run, describing the following good reasons for the user to register:

- You get the latest revision without an annoying message.
- You receive a manual / documentation.
- Next major version is sent automatically when it becomes available.
- The "retail" price is $79, but shareware users can get it for half price, $39.50.

This author publishes utilities. Notice there are no threats and no messages about crippled software—only positive incentives to register. Negative tactics might ensure a higher ratio of paid users, but they also cut down on the total number of users. Don't worry about people stealing your software. If they're going to do it they'll do it, or else they'll steal another program that works all the time.

Surveys have shown that one of the biggest reasons users register is to get printed manuals and updates. The previous author offers both of those and is very successful.

The best approach for encouraging registrations is to offer positive incentives. The following positive incentives have worked for other authors.

Paying registered users a "distribution" royalty To do this, the shareware version and registered version must be the same. When registering, a user receives a disk with a serial number that appears on the first screen. This user can then share that disk with other users. When new users register, the serial number will identify where the disk came from so you can pay the appropriate royalty.

This type of positive incentive was used in the early days of shareware and was one of the incentives that lead to PC-Write:'s success. However, as shareware has become more of a mainstream product, offering a commission or distribution royalty has lost its effectiveness as a registration incentive. People buy software because the software helps them in some way, not to become a salesperson for that software.

Offer additional software free with registration This is the approach Apogee Software has used to become a multimillion dollar game publisher using shareware. Apogee publishes games such as the Commander Keen series and Wolfenstein 3D. Apogee creates a series of three games and then releases only the first game as shareware. Once you get hooked on the first game, you have to register in order to get the other two games.

Apogee's success proves that offering other software can serve as a powerful incentive to get people to register shareware. They are now the second largest shareware publisher in the world and they keep getting bigger and more successful every year. (McAfee Associates Inc. is the largest shareware publisher, with over $15 million in sales in 1992.) However, while this incentive works well for games, where a three-part trilogy can be created, it's difficult to use in other areas such as business software.

Offer a free premium bundled with the software   A book related to your target market is an excellent premium.

Customize the registered version to include the user's name   Users love this. Having their names appear as a part of the title screen makes them feel important and increases their ownership feelings. The problem with this incentive is that the number of registered copies you can ship is limited by how many you can customize each day.

Offer free technical support   This is very important because users need to feel they can get help when they need it. One of the advantages for users of shareware is the ability to call the author directly for help.

My user survey showed that technical support is a powerful incentive to get users to register. Users feel it's important to have access to technical support. However, technical support is a two-edged sword. If you withhold support from unregistered users, you'll be cutting down on the number of registrations. People who are having trouble using your software won't pay for it. However, if you provide free, unlimited support to both registered and unregistered users, there's no incentive to register.

My author survey showed that nearly all authors provide free support either by phone or by mail. In addition, most authors provide support for users who aren't registered. They generally have a stated policy of providing support for registered users only, but in reality they support anyone who calls. One way this can be stated in your documentation is to say "I provide technical support for all users of my software. However, registered users receive priority support."

Although you have no obligation to offer any type of support to shareware users, it's one of the best ways to sell your software. My experience has been that over half the unregistered users calling for help became registered users at the end of the phone call.

Free support doesn't mean installing an 800 number and paying for the phone call. Free support means you don't charge for the time spent answering questions and helping users. Most authors don't put a time limit on providing technical support, while most retail software publishers provide free support for just a few months, possibly up to a year. Shareware authors typically provide support to anyone who calls, without regard to when they purchased the software and whether or not they're a registered user.

Be friendly   Some of the reasons users register have nothing to do with the direct incentives you offer. Some people will like your software and want to support your software company. Others feel a personal obligation to follow the rules or want to feel honorable about paying for software. Possibly the number one reason users register is because they like the author. You should do all you can to encourage these positive feelings and make your users feel good about registering your software. Even if you don't offer a printed manual, you should acknowledge each registration you receive. For example, I don't provide a printed manual for my Play 'n' Learn software (which sells for $10). Each registered user receives a new disk with the current version, even if it's the same as the shareware version, and a thank-you note. Figure 3-2 shows the thank-you note I send with Play 'n' Learn.

HomeCraft Software
P.O. Box 974
Tualatin, OR 97062
(503) 692-3732

Dear Play 'n' Learn user:

Thank you for becoming a registered user of *Play 'n' Learn*. I hope your children are enjoying this software as much as mine did. I very much appreciate your support of my software and shareware. People such as yourself are what make user supported software work. Your registration will help us to continue to improve *Play 'n' Learn* and develop new software for very young children.

Enclosed is a disk with the latest version of *Play 'n' Learn*. The files on this disk will directly replace those you currently have without altering the award settings for Amanda's Letter Lotto.

THANK YOU!

Steve Hudgik
President, H.C.P. Services, Inc.
HomeCraft Software

3-2 The best approach for encouraging users to register is to use positive incentives, such as this thank-you note.

Many people tend to look at shareware as being a special type of business in which you have to offer incentives to get people to buy your product. However, shareware is no different than any other type of product. Each of the incentives I've just listed are used by other types of businesses. The first one is the basis of Amway's success. The second is similar to a "buy one, get one free" offer for pizza. Even the last is common outside of shareware—think of the stores you prefer to shop in because you like the friendly, helpful people who work in them.

Shareware is no different from any other business or service—you need to give people a reason a buy your product. For additional information about incentives to encourage registration, see chapter 15, in which I've reprinted the ASP guidelines on crippling shareware.

Be patient

I've mentioned it before, but it bears repeating. Be patient. Here's an excerpt from a letter I received in today's mail:

"We are very interested in your software program Book Minder and have a shareware copy of version 1.4. Before sending the registration fee, I have a question . . . "

Version 1.4 of my Book Minder software was discontinued 2½ years ago. It took a while for this person to get a copy and try it. Be patient; sometimes it takes a while for your program to reach people and for them to look at it.

"Be patient and persistent. In the beginning keep trying. If it looks like it won't go, improve your software and keep pushing it at anyone who will look at it."
— Survey response from a shareware author with $100,000 in sales.

"Don't give up. Spend time to build in quality."
— Survey response from a shareware author with $30,000 in sales.

"Don't expect much during the first 9 months to a year."
— Survey response from a shareware author with $16,000 in sales.

"Stick with it and respond to every letter and call you get."
— Survey response from a shareware author with $5,000 in sales.

"Be patient."
— The most frequent comment on the shareware author survey

Shareware does require patience. It takes time for disk vendors to review your software and get it into their catalogs. It takes time for people to find your shareware, get a copy, and then try it until they feel comfortable that this is a program they want to buy. But don't just send your first program out to disk vendors and BBSs and then sit back and wait (because you know it will take time). Keep working to get user feedback and to improve your program. Promote it with press releases, by talking at user group meetings, and by attending trade shows and conferences.

Old versions never die

The biggest drawback of shareware is that once you release a disk, it keeps circulating forever. I first released my Home Insurance software in 1986. In 1987 I released a completely rewritten and expanded version and increased the registration fee from $25 to $60. It's now 1993 and I still get registrations for the old version, but I no longer have manuals or copies of the software, and I don't want to continue supporting the old version. What can you do to avoid this problem?

The solution I came up with is to have the main program file display a message beginning 2½ to 3 years after the date I released the software. The message informs users that the software is out of date and they should contact me for a new copy. To accomplish this, the software is designed to check the date in the computer's clock. If it's more than three years from when I issued the software, the out-of-date message is displayed when the software is started.

The date-related message states that if users send their disks to me I'll mail them the latest version. I also include a warranty statement with my shareware that lets users know that if they have any kind of problem, even if the disk they have is physically defective, they can send it to me and I'll update/replace it at no charge. By doing this I accomplish several things:

- I inform users that the version they have is an old version and that both the software and registration fee might have changed.
- I eliminate old versions from distribution. However, I've found that this isn't as effective as I'd thought. I've run into vendors who continue to sell the old version. Sometimes it takes the threat of legal action to get them to stop selling the out-of-date software.
- I get the names and addresses of people who are trying my shareware, and by getting the disk from them I'm sometimes able to get the name and address of the vendor who is selling the out-of-date version.
- I ensure that people are looking at the latest and best version of my software. I don't want users basing their evaluation of my software on an older version. They're looking at software that no longer exists and not seeing the enhanced features, improved speed, better user interface, and all of the other good stuff in the most recent version.
- I identify the software as date-limited in the READ.ME file with the following paragraph:

This version is valid through 1997. It will run in 1998 and later, but at that time the software will display a message stating that it is outdated. We want to be sure that only current versions are circulating. This allows us to be sure that you get the best, most current software. If you wish to have software without this message after 1997, please send us your disk and be sure to include your name and address with the disk. We'll return your disk with the latest shareware version of the software on it.

In putting a dated message in the software, I don't do anything to destroy files or prevent program operation. The program functions fine with no limitations. Users can also run the program without the date-related message by resetting the date in their computers to a year that falls within the functioning range.

Another important part of putting a date-timed message in the software is to provide updates to all shareware dealers every year. These updates extend by one year the date on which the message appears. This has the additional benefit of discouraging unauthorized dealers from selling old versions of software because their disks will go out of date.

The two-year time period is important because it might take up to a year for your software to work its way through the distribution channel and another year or two before a user tries the software. If you don't feel comfortable with two years, or don't expect to be updating your software in the near future, you can use three, four, or five years.

I haven't had any problems with date-limiting my shareware in this way. I've discussed it with vendors and they feel that a two- to three-year trial period is long enough, as long as they get regular updates. The first time my three-year limit expired, which was at the end of 1992, I received lots of disks from users who wanted them updated, but only one complaint. The complaint was from a person who had used one of my programs to create a database with over 10,000 records. He was concerned that he had lost all of his work. I sent him the latest version and included a note that explained that his existing data was fine, but creating a 10,000 record database was doing more than just evaluating the software. Many of the people who sent disks to be updated included notes that said they had just purchased the software. Most of the disks seemed to come from flea-market vendors, although I did find several disk vendors who were carrying both the current and old versions of my software.

Don't do this

A negative approach that's similar to the previous approach is to put true date limitations in the software. Some authors limit their software to thirty days of use from when it's first booted. Others stop the software from running when a specified year arrives. Similarly, some programs limit the data files it generates, for example, a check-writing program that allows only 100 checks to be written. Others limit features, for example, a label-printing program that allows you to design a label but not save your design for future use. These all fall into the category of crippled software. Putting out crippled software is bad business and limits the potential of your software. Magazines and reviewers will ignore it, and few users will use it long enough to get interested in registering.

The best way to get the most registrations is to write quality software that's easy to use and has no limits or crippled functions. If you don't do that, it doesn't matter what type of registration incentives you have—you won't get many people registering your software.

4
Why people register shareware

"Somehow we get blinded by the fact that our 'product' is a computer program. If we were making hand-painted china plates, the importance of marketing would be immediately apparent. We would decide what patterns would sell best and where the best outlets would be, Macy's or K-Mart, and so forth. It would be the first thing we did. We would not paint up a warehouse full of them and then try to figure out how to sell them. Since I started to treat my programs like hand-painted china plates, I am discovering all kinds of smarter things I could have done."

— "Doc" Wright, shareware author

I am astonished at the number of shareware authors who think shareware is a special type of business—a type of business in which normal business practices and rules of success do not apply. I assume they're either unaware of what's involved in running a successful business or choose to ignore business fundamentals—fundamentals such as doing market research, creating a product people need, making it easy for people to buy, and actively promoting that product.

The reasons for this survey

There were several reasons why I conducted the survey on which much of the information in this chapter is based. They are as follows:

Questions that need answering

Since writing the first edition of this book, I've talked with many people who wanted to show me their program and get my advice. (Please note that

I don't run a free consulting service and cannot talk to everyone who calls.) In most cases I found that, although they tell me the advice in this book is excellent, their software and our conversation indicates that they're ignoring much of what this book recommends. For example, a fundamental key to success is to know your customers and listen to what they say. However, really listening and paying attention to customers seems to be a problem for many new shareware authors. Some of the authors I've talked with feel they're the experts. They feel they know better than anyone else what needs to be in their software and how the software should work. They seem to be unwilling to accept that "lowly users," who are not experts in software design, would have anything useful to say.

I spoke with one author who felt he had listened to his users and they had told him they wanted educational software for the junior high school level. He thought he knew what was needed, and called me because he couldn't understand why no one was buying his software. The problem was that he stopped listening after finding the answer to just one question. He never found out what type of subjects people wanted covered, how the material should be presented, or even what features should be in the software. However, when I pointed this out to him he told me that he was the expert and that people should recognize this and buy his software because of his expertise. Unless you have a highly recognizable name and can sell software on the strength of your name alone, business doesn't work that way.

I work very hard to listen to the users of my software and encourage them to tell me what they think about it. How do I do this? I ask them questions. Not just one question, but lots of questions. Instead of assuming that I'm the expert and that I know the answers, I ask. And I usually find that some of the answers are different than what I thought.

One of the questions I wanted answered was "Why do so many people who get copies of my shareware not register it?" That's a fundamental question for all of us in the shareware industry and it's the first reason that I conducted a survey of people who had tried my shareware but who had not registered as users.

Reaching conclusions without facts

I'm surprised by an ongoing debate that has been raging on Compuserve. Some shareware authors have gotten figures from disk vendors that show they're getting only one or two registrations for every 1,000 shareware copies sold. In some cases, the ratio is one registration for every 10,000 shareware copies sold. Their conclusion is that shareware doesn't work—people don't register shareware.

Let's stop and think about this for a minute. This is a program that is catching people's interest. People are buying thousands of copies. Disk vendors are making a lot of money selling this shareware program. Yet the author is essentially getting no registration payments. What should this author do?

- Get on Compuserve and complain that people don't register shareware.
- Quit working on the program and get a night job flipping hamburgers because the pay is better.
- Rewrite the software to improve its performance, add features, and clarify the documentation.
- Ask the people who have the shareware version why they didn't register.

I hope you said that the first two answers are not correct—at least if you want to make some money with your software.

The third answer is also incorrect. Immediately getting to work improving the software and documentation without knowing what users want is like going deer hunting on a moonless night with a shotgun. It's too dark to see where you're going and you don't know where your target is, but you figure that maybe, if you scatter buckshot in a wide enough area, you'll hit something. I'm not a hunter, but I know enough to be sure this isn't the way to bring home a deer. That's what you're doing when you start upgrading your software without knowing what your customers want. You're taking shots in the dark and hoping that if you add enough new features one of them will "hit the target" and be a feature users really want.

The best way to get a deer is to go hunting during the day and use a rifle. You can see your target and hit it with a single shot. And that's what you need to do with your software. Feedback from your customers will identify the areas you need to target, and then you can focus your efforts on those areas to produce a product people want to buy.

The correct answer is the fourth one: start by asking people why they aren't registering your shareware. There are so many people debating the "why users don't register shareware" question, none of whom had any facts to backup their claims, that I decided it was time to get some facts. That was the second reason I decided to do the survey presented in this chapter.

Getting customer feedback

My shareware programs are fairly successful, so I hadn't thought of contacting people who had used but not registered my shareware. But I had a mailing list of over 800 people who had requested shareware disks from me and then never registered the program. So here was a group of people I could contact.

One of the complaints many shareware authors have with disk vendors is that they'd like the disk vendors to give them the names and addresses of people who have purchased their programs. But disk vendors prefer not to give out the addresses of their customers because they feel that doing so would hurt their relationship with those customers. So how did I get the names and addresses of people who had tried my shareware, but had not registered? I provide users with a warranty that says, without regard to where they got it, that they're guaranteed to have the latest version. If users have an older version, have a problem using the software, or even have a defective disk, they can send the disk to me and I'll put the latest version of the software on their disk and return it to them at no charge.

That's how I got the names of people who had tried my shareware, but for a survey to be valid I needed to contact more than just people who had tried my shareware. If I surveyed just those people, I wouldn't be able to tell whether the results of the survey applied just to my software or to shareware in general. I needed to get the names and addresses of people who had tried other shareware and had not registered. So I contacted other shareware authors to see if anyone else had a mailing list similar to mine.

All authors receive requests for shareware disks directly from users. When I started contacting other successful shareware authors, I found that most of them had mailed a lot of disks to users. But I also discovered they weren't using this information. I had trouble finding someone who had the names and addresses of unregistered shareware users in a usable form. One author had all of the names on tiny slips of paper thrown in a shoe box. Several other authors didn't even bother to keep the names of people who had requested disks. Out of the fourteen authors I contacted, only one kept a mailing list of people who had requested shareware disks.

It's hard to believe that people who are in business could ignore potential customers this way. If people takes the time to write or call you and request a shareware copy of your software, they're interested in it. They have a need for your software. They want your software and are some of your best prospects.

In any other business, and in particular in direct marketing businesses such as shareware, a mailing list is recognized as one of the most important assets a business has. Yet it turns out that most shareware authors aren't using their mailing lists and, in many cases, are throwing them away!

The information wasteland

As I've talked with shareware authors, a common complaint I've heard is that it's difficult to get information about what's going on in the industry. There's no source of current news and information. One of these reasons is that there's no one, other than myself and people writing books like this, who is collecting and publishing information about shareware.

I've also found that most shareware authors don't stay in touch with their customers. For example, I have registered as a user of fifteen shareware programs. Yet, in the past five years I have received a newsletter from only two of them, plus a letter announcing the release of an upgrade from one other. That's not how to stay in touch with your customers.

An article in the May 21, 1993 issue of *USA Today*, "Customers to IBM: Keep us informed," describes a 2 1/2-day meeting IBM had with 175 of its largest customers in which "some [customers] suggested that IBM might have a better image and balance sheet now had it spent more time keeping customers informed."

Even the mighty will fall if they get out of touch with their customers. If you're to succeed as a small software publisher, if you're to beat your bigger and better-financed competition, you need to be very close to your customers.

As a result of this poor approach to marketing and communicating with customers, shareware is a wasteland as far as marketing information is concerned. Authors generally have not bothered to ask their customers or potential customers about either their products or shareware. That's the third reason I decided to go ahead with a survey of people who had tried a shareware program but not registered it. A motto I use to provide guidance in this type of situation is "make something happen." If there are questions to be answered, then you need to go out and do something to get the answers—don't run your business based on assumptions.

The survey

I did, eventually, find another author who had maintained a mailing list of people who had received shareware disks but who hadn't registered. The other author's programs, I felt, were all high-quality, well-written, excellent examples of shareware. In addition, they were targeted at home users, as is my software, so they provided a good comparison.

As the results from these surveys started coming in, I realized that to get a good comparison I needed a survey of shareware users in general. So I contacted a shareware vendor who was kind enough to send me 300 names from his mailing list, and I sent the survey to those people also. This provided a three-way comparison.

To make it easier to discuss the results of these surveys, I'm going to call the survey based on the vendor's mailing list the *general* survey. The survey of the other author's shareware users will be called the *author* survey, and the survey of my shareware users will be called the *HomeCraft* survey, which is my company's name.

Why some people don't register shareware

Let's get right to the main point of these surveys, answering two key questions:

- Are there a lot of people using shareware who aren't registering it?
- Why don't some people register the shareware they've tried?

Once these questions are answered I'll discuss how I solved the problems the answers to these questions revealed. The last half of the chapter will provide the complete survey results.

The survey of people who had tried my shareware found that users weren't continuing to use shareware programs they hadn't registered, and there were two primary reasons why people had not registered my shareware:

- 22% percent of the people surveyed found the software to be too difficult to use or felt it didn't work properly.
- 18% didn't like the software.

Other reasons people gave for wanting to look at the software but not registering it were that they were just curious about it (13%), they had decided to use another program (8%) or they hadn't tried it yet (8%).

Did these reasons point to a problem with my software, or is there always going to be a certain percentage of people who will either not like a particular program or find it difficult to use? The answer to this question is found in the other two groups I surveyed. The top two reasons that users of the other author's software didn't register were:

- 22% found the software to be too difficult to use or felt it didn't work properly.
- 43% didn't like the software.

Other reasons people gave for not registering where that they use only a few of the shareware programs they try, they had decided to use another program, or they never even tried using the shareware. The general survey also showed similar results—most people didn't register the shareware they had tried because it was too hard to use or they didn't like it.

It appears that, at least for users of home software, most of the people who don't register either don't like the software or don't know how to use it. What does this conclusion imply? It says that shareware has to be incredibly easy to use. The basic test I apply to any new shareware I'm reviewing is that I've got to be able to use it without reading the manual. I think that's also what most users do.

What now? The surveys show that I'm losing a lot of potential registrations because people think my software is too difficult to use. But the other shareware author has the same problem, and it appears to be a generic problem with shareware. I suppose I could just accept this as a characteristic of shareware, that some people won't understand how to use the software. But I see no reason why I should give up on these potential sales. Now that I know what the problem is, I need to do something about it.

Solving the problem

The software I sell is a large, fairly complex database program. Database software has the reputation of being one of the most difficult types of software to use, yet my software has already been rated by the press as being one of the easiest-to-use database programs available.

The reaction many authors have to this type of situation is "These people are stupid! They don't know how easy to use my software really is! I don't need to change anything." I've most frequently heard this reaction from people who are outstanding programmers. However, by making a statement like that, they're showing that they either don't care about or don't know about marketing. And it's marketing that sells software.

Another reaction I've heard is "I don't know how to make my software any easier to use. There's nothing I can do." This simply isn't true. There's always something you can do. I did two things in response to learning that some people found my shareware difficult to use.

First, I hired an editor to go through my documentation in order to correct both grammar and punctuation errors and to ensure that the documentation was clear and easy to understand. The editor was someone I felt was close to the type of person in my target audience, someone with limited computer experience. As a result, her comments were not biased by a lot of background knowledge about computers. In addition to correcting grammar, punctuation, and improving my writing, she identified the sections in my manual that needed to be clarified.

How do you find an editor? I've been lucky. In the past three years I've hired two editors, and I found both people as a result of meeting new people and asking them about themselves. I hired the first editor to help me with the first edition of this book. She was a user of my software. She had written to me asking for information about my software, and I noticed that she had identified herself as a *wordsmith* on her stationary. I was curious as to what a wordsmith was, and it seemed like it might have something to do with writing. So I called her and asked. It turns out that she was both a writer and an editor. She had even already edited some software manuals, but she wasn't a computer expert. Just the type of person I wanted to find.

In the spring of 1992 I started working on the research for a new book about computers and collecting. I intended to have the same person edit that book. However, when I met another editor who lived here in the Portland area, I hired her to edit the new book. When I needed someone to edit my software manuals, she was able to take on that job also.

You probably won't be lucky enough to just run into people who are qualified to edit your manuals. But you can find a qualified editor fairly easily. The best place to look is at a local college or university. Check with the English department and ask them to recommend a student who would be qualified to edit technical manuals. If you don't live near a college or university, contact your high school and see if any of the English teachers are interested.

How can you tell whether someone will do a good editing job? Ask a lot of questions and ask to see something he or she has written (and preferably published). If you can't find or afford an experienced editor, look for people with the necessary educational background—those who are intelligent and who care about doing a good job. Ask about their job and try to find out about their work attitudes and the quality they put into that job. It doesn't matter what type of work they're now doing; people who care about doing quality work will put the same care into the work they do for you.

The second thing I did was to think about the group of people who didn't register my shareware because they didn't like it. I said to myself "There is no one style or design everyone likes, so what do the car companies do in order to satisfy the needs of a variety of people?" The answer is that they make a variety of cars! So that's what I'm doing with my software.

I started by designing a new, "lite" version of my software. It's a simplified version of my main program; it only has about half the features of the main program. Instead of a 100-page manual, it has a 40-page manual. When I send a copy of my shareware to someone, I now follow up about a month later with a brochure describing the lite version. So far it's going very well; I estimate that about 25% of the people who in the past would not have registered my shareware are now buying the lite version.

Surveys are a useful means for getting the information you need to help run your business. They encourage your users to provide feedback and suggestions that will help you increase your sales. For example, if you've released a shareware program and no one is registering, you need to find out why. If you can't get the names of people who have tried your shareware, then survey people who might be interested in your software. Remember, it's up to you to make something happen. You need to find ways to reach the people who can give you the feedback you need to make your software successful.

Survey results

As with any survey, my survey of shareware users didn't provide direct answers or hard rules that can be followed in every situation. The results only help to identify problem areas and provide some direction and understanding of what users are thinking. Also, remember that the people in the HomeCraft, author, and general surveys were people who had been identified as not having registered a shareware program they had obtained from one source or another.

I mailed a total of 900 survey forms: 300 to people who had received copies of my shareware, 300 to people who had received copies of the shareware written by another author, and 300 to shareware users in general.

Out of the 900 surveys, 329 were completed and returned. I received close to the same number of returns from users of my software and users of the software by the other author. A slightly higher number of people returned the general survey. Table 4-1 shows the return rate for each group.

Table 4-1   Shareware user survey response rates.

Target group	Surveys mailed	Surveys returned	Return rate
HomeCraft	300	108	36%
Author	300	102	34%
General	300	119	40%

People like "try before you buy" software

I used the first two questions to find out whether people understood that the disks they received were shareware disks. The first question asked people if they were familiar with the term *shareware*. On all three surveys, nearly everyone answered yes. The second question asked whether they had ever tried a shareware program, and the answer again was overwhelmingly yes. These are the people you need to understand—they think they know what shareware is, and they are trying shareware.

Question two had several additional parts whose purpose was to determine whether people register the shareware they've tried. The answers show that people like the concept of "try before you buy" and they tend to try lots of programs. The 329 people who responded to the surveys reported having tried a total of over 11,000 shareware programs. They said that of those 11,000, 1,365 were still on their hard disks, and 803 of those were registered. Table 4-2 summarizes this information.

In addition to what is shown in TABLE 4-2, 25% of the HomeCraft survey, 16.7% of the author survey, and 11% of the general survey, respondents said they currently had no shareware on their hard disks.

Table 4-2   Number of shareware programs users have tried, versus the number that are registered.

Target group	Total number of programs	Average number of programs	Median number of programs
Number of shareware programs users have tried			
HomeCraft	3084	30.84	10
Author	3925	41.76	24
General	4262	40.21	20
Number of programs still on users hard disks			
HomeCraft	452	4.57	2
Author	442	4.80	2
General	471	4.44	2
Approximate number of programs that have been registered			
HomeCraft	260	2.57	1
Author	253	2.66	2
General	290	2.73	2

Overall it appears that people register about 60% of the shareware they have on their hard disk and about 10% of the shareware they try. Ten percent of the people commented that they were still evaluating the shareware that was on their hard disk. Another 5% mentioned that they where no longer using some of the shareware on their hard disks, but they hadn't yet gotten around to erasing it. A later survey question revealed that about 10% of shareware users feel they paid for the software when they bought the shareware disk, and another 3–4% feel they don't need to register shareware. However, before you draw any conclusions, let's go over the rest of the survey.

People's attitudes toward shareware

Question three gave a series of statements about shareware and asked people whether they agreed or disagreed with each statement. The three interesting results from this part of the survey were that most people know that shareware is "try before you buy" software and they need to pay for it if they continue to use it. However, it also showed that 30% of the people responding to the survey don't feel under any time constraints to register shareware and they don't feel they need to register within the 30 to 60 days allowed by most authors.

The third interesting result was that just over 50% of the people responding to this survey agreed with the statement "If I only occasionally use a shareware program and it isn't really very good, I don't need to register it." This is disturbing, but don't let it bother you. Complaining about users who don't register doesn't accomplishing anything. Understanding why they don't register and then doing something about it is the best approach. As a result of this survey, I know that it will be more difficult to get people to register software they only occasionally use. If you make this type of software, you need to take this into consideration when designing your software. (Chapter 16 shows how one successful company handled this problem.)

Background information

Questions four through seven were used to get background information on the people who responded to the survey. These questions determined that 75% had registered at least one shareware program. These questions also showed that some people were either confused or didn't understand the difference between a shareware author and a shareware vendor. When asked to write in the name of the shareware author of the last program they had registered, 4% of those who answered wrote in the name of a disk vendor. While this isn't a big percentage, it does show that some people don't fully understand the shareware industry.

Why users register or don't register shareware

Questions six and seven asked users to identify the last program they had registered. Question eight then asked them to give the specific reasons why they had registered that program. The results are shown in TABLE 4-3. Some people provided more than one answer, so the percentages will add up to more than 100%.

Table 4-3   Users' reasons for registering a specific shareware program and the percentage of different types of users with those reasons.

Reason	HomeCraft	Author	General
Liked the software	27.7%	33.0%	32.4%
To get additional programs	7.9%	10.1%	29.6%
To get additional program features	15.8%	19.2%	21.5%
It's the right thing to do	11.9%	18.2%	17.7%
Support the shareware concept	8.9%	20.2%	16.5%
Wanted the printed manual	12.9%	15.1%	14.2%
To get a more recent version	13.8%	13.1%	12.9%
Needed technical support	6.9%	9.1%	8.9%
Liked the author	2.0%	4.0%	3.1%
The shareware version had bugs and I wanted a better version	4.9%	2.0%	2.8%
Other	3.0%	2.0%	2.0%

Note that the number one reason people say they register shareware is because they like the software. The high rating (29.6% in the General column) of "to get additional programs" comes from people who said the most recent program they registered is an Apogee game. The major registration incentive with Apogee games is that when you register you get additional games that aren't available as shareware. Many shareware authors discount this approach as being valid only for games. However, a few have come up with ways to apply the trilogy approach to business applications. It's too early to tell whether it'll work, but this is an area to watch.

The third most important reason people register shareware is to get additional program features. This is becoming one of the most common registration incentives. A fully functional program is distributed as shareware. Then when users register, they get additional utilities or add-on software that works with the main program.

In my survey, I try to ask important questions in two different ways. I can then compare the results from the two questions and see whether they're consistent. Question eight provided a checklist of reasons for registering shareware. Later on in the survey I asked people to write in the reasons they had for registering shareware. Their top five answers are shown in TABLE 4-4.

Table 4-4 Users' reasons for registering shareware in general and the percentage of different types of users with those reasons.

Reason	HomeCraft	Author	General
I use the program	24%	22%	36%
It's an excellent quality program	20%	16%	28%
To get updates	21%	12%	28%
To get additional programs	2%	8%	9%
It's the right thing to do	6%	3%	6%

The answers people wrote in response to this question are consistent with those they gave in question eight. The check boxes for question eight didn't include one to indicate that updates were an incentive to register, but updates show up as a strong incentive in TABLE 4-4. I made some follow-up phone calls to get a better understanding of what people were meant when they said that updates were one of the reasons they registered shareware.

What I learned is that many users want to stay in touch with the author of the software. They want to learn about new developments and improvements in the software, and to have access to those improvements. They like receiving regular newsletters that contain information about updates, add-on products, and other software the author has created. I was surprised by this. I expected that users would want newsletters that provided hints and tips about using the software. But this isn't the case.

Whether the author offered free updates or charged a small fee for updates didn't make much difference to the users I interviewed. If there was any bias, it was that users felt there was more value in updates they purchased. (Note: If you're going to send newsletters to your users, then using the newsletter to sell updates is a good way to pay for the newsletter. However, in promoting your software keep in mind that it's not the newsletter that users want, it's the updates.)

It's not only useful to know why people register shareware, it's also useful to find out why they don't register some shareware programs. Question 9 asked people to identify the last shareware program they had tried and not registered, and then identify the reasons they hadn't registered that program. The results are shown in TABLE 4-5. Some people gave multiple answers, so the percentages will add up to more than 100%.

These results provide some interesting information. All three groups give "I tried the software and didn't like it" as the #1 reason for not registering a shareware program. Combine this with the people who said they never got around to try the software, and you see that over 90% either

Table 4-5 Features that encourage users to register.

Reason	HomeCraft	Author	General
I tried the software and didn't like it.	65.5%	52.3%	70.1%
I was curious about this software, but it's not something I need.	47.2%	7.7%	46.5%
The software didn't work, and I wasn't able to try it.	23.8%	24.5%	36.6%
I tried this program, but found another I liked better.	29.3%	38.4%	36.6%
The software didn't work.	32.6%	38.4%	35.2%
Tried the software and found it too hard to use.	27.4%	23.1%	31.8%
I already use another program, and just wanted to see what this one was like.	27.8%	12.4%	24.0%
I buy a lot of shareware programs, but use only a few.	12.8%	6.2%	24.0%
I never got around to trying this software.	12.8%	18.4%	22.9%
I'm planning to register as a user, but haven't gotten around to it yet.	12.8%	2.9%	14.1%
I'm still using this program and will eventually register.	9.1%	9.1%	10.9%
I collect shareware programs.	9.1%	46.1%	10.9%
The program is available to everyone and you need to pay for it only if you want to.	3.6%	10.6%	10.2%
Since I already have the program, and it does everything I need, there's no need to register it.	3.6%	9.2%	9.9%
I paid for the program when I purchased the shareware disk.	11.0%	6.2%	9.9%
I feel the author is trying to "rip me off" by asking for too much money.	5.5%	9.1%	7.5%
Other	18.3%	9.1%	24.0%

didn't like it or didn't try it. This begins to show why authors see large numbers of their programs being sold, but only a small percentage of those turning into registrations.

It's also interesting to note that about 10% of the people feel, in one way or another, that they don't need to pay for some of the shareware programs they use.

It's interesting to note that the questions relating to both quality and the ability to use the program were consistent for all three group. About 30% of the people in all three groups said that either the software was too hard to use, or that it did not work. I know that the shareware I was sending out was functional, and I've been a user of the shareware written by the other author, so I know that shareware works. This means that the problem isn't with bugs in the software or with the software not working, but that a large percentage of users can't figure out how to use it. Which means that shareware authors need to put a lot of effort into making software as easy to use as possible.

Be careful with the results from this question. Because so many people provided multiple answers, the results are fuzzy. For example, you can't say that 70.1% of people who try a program won't like it. The only conclusion you can draw is that a significant number of people responded in a certain way.

As I did when trying to find out why people register, I asked a second, open-ended question to get more information on why people don't register some shareware programs. The question I asked was "What would encourage you to register a shareware program." The most frequently given answers are shown in TABLE 4-6. Again you see that a useful, quality program is the top incentive.

Table 4-6   What users expect to get when they register shareware.

Incentive	HomeCraft	Author	General
Better quality software	10%	13%	16%
Software that fits my needs	8%	6%	10%
Availability of upgrades	4%	0%	4%
Lower registration fees	3%	3%	3%

What users expect to get

Sometimes when you ask a question from a different perspective you can learn something that wasn't apparent from asking the question directly. The previous two questions directly asked users why they register some shareware programs. There was a third question in the survey (these questions where scattered throughout the survey) that asked the same thing, but in a different way. It asked people to list the things they expected to get when they registered a shareware program. As you can see in TABLE 4-7, people feel that updates and technical support are very impor-

Table 4-7   Users' reasons for not registering a specific shareware program and percentages of different types of users with those reasons.

What they expect to get	HomeCraft	Author	General
Updates and technical support	11%	10%	12%
Additional programs	1%	1%	9%
Updates	9%	6%	7%
Updates, user manual, and support	4%	5%	7%
Updates, support, and latest version	6%	0%	5%
User manual and latest version of the software	2%	3%	3%

tant and they expect to have access to them when they register a shareware program. That's what they want.

The number two answer, showing that people register in order to get additional programs, came exclusively from people who had registered an Apogee game. Games generally don't have updates, technical support, or printed manuals. But Apogee has proven that by offering a series of three games, with only the first one available as shareware, you can sell millions of dollars of software.

What users like and dislike about shareware

One of the survey questions asked people to list what they like about shareware. The top answers are shown in TABLE 4-8. As you can see, users like being able to try a program before they have to pay for it. And, as you can see in TABLE 4-9, the issue of quality comes up again when the survey asked users to name the things they most disliked about shareware. The top two answers—poor-quality software and poor documentation—are both quality-related issues.

Table 4-8 Aspects of shareware that users like.

Aspects of shareware users like	HomeCraft	Author	General
You can try it before you buy it	42%	45%	52%
It's inexpensive	21%	14%	21%
There's a wide selection of software	8%	7%	14%

Table 4-9 Aspects of shareware that users dislike.

Aspects of shareware users dislike	HomeCraft	Author	General
There are many poor quality programs	21%	24%	28%
Poor documentation	3%	7%	8%
Lack of technical support	1%	7%	7%
The registration messages	4%	1%	4%

Where users get shareware

Since the mailing list for the general group came from a catalog vendor, it's not surprising that TABLE 4-10 shows that so many users get shareware from shareware catalogs. What I found interesting was that many people who had received disks directly from HomeCraft and the other author said that they frequently get their disks from flea markets and computer shows. Yet, few people on the catalog vendor's mailing list said that they get shareware from flea markets and computer shows. There's not enough information to draw any conclusions, but I do wonder whether people are

Table 4-10 Where users get shareware.

Source of shareware	HomeCraft	Author	General
Shareware catalogs	56%	65%	98%
BBSs	34%	22%	14%
Flea market/computer shows	22%	23%	4%
Direct from author	17%	15%	2%
Compuserve	8%	4%	2%
GEnie	3%	2%	—
Retail stores	5%	11%	6%
Friends	7%	6%	5%
Prodigy	2%	—	—
America On Line	2%	—	—
Public library	2%	—	—
User groups	1%	4%	1%

getting out-of-date disks at flea markets and computer shows and then contacting the author in order to get new disks or when they're having a problem.

Summary

What the survey shows is that people aren't going to send shareware authors money unless they feel that the author has a high-quality, useful program. That's the advantage of shareware for users—they get to try the software before they buy it. Based on this survey of shareware users, it appears that shareware is being used exactly in the way it was intended.

That also means that shareware isn't a free ride for the author. Just like any other business, you need to work for your success. You must produce a quality product that users need, and you must include registration incentives that have value to the user.

My experience in reviewing shareware programs agrees with the results of this survey. In my opinion, I feel that 19 out of 20 shareware programs need a lot of improvement. Sometimes the software is good and the documentation is lousy. And sometimes I can't see that the program does anything useful. Or there are no incentives for people to register. Or the fact that it's shareware is not clearly evident. Or the author doesn't include his address. Or many, many other kinds of mistakes.

Chapter 3 told you that you needed to do market research. This chapter has given you some valuable market research information. Now let's go on and learn how shareware is distributed.

5
Distribution channels

In marketing your programs as shareware, one of the prime objectives is to get copies of your disk to as many people as possible. Do this by sending disks to shareware distributors, user groups, BBSs, and electronic information services, and giving away as many copies as you can.

I remember reading about a major shareware publisher several years ago. I cannot remember his name now, but the article talked about how he gave away copies of his shareware to anyone who asked—30,000 copies in a year. "How can I afford that?" I thought. I would go broke just giving out disks. You don't have to give out 30,000 free disks, but you should be generous in giving away free copies of the shareware version of your program. For example, in the previous section, I mentioned that I will send a new disk to anyone who sends me their old disk. Some people don't send a disk, but I still send them a free copy of the latest version. It's good business.

"Send out as many disks as possible to dealers."
— Shareware author survey response

"Send it out to everyone. Put it on every board (BBS). Talk it up."
— Shareware author survey response

Yes, it's good business and simple psychology. If you help people, they'll want to help you and will feel better about purchasing your software. Giving out disks one at a time is fine, but then you can't reach large numbers of people. You need the help of organizations that distribute shareware.

Shareware disk distributors

Disk distributors have their roots in the user groups and public-domain software of the early 1980s. For example, I was the librarian for the Portland Epson Group (in the days of CP/M computers). When I took over the user-group library, it was a mess. We had only about 250 disks, but it was an impossible task for one person to keep the library organized and up-to-date. Since that time, for-profit disk libraries have replaced user groups as the primary means of distributing public-domain software and shareware. By charging a fee for their disks, the distributors are able to hire a professional staff whose full-time job is to maintain the disk library.

Disk distributors range in size from companies that sell 100,000 disks a week to small home businesses that sell 50 disks a week. The quality of service provided by disk distributors varies. Some small distributors provide excellent service to both authors and users, and some large distributors never return calls and sell crippled software. Send copies of your program to as many distributors as you can afford. The more distributors who sell your program, the greater the number of people who will see it and the more registrations you'll get.

Include a cover letter with a short description of your program, the system requirements, the amount of the registration fee, and your name and address. If you decide to time-limit your software, you should describe those limits so vendors will know when to pull this version from their library. It's also a good idea to include a list of what users get when they register. Some catalogs indicate whether users get a printed manual, technical support, updates, a newsletter, etc. Also, if you're a STAR or ASP member, be sure to include that information in the cover letter.

The VENDOR.DOC file

Each of your shareware programs should have a VENDOR.DOC file. This file is used to provide information to vendors, BBSs, and other people who want to distribute copies of your shareware. An important component of the VENDOR.DOC file is your distribution license. The distribution license gives the terms and conditions under which your shareware can be sold or distributed. It's important that your shareware include a good, complete distribution license. Without it you can lose control of the distribution of your shareware. At a minimum, the distribution license should do the following:

- Place a limit on the fee distributors and dealers can charge for copies of your software. A typical limit is about $10, including shipping and other charges. I have seen some authors who allow fees as high as $20 and as low as $3. Many of the major dealers charge $4 to $5 for a disk, so setting limits lower than that might restrict the distribution of your disk. Lower limits also make it difficult for dealers who supply retail stores to carry your software. Typically, shareware sells for $4.95 to $9.95 in a retail store. A distributor sells it to the retailer for about half of that. If your limit is under $10, it will be difficult for the retailer and distributor to make a profit. Thus, they won't bother with your program. You don't want to eliminate this channel of distribution. It's growing rapidly and reaches people that don't generally buy shareware. I now get more registrations from users who purchased their disks from a retailer than I get from those who purchased disks directly from distributors.

- State that the software must be identified as shareware. The term *shareware* must be explained so that users know the software is copyrighted and that an additional fee must be paid if they use it. This explanation should be displayed so that all disk buyers have the opportunity to read it. Thus, it should be in all catalogs and on all retail packaging or point-of-purchase displays. In the past, some dealers created problems because they didn't identify the disks they sold as shareware. Intentionally or not, that led people to believe they were buying the program when they purchased the shareware disk. This is turning out to be a particularly difficult problem for shareware sold in retail stores. The shareware display might fully identify the software as shareware, but some people don't take the time to read the display. I continue to get calls from both people who have purchased disks from catalogs and those who got the disk in a retail store who were upset because they thought they had purchased a copy of my $59.95 program ORGANIZE! Your Sports Cards for $3. I also have users complain because they think I get the money they paid to the dealer and they want a refund when they pay the registration fee. When people with these problems call I describe how shareware works and the benefits of registering my software. If they are particularly angry, I might offer to give them a reduced price or throw in some additional software if they register. If I'm patient, listen to their complaints, and am sympathetic to their problem, the call usually results in the person registering the software.
- The distributor must stop selling copies of your program upon written notification from you. Without this requirement, it can be difficult to quickly stop someone who is misrepresenting your shareware from selling it.
- None of the files on your disk may be modified in any way. All the files must be distributed together, although other files may be added.
- The dealer must correctly use and identify any trademarks you have. This is important to protect your trademarks. If you don't protect them, you can lose them. The previous five items are musts in any distribution agreement. In addition, you might want to include one or more of the following.
- The distributor must provide you with copies of any catalog listing

your software. This allows you to check the description of your software to ensure that it's correct. It also lets you see whether or not the catalog properly identifies the software listed in it as shareware.

- Describe any restrictions on distribution of your software. For example, you might not want it sold outside the U.S. in order to protect the rights you have given or sold to foreign distributors.
- The distributor must refer any customer complaints or problems to you. This ensures that customers are not getting upset over problems you never hear about. You need to know what users are saying about your software and whether or not they're having problems with it.
- If you don't want your shareware sold in certain ways, such as on retail racks or CD-ROM disks, include that restriction as a part of your distribution license.
- You might want to require that certain types of distributors, BBSs, user groups, etc. have written permission from you before distributing your shareware. This has several advantages. For example, if you require written permission, you know who is distributing your shareware and can send them new updates. It also provides you with better control of your software. Every year I find two or three companies who are selling my software in ways I don't approve. In one case, a computer supplier was putting copies of my shareware on the hard disks of their computers and claiming they wrote the software. I take action to stop people who do this and, if appropriate, collect damages. My requirement that vendors have written permission before distributing my software has made going after copyright infringments easy. If they haven't received written permission from me, it's an open-and-shut case that's quickly settled.

A copy of the distribution license I put in my VENDOR.DOC file is provided as a part of the sample VENDOR.DOC file shown in chapter 13.

What you should provide to disk distributors

Based on my shareware distributor survey, the two biggest complaints shareware distributors have are that authors don't provide descriptions when they send a disk and that they don't keep distributors up-to-date with current shareware versions. If you don't provide a description of your software with your disks, distributors will have to write their own for their catalogs. No one knows your software better than you. You're the person best qualified to write a description that will help sell your program.

Here are some of the comments distributors wrote on my survey forms in response to a question that asked what shareware authors could do to help dealers:

"Send better cover letters with programs; list registration fee, system requirements, if it replaces an earlier version; and include a short description."
— Dealer who sells 2,000 disks per month

"Listen to feedback on how to improve the product. Include a user survey on each disk."
— New dealer just getting started

"Send new programs/new versions as soon as available with no strings attached, i.e., if a distributor is willing to catalog, copy, and distribute at his expense, then the author should not request payment in any form from the distributor."
— Distributor with 1,500 disks in his catalog

"Leave room on disks for dealers to put their menu program and logo."
— Dealer who sells 350 disks per month

"Keep us updated and send complete descriptions of products."
— Most common response

Tracking sales

If you want to find out which distributors reach the users most likely to register your software, you might find it helpful to put something on your disk that allows you to track who distributed it. I use a system where I put the name and address of the distributor, BBS, information service, etc., in a file on the disk. When my software boots it reads the name and address from this file and displays them as a part of the introductory screen. When the user prints the registration form, the software puts the distributor's name on the form. Combined with my asking people who register by phone where they got their shareware disk, I can tell which distributors bring me the most sales. Two notes of caution:

- It takes a lot of work. I put the distributor's name and address on a disk to help publicize the people distributing my disks. I feel it's worth the extra effort. A simpler approach is to code your disks with serial numbers and keep track of which number is assigned to which distributor.
- Don't eliminate distributors because you haven't received registrations that can be identified as coming from disks they sold. I've supplied disks to distributors for over two years before I received registrations coming from disks they sold. In one case, I received no registrations that I could track to a specific distributor until the distributor began supplying disks to a retail chain. Now this same distributor is the leader in generating registrations for several of my programs.

CD-ROM disks

I'll go out on a limb here and predict that a significant part of the future of shareware lies with CD-ROM distribution. I used to buy three or four disks every month from various shareware catalogs, just to help me stay up-to-date with what other authors are doing. I'd also download several programs a month from CompuServe. Since I purchased my CD-ROM drive, I haven't downloaded or purchased another shareware program. When I need to look for a certain type of program, I go to my CD-ROM disks. I have only four CD-ROM shareware disks, but each has over 3,000 programs. So far one of them has always had the program I've wanted to look at. When I can immediately find the program I'm looking for on a disk I already have, there's no reason to download programs or order disks from catalogs. For me, the convenience provided by a shareware CD-ROM probably means I'll never buy another shareware disk again—and I'm betting that most consumers will agree with me.

As I'm writing this it's the summer of 1993 and CD-ROM disks have not yet made a significant impact on the software market, but they've stirred up a minor controversy in the shareware industry. Some shareware authors don't want their programs placed on CD-ROM disks. They see vendors who are selling thousands of disks that include their programs, but they don't get a single registration.

To me this is only a natural characteristic of CD-ROM distribution of shareware. CD-ROM disks have thousands of programs on them and it's unlikely that any one CD-ROM owner will be interested in your software. If your software targets a niche market, instead of a broad horizontal market, very few people who get the CD-ROM will be interested in your software.

There's another characteristic of CD-ROMs that can hurt some authors. Not only do CD-ROM disks include your software, but they include all of your competitor's also. CD-ROMS make it easier for users to do a side-by-side comparisons of various shareware programs and pick the one that's best for them. This means that it's even more important that your software be high quality, good looking, and easy to use. When people have a variety of programs already in front of them, they're unlikely to spend a lot of time with a program they can't immediately understand. They'll just move on to the next program. This puts more emphasis on the need to make your shareware very easy to use.

CD-ROM problems

Everyone seems to be trying to jump onto the CD-ROM bandwagon, and this is leading to some problems. For example, some BBS operators who have built large libraries of files are putting their libraries on CD-ROM disks and marketing those disks. However, in some cases they're publishing disks with out-of-date files and programs that authors don't want distributed. People who have never been involved in shareware are trying to jump into the market for CD-ROMS and many are paying little attention to what they put on their disks. For example, I have a CD-ROM that includes five separate versions of my Play 'n' Learn software, all out-of-date. It also includes version 1.05 of my Home Insurance software, which was discontinued in 1988.

Even when a CD-ROM is published with current, up-to-date shareware, it might take a year to sell all the disks that were pressed. If you have a program on that CD-ROM and you discover a bug in it, there's nothing you can do. The buggy version will continue to be distributed until all the disks are sold. Before authorizing your software to be distributed on CD-ROM, be sure it's completely bug free.

BBSs, user groups, and magazines

Besides shareware dealers, you should provide copies of your shareware to BBSs and electronic information services. My survey shows that most authors upload their shareware to CompuServe. You should also consider other services such as GEnie, Prodigy, and American On-Line. They all have substantial subscriber bases. With these services, you can upload your shareware using a modem. You can also mail your shareware to all of these services. (Addresses are on the disk included with this book). However, when you mail your programs someone else will decide where they're posted. When you upload your software, you decide where you want it placed. If you don't have a modem or don't want to spend time calling individual BBSs, Andrew Saucci, Jr., runs a service that will upload your program to a variety of BBSs and information services. You can contact him by writing to him at:

Megapost
641 Koelbel Ct.
Baldwin, NY 115103915
800-538-8461

Uploading your software to BBSs is also an effective way of getting it to as many users as possible. For some types of software, BBS distribution is the best source of registrations. I'm finding that as BBSs become more popular and modems become faster, even large programs are getting wide BBS distribution and large numbers of downloads. BBSs should be a key part of your shareware distribution plan. However, if you don't have a high-speed modem, uploading your software to a large number of BBSs can produce some big phone bills.

To learn about BBSs and information services, I recommend reading *Dr. File Finder's Guide To Shareware* by Mike Callahan and Nick Anis (Osborne/McGraw-Hill, Inc., 1990). This book not only includes the phone numbers for several hundred BBSs, but it also provides detailed instructions on using both BBSs and information services. And it's packed with information about shareware. If you're going to be involved with shareware, you should have a copy of this book.

I also recommend you send a copy of your program to Dr. File Finder, Mike Callahan. His address is:

Dr. File Finder
c/o FF&P Enterprises
P.O. Box 591
Elizabeth, CO 80107

Dr. File Finder's BBS number is (901) 753-7213.

Running your own BBS

An excellent way to distribute your shareware is to run your own BBS. I consider myself to be telecommunications impaired—I have a terrible time getting my computer to do things that involve telephone lines—but I have been able to set up my own BBS. With some of the new BBS software that's now available, setting up a BBS is relatively easy.

The main advantage of running your own BBS is that it provides you with a means to get the shareware versions of your software to users immediately. If someone who's interested in your software needs a copy immediately, just have him call your BBS. And it's a great asset when providing technical support. For example, if users call with questions, and you find they're using an older version of your software (possibly a version that had some problems), you can have them call your BBS to get the latest version. I've even had situations in which an unregistered user had discovered a problem with my software, and a half-hour later I had the fixed version on my BBS ready for him to download.

If you don't want to run your own BBS, many times you can set up an arrangement with the sysop of a local BBS. Most sysops are happy to make their board available as the home BBS for a shareware author. They'll generally agree to provide your shareware so that first-time callers can download it, and let you use the BBS for technical support. In return they get more traffic and publicity for their BBS.

However, I prefer to run my own BBS because it gives me the flexibility to do want I want, when I want to do it. In my case I use the BBS to post announcements about new products, distribute the latest versions of my shareware, and exchange files with users and beta testers. And I have a subscription section that provides software updates for registered users. Registered users pay a $25 annual subscription fee that gives them access to a private section on the BBS. The private section has the most recent versions of my software, plus utilities that work with my software—all available for subscribers to download.

If you want to run your own BBS, I recommend the Tri-BBS software. I've found it to be very easy to use, and simple to set up. You can actually install the software and have your BBS running in about ten minutes. Tri-BBS is available as shareware.

User groups

User groups have generally not been a good source of registrations for shareware authors and, unless you have a special reason that leads you to believe that user groups will generate registrations for your shareware, I don't recommend sending disks to users groups. You might want to send disks to a couple of the major groups such as HAL-PC and the Boston Computer Society. But, in general, I'd focus my distribution efforts on disk vendors and BBSs.

If you're going to send copies of your shareware to user groups, the best source of user group addresses and BBS numbers is *Computer Shopper*. They publish a comprehensive list of user-group addresses on a regular basis. Even if it isn't an issue with user-group addresses, pick up a copy of the magazine. It's filled with useful information for shareware authors.

No one seems to know the reason why user groups generate so few registrations. A survey of user groups conducted by Arthur Saltzman, Ph.D. (California State University at San Bernardino, Marketing Department) showed that user-group members feel they register shareware in large numbers. But the general experience of authors has been that few registrations result from disks distributed by user groups. Unless your software has a proven capability of drawing registrations from user groups, you'll do better to stick with shareware disk vendors and BBSs.

Magazines

How you approach magazines depends on your budget and the amount of time you want to put into marketing. My general experience has been that sending shareware disks to magazines for review will probably not result in a review. However, it can be worth the cost of mailing 30 or 40 extra disks.

It's worth the extra effort because sending your shareware disks to editors makes them aware of your existence. Keep in mind that if you don't put your software in front of these editors, no one else will do it for you. I also suggest that you include a printed copy of your documentation with any disks you send to editors. These are busy people and they'll tend to look at software that can quickly be installed and used. Forcing an editor to print the documentation puts a barrier between your software and the editor.

Don't expect much feedback from the disks you send to editors. Over 100,000 shareware programs are already in circulation and a flood of new shareware is being released (150+ disks per month according to George Pulido, librarian for PC-SIG). Plus, the volume of retail software released each month is even greater. It's very difficult for your software to get noticed.

"Increase the frequency of contact—if a major new version is released, send out a press release. Also include the product along with your release—even interesting releases often go without follow up, but I'll always boot a disk."
— Editor of a computer magazine with 100,000 readers

Watch out for bugs

Be sure that your software is bug-free before sending it out to disk vendors, BBSs, and user groups. If you're still in the bug-fixing stage, keep it among friends, local user groups, and local BBSs. It's always best and cheapest to do things right the first time. You don't want to send out a lot of correction disks to fix a bug. Serious bugs give your software a bad reputation from which it might be difficult to recover. If you're trying to get feedback, be sure to identify the disk as a beta test version or early version. If you don't properly identify your disks, you might end up having some very angry users and a reputation for producing buggy software. Plus, remember that old versions will circulate forever, so you don't want a version with bugs in it to be widely distributed.

Selling through retail stores

Going through retail channels is difficult and expensive. You need brand-name recognition and a list price that allows dealers and others in the distribution channel to make a reasonable profit. Next time you're in a software store, look for the lowest-priced software you can find. You're unlikely to see anything priced under $25, and most items will be priced well above that.

I've already discussed the retail channel in the previous chapter, but there are a few additional suggestions I can add. If you're determined to try retail stores, first contact a few local dealers. Usually, they won't be interested. It isn't worth their effort. But if you have a unique program, you might find one who's willing to give your software a try. Your best opportunity might be to get to know someone who works in a software store. You might be able to get the store to put out a few copies of your software on a consignment basis. Don't think that this won't cost them anything, however. Shelf space is very valuable. Some of the fiercest battles in retail stores are fought over shelf space. By putting your software on his shelf, a dealer might lose sales from another, better-selling program.

If you really want to get into retail channel work, create both a "push" and a "pull" for your software. Go on the road and push your software at trade shows and conventions. Talk to dealers and distributors. Show them how they can make more money carrying your software. Become a non-stop whirlwind of promotion for your software. Create a pull for your software by referring users that want to register to retailers. These retailers will order your software for the user. You run the risk of the user not bothering to buy a copy of your software, but you'll also show dealers that there's a demand for your programs.

Pushing your software into the retail channel is tough and the risk of failure is high—especially if you don't have big money backing you. However, even if you want to stick with just the shareware channel, you shouldn't hide from the retail channel. Many users feel more comfortable buying from a dealer, and many dealers will special order software for users. Be sure that your software is listed in several directories that dealers use for locating names and addresses of software publishers. I'll discuss directories and will provide you with the names and addresses of several.

If you want to contact computer dealers directly, here are several directories that provide the names and addresses of dealers:

Chromatic Communication Enterprises, Inc.
P.O. Box 30127
Walnut Creek, CA 94598-9878
The cost is $495 for a list of 5,135 computer stores in the U.S. A second list of 1,126 Canadian dealers is available at $425. Their phone number is 800-782-DISK or 415-945-1602 inside California.

CSG Information Services
425 Park Ave.
New York, NY 10022
The cost is $289 for a directory of 2,800 computer/software resellers. A list of 5,000 VARs also is available for $289.

PC Computer Source Book
21684 Granda Ave.
Cupertino, CA 95014
They publish regional listings of computer distributors and dealers. Each book costs $14.95.

The NACD National Directory:
The Official Computer Yellow Pages
NACD
13103 FM 1960 W. #206
P.O. Box 690029
Houston, TX 77269
This is a compilation of names, addresses, and phone numbers for distributors, manufacturers, publishers, rental companies, retail stores, service companies, VARs, and used-computer dealers. The cost is $69.95.

Software catalogs

If you've seen mail-order catalogs from companies such as Tiger Software, you might think that it'd be great if you could get your software into one of those catalogs. The problem is that it takes a lot of money.

There are two types of mail-order companies: those who sell space to anyone wanting to sell software, and those who sell software themselves. If it's a company who sells space, it will cost you between $8,000 and $25,000 to get into the catalog. Those are minimum figures; the larger advertisement you have, the more it will cost. If it's a catalog company who sells software, they will consider only software that already has a successful advertising campaign going and is already in retail stores. Catalog companies aren't in the business of introducing new software; their business is to move high volumes of programs that are already popular.

Low-cost retail (LCR) software

Another route into the retail market is through low-cost retail (LCR) software. This is software that'is usually sold for under $10.00 in mass-merchandise and discount stores. You'll find LCR software in stores such as Walmart, Office Depot, and even Home Base.

Many of the LCR software publishers had their start as shareware disk vendors and they maintain very strong ties to the shareware industry. Just by releasing your software as shareware, you'll be putting it in a position where it will be seen by LCR software publishers. The LCR software business is fairly new and there are new publishers starting up all the time—and I assume many of them will go out of business just as quickly. If you want to send your software directly to some LCR publishers, check your local discount stores for LCR software and get the addresses of the publishers from the software packages. In addition, here are the addresses for two of the larger LCR publishers:

Expert Software
800 Douglas Road
North Tower, Suite 355
Coral Gables, FL 33134-3128

UAV Corporation
P.O. Box 7647
2100 Carolina Place
Fort Mill, SC 28241

You have a much better chance of getting your software published as an LCR program than as a traditional retail software package. LCR publishers are in the business of selling large volumes of a variety of low-cost software and they're always looking for new products. However, they're typically interested only in software that has some very specific characteristics—it must be fully usable without a printed manual, it must have a mass-market appeal, and it must not require technical support.

Selling your software internationally

"It is difficult to get recognition from U.S. shareware authors; our letters go unanswered."

— A shareware distributor in England

Offering your software to users in other countries can be a significant source of sales. Many software companies report that 25% to 35% of their revenues come from sales outside the U.S. My experience is that about 25% of my registrations come from foreign users.

Selling your software outside the U.S. does involve some problems. The biggest problems have to do with U.S. shareware authors not responding to inquiries from users outside the U.S. and the difficulties U.S. authors have with banking and currency exchange.

Unfortunately, many U.S. shareware authors don't respond to letters from foreign dealers and users. This has led foreign users to be hesitant about registering shareware with U.S. authors. In many cases, these users pay the registration fee by purchasing a money order in U.S. dollars. If the author doesn't respond, or even if the author sends the money order back, the user can't get a refund. The money is lost, and the user gets nothing in return.

If you aren't going to accept registrations from outside the U.S., then say so in your documentation. If you want to include Canada but exclude all other countries, state that you accept registrations from the U.S. and Canada only. If you don't do this, you might build a reputation for unresponsiveness to foreign users. This reputation could hurt your business if you to expand outside the U.S. in the future.

If you're going to accept registrations from other countries, handle all correspondence, letters, and software shipments just as you do for your U.S.-based customers—with the exception of using air mail for anything you send. Answer all letters the same day you receive them. Ship all registered versions of your software as soon as possible. To cover the higher shipping costs, you can charge two to three times more for shipping and handling than you do for U.S. orders. Don't get carried away, however. One of the sore points with users in other countries is the high shipping and handling fees some U.S. authors charge. You should charge more, but be reasonable.

In responding to foreign inquiries for information, if you don't want to pay the extra cost of air-mail postage, you can require that your users pay for it. Ask your users to purchase international reply coupons and include them with any request for information. International reply coupons can be exchanged for the minimum postage of an overseas letter. However, they're relatively expensive for your users to buy. For example, a coupon costs 60 pence ($1.00) in the U.K. I do not recommend this as a good way to encourage foreign users to register. The best advice is to treat foreign users the same as U.S. users. This means you pay the cost of air-mail postage. The same rule discussed earlier applies here—the easier you make it for users to register your software, the more registrations you'll get.

Getting paid

The easiest way for you to handle registration fees is to have your customers use Visa or MasterCard. To accept credit cards, you need to establish yourself as a Visa/MasterCard merchant. (I discuss how to get merchant status for credit cards in chapter 8.) Credit card company will handle the necessary currency conversion.

Don't expect all foreign users to have credit cards. For example, some countries don't allow their citizens to have Visa or MasterCard accounts that are valid internationally. This was true in Argentina for quite a while. In other countries with differences in culture, very few people have credit cards. They aren't an accepted way of doing business in that culture.

An alternative is to require checks, or money orders in U.S. dollars drawn on a U.S. bank. Be sure your documentation specifies that the check must be drawn on a U.S. bank. If you don't require the check or money order be drawn on a U.S. bank, you can get into some hefty bank fees when you try to cash it. This has happened to me only once. I received a $67 check in U.S. dollars drawn on an Italian bank. My bank charged me $20 to cash the check. The Italian bank added another $20 in fees. I ended up with $27 out of a $67 registration payment.

The ease of cashing a check or money order drawn on a foreign bank depends on the country from which the check comes. Most of my foreign registrations come from nine countries: Canada, Australia, New Zealand, England, Ireland, Germany, Sweden, Norway, and France. I have never had any problems with checks from these countries, regardless of whether or not they're in U.S. dollars or the local currency. To handle checks from foreign countries, you need to work with a bank with a foreign currency department. In addition, as with most other banking services, you need to establish a personal relationship with your banker. The manager of the branch you visit should know you personally and feel comfortable working with you. You know you've accomplished this when the branch manager says "hello" to you in a grocery store (or other nonbanking location).

Checks from some countries, in particular Australia, will have NOT NEGOTIABLE either printed or written on them—even if they're in U.S. dollars. This can cause problems for some U.S. banks who don't understand how the banking systems in other countries work. You might need to explain to the bank that, in Australia, NOT NEGOTIABLE doesn't mean that the check cannot be cashed. The check is good. What it means is that the check can be deposited only by the person or company named as the payee on the check. It means the same thing as For Deposit Only does in the United States.

Another alternative is to ask people to pay in cash. You can request U.S. dollars or accept foreign currency. You can get foreign currency converted at your local commercial bank. Don't add a hefty surcharge to cover the cost of currency conversion. In many cases, you can convert cash payments in foreign currency at about the same rate your bank charges to handle a credit card transaction.

Accepting registrations through foreign dealers

You can also work through a foreign shareware disk dealer who's set up to sell registered versions of software. This provides users with a local contact for purchasing your software, and it eliminates the problems of currency conversion for you. If you're interested in finding out more about this type of arrangement, write to the foreign shareware distributors. To find out which distributors handle registrations for authors in other countries, check the documentation files included with some of the better-selling shareware programs. They'll typically list the names of the distributors who are representing that software in other countries.

You'll probably find that the best way to get distributors in other countries to represent your software is to send your shareware to as many shareware vendors in other countries as you can. As I've talked with other shareware authors, I've haven't found a single one who has "sold" his software to a distributor in another country. In every case the distributor has noticed the shareware program and contacted the author.

Encouraging foreign registrations

If you're going to pursue foreign registrations, make foreign users as comfortable as possible. Put a statement in your documentation or READ.ME file that welcomes foreign users. Let them know you'll answer their letters ASAP and that you'll return their phone calls (if you provide phone support). Overseas calls aren't as expensive as you might think. If your software includes the dollar sign or anything else specific to the U.S., make a version that includes the pound sign for the U.K. or eliminate the $ symbol in foreign versions. Also keep in mind that most countries use a different format for the date. Instead of mm-dd-yy, most countries use dd-mm-yy.

To encourage foreign users to register, I even go as far as offering to accept personal checks in their local currency. My bank can handle most foreign checks, so this isn't a big problem. In two years, I've received only a few personal checks in a foreign currency, but making this offer is a good marketing strategy that shows I'm seriously interested in foreign registrations.

International support

You must support foreign users the same way you support U.S. users. I received the following comment from a user of my software in London: "I wish U.K. suppliers of hardware and software were as efficient and helpful as you." If you get letters with comments like that, then you're properly serving the foreign market. Just remember to treat everyone the same, providing super service across the board, and you'll be going in the right direction. The following are some helpful hints for doing business internationally:

- There's a helpful booklet from the post office on international postal rates. Ask for Publication 51, International Postal Rates and Fees, at your local post office.
- When mailing catalogs, software, or other small packages to a foreign country, use small-packet air mail. It's significantly cheaper than regular air mail.
- Include the phrase "All Rights Reserved" as part of your copyright notice on your disks and in your manuals. Some countries require these words to protect your copyright fully.
- According to the Commerce Department, to provide complete protection for your copyright on an international basis, you should also mark any package containing software with the letters GTDR. This stands for General Technical Data Restricted.

6
Shareware on retail racks

I've already talked about what were, in the past, the traditional means of distributing shareware disks: catalog vendors, BBSs, and user groups. But over the past few years, an exciting new method of shareware distribution has developed: retail rack sales. Since then, retail rack sales of shareware disks has become the biggest controversy in the shareware industry.

"Shareware sold in a retail setting is either a great opportunity, or a great disaster, for a shareware author. If your product is not available anywhere as a royalty-paying retail title, then shareware racks offer you an opportunity to crack the retail barrier. You will receive increased exposure and with it the opportunity to reach a whole new audience. One that doesn't have modems and doesn't buy from catalog vendors.

However, this increased exposure doesn't automatically guarantee increased registrations. Some authors have reported registration rates as low as 1 in every 2,000, or even 4,000 shareware disks sold at retail. Others have reported receiving angry calls from consumers who didn't understand shareware and thought the registration fee was a nasty 'bait and switch' tactic. Still, a new author can't easily dismiss the opportunity that mass distribution brings."

— Dave Snyder, MVP Software

Shareware racks: controversy and opportunity

The term *rack sales* refers to the sale of shareware disks in retail stores—usually in some form of a rack or bin. You've probably seen them; shareware racks seem to be everywhere: In K-Mart and Walmart, in bookstores and drug stores, in airport gift shops, and sometimes even in computer stores. Shareware rack vendors are selling millions of copies of shareware disks through retail stores.

These are the same disks that shareware vendors sell in their catalogs. For retail sales, however, the disks are usually packaged with a bright, color graphic (to catch the consumer's eye) and sealed in some sort of package (to prevent people from handling the disks). Retail prices range from about $1.99 up to $9.99.

The source of the controversy, and the problem some shareware authors have with shareware disks being sold in retail stores, is that they feel they're getting very few registrations from this method of distribution. In 1993, 40 authors, representing over 180 shareware programs, felt serious enough about this problem to send a letter to all shareware disk vendors. This letter said, in part:

Dear Shareware Vendor:

The shareware authors listed below want to express their appreciation for the services provided by shareware vendors. You promote and distribute our products, you help us reach markets we would not otherwise reach, you educate shareware users, and in general you do a terrific job. We also appreciate the traditional goodwill between shareware vendors and authors, and in this spirit we are sending this letter to you.

Recently an issue has become important to many shareware authors, and we wish to tell you about this issue and remind you of the distribution policies adopted by some authors for their products. The authors whose names appear on this letter are by no means the only authors with an interest in the issue.

In recent years shareware rack vending (SRV) and CD-ROMs have become popular methods for vendors to sell shareware disks. We authors certainly applaud efforts to expand shareware awareness and usage. However, SRV and CD-ROMs have caused a number of problems for some authors. For one thing, they may conflict with retail sales on which authors receive royalties. In addition, some authors report getting irate calls from users who did not understand that the shareware disk they bought from a store requires separate payment to the author.

But the biggest problem is that many authors report very few registrations from SRV and CD-ROMs. Dave Snyder of MVP Software reports that he receives fewer than 1 registration for every 2,000 SRV disks sold. Mike Prestwich of Imagisoft reports that a major rack vendor shipped 12,000 SRV copies of Chinese Checkers, and to date Mike has received only three registrations that can be traced to that distribution. Other authors can trace no or very few registrations to CD-ROM distribution.

These dismal statistics are bad for all of us. When authors don't make money from shareware they abandon it, leaving unsupported software behind. Or they simply stop developing new shareware.

This letter does a good job of describing the problem and expressing how some authors feel. As a solution, the letter goes on to explain that shareware vendors need to honor the distribution licenses of shareware authors and, in most cases, get written permission from the author before distributing shareware on a retail rack or CD-ROM. In other words, it told vendors that the author of a shareware program has control over how that program is distributed; If the author does not want the program sold on retail racks, then the vendor may not sell it on retail racks.

The source of the problem

The only real difference between rack sales of shareware disks and all other forms of shareware distribution is that the racks are in retail stores—which is the source of the problem for many shareware authors.

These authors feel that, when someone buys something in a store, the person expects that he or she then owns it. Imagine how you'd feel if, when you purchased a box of cookies, there was a message inside that said "You may try a few of these cookies to see whether you like them. But if you eat more than five cookies you're required to send $5.00 to the Amarillo Cookie Company." Or imagine purchasing a hammer in a store. Engraved on the handle is the following: "You may try this hammer for 30 days. If you use it after that, you must send $10 to the Acme Hammer Company."

The feeling of many shareware authors is that when people buy something in a store, they expect to own that item. People don't expect to have to pay for it again.

But is this really the problem? Stores sell trial versions of many things. It's common to find small packages of many types of products. My son loves going grocery shopping on Wednesdays because that's the day the deli counter puts out a lot of samples. You can try a sample of each meat and cheese before you buy it. And there are almost always small, trial bottles of shampoo, soap, and other products for sale. You can buy a small sample and try it before buying a large bottle. Try before you buy—isn't that the basic principle behind shareware?

The problem isn't that people don't expect the "try before you buy" concept in retail stores. The problem is that people aren't familiar with the concept in relation to shareware. And it doesn't help when, in many cases, the sign above the shareware rack says "low-cost software." What if a grocery store display of two-ounce trial-size bottles of shampoo had a sign over them saying "low-cost shampoo?" You'd probably consider that to be misleading. Shareware should be treated the same way.

We all love finding a bargain that's almost too good to be true. And that's how many people see shareware in stores—as bargain-priced software where you can get a full-featured word processing program for $3.99.

The way shareware is marketed in stores makes overcoming this problem very difficult. It's generally marketed as an impulse item. Impulse means that people buy it on impulse with very little thought (or reading of the package). People see the "low-cost software" sign on top of the rack, spot a package that looks interesting, and buy it. Some people might read the information about shareware that's usually on the back of most vendors' packages, but others never take the time to read the package.

Even when the shareware racks have signs that identify their contents as shareware, most people don't know what the word *shareware* means.

Some rack signs include "try before you buy," but some people, when they're hot on the trail of a bargain, never notice the sign. The bottom line is that, until the word *shareware* becomes an ingrained part of our culture, a word that everyone understands without thinking about it—there will be people who buy shareware disks expecting that they've fully purchased the program.

What shareware authors really want

Let's stop and think about what's happening. Before shareware rack vending exists, shareware authors want two basic things from vendors who sell our disks:

- We want them to sell lots of our disks.
- We don't want them to misrepresent shareware as being free software nor do we want them to give their customers the impression they can use the software forever without paying the author for the program.

Shareware rack vendors are doing a very good job with the first of these; they are selling lots—make that millions—of copies of shareware disks. That's good. We can't get people to register our shareware until we get them to try it first.

The rack vendor's side of the story

Most shareware rack vendors are also doing a fairly good job of not misrepresenting shareware. However, they also have several constraints that limit what they can do to better inform people about what they're buying. First, keep in mind that in order to sell lots of copies the vendor has to position the rack as an impulse item. People browsing through a store aren't going to spend a lot of time reading signs and paragraphs of information. Also, rack vendors have only a limited amount of space to work with on shareware packaging and on the signs that go on the rack.

I'm not trying to make excuses for rack vendors, but we have to deal with reality. Both the rack vendor and the author want lots of people to buy the shareware disk, and accomplishing that puts constraints on the rack vendor. However, this doesn't mean that shareware should be misrepresented as low-cost software.

Things you can do to protect your shareware

Most shareware rack vendors put a definition of shareware on the backs of their packages. Even rack vendors who sell $3\frac{1}{2}$" disks (which have a much smaller package size than $5\frac{1}{4}$" disks) and even those who must put everything in two languages are able to find room to put a description of shareware on the packaging (see FIG. 6-1). So there should be no excuse for vendors not putting a description of shareware on their packages.

6-1 A full-sized reproduction of the back of a retail rack shareware package, published by Universal Shareware Alternatives. Not only have they included all the necessary information, but they've put it in two languages.

One thing you can do is to put a requirement in your vendor license that requires retail vendors to explain shareware on their packaging. My attitude is that, if I'm going to give vendors permission to sell my shareware in a retail store, they must have an explanation of shareware on the package.

I also feel that shareware should be properly represented by the signs placed on the rack. A sign that says "low-cost software" is not acceptable to me. The word *shareware* or the phrase "try before you buy" or similar wording should appear somewhere on the sign, even if it's in small print.

To ensure that my software is sold only by shareware rack vendors who meet my requirements, I require that they contact me for written permission before they distribute my software and that they send a sample of the packaging they use. If their packaging contains an explanation of shareware, then I give them permission to sell copies of my shareware. I also inform them that the signs on the racks or bins carrying my shareware must not misrepresent shareware as low-cost software.

You are in control

As a shareware author, you have control over how your software is distributed. If you think certain retail racks will cause problems for your software, you can prevent it from being sold on those racks. You can require that shareware rack vendors send you copies of their packaging before you allow them to sell your disks. You can require that they be ASP members. You can require that they pay you a royalty. You can require that your trademark or logo be featured on any packaging. If you don't want your shareware sold on retail racks at all, you can prohibit it. You own the copyright and you control what is done with your software.

However, before you start deciding on the limits you want to put on shareware rack vendors, here's a little more information about the SRV channel.

Characteristics of shareware racks

There are several characteristics of shareware racks that limit what shareware rack vendors can do. For example, they are limited in the type of software they can carry. They are limited in the number of programs they can carry. They are limited by the high cost of creating a slick-looking retail package. They have only limited space on the package to promote the product, include necessary information (such as a bar code), and explain shareware. They are limited in that they can carry only programs that fit on a single disk.

Limited space

The key characteristic of shareware racks is that they have limited space. Rack vendors typically will put between 40 and 60 titles on a rack in a store. There just isn't enough space for more. Shareware catalogs, on the other hand, can have up to 3,000 or 4,000 titles, with the average catalog size being about 2,000 titles.

Mass-market products only

In general, shareware racks are targeted at mass markets. They carry only titles that appeal to large numbers of people. The next time you're in a store that has a shareware rack, notice the type of software you see on that rack. It will be mostly games and educational software, with a few other programs such as utilities, tutorials, astrology, and possibly one or two of the big-name word processing or spreadsheet programs.

These are the kinds of programs people in stores are interested in buying. You won't find payroll software, project management software, or programming utilities. You won't find software designed for small niche markets. As the retail market for shareware expands, you might start to see shareware sold in specialty stores (in which case specialized programs will find a market), but as things stand now shareware rack vendors are interested only in programs that can be sold to large numbers of people.

"The market being addressed by shareware racks is one that is likely to be less familiar with shareware than folks who get their shareware from catalog vendors, BBSs, or user groups. The products that do well on racks are games, home and hobby applications, and general-purpose applications such as word processors and spreadsheets. Shareware rack sales are an impulse buy, usually by someone who is attracted solely because of a catchy program name or flashy screen shot. Therefore, it is important for the vendor and the author to educate the user about shareware. And it is very important for the author to make the program easy to understand and use."

— Bob Burns, Product Line Manager for Gold Medallion software

Expensive retail packaging

It's expensive for a shareware rack vendor to put a program onto a rack. They have the cost of creating a sharp-looking color package and then having to manufacture thousands of copies of a program for which they might not get paid for two or three months. Shareware rack vendors need to put out a lot of up-front money before they see any return on their investment. This means they must feel fairly positive that a program will sell well before they're willing to invest in the up-front costs of creating a retail package for that product.

Multiple disk programs

The profit margins on shareware disks sold on racks are very small. Vendors make their money by selling large numbers of disks. This means that they cannot afford the extra cost of putting two or more disks in one package. Shareware programs that require multiple disks won't make it onto retail racks. However, the current trend is away from 360K 5$\frac{1}{4}$" floppy disks and toward 720K 3$\frac{1}{2}$" disks. This means that nowadays you can have up to 720K of disk space to work with. If your program is larger than that, however, it has little chance of getting onto a shareware rack.

Getting your software on racks

All these characteristics of shareware retail racks mean that it can be very difficult to get a program onto a shareware rack. Each rack has only limited space and rack vendors want to invest their money only in programs that will sell to large numbers of people. Only high-quality programs that appeal to a mass market have a chance of getting onto a shareware rack. When you're deciding on the requirements you want to place on rack vendors, you need to keep this in mind. The more requirements you place on the vendor, the less likely it is that your shareware will make it onto the rack.

If you have a high-quality game that's popular and is receiving a lot of good press coverage, you're in a good position. If you make a DOS shell program, you should keep in mind that there are a lot of other DOS shell programs and that you're therefore not in a position to place many requirements on a rack vendor.

That's the bad news. There is one characteristic of retail sales that will help you get your shareware onto a retail rack, however: the product life cycle.

Product life cycle

One characteristic of retail products is that they always have a life cycle. Most people continue to come back to and shop at the same stores. Once they've looked over the disks on a shareware rack and tried the programs they found interesting, they have no reason to continue looking at the shareware rack. To maintain shoppers' interest, rack vendors must have a continual supply of new shareware to offer their customers. As sales of old programs drop off, they must be replaced with new software. As a result, rack vendors are always looking for new software, and this opens opportunities for your shareware program.

Advantages of shareware racks for authors

Shareware racks offer one big advantage to shareware authors: they get copies of your program into the hands (and computers) of tens of thousands of people who would otherwise never see or hear about your program. Shareware catalog vendors and BBSs reach only a small percentage of computer owners. Catalog vendors send out millions of catalogs, but there are tens of millions of computer owners who never see a shareware catalog. A large majority of computer owners don't have modems, and many of the people who bought computers that came equipped with a modem don't use their modems. However, nearly everyone goes to a grocery store, and shareware racks are showing up in grocery stores right next to the cash registers.

If you want to get your shareware into the hands of as many people as possible, then having it on shareware racks is one of the best ways to do it.

Another advantage of shareware racks is that many of the major shareware rack vendors are now paying royalties to the authors of the disks they're selling. Ten cents per copy sold has become the standard royalty, although this number can vary depending on the vendor and the popularity of the program.

Shareware rack royalties

Should you expect to get a royalty from every shareware rack vendor? That depends on how good your software is, what type of competition exists for it, and how popular it is. In other words, like anything else in business, it depends on the situation. If you want to get your shareware into retail stores, and there are many similar programs, you might want to undercut the competition and offer your software to vendors on a royalty-free basis. This gives them an incentive to carry your program instead of someone else's.

By the way, not all shareware authors feel that royalties on the sale of shareware disks are a good thing. Keep in mind that vendors who pay royalties not only have the added cost of royalty payments, they also have the added bookkeeping expense of having to track the royalties of the authors whose programs they carry. This means that vendors might tend to favor authors whose programs they're already carrying, so as not to increase their accounting costs. It also means that they'll tend to focus more intensely on finding software that will sell large numbers of disks, and they'll be less likely to consider a "marginal" program that might have been acceptable before they were paying royalties.

Don't count on making a significant amount of money on the royalties from the sale of your shareware on racks. It can be a nice source of some extra money, keeping in mind that none of the authors who responded to my 1993 survey reported more than one or two percent of their income coming from royalties paid on the sale of shareware disks. This might change in the future, but at present getting people to register your software is the best way to make a lot of money.

License fees

One of the biggest problems rack vendors have with paying royalties is the amount of paperwork required to track the royalties being paid to authors. There are a few retail vendors who stock a large number of titles. These are usually displayed in bins that can hold several hundred titles. For these vendors, in particular, the paperwork problem can be significant. To simplify the paperwork, some vendors will offer to pay a flat fee for the right to sell copies of your software over a set period of time, such as one year.

The advantage of this is that the vendor doesn't have to track the sales of individual disks and write a large number of quarterly checks. As an author, you don't need to depend on the vendor selling the disk; you get your money up front.

The disadvantage for the shareware author is that the vendor could sell a lot of copies of your program and you might make a lot more money if you got ten cents for each copy sold. You must decide whether the amount of money the vendor offers you is worth it to you. But keep in mind that the vendor is the one taking the risk. The vendor pays you up front and might not sell even a single copy of your program. In business, someone who takes a risk is usually compensated by having the opportunity to achieve greater profits.

Summary of advantages of shareware racks

I've spent a lot of time discussing the negative side of selling shareware in retail stores. However, there are many good reasons for allowing your shareware to be sold on retail racks.

- One of the keys to success in shareware is to get your software into the hands of as many people as possible. They can't buy your software until they try it. Retail racks move a huge volume of disks. While catalog vendors talk about selling thousands of copies of a program, rack vendors talk about selling tens of thousands of copies.
- With retail racks, you reach a mass market that generally doesn't buy from catalogs or download software from BBSs. Not only is this a huge market, but you're getting your software into the hands of people who otherwise will never hear about it.
- Shareware racks are excellent for software that people use only once. It's difficult to get people to register software that they use only once. They tend to use it and then forget about it. With shareware racks that pay a royalty, at least you can get some income.
- Even with software that's used every day, getting a royalty payment is nice. Just keep in mind that royalty payments don't replace the money you'd receive from registrations. But if you have the secret to success on shareware racks, you can get people to register and have the added bonus of getting a royalty payment on every copy of your shareware program that's sold.

Shareware rack examples

The secret to success on retail racks is to create a high-quality mass-market program that people need. Be sure you have good, strong registration incentives, and be sure that your software makes people aware that it's shareware and that it fully explains shareware. In other words, it's up to the rack vendor to sell lots of copies of your shareware and to not misrepresent it. And it's up to you to sell the user on buying your registered version and to protect your shareware from rack vendors who misrepresent shareware.

Here are some examples showing different SRV (shareware retail version) situations:

A new high-quality, mass-market program This is a high-quality program (as evaluated by other people such as the press—your evaluation of your software won't be objective). If you have a program like this, one that most people would find useful and that has no competition, then you can probably require a royalty if you offer it to rack vendors. However, you might need to promote your program to vendors by doing things such as including copies of reviews and letters from users. If your program has no track record, you'll probably need to convince vendors that it would be a good product for them to carry.

A proven game   If you have a game that is already a good seller on other racks, you're in a position to require that all rack vendors pay you a royalty. You might also require that they include your logo as a part of the package design (this will help to increase your brand-name recognition). In this case, you have a program that the rack vendors want, one that sells.

A high-quality, multidisk, business accounting system   It's almost impossible to get this kind of program onto a shareware rack. Multiple disk sets are too expensive to produce, and business software doesn't appeal to a mass market.

A set of hard disk utilities   There are a lot of hard disk utility programs available, and most rack vendors, if they want to carry this type of software, already have someone else's utilities on their racks. You first need to convince vendors that your software is better than the competition's, and you might need to give your software a competitive advantage by offering it on a royalty-free basis. If a vendor is paying a royalty to another author, the additional profit they can make by switching to your program could help get your program on the rack.

If these examples make shareware sound like any other business, then you're starting to understand retail sales. Most shareware authors write a program and send out copies to disk vendors and BBSs—and then their marketing efforts stop. They wait for something to happen. Such an approach to running a business doesn't work, and if you want to be successful you can't treat your business like a hobby. If you want financial success, you must make something happen. You must sell your software to both vendors and users. Instead of waiting for success, you should be actively working to promote it.

Ways to approach shareware rack sales

As the author of your software and the owner of the copyright on your software, you control what other people do with your software. You can allow your shareware version to be sold in catalogs but not on retail racks. Or you can allow your shareware to be sold on racks when they pay you a royalty. The VENDOR.DOC file is used to inform vendors, BBSs, users groups, and anyone else who wants to distribute your shareware version about the limits and requirements you've placed on its distribution. (This is discussed in more detail in the previous chapter.)

There is also a service offered by the Copyright Office called the Shareware Registry. The Shareware Registry provides a way for you to publicly announce your distribution license requirements. The Shareware Registry will be discussed in detail in the chapter 11. All you need to remember is that this is your software, you own it, and you can control how it's distributed. With that in mind, there are several approaches you can take toward the sale of your shareware on retail racks.

My approach to retail racks

I have the attitude that rack sales provide an opportunity to reach a lot of people; I just need to find a way to take advantage of that opportunity. Once they start using my shareware, then I worry about step two—getting them to send me the registration payment.

This attitude works well for me because I publish database software. If I can get people to use my software to establish a significant database of information, they're likely to continue using it. Switching from one database to another can be difficult and most people don't change programs once they get started. Understanding this is part of knowing my market and the people who use my software. Based on this understanding, I can design my software and its registration incentives so that most people will want to register the software.

However, my software does have a problem as far as retail racks are concerned. Most of my programs are niche programs, not mass-market software. Although some of the niche markets served by my software are very large (I make software for cataloging stamp collections, and there are over 20,000,000 stamp collectors in the U.S.), some rack vendors are either not interested in carrying my shareware or are interested in carrying only one or two programs. As a result, my approach to rack vendors is to let rack vendors carry my products without requiring them to pay a royalty. To ensure that shareware is properly explained on the disk package, I do require that rack vendors send me a sample of the packaging they use. I also require that they obtain written permission from me before they start to sell my programs.

So far, I've rejected only about 1 in 10 vendors for having an inadequate description of shareware, or no description of shareware, on their packaging. These have all been small, individual retail stores that put out a bin filled with shareware disks. The disks are not individually packaged, and there's no definition of shareware included with the disk the customer purchases. By requiring that a description of shareware be included with the disk, if someone calls to complain, I can always have them read the package the disk came in. Then they have no excuse for thinking they purchased a $60.00 program for $3.00.

Some software should receive royalty payments

I have several programs that are attractive to rack vendors and that, due to the nature of the market, don't generate many registrations. My software for cataloging baseball cards falls into this category. Because there are lots of baseball card collectors, this software has a large mass market. But most of them are young kids who don't have money to spend on a $60 software package. As a result, I get few registrations for this software. Even the copies sold through catalog vendors generate very few registrations.

My policy for this software is that, if rack vendors wants to carry this program, I require that they pay 10 cents per copy. The royalty payments partially compensate me for the lack of registration payments. In the meantime, I'm working to improve this software and find better ways to encourage users to register.

As you read this, you might say to yourself "Why doesn't he just reduce the cost of the software to something kids can afford?" The reason is that the software is based on a standard database engine that I don't feel I can sell for less than $60.00 and make a enough of a profit to stay in business. What I have done is create a new "lite" version of this software that costs only $24.95.

Authors who don't like royalties

Some authors feel that by accepting a royalty payment from the retail rack vendors, they're reducing the likelihood that users will register. In the past, some authors have encouraged people to register by telling them that what they've paid for the shareware disk goes exclusively to the disk vendor. To encourage people to register, they tell their users that they don't receive any part of the money paid to buy the disk. They get paid only if the user registers the software. These authors feel that if users know the author has received a royalty, they'll think the author has already been paid and they won't register the shareware version.

There are many attitudes authors have taken concerning retail sales of shareware. That's why it's a controversial subject. But it's also an area that's growing and provides a lot of opportunities for both authors and vendors.

The future

Because this is such a new area, you'll need to stay in touch with future retail rack vending developments. One of the best ways to learn about new developments is by attending the Summer Shareware Seminar (SSS) held each June. Or, if you can't attend, buy the audio tapes of the SSS sessions. (Chapter 17 has information on the SSS and SSS tapes.) Another good way to stay in touch is by joining one of the trade associations such as STAR or the ASP.

A low-cost way to see what changes are taking place is to watch what successful shareware authors are doing. When you're in a store, look for shareware racks and notice the type of programs on the rack. Make a note of new racks that appear in stores where you haven't seen them before. Buy several shareware programs off a rack now and then and look at the terms of distribution in the VENDOR.DOC file. Buy copies of shareware programs that aren't on racks and look at their VENDOR.DOC files. By watching what successful shareware authors are doing and what they put in their distribution licenses, you can get a good feel for the direction the industry is heading.

Low-cost retail (LCR) racks

"Take everything rack vendors tell you with a large grain of salt. Talk to authors who have negotiated these waters before you. Remember you have more in common with another author (even if he/she is a direct competitor) than you do with a vendor.

If your product is available as a royalty-paying retail title, or if you hope it will be, shareware racks may be detrimental to those sales. And that will cost you money."

— Dave Snyder, MVP Software

The subject of low-cost retail (LCR) racks is related to shareware only in that LCR vendors get most of the software they sell from shareware authors. But LCR racks don't sell shareware. Typically, LCR vendors take a shareware program and have the author remove all references to shareware. The program then becomes a retail program—the purchaser doesn't need to register with the author—and is generally sold at a price of $6.00 to $12.00. The author receives a royalty on each copy sold—typically 5% to 10% of the net price the LCR vendor receives.

There are major differences between LCR software and shareware sold on racks. For example, since customers own the LCR software they buy and don't need to register with the author, the author can't expect additional money from them. This is important when you consider the cost of providing technical support, for example. As an author, you cannot afford to support thousands of users when you're getting only 30 or 40 cents per copy. For that reason, the publisher of the LCR software should always be responsible for support.

"In my opinion, when authors are designing programs for LCR sales, they should plan for the following features:

- No technical support required.
- No printed manual required.
- Mass-market appeal.
  - easy to recognize (no esoteric software)
  - appeals to impulse buyers
  - appeals to kids and their parents
- Good art, allowing for good screen shots.
- Games work best.
- Use code that you can reuse to generate many smaller programs in order to get on multiple racks and maximize profits.

When designing a program for shareware, the formula changes:

- A printed manual and technical support make excellent registration incentives.
- Your buyers are comparison shoppers, not impulse buyers.
- Application programs work well, as do many other kinds of programs. Sometime even complicated, technical, and esoteric programs sell well.
- Writing and supporting a single larger program, selling for a higher price, will maximize profits."

— Diana Gruber, of Ted Gruber software and a founding member of STAR

The sale of LCR versions of software is always covered by a written contract. If someone approaches you who wants to sell an LCR version of your software, but doesn't offer a written contract, stay away! And any time someone offers you a contract, get a lawyer to review it.

LCR software contracts

"Get a lawyer who specializes in intellectual property contracts (preferably software) to review the contract before you sign it."
— Gary Elfring, Elfring Soft Fonts

Finding a qualified lawyer is important. Don't use your family attorney or someone who has a general business practice. You need an attorney who is familiar with intellectual property contracts for software.

As an experiment, I brought two LCR contracts to my family attorney for his review. He was happy to go over them for me and he charged me $300 for his efforts. The results, however, were dismal. He was not able to offer any comments that helped improve my negotiating position, and he caught none of the areas in the contracts that would have created problems for me. He's an excellent attorney for handling wills and family law, but he didn't have the background required to understand a publishing contract.

I found a good intellectual property rights attorney by attending a seminar on intellectual property rights for computer software run by the local community college. (Several attorneys attended the seminar.) When this attorney reviewed the contracts, he found several major problems: a clause that was in violation of anti-trust laws and several points lacking in the contract that were needed in order to protect me. The total bill from this attorney was $200—in spite of the fact that the intellectual property rights attorney charges $200 an hour and my family attorney charges $90 an hour. Since license agreements are what intellectual property rights attorneys work on every day, it took him only an hour to do the job.

If you live in a metropolitan area, you can find an attorney by contacting your local lawyer referral service. Get several names and ask them, first, whether they specialize in intellectual property rights and, second, whether they've handled software contracts in the past. If you live outside a major city, you can look for an attorney in a city near you or ask other shareware authors for the name of the attorney they use. Your attorney doesn't need to be located near you. I live in Oregon and one of the best intellectual property rights attorneys I've hired lives in Florida. That's about as far apart as you can get.

Keep in mind that contracts are always negotiable. You won't sour a deal by asking for changes in a contract. In fact, you should expect that any contract given to you by a vendor is written to favor that vendor. After all, the vendor paid an attorney to write the contract and that attorney is going to do his best to create a contract that gets the vendor the best possible deal. As a result, there will be things you need in the contract that aren't there. And there will be things that are to your advantage to take out of the contract or to modify. Vendors know this, and they expect that you'll request modifications to the contract. So don't be afraid to ask for changes. The worst that will happen is they'll say "no" to your requested modifications, in which case you and your attorney have to decide whether you can live with the contract as it is. Here are a few key points to watch for in LCR contracts:

Geographical area covered

What geographical territory does the contract cover? Are you selling the rights for U.S. distribution only, or is Canada included as well? (Usually the term North America is used when the territory covered by the contract consists of both the U.S. and Canada.) Does the contract give world-wide rights to the LCR vendor?

The geographical area covered by the agreement will affect other parts of the agreement. For example, you don't want to sign a contract granting world-wide rights unless you know the vendor has the capability and experience to generate significant sales on a world-wide basis. If you sign a contract granting world-wide rights to one vendor, you might cut yourself out of a better deal with a more experienced international vendor who requires some form of exclusivity.

Exclusivity

Try to avoid exclusive contracts. They tie you down to one vendor and eliminate your ability to sign contracts with other vendors. In the early days of LCR software, many shareware authors signed exclusive contracts and have been sorry ever since.

However, some limited forms of exclusivity are acceptable. For example, you might grant a vendor a regional exclusive or a market exclusive. This means that you might give one vendor the exclusive right to sell a program in a specified geographical area, such as New England. Or you might give a vendor the exclusive right to sell a program through a specified chain of stores.

You, as the author of the software and owner of the copyright, determine what *exclusive* means. For example, you can create various versions of the same program and license them to different LCR vendors.

You can also give vendors exclusive rights to rack sales only, or CD-ROM sales. You can give exclusives for specific price ranges or types of packaging—such as allowing an LCR vendor to have exclusive rights to sell copies of a specific version of your software in clam shell packaging.

Noncompetition clause

A noncompetition clause says that you agree not to create any products that will compete with the software you're licensing to the LCR vendor. This means that you can't make any other version of the software you're licensing, nor create new programs that perform similar functions. A noncompetition clause severely restricts what you can do and could put you out of business. Never agree to a noncompetition clause in a contract unless the LCR vendor is willing to give you a lot of money up front. You want to have the right to create other versions of your software that can be sold elsewhere, including via shareware.

Right of first refusal

Never agree to a contract that includes a right of first refusal clause. A right of first refusal means that you have to offer any new versions of your program, and sometimes any new software you create, to the vendor before you can offer it to anyone else. That vendor has the right to look at your software first, and you cannot sell or license it to anyone else until the first vendor refuses to publish it.

There are many variations on the right of first refusal clause. Some might include a limit to the amount of time a vendor has before they must make a decision about your software. Or the clause might give the vendor the right of first refusal for only a few specified product areas. Don't agree to any of them unless your attorney tells you they're acceptable.

Technical support

Any LCR contract you sign must say that the LCR vendor provides all technical support. When you're receiving only a small amount of each copy sold, you don't want to have to provide technical support to thousands of users. The contract might require that you provide technical support to the vendor, and that's acceptable. However, never agree to directly support users. Keep in mind that if the contract doesn't specifically require the vendor to provide support, you'll find yourself providing all the technical support.

Right to audit

The contract must give you the right to audit the vendor's books to verify that you're being paid the correct royalty. A good way to do this is to say that you, as the author, have the right to hire a third-party accounting firm to audit the vendor's books. Notice that you're paying for the audit. However, if the audit reveals any significant underpayment of royalties, then the vendor must pay the cost of the audit as well as all additional royalties owed to you.

Author copies

You have the right to some free "author copies" of the LCR package produced by the vendor. Make sure that the contract stipulates that you get at least 10 or 15 author copies.

Most favored nation clause

A "most favored nation" clause in a contract gives you the right to buy copies of your software at a price lower than that offered to anyone else. This can be very valuable because a vendor who's publishing your software in large qualities can probably sell you copies at a lower price than you can make them yourself. You can then resell them, provide them to registered users, or do whatever else you want with them.

Ask for a most favored nation clause in any contract you're offered. It might sound simple for the vendor to give this to you, but it might not always be possible. An example is if the vendor has a conflicting agreement with someone else. Often one of the vendor's high-volume customers, such as Walmart, will require their suppliers to sign an agreement stating that the vendor will not sell to someone else at the same or a lower price than Walmart gets. This would prevent the vendor from granting you most favored nation status, in which case you might ask for the Walmart price plus 5%.

Performance clause

When you sign a contract with an LCR vendor, you typically won't receive your royalties until the vendor sells copies of your software. What happens if a vendor gets so busy producing another software package that it doesn't have time for yours? You still have a contract, but you aren't getting any income and the contract might be limiting your ability to sell your software to someone else. That's why you want to be sure your contract has a performance clause.

A performance clause requires vendors to start selling your software within a set period of time. It might even include a minimum quantity they must sell, such as "the vendor must sell x copies per month, starting six months from the date of this contract, or the contract is canceled."

Another variation on the performance clause is to require a minimum royalty payment per quarter. If the publisher doesn't pay the minimum royalty, the contract is no longer in effect and you can sell your software to another publisher.

You need vendors to start producing and selling copies of your software now, not in two years. The performance clause provides a way for you to cancel the contract if the vendor doesn't perform.

Indemnity

This is a legal term that means the publisher will pay the coast of correcting things should they make a mistake that results in financial damage to you. You want to have the publisher provide you with an indemnity.

The publisher might also require you to provide them with an indemnity to cover any problems that could result if, for example, you have copied parts of your software from someone else's program and violated their copyright.

Termination

All contracts have a clause that describes the conditions under which the contract can be terminated. You need to watch out for the "sell off stock" part of the termination. This clause allows the vendor to sell off any remaining inventory of your software. However, such a clause, with no limits, could allow the vendor to sell your software over a long time period. Put a time limit on it. Generally, if you want to stop a vendor from selling your software, they're doing something that's damaging your image, your company's image, or your software. In that case you want to be able to stop that vendor, within a reasonable amount of time, from selling your software.

There are two kinds of contract terminations: one is for cause and the other gives a vendor time to sell off stock.

When a contract is terminated for cause, that means that one of the parties has violated the terms of the contract, and the other party no longer wants the contract to continue. In this case, the contract is terminated immediately, and the vendor must immediately stop selling all copies of your software.

The termination clause of a contract also usually allows either party to terminate the contract for any reason, without cause. For example, you might want to terminate the contract if the vendor is misrepresenting your software. This misrepresentation is hurting your image, but it isn't in violation of the contract. In that case you can terminate the contract, but the vendor will be given a limited amount of time to sell any remaining inventory.

Assignment

It's important that the contract includes a clause saying that the license cannot be assigned to anyone clsc. This prevents the publisher from assigning the contract to a friend or relative, charging that person a low licensing fee (meaning you get essentially nothing). Or the publisher might assign the contract to another company that doesn't have the financial resources to pay your royalty. You'll end up with a lot of users who have legitimate copies of your software, but you don't get a dime.

Royalties and advances

The royalty is the last thing you want to negotiate. Neither you nor the vendor can determine what an acceptable royalty is until you know the terms of the contract. Once you know what rights you're licensing to the vendor and what your responsibilities are, then you can determine what the royalty should be.

In most cases, royalties are based on the amount the vendor receives for your software. For example, the software might have a $7.99 suggested list price. However, the vendor sells the software to the retailer for $4.00 per copy. Your royalty will be based on $4.00 per copy.

The amount of the royalty will vary depending on how badly the vendor wants to carry your software and the terms of the contract. Typically, however, you can expect royalties to be in the 5% to 10% range.

The royalty clause in the contract also needs to state when the royalty payments are to be made. Typically, royalties are paid quarterly within 30 days of the end of the quarter.

If you have a very popular program, you might be able to get an advance against future royalties. This means that the vendor pays you some money when you sign the contract. Then this advance is deducted from the royalties your software generates. If you want an advance against royalties, you have to ask for it. However, at this time, advances are unusual for LCR software, unless the software is very good, unique, and very much in demand.

Other tips

Before you sign a contract, find out a little about the vendors. What type of stores are they in? How many? Are they selling software on a regional or national basis? When they say they're in K-Mart that could mean they're in one K-Mart store in Montana, or in all K-Marts across the country. Be sure you know exactly what they're saying and don't be afraid to ask questions. Remember, no one will tell you the answers to these questions unless you ask.

When you're discussing an LCR contract with a vendor, don't give all the rights to all of your programs to that one vendor. Just like any other business, you can expect half the LCR vendors to be out of business within a year or two. You don't want all your programs tied up with a vendor who is no longer generating income for you.

This has turned out to be a rather long chapter, but selling software on retail racks is a big subject. This method of selling software only started to become widely used in 1993, so it's relatively new. Both authors and vendors are still learning the best way to use this channel. Keep an open mind, and pay attention to what you see happening with shareware and LCR software in stores; this is a market with big opportunities.

7
"Free" publicity

I once saw a CompuServe message from a shareware author that contained the following listing of best response rates for different kinds of publicity:

- Review in magazine (even negative review generates sales)
- Direct mail
- Large ad in major publication
- Small ad anywhere
- Trade show/convention
- Classified ads
- Listing in a directory

Reviews are the best means of increasing sales. A good review can provide the initial boost it takes to get started, and has done so for many shareware authors, including myself. How do you get magazines to review your software? You must tell them about your software. Don't wait for them to find it in a shareware library. How do they find out how good your software is? You tell them.

Here's a key point: Announce all your products with a press release. Even if your software has been out for a while, it's better late than never. If you've never sent out a press release, get ready to write one now.

Writing a press release

"I've never seen a press release from a shareware author that I would classify as outstanding."

— Computer magazine editor

In my survey of magazine editors, almost all said they wanted press releases from shareware authors. However, the quality of the press releases they've received in the past was described as poor. Here's one magazine editor's response to a survey question about what shareware authors could do to improve their press releases:

Stop using dot-matrix printers! Use laser printers with a proportional typeface; anything less looks unprofessional. Be sure to include capsule overviews of the product described, along with addresses, phone numbers, prices, and requirements to run the program. This is obvious, but use a spelling checker (sometimes even PR writers forget to do this, it seems).

Pay attention to grammar. Most importantly, start with the most important information. If a press release rambles, it has likely lost its reader a few paragraphs back. Finally, don't over-jargon the reader and keep a humorous touch.

Nothing turns me off faster than the things I mentioned. I receive hundreds of press releases a week, and I look for excuses to pitch them in the trash (or else I'd have time to do nothing but read them).

Since only a few of the hundreds of releases can be printed, editors try to select those that are concise, well organized, and well written.

"Make press releases more concise, easier to read. Include more facts and features (remember, everyone calls their program the best). What sets this program apart from others like it?"
— Survey response from a magazine editor

Remember, magazines are always constrained by time and space. Include a short version of your press release, possibly in a cover letter, and a longer, more detailed version. Make it easy for editors to reprint what you've written; it saves them time. They'll tend to make a quick judgment of whether or not your product will interest their readers and how easily your press release can be edited down to the essential information. Concise writing and careful organization of the press release are crucial. If you have black-and-white photos, slides, or screen shots of your products in action, be sure to include them.

Write two versions of your press release

First write the long version. Put it on company letterhead or have special letterhead printed. Then write a one-page version. If you provide two versions of your press release, you make it easier for the editor to find a space where it will fit. I always write a one-page cover letter on my company stationery that provides a short summary of the press release. The longer press release is typed on stationery with a big green NEWS banner across the top and is usually just under two pages long. Try not to write press releases longer than two pages. If editors need additional details, they'll call you.

Since I am giving examples of how to write press releases, I should mention the success I've had with them. During the past twelve months, my software has been reviewed or discussed in articles in national publications or syndicated newspaper columns at least once every month. During the past week, I've been interviewed twice for articles about my software and contacted by two publications reviewing my software. Of these four publications, only one is a computer publication (*PC Sources*); one is a news magazine (*Business Week*) and the other two are special-interest magazines.

Getting back to the guidelines for writing a press release, include only the necessary details in your press release. Don't use superlatives or make extravagant claims that can't be verified. Editors have seen it all and extravagant claims and superlatives only detract from the chances of your press release getting published.

A step-by-step guide to writing press releases

"The press release must tell us what it is about the product that sets it apart from the competition."

— Survey response from a magazine editor

"Professionalism. I cannot emphasize that enough. Editors can get nervous if the company looks like it's fly-by-night. The product might look interesting, but if it looks like the company's going to fold—they don't have letterhead, it's printed on a dot-matrix printer—we don't want our readers to call a company a few months later and find nobody answering the phone. It makes us look bad."

— Marilyn Young, *Shareware Magazine*

Here's a step-by-step description of how to create a good press release (see FIG. 7-1 for an illustration of a sample press release; the numbers in the following list correspond to the bold numbers in the press release):

1. Give a date when the information in the press release can be published. Some editors mentioned that they like to receive press releases two to three months before the product will be available to accommodate publishing lead times.
2. Give the name of someone who can answer questions. This will most likely be you, but if not be sure it's someone who's knowledgeable and very familiar with your software. When I was talking with Marilyn Young, editor of *Shareware Magazine*, she mentioned she sees a lot of press releases that don't include a phone number. Don't forget to include your phone number. Even if you have only an answering machine, give your phone number; if someone from a magazine calls, they'll leave a message.

3. Magazines like to keep their readers up-to-date with the latest information. They're looking for new software, new ideas, and anything on the leading edge of the market. The word *new* will tend to catch an editor's eye. If your press release is announcing a new product, include the word *new* as one of the first words in the first paragraph.

4. List the computer system(s) with which the software will work. This allows editors to immediately see whether or not your software runs on the systems their magazine covers. Incidentally, make sure you target your publications carefully. It's a waste of time to send a release about a PC-only program to *MacUser*, or information about a Mac program to *PC World*.

5. Give a short summary of the advantages of your software. Highlight the key benefits and features. Don't try to cover everything. Your press release needs to be focused. What are the unique benefits of your software and why would the magazine's readers be interested? Describe the technical features of your software and then explain the benefits of each. Don't just list features. Editors and potential users are interested in benefits. Ask yourself why someone would pay for your software. Why should a user put time into learning to use your program? If you already have people using your program, conduct a survey or ask about it when they call for help. Find out why your current users like your program and include that information in your press release. When describing the benefits of your software, be specific. Terms such as *faster*, *cheaper*, and *better* don't mean anything. All authors make these types of claims for their software. Document your claims and make them quantitative, such as 25% faster than . . . .

In describing the benefits of your software, the key question you're trying to answer is "Why should a user choose your software rather than similar programs?" As a salesman, I once gave a presentation to a group of engineers at a utility company. I was working to sell a software package priced at $250,000. I was well prepared, with slides and demo programs, and I was rolling along feeling good about my presentation when one of the engineers stumped me with a simple question. "Why should we buy your software instead of someone else's?" I knew all about the features and benefits of the software, but I couldn't answer his question. I didn't get the sale, but I always knew the answer to that question before starting another presentation. You should always know the answer to that question and put it in the first paragraph of your press release.

It's a good idea to write your press release so that the first paragraph and last paragraph will stand alone if the editor is really cramped for space. Typically, the first paragraph should describe what type of software it is and the key benefits it provides. The final paragraph should list your phone number, address, and ordering details.

6. Except for the rule about repeating the contact information in the final paragraph, always write press releases in an inverted pyramid, i.e., from most important to least important. Describe secondary, less important features later in the release. Descriptions of less important features might need to be edited out to fit the available space in the magazine. Try to write your press release so that it can be cut off at the end of any paragraph and still make sense. Newspaper stories are written in this manner. The writer gets all the key information into the first paragraph. The next few paragraphs discuss secondary information. Once all of the key information has been concisely presented, the writer will go back and discuss the story in detail from the beginning.

7. The last paragraphs should describe other products such as add-on modules because this is the information most likely to be dropped. Many times, if you do offer add-on products, these can be discussed in a separate press release. A press release should be concise, short, and to the point. Discussion of add-on products might take the editor's attention away from your software's key benefits and features.

8. At the end of your press release, give a complete description of the system requirements. These include the types of computers the software will run on, the earliest version of DOS the software will work with, memory requirements, hardware requirements, and any requirements for additional software. Also include list prices and purchasing information. Provide an address and phone number the magazine's readers can use to contact you.

Choosing target publications

First, identify the magazines your potential customers read. How do you do this? You can ask them. When you first release your shareware to a limited group of people, ask users who register about the magazines they read. If people expresses interest in your software in BBS messages, ask them what magazines they read.

Sometimes it will be be obvious what publications your users read. If you've written a utility program, then computer magazines immediately come to mind. If you've written a specialized program, for example software to track thoroughbred genealogy, then you should be aware of the special-interest magazines that serve this market. One of the most effective approaches is to send press releases to publications and newsletters that focus on a special-interest area in which your software is useful. Sending press releases to noncomputer magazines generally gets more attention because computer software is unusual to them and their readers. For example, I send press releases for my record cataloging software to *CD Review*, *Audio*, *Stereo Review*, and about a dozen other publications related to music and record collecting.

1
For Release: 11-30-90

2
Contact: Steve Hudgik
(503) 692-3732

3 NEW RESOURCE FOR POTENTIAL
SOFTWARE AUTHORS
4 Who Use IBM and Compatible Computers

5
Writing and Marketing Shareware by Steve Hudgik is the first
reference book that includes, in a single volume, all the key
information a potential software author needs to know. It starts
by explaining why shareware is the best way for individuals to
market their own software. It then provides specific and practical
information on how to market a program as shareware. It describes
how to set a price for software, how to encourage users to
register, how to get free publicity, and how to run a small business,
and it provides answers to legal questions.

6
A disk is included that provides a mailing list of over 170
shareware dealers and 90-plus magazine editors. A sample shareware
mailing list program will search, sort, print mailing labels.
To help shareware authors find the supplies and services they need
a resource directory provides a list of vendors categorized by the
type of product or service they sell. All the information a
shareware author needs to run a successful shareware publishing
business is included in *Writing and Marketing Shareware*.

7
Also available is an audio cassette on which the author summarizes
key topics and talks with successful shareware authors.

8
System Requirements for the accompanying disk are: an IBM PC, XT,
AT, PS/2, compatible computer with 256K RAM, DOS 2.11 or later,
and a 3-1/2″ disk drive. (5-1/4″ disks may be ordered for $5
extra.)

Writing and Marketing Shareware is available for $24.95 (plus $3
S&H within the U.S., $10 outside the U.S.) from: **HomeCraft, P.O.
Box 974, Tualatin, OR 97062**. Telephone orders can be placed by
calling (503) 692-3732. Visa and MasterCard are accepted.

The audio tape is available for an additional $9.95.

7-1 This press release was written for an earlier version of this book. It illustrates the key
components of a good press release.

If you need help finding publications that target the audience you're trying to reach, use a directory of magazines. A good one is *The National Directory of Magazines*, published by Oxbridge Communications, Inc., at 800-955-0231 or 212-741-0231. Another excellent source is the *Standard Periodical Directory* also published by Oxbridge Communications. You should be able to find these or other similar directories at a public or university library.

Most people are too stingy with their press releases. Be sure you cover all publications whose readers might be interested in your software. For example, this could include the *Wall Street Journal, Business Week*, and *U.S. News & World Report* for business software. Although they might not publish a news announcement based on your release, you'll increase your name recognition. When they need to interview someone concerning shareware or your type of business software, they might remember your name and call you. I've been interviewed twice concerning software for home use on this basis.

Where to send press releases

If possible, address press releases to specific people. It's alright to send releases to the news editor or software review editor, but if you can get it directly into the hands of the person interested in your type of software, you'll be better off. It's important to find out who's interested in your type of software. Hardware editors aren't going to be interested in software press releases. Entertainment editors don't want to see sales management software. How do you find out who the right person is? Consider the following:

"First look at the masthead. If it's not evident from that, probably the person to call is the editorial assistant. Just ask for the name of the person who takes care of the software press releases. Or ask for the person who's in charge of software product listings. Or talk to the receptionist. When you call you might also double check editors' titles and the spelling of their names."

— Marilyn Young, editor of *Shareware Magazine*

"Read the magazine and pay attention to who writes articles and reviews about your type of software."

— Computer magazine contributing editor

Both of these are excellent suggestions. A third approach I've used is to ask an advertising salesperson. If you get a call from a magazine trying to sell you ad space, ask the caller to help you identify any editors who might be interested in your software. Salespeople are usually eager to please potential customers and generally will be glad to help.

How often to send out press releases

You should send out a press release only when you have news. Some companies send out a press release every time someone in their company burps. Editors eventually start to recognize the return address as coming from a company that has nothing important to say. To get the most impact from your press releases, send them only when you have something to announce.

For example, always send out press releases when you announce a new product or update. If your company is doing something interesting related to an industry trend, you might also send out a press release. Don't send press releases to announce that you've hired someone, unless that person is a recognized name in the industry. Don't use press releases to announce minor changes in your software or an upgraded manual.

Don't forget local publications

Include local and regional newspapers and magazines on your press mailing list. It's often easier to get a feature story written about your software in a local publication than in a national magazine. These stories are excellent sources of quotes you can use to promote your software. Here is an example taken from a newspaper review of one of my programs:

"I found data entry to be simple and the file-saving process to be crisp and speedy."

— *Monterey Herald*, February 26, 1990, regarding HomeCraft's software For Record Collectors

You can use quotes such as this to build interest in your software and to demonstrate to larger publications that you have a worthwhile product that's getting attention. Quotes from reviews or articles are your most effective means of selling your software to both end users and the press.

Should you include copies of your shareware with your press release? Some editors in our survey said they would like copies of shareware with press releases. Be careful with this technique. Don't send out an incomplete version or, if you must, be sure to identify it as an alpha or beta version. Be aware that a magazine's testing of a beta version can result in negative comments.

If you send copies of your shareware to reviewers, include a printed copy of the documentation. Reviewers are generally working to meet tight deadlines. Not only will they appreciate having the documentation immediately available, if they're running out of time (as is typical), the program with the preprinted documentation is more likely to be reviewed.

Usually, it isn't worthwhile to send your complete software package (registered version) to editors unsolicited. I've tried it several times and it has never prompted a review or article. Sometimes the magazine returned my package with a statement saying, in effect, "Don't call us, we'll call you if we want your software." And they will call. If something happens that makes your software interesting, the magazine will call. If it's important, they'll give you their Federal Express number so you can ship them a copy as soon as possible. Unless there's something unique about the way your software is packaged or what you've included in your package, a press release is probably more effective.

Giving out review copies of your software

When someone requests a review copy of your software, don't be stingy. Give out free copies of your complete registered version to anyone who asks, even if the name or publication is not familiar. You never know what will come of it. Reviews that catapult your software into six-figure sales can come from unexpected places.

When you send copies of your software for review, never expect to get them back and never ask for them back. It makes you sound cheap and unprofessional. Even if reviewers offer to return your software, tell them they can keep it or donate it to a nonprofit organization if they want. Usually, once they no longer have use for it, magazines destroy software they've received for review. They do this because they don't want to be seen as an illegal source of software.

Media kits

If someone from the press expresses interest in your software, you want to have a media kit available to send. A media kit is a complete package that gives an editor everything he needs to know about your software, your company, and you. The purpose of a media kit is to make it easy for an editor at the magazine to write about your software. Editors are always rushed, and if you can provide them with a ready-made article that will fill a couple of inches of column space, you're more than halfway to getting publicity for your software.

A media kit should include a cover letter introducing your company, your software, and the contents of the media kit. If your software has won any awards, be sure to mention them in the cover letter. Your media kit should also include copies of your latest press releases and any brochures or catalogs you use to promote your software. If you publish a variety of software, you might also want to include your line card (a complete listing of all of your products).

Include a copy of the registered version of your software, and a short one-page fact sheet that describes the software and its capabilities. You don't need to include the shareware version of your software or even mention that you offer your software as shareware. The media kit is about your software and your company, not about your marketing strategy. If you have any add-on products that go with your software, you should also include those.

The key part of your media kit is the press release. It should essentially be a short article about your software that the editor can directly place into the magazine. The style should be appropriate for the target publication and it should be no longer than one or two double-spaced pages.

The final part of your media kit is background information about your company and yourself. Include a short biography of both yourself and your company, sticking to information that's relevant to your software. Also include any product photographs, screen shots, copies of other reviews, and any other background information you have available.

Other ways to get free publicity

A multipronged approach to getting free publicity is often the best. If sending press releases and review copies of your software doesn't get a response, try some of these different techniques:

Writing articles

A good approach for getting free publicity is to write magazine articles yourself. These should be related to your product or be articles about your users. (To do this, interview users. It's a good way to get both feedback and an article.) The best place to submit these articles is to noncomputer publications. Often, these publications don't have anyone qualified to write about computer-related topics and you might that find your article is happily accepted.

Using directory listings

Directories are books that list available software. Some just contain listings of program and publisher names, others include descriptions of software. If you want to see what a directory looks like, you can usually find them in major book stores such as B. Dalton and Waldenbooks.

You won't get many sales from a listing in a directory and any leads will generally be of poor quality. However, most directories will list your software for free. Purchasing the listing enhancements, such as additional headlines or bold type, generally isn't worthwhile. The main advantage of being listed in the top directories is that a dealer can then look up your name and address should a customer request your software be special ordered. The following directories will list your software at no charge:

Software Encyclopedia
R.R. Bowker
245 W. 17th St.
New York, NY 10011
212-645-9700
(fax) 212-242-6987

TPS Software Directory
Technical Processing Services
Montague Publishing Co.
P.O. Box 3159
Gardena, CA 90247-1359
213-770-6929
This company is also interested
in receiving press releases and
provides software testing services.

To be included in these directories, write to them and request the required forms for a listing in their publication.

There are also industry-specific publications that specialize in computer news and publish yearly buyer's guides. You should make it your business to be aware of all publications that target markets related to your software. Don't hesitate to purchase a magazine that might target a market related to your software or area of interest.

Giving away your software

One of the best ways to build a user base is to give away copies of the registered version of your software. Give it away to any interested groups from whom you might get free publicity. For example, be very liberal in giving away copies to user groups. A user group can use your software as a prize in a raffle or as a door prize at a meeting. You get publicity because your software will be announced as "the prize" during the meeting.

The author of the *Home & Business Legal Guide*, Herb Kraft, has provided another good approach to giving away software. He has an idea that helps authors get publicity for their software and, at the same time, helps small BBSs to continue to operate. He suggests that authors donate copies of their software to BBSs to give away as part of a fund-raiser. By posting the name of your software "prize" as an announcement on a BBS, your software gets free publicity. You might try contacting some of the BBSs you'd like to support and see if they would be interested.

Keep your mind open and watch for opportunities. I've donated copies of my software to my children's elementary school for prizes at their annual carnival. I've given software to church fund raisers, charity auctions, and other fund raisers run by nonprofit groups. It takes time, but each copy is another small step in the process of building the reputation and name recognition of your software.

Business Software Database
Information Sources, Inc.
P.O. Box 7848
Berkeley, CA 94707

Microleads
Chromatic Communications
Enterprises, Inc.
P.O. Box 30127
Walnut Creek, CA 94598

8
Paid advertising

The best form of advertising is a quality product. If you don't have a quality product (software), then don't use shareware as one of your marketing tools. You'll only reach a market unwilling to pay for your product and you'll damage your reputation as a software author.

"Advertising does a good job of reaching a specific target market."
— Shareware author survey response

Many shareware authors don't consider advertising. In my surveys of shareware authors over the past four years, only about one-third say they've tried advertising. Don't rule out advertising without considering your market objectives. Shareware reaches a certain group of people who might be only a small percentage of your potential users. Advertising will help you reach more.

Of those authors who answered surveys by saying they tried advertising, almost all of them said it was a waste of money. Typically only authors selling more than $50,000 of software a year reported getting good results from advertising. You might conclude from these responses that advertising isn't worthwhile. But this isn't a valid conclusion. Although most shareware authors haven't had a good experiences with advertising, it's likely they weren't approaching it correctly. The ability to create a good advertisement that gets results isn't a skill most people have. You can't just write something that describes how good your software is and place it as an ad in a magazine. You need to create your ad with a basic understanding of how advertising works.

You need two important ingredients to achieve good results from advertising. For it to be effective, it has to be directed at the correct target audience and the ad itself must achieve the objectives you set. Notice that I didn't say the ad must sell a lot of software.

Advertising basics

Discard the notion that readers of magazines with the largest circulations are your ideal buyers. Start by finding out what your current users read. Also, find out where other software companies that sell the same or similar products as you have advertised on a regular basis (for more than six months).

To get a feel for what types of ads work and what types don't, look through the direct marketing section of any major computer magazine. Take notice of the ads that catch your eye and the ads you actually read. To gain an understanding of how they work, pay attention to those techniques that make you want to respond. Try to apply the same techniques in your ads.

When people respond to your ad, follow up fast. The longer you take to get information to people, the less likely they are to buy (or they might purchase software from someone else in the meantime). A good policy is to respond to all requests for information the same day you receive them.

Choosing a publication

In choosing a specific publication, know your potential users. Determine the demographic characteristics that distinguish them. (Demographics are statistics that characterize a group of people. This information might include age groups, personal interests, education, and job experience.) Then look at the advertising in the magazine to find out who its readers are and match their characteristics with your existing customers. For example, are they business or home software users? What types of things do they buy? How much time do they spend with the computer? Do they buy or plan to buy products similar to yours? The quality of your target audience is of prime importance.

Magazines can give you survey results that provide a profile of their readers. Read these magazines (you might already be a subscriber to the appropriate publications). If you've written software to meet a need you had, then people who read the same magazines might have the same need.

Publications can also tell you how their readers use their PCs. They can tell you whether or not their readers make recommendations on product selections and whether or not they actually make buying decisions. (It's important to reach the decision-maker, especially when selling software to businesses.) Publications can also tell you what their readers do with the magazine. Whether or not they read and discard it or keep it as a reference has a big impact on the durability of an ad. A magazine that's retained is the first place a buyer will go when making a buying decision.

You should be aware, though, that the information you obtain might not be completely reliable. For example, every publication I've talked to claims to reach decision-makers. They're not lying. This is what their surveys tell them. But in 10 years as a salesman, I found that many people like to say they're the decision-maker, but few really are. There's no way for you to tell whether or not you're reaching a decision-maker other than by trial and error.

Finding out how well a magazine's audience will respond to your software is also a trial-and-error process—in most cases. About the only way to get a feel for how well a magazine will work for your software is to gauge the response you get after the magazine publishes your product announcement or does a review of your software.

Choosing specific media

Up to this point, I've talked about magazine advertising. However, a variety of media is available and the same advertising principles apply to all of them. The different types of media you could advertise with include the following:

- Radio and TV
- Newspapers (national and local)
- General-interest magazines (*Newsweek*, *People*, etc.)
- Computer magazines (*PC Magazine*, *Byte*, *PC World*, etc.)
- Special-interest magazines, like hobby magazines and industry journals
- All advertising magazines, for example *Computer Bargain Line*
- Card decks
- On-line services, like Prodigy
- Disk advertising

The closer you match an audience to your typical user, the better response you'll receive. Radio and TV are very general media. Products that everyone uses, such as soap and breakfast cereal, do well, but you almost never see software advertising on TV. Newspapers are also general in nature, but some have targeted audiences. You'll see some advertising, though, by the major software companies in newspapers such as the *Wall Street Journal* and *USA Today* because both have many business readers. General-interest magazines also have broad audiences.

You pay for advertising based on a dollar rate per thousand readers (or viewers). The more people your ad reaches, the higher the rate you can expect to pay. If you advertise in any of these more general media, you pay for a lot of readers who aren't potential users. Consider the following specialized media:

Computer magazines Most shareware authors' first inclination is to advertise in the big computer magazines. After all, they're selling computer software and the readers of these publications are all computer users. But that's true only if they have a software product that all computer users need. Think very carefully about your market. If you publish a hard disk utility, then the general computer publications might be right for your product. If you publish C libraries, then maybe *Byte* or *Dr. Dobbs Journal* are better.

Special-interest magazines Special-interest publications target very specific audiences. If their audience coincides with your typical user, then this is probably the most effective place to advertise. If, for example, you've written a word processor designed for fiction writers, advertise in magazines that fiction writers read, such as *The Writer* or *Writer's Market*. Your target market is not necessarily computer users. Your target market is people who will find your program useful, even if they currently don't use a computer.

All my software is specialized. I've found that advertising in publications targeted at specific audiences is very effective. For example, I advertise my software for cataloging CDs, albums, and tapes in publications such as *CD Review* and *DISCoveries*, both of which are publications music lovers read. My stamp-cataloging software is advertised in *Stamps Magazine*. Find the publications that your users read; that is the place to advertise.

When purchasing advertising, look at what the ad will cost you per thousand readers in your targeted group. An ad in a computer magazine might draw a lot of responses. But if that magazine targets Amiga, Commodore, Apple, and IBM users, and your software runs only on IBM and compatibles, most of your responses might be from people who have computers on which your software won't run. The result is that you've wasted a lot of money on an ad and a lot of effort responding to people who can't use your software.

All-ad magazines Several magazines publish just advertising, with little or no editorial content. Before purchasing an ad in a publication such as this, look at an issue for the types of things that are being advertised. Most of the ads I've seen are for hardware, components, chips, etc. If this is the case, the audience the publication is reaching is a hardware-buying audience. Unless that's the market at which your software is directed, an ad in this type of publication woudn't be very effective. If you want to take a look at an all-ad publication, write to:

Computer Bargain Line
P.O. Box 1662
Ft. Dodge, IA 50501
800-654-3129
515-955-7231 in Iowa
(fax) 515-955-8235

Card decks   Card decks are those stacks of postcards you receive with a single ad on each postcard. If you can find a card deck that targets the specific audience you want to reach, then they can be very effective. Typically, specialized software sells better in a card deck than general applications.

Card decks have proven to be a very effective means of generating leads for some shareware authors. I discuss card decks and direct marketing in more detail later in this chapter.

Electronic media and disk advertising   Electronic media services such as Prodigy are probably not appropriate for most shareware products. Advertising on a general-interest service reaches a broad, general market of computer users. It might be good media for advertising products that all computer users can use such as cars and printers, but my feeling is that it isn't targeted enough to be effective for shareware authors. To advertise your software on a service such as Prodigy, it should have a unique feature that users need, and that can be described quickly in a line or two that will catch the user's eye.

At one time, several companies were promoting advertising on floppy disks as the media of the future. You could purchase several screens on a floppy disk to describe or demonstrate your software. Other than disk-based magazines, disk advertising seems to have died. However, with the arrival of multimedia and the growing popularity of CD-ROM disks, this media might make a comeback. For example, Ziff-Davis is putting together a CD-ROM containing software demos and advertising.

Defining your advertising objectives

The first step is to find the best publications for your ads. Step two is to determine the objective of your advertising. Are you building an image for your software? Are you announcing a new product or upgrade? Are you trying to sell your software directly? Are you trying to expand your mailing list? One of the main reasons advertising doesn't work for some authors is that they don't have an ad designed to meet their objectives.

There are four types of objectives advertising can achieve. First, advertising can produce sales by calling attention to your software. This is the objective most people have in mind when they buy an ad. To do this, the ad must be clear and simple, and it must get and hold the reader's attention.

Second, advertising can get people who might be interested in your software to request additional information. These are called *literature ads*. The most effective ads use this as their objective, although they might also list a price and provide purchasing information. Instead of trying to sell software directly, the ad offers a free catalog or brochure. If you have good, strong promotional material, such as copies of reviews, articles about your software, outstanding references, etc., then this is a good way to identify potential users for a subsequent direct-mail campaign.

Third, advertising can create a positive image of your software in the reader's mind, and increase your brand-name recognition. This is called *image advertising*. You should realize that most readers are not making a buying decision when they see your ad. Therefore, the ad should, as at least a second objective, produce a lingering, positive image in readers' minds. When they become interested in buying software, this image will predispose them toward purchasing your software. Many of the full-page ads you see in computer magazines are solely image ads. For example, Microsoft generally doesn't advertise to sell their software directly to you; it advertises to create a positive image of the products.

There is another reason for using image ads. After a reader buys your software, an image ad reinforces the decision. This helps the buyer to continue to feel good about purchasing your software.

Finally, advertising can help establish you as a serious business. By advertising, you're announcing to the world that you're in business and paying your bills. Magazines won't run your ad for long if you don't pay for it. I've found that having an ad in a major publication helped my business establish credit. One of the biggest problems you might face as a home business is having banks and suppliers take you seriously. An ad in a major magazine shows that you're serious about being in business, that it's not just a hobby you'll abandon on a whim.

The best advertising is either a literature ad or an ad that combines all four objectives. Your ad should be professionally typeset to produce a quality image. Don't run ads printed on a dot matrix printer—even a 24-pin printer. A laser printer is an acceptable alternative if you have some experience with fonts and advertising design. Your ad should offer free literature, quote a price, and provide ordering instructions.

Designing your ad

Display ads are the most effective type of ad. If a magazine has a direct-marketing section, that will generally be the best place to run your ad. Unless you can afford a $1/3$-page or bigger ad, avoid the main body of a magazine. Small ads become lost among larger ads in the main body of a magazine.

Classified ads are usually the least expensive form of advertising. They work well for reaching those people who are looking for your type of product. They don't do especially well at selling your product. The most effective ad, in either the classified or direct-marketing section, is a display ad.

A display ad should include a headline, printed in larger type, that captures what your software does in two to five words. The heading should be designed to catch the reader's attention as he scans the page. For example, I use the heading "Organize Your Collection" at the top of my ads.

8-1 A literature ad used by Crescent Software to make potential users aware of their programming tools.

The Crescent Software ad shown in FIG. 8-1 is a good example of a literature ad. It makes no attempt to directly sell software. The headline is eye-catching and will get the interest of anyone who programs using BASIC. The body of the ad gives you reasons to learn more about Crescent Software. It sells Crescent Software as a company; it doesn't sell any specific product Crescent Software publishes.

Graphics also help to call attention to an ad. If you have a good logo or graphic art that will produce a quality image when reduced to a small size, include it in your ad.

If you're trying to sell software directly, the body of the ad should describe what you're selling and why the user should buy your software. Quotes from reviews or user comments are usually very effective sales tools. An ad I've run in several magazines, shown in FIG. 8-2, is a good example of this.

8-2 This is one of my ads that has worked well. It's a good example of an ad that's designed to sell software: it includes a price, ordering information, and a money-back guarantee.

Pricing ads

How much should you pay for an ad? There are no set guidelines. If a $10 ad has no response, then it's an expensive ad. If a $10,000 ad sells $1,000,000 of software, then it's cheap.

Getting a discount

When purchasing an ad, try to get several discounts off of the published rates. Ask for a 15% discount for camera-ready art. This means you supply your ad typeset and ready to be inserted in a magazine. It's cheaper for you to have the typesetting done locally than it is to pay 15% extra for your ad. For example, a two-inch display ad can cost $500 per month. Fifteen percent of this is $75. Having the ad typeset locally might cost $30 to $40. You save at least $35 the first time you run the ad and $75 each time after that. Sometimes this discount is listed as an agency discount. Ask for it and most publications will give it to you as long as you have camera-ready art. If they won't give you the agency discount, form your own advertising agency. All you need is printed letterhead. You can typically get letterhead and business cards for under $100, an investment that can easily be recouped in one or two ads!

Discounts for multiple insertions

Magazines also offer discounts for multiple insertions. The more times you run an ad, the less it costs per issue. To be effective, you need to run your ad in at least three consecutive issues, preferably six. Ads generally don't get noticed the first time they're run. It takes about three issues before you'll start to get a good response. If the ad isn't paying for itself after six issues, you should evaluate both the publication and whether or not your ad is written correctly.

Prepayment discount

You might also be able to get a discount of up to 15% for prepayment. If you have the cash available, this can save you some money. However, with smaller publications, judge the value of this against the durability of the magazine. Will the magazine be around a while or fold and take your money with it? If a major magazine stops publication, they'll usually arrange for another magazine to carry your ad for the duration of your contract. *PC Resource* did this when they stopped publishing in August 1990. Small publications can just disappear and take your money with them.

Typical ad costs

The cost of an ad is normally measured in dollars per thousand readers. Table 8-1 shows the rates four magazines were charging in 1990.

Table 8-1 Typical advertising costs in 1990. Actual costs per issue for a 2-inch ad in the mailorder/direct-marketing section of magazines before discounts, at the 6X rate.

Magazine	Cost of 2" ad	Cost per 1,000
Small-circulation computer magazine (40,000 readers)	$132	$3.30
Large-circulation computer magazine (362,000 readers)	$600	$1.66
Small-circulation specialty magazine (10,000 readers)	$23	$2.30
Large-circulation specialty magazine (102,000 readers)	$72	$0.70

You should also ask magazines what they mean by *prepayment*. Do you have to prepay the entire contract, or can you prepay each ad on a month-by-month basis? If you don't have the cash to prepay your ad, you can still get a discount if the magazine bills on a 2-10 net 30 basis. This means you get a 2% discount if you pay your invoice within 10 days, otherwise the balance is due in 30 days. Depending on the magazine's prepayment discount, you can sometimes save money working on a 2-10 net 30 basis.

Large software companies spend up to 50% of their revenues on advertising. For a small company, it's usually the largest single budgeted item. It's also an item where it's difficult to start small and work up. If you're going to advertise in the major computer magazines, plan on spending at least $2,000 to $3,000 to start.

A fatal advertising error

If you have a good ad and you place it in a publication your target market reads, there's still one fatal error that will result in your ad not being effective. It takes time for advertising to work. You can't run an ad in one issue of a magazine and expect to get a response. Most magazines will recommend that you run your ad in three consecutive issues. Based on my experience, I'd even consider three issues to be too few. I've found that my most effective advertisements are the ones that run for a year or more. People have to see your ad in issue after issue before they believe both that you're not a fly-by-night company who will quickly disappear and what you say in your ad.

When you're planning an advertising campaign, budget enough money to pay for at least six month's worth of advertising. If the ad generates sales, use that money to keep the ad running for another six months.

Selling by direct mail

Another effective advertising method for shareware authors is direct marketing. As a shareware author, direct marketing is your primary method of selling software. Using shareware to market your software is a form of direct marketing. You're promoting your software directly to the end user. But that isn't the type of direct marketing I'm talking about. The traditional way people define *direct marketing* is as direct mail or telemarketing. Telemarketing is using the telephone to call your prospects directly. An example of telemarketing would be those phone calls you get, usually at dinner time, from people selling carpet cleaning, insurance, and investment opportunities. Another aspect of direct marketing that many shareware authors have found to be the most useful is direct mail.

There's no way around it. As a shareware author, you'll be using direct mail to promote your software. If you send out a newsletter, that's direct mail. If you mail upgrade announcements, you're using direct mail. This section will help you understand and use direct mail more effectively.

Direct-mail uses

You can use direct mail to sell your software. When most people think of direct mail, they usually think of "junk" mail—third-class mail used to sell something. Although this term has a negative image, direct mail is a very effective way to sell software.

Upgrade announcements are usually sent using direct mail. One of the reasons people register shareware is to get access to upgrades. Upgrades are important to users and most users look forward to getting upgrade announcements—as long as they don't come too frequently. Whether you send out postcards or color brochures, direct mail is the most effective means of letting your users know about upgrades.

Direct mail announces new products. How do you let the world know about your new software? One of the best ways is to put a product announcement in front of prospective users. Use their mailbox with direct mail.

Direct mail helps you maintain contact with users. You should stay in contact with your registered users. They are a source of feedback that will help improve your software, identify bugs, spot market trends, develop ideas for new products, and spread the word about your software. Some authors publish newsletters. Others send marketing surveys to selected users. Regardless of the method you use, staying in touch with your users provides a valuable source of feedback.

Direct mail is an excellent way to get names of prospective users and build your mailing list. Shareware disks reach only a limited number of the millions of computer users. Most computer users are not familiar with shareware. Direct mail is one way of reaching them. Use direct mail to build a mailing list of prospective customers. Then use direct mail again to tell these people about your software.

Use direct mail to build your image. People follow companies and products they consider leaders in a product category. If you can build an image of leadership and stability, people will feel more comfortable buying your software. Regular direct mailings to users, for example a biannual newsletter, is a good way to build your image.

Direct mail can create a demand for your products. Once you achieve success and dealers across the country carry your software, direct mail is an effective way to tell people about it and encourage them to buy your software from their local dealer.

Why direct mail works

Whether you're announcing a new release or prospecting for new sales, if done correctly direct mail works. Direct marketing is big business. People like to buy through the mail. The Direct Marketing Association reports that over 98 million people shop by mail every year. This is a 72% increase over the past seven years.

One of the reasons direct mail is successful is that it has little competition within the medium. For example, according to the Radio Advertising Bureau, each day the average person hears 42 commercials on the radio. The Newspaper Advertising Bureau says the average newspaper reader sees over 180 newspaper ads every day. Almost 60 billion inserts are included in newspapers every year. An average adult watches 3.6 hours of television and is exposed to 95 TV commercials every day. The March 22, 1991 edition of the *Wall Street Journal* reported that every day the average American is exposed to about 300 advertisements.

On the other hand, a U.S. post office study has shown that U.S. households receive an average of 10 pieces of third-class mail per week. That is about three advertising messages every two days. Businesses receive an average of 25 pieces of third-class mail per week, a number that's still much less than any other media. The point is that direct mail puts your message in front of a potential user without a lot of competition from other messages.

A recent U.S. post office study done by the University of Minnesota showed that the term *junk mail* is a misnomer. People don't consider direct mail as junk mail. Seventy-one percent of all third-class mail is immediately opened and read. Fifteen percent is set aside for later reading and 91% is eventually read. People like to receive mail, especially if it's about a subject that interests them. This is why direct mail works.

Characteristics of direct mail

Direct mail has some unique characteristics that can work to your advantage. For example, it's personal—your message can be designed for specific types of readers. In fact, that's a key ingredient of direct mail. Your mailing must be about a subject that interests the recipient. If you mail information about Pascal utilities to people interested in gardening, you're wasting your money. However, if you send it to Pascal programmers, you're directly reaching people with a personal interest in what you have to say.

A good use of direct mail, one that adds a personal touch to your software and your company, is a newsletter. Users like to hear from you. They want to know what's going on. They want to know about updates and upgrades. A newsletter is a great way to stay in touch with your users, and if you use it to announce new products and upgrades, you should be able to get it to pay for itself.

Direct mail is flexible. With direct mail, you can adapt your message to the needs of the recipient. Unlike other forms of advertising in which the same message goes to everyone, you aren't limited in what you can say in a direct mail piece. You can change the contents of your mailing to adapt it to different types of people. If you have the time or are selling high-priced software, you can even write a personal letter to each potential user. And you have as much room as you need. If your message takes six pages, that isn't a problem. (Try paying for six pages of advertising in a magazine. That bill would put most of us out of business.)

Direct mail is measurable. You can evaluate the results from direct mail and run tests to find what brings the best response. You can send a mailing to a group of potential users and measure its effectiveness by counting the number of people who respond. Of course, you have to know what you're measuring, meaning you need to know the objective of your mailing. I cover direct mail objectives in the next topic.

Direct mail is selective—you can send your offer to the people most likely to be interested in your software. This provides the same advantage as advertising in specialty magazines—you don't pay to reach a lot of people who aren't interested in your software.

Direct mail has the reader's full attention. Generally, you look at one piece of mail at a time and at a convenient time. Unlike magazine advertising, where competing software might be advertised on the same page as your software, direct mail doesn't have your competition's message present to distract your potential customers.

With all the good aspects of direct mail, why did I bother talking about advertising in the first part of this chapter? The answer is that they both have their place in a good marketing plan. For example, you can't use direct mail until you have a mailing list of interested prospective customers. You can use magazine advertising to identify these people, and then direct mail to contact them. In fact, this is where many people make a mistake.

They place an ad in a magazine and expect sales to soar. When nothing happens, they declare magazine advertising a waste of money. The problem, in many cases, is not that the ad didn't work; the problem is that the advertising objectives weren't correct. With an advertising objective aimed at building a mailing list, a combination of advertising and direct mail can be very effective.

Getting started with direct mail

By now, you're probably getting tired of hearing that the first step is to identify your objectives. But if you don't know where you want to go, you might never get there. In direct mail, as with anything else, the first step is to set your objectives. I've given you a list of ways direct mail can be used. Now, you need to determine what you want to accomplish. Do you need to inform your users of an upgrade? Are you trying to sell more software? The design of your direct-mail package will depend on what you're trying to do. For example, if you're announcing an upgrade you can do it with a postcard. However, if you want to announce an upgrade and a new product, you'd be better off mailing a newsletter.

When determining your objectives, keep in mind that it will take several mailings to sell your software by direct mail. My experience has shown that people generally need to be contacted five times before they buy. Table 8-2 shows a typical response to a direct-mail campaign. If you target 100 people with your direct mail campaign, 6% will buy the first time you contact them. When you contact the remaining 94%, about $2\frac{1}{2}\%$ will buy. By the time you send out the sixth mailing, there are about 80 people left who haven't purchased your product and typically about 79% of them will buy at that point.

This buying pattern doesn't hold true in all situations, however. Using direct mail to announce a software update will typically generate a much higher response with just one mailing. Some authors have told me they get

Table 8-2 This table shows that the typical qualified customer generally doesn't make a purchase until he has been contacted five times.

Number of times a customer is contacted	Number of customers who buy
1	6%
2	2.5%
3	3.5%
4	9%
5	79%

70% to 80% of their users upgrading each time they send out an upgrade announcement.

To help you identify your direct-mail objectives, here are some questions you should answer before you mail anything:

- Is your mailing a bug-fix that needs to get out as soon as possible, or a regularly scheduled newsletter? Are you trying to coordinate your mailing with the release of a new shareware disk to distributors?
- What is your budget for this mailing? Can you afford to send a four-color brochure to 30,000 people or just a photocopied letter to 50 people?
- Who is your target audience? Do you want to reach your registered users or find people who don't currently use your software?
- What is the message you want to get across? What do you want to tell the recipients and what action do you want them to take?

Once you've put your objectives in writing and answered these questions, you're ready to start designing your direct-mail package.

Direct-mail package design

To be successful, direct mail must do certain things. It doesn't matter whether you're mailing a postcard or a two-pound box of brochures. The following things must be incorporated into your direct-mail package.

It must attract attention If your prospective customers throw away your mailing without reading it, you've wasted your money. Getting them to open the envelope is the first key step. Once the envelope is open, you must then hold their attention.

Studies have shown that the best way to get a recipient to open an envelope is to do nothing. Use a plain white envelope with only your return address printed on it. Don't include advertising copy on the envelope. Of course, there are exceptions to this rule, as there are exceptions to everything I've talked about. However, in general, a plain white envelope with no advertising copy will generate a better response than an envelope with advertising.

Although special classes of mail and services such as Federal Express can be attention-getting, don't use them for direct marketing. Special-delivery services will decrease the response to your mailing because people will feel deceived. With direct mail, always do what people expect. People expect Federal Express deliveries to contain important and necessary information. They don't expect a sales pitch.

When reading a piece of direct mail, most people glance at, more often than read, what you present to them. Your package must be designed to catch and hold their attention as they scan it. A good approach is to use bold headlines and bulleted points that provide key information.

Include a direct-mail letter   When selling something, whether a new product or an upgrade, always include a letter. (An exception to this rule is when you're sending out a newsletter. Newsletters don't need an accompanying cover letter, although you can include one if you want to.) A letter is the first thing people will read. The copy style should be informal and written to a single reader. Write the letter as if you were writing to a friend. You don't have to follow the formal rules of grammar as if it were a business letter. In addition, the title of the person signing the letter is very important. One of the first areas people check is the signature block. Be sure the letter is signed and that your title is included. A letter from the president or owner of a company is much more impressive and effective than one from an unknown name or a lower-level person.

Always include a P.S. as a part of your letter. The P.S. is the most often-read section of a direct-mail letter. Use the P.S. to summarize your offer and the action you want the person receiving the letter to take.

In designing your letter, don't try to be creative. As I've already stated, do what people expect. The most effective letters use black ink on white paper. Although purple ink on yellow paper might be eye catching, it isn't an effective way to get people to read your letter. When selecting a typeface for a letter, always use a standard typeface. Don't use small or fancy print. Again, the key point is to do what people expect; a letter should look like a letter.

The layout of your letter affects its readability. Use short sentences and bulleted (or numbered) points. Sentences should be no longer than 25 syllables. Use as many pages as you need to explain your offer and tell readers what you want them to do. Long letters get as good a response as short letters. The content should be based on the proven rule of thumb that you need to first tell people what you're going to tell them, then tell them, and finish by summarizing what you told them.

Include a variety of materials   Your direct-mail package should include several different types of material, such as a letter, brochure, catalog, coupon, and reminder note. Plus, don't match all the pieces in your package in style, color, paper stock, and typeface. Design variety into your direct-mail package. With each piece handled separately, providing a variety of styles results in a better chance of having the recipient read each message. Also keep in mind that people are different and different people will be attracted to different parts of your package.

Include a message of interest   For a direct-mail piece to hold someone's attention, it must relate to that person's interests. The key to doing this is to use the correct mailing list. As I said before, don't mail information about Pascal programming utilities to people interested in gardening.

A good way to get and hold people's interest is to use real-life testimonials. In fact, testimonials are the best and most effective means of communicating your message. They're better than anything the best copywriter can write.

Another way to catch people's interest is to include pictures. People like to look at pictures. For example, when scanning through a brochure, people will first look at the pictures and read the captions before they read the rest of the brochure. Don't write off picture captions as being unimportant. Picture captions are one of the best ways to deliver your message. The best brochure includes a photo story. Include photos, if you can, and use screen shots to illustrate the key benefits of your software.

When a brochure is about computer software, how do you include photos? What else can you show other than a computer screen? Some software easily brings photographic possibilities to mind. For example, a brochure for genealogy software might include a family photo that has three generations of family members. For my Play 'n' Learn software, I used a photograph of a baby in a highchair using a computer. A brochure for word processing software can contain pictures of people using the software in an office setting. But what do you do if, for example, you publish programming utilities? Falk Data Systems (publishers of shareware such as the Programmer's Productivity Pack) came up with an excellent and creative approach. Its brochure shows recreational activities you could enjoy as a result of the time you save using Falk Data's ProPak 2.0. The photographs are attention-getting and they deliver a message that says you'll save time if you use this software.

Suggest a course of action Don't assume the reader knows what you want them to do. Explain everything fully and in detail and then ask the reader to perform a specific action. Don't assume that anything is obvious to the reader or that the reader will know what to do.

Also, keep in mind that people always have questions about the next step. People want to know both what they need to do and what you'll do in return. For example, when they order your software, will they have to wait four to six weeks or do you ship the same day you receive the order?

Another fact of direct mail is that most people procrastinate over making decisions. Twenty-nine percent of direct mail sales are impulse sales, meaning that people read your material, like what you're offering, and order it immediately. The remaining sales come from people who put off responding to the offer. In addition to procrastinating, people tend to keep only the reply vehicle (e.g., coupon, business reply card, order form) and throw out the rest of your materials. Be sure to include a reply vehicle with a complete recap of your offer and specific directions telling what to do. You might also include a testimonial or a captioned screen shot on the coupon or order form.

Encourage a positive response Don't forget to ask for an order. Tell people what you want them to do. If you want people to buy your software you might say "Call 555-555-5555 today for immediate shipment of your new software." This tells people specifically what they need to do.

If you want people to give you their name and address for your mailing list, you could say "Mail the enclosed coupon today for a free shareware copy of the QuickPay Accounting System."

Here is another approach: "The QuickPay Accounting System is so easy to use that we know you'll want to get started right away. Check the YES box on the enclosed coupon, mail it to us, and we'll ship your copy of the QuickPay Accounting System via Federal Express at no extra charge."

Notice that all of these tell people what they need to do and encourage the prospect to take action now instead of procrastinating.

Sometimes, asking for an order seems difficult. But, people want you to pursue them. When you ask for the order, you make people feel that you care and that their business is important to you. If you do not ask for an order, you give the impression that you do not care whether the prospect orders your software or not. If you do not care, why should the prospect care about ordering your software?

The list

The key factor in the success or failure of a direct-mail campaign is the quality of the mailing list. Your mailing must reach your target market. There are two types of mailing lists. Those you generate internally and lists you purchase from outside vendors. With a list you have put together, for example a list of your registered users, you know the people to whom you are mailing. If you send an upgrade announcement to your registered users, you know you are reaching the right audience.

When you prospect for new users, you most likely will buy or barter for a list from an outside source. The only way to know whether or not you will get a good response from this list is to test it. Never do a large mailing using a list from outside sources until you have tested the mailing list and the material you are including in your mailing.

List testing

Statistically, to have a valid test you need to get at least 56 replies. This will provide you with an 85% confidence level that the results from a repeat mailing will not decline more than 12.5%.

Unfortunately, no rule of thumb gives a percentage response rate for direct mail. Responses can vary from a fraction of a percent to 70 or 80% for software upgrades. Until you have done some testing, you have to guess at what your response rate will be (a classic catch-22). However, as an example, if you anticipate a 2% response rate, you must mail 2800 pieces to get a valid test. But, if you think you will get a 10% response rate, you need to mail to only 560 people.

Testing is critical for companies with big direct-mail programs. Companies that mail hundreds of thousands or even millions of pieces of mail do not want to make mistakes that render their mailings ineffective.

However, if you are a small, one-person company with a limited budget, how can you run a test involving 2800 pieces of mail when your budget only supports a total mailing of 500 pieces?

One nice thing about direct mail is that if your budget will not support a mailing to several thousand people, you can still effectively use direct mail. To take advantage of bulk mail rates, you only need to mail 200 pieces at a time. For many years, I routinely built my mailing list by trading names with other authors and adding them to the names of people who responded to my advertising. Each time I collected 200 names I would do a bulk mailing. Sometimes, I would get a good response. Other times, my mailings generated no response. I did not have the resources to test my mailing lists. But, unlike mailings involving possibly millions of pieces of mail, when you mail just a few hundred pieces and do not get a good response, you will not have lost a fortune. The risk is very low.

Getting no response to a mailing does not mean the mailing was a failure. At a minimum, you are building brand recognition and your company image. You are letting people know you exist. That is an important part of building your business.

Building a mailing list

There are companies that rent or sell mailing lists, but it might not be necessary for you to purchase a list. If you are a member of the ASP, you can use the mailing lists the ASP has generated from their trade-show booths. Some authors have reported success using the ASP mailing lists.

If your software serves a niche market, you might be able to purchase the subscriber list of a magazine serving that market. Give the magazine a call and ask.

Another source of lists are professional association directories. You might be able to find these directories in your library or you might be able to purchase a copy from the professional association. Some libraries also have industry directories that can be used for compiling a mailing list.

If you sell software to businesses, you can compile a list of prospective customers by looking at the ads in trade magazines and publications. If, for example, you publish software for cataloging software disk libraries, check computer magazines for the addresses of shareware disk distributors. And, of course, you can use the mailing list included with this book for sending disks to vendors and BBSs, and for your press releases.

Anytime someone calls you with questions or a request for information about your software, be sure to get their name and address. This is your most valuable source of names. People who take the time to call are interested in your software and are the best prospects for becoming registered users. This list becomes one of your most valuable resources.

"We get a lot of technical support calls from copies of our disks sold by other vendors. Of course, we give them technical support, but I'll tell you something—we try not to let that customer hang up without giving us their name and address so we can send them a catalog of ours and make them our customer."

— Roger Jones, president of Software To-Go

A good way to build a mailing list is through a booth at a trade show. For example, COMDEX is a great place to collect all sorts of toys and trinkets. Last fall, I came back with hula hoops, a slinky, a globe, sunglasses, and all sorts of buttons, badges, and letter openers. Why do COMDEX exhibitors give away all that stuff? They want to attract people to their booths so they can build their mailing lists.

Some magazines can be good sources of names. For example, Computer Shopper publishes a list of user groups, providing you with a current list of user group names and addresses. Some trade magazines publish industry directories that can also serve as a good basis for a mailing list.

If you know of someone who targets the same market as you do, consider swapping names with that person. It is an inexpensive way to build a great mailing list of prospects already identified as being in your target market.

Finally, you can purchase lists from list brokers. There are several brokers listed in chapter 17.

Renting/buying a mailing list

When you "buy" a list, you are usually renting the right to use it for a specified number of times. The list broker will send you a set of mailing labels, and you may use each label one time. When can you add names you receive from a list broker to your permanent mailing list? As a general guideline, after you have contacted someone, and that person has responded to your offer, the name is yours.

The cost to rent a mailing list is typically in the range of $40 to $150 per thousand names, and, in many cases, there is a 5000-name minimum. Some premium mailing lists will be priced higher than $150. The average list cost is in the $90–$100 range per 1000 names. In a few cases, you can buy the mailing outright and make it a part of your permanent list. Typically, expect the cost to be anywhere from 3 to 10 times the rental rate.

Keep in mind that when you rent a list, that list is the customer file belonging to some other company. Most companies do not want to jeopardize their relationships with their customers. In some cases, you will be asked about the product you are selling and there might be a request for a copy of the material you will be mailing. If you have a competitive offer, you might not be able to rent the list. For example, I do not think PC Magazine would rent its subscriber list to PC World.

Producing your direct-mail material

Here are a few guidelines for the actual production of your direct-mail material.

- Study the direct-mail packages you receive. What catches your eye? What do you like about them? Which ones do you throw in the trash and why? Model your package on the ones you think are most effective.
- When you start, talk to your printer early in the design process. Discuss what you are planning to do and find out what you can do to minimize costs. For example, if you are including a multiple-page flyer, find out from the printer what would be the optimum number of pages. Many times the printing process results in catalogs/flyers of eight pages (or multiples of eight) as the most cost effective to print. Be careful that you do not design aflyer that is hard to print.
- To save money, you can do as much of the work as possible yourself. If you have a laser printer and good font software, you can handle the typesetting. Folding and envelope stuffing are simple jobs that you can do, but because many printers have automated equipment, sometimes the money you save is not worth the extra time you would have to put into it. Weigh the value of your time and your ability to produce quality material against the cost of paying someone else to do the work.
- Before bringing your material to the printer, make a dummy of your package with everything cut and folded as it will be in the actual package. This will give you a chance to see if your package is within the post office's weight limits and whether or not the materials will fit in the envelope you are using. There is nothing worse than designing a super package, printing 5000 copies, and then finding it will not fit in the envelope.
- Where possible, use standard materials. It might be exciting to use odd-shaped envelopes or inserts, but it will cost more. Also, you should avoid special inks. Some printers have a regular schedule of when they run certain standard colors. If you can build enough time into your schedule, you might be able to save the extra costs of special print runs for additional colors. Also, if you specify a color background, some printers will print the background. If you are thinking that you want your flyer printed on colored paper, be sure to tell the printer to specifically use colored paper.
- When working with vendors, put everything in writing. For phone calls, always send a follow-up letter to confirm your understanding of the conversation.

Using card decks

A card deck is a package of post cards sent to a targeted group of people. Each post card contains an advertising message. To respond to the ad, you can generally put a stamp on the card, write in your name and address, and drop it in the mail.

Card decks are effective in two ways. They are good for selling inexpensive impulse products. For example, some shareware distributors have found card decks to be very effective in selling disks priced at $3 or $4 each. Card decks are also excellent at generating leads in highly specific target markets. Advertising in a card deck can be excellent for generating leads at a low cost. What is a lead? A lead is the name and address of someone who is interested in your software. It is the first step in selling your software. Lead generation is the most effective use of a card deck for a software publisher.

Before you advertise in a card deck, know your objectives. What do you want to get for the money you are spending on card-deck advertising? Do you want to generate leads? Are you trying to sell copies of the shareware version of your software?

Next, be sure the card deck is targeted at a group of people who need your product. For example, if you sell programming utilities, the Byte magazine card deck would be an appropriate place to advertise. However, it would be better to advertise software for cataloging book collections in a card deck going to Book-Of-The-Month-Club members.

One of the big advantages of card decks is that it costs a lot less to use than it does to mail a letter to everyone receiving the card deck. A typical cost might be $0.04 to $0.05 per prospect.

What type of response can you typically expect from a card deck? As with direct mail, the response will vary with different card decks and products. A typical response might be in the 2% range for requests for additional information and an additional 0.05% for immediate purchase of your software. With card decks you can expect to receive 50% of the responses within three weeks of the mailing date and 90% within eight weeks.

The design of your card is important for achieving a good return rate. The elements of a good card-deck design follow.

The headline and visual are the most important elements. They must work to stop the prospect at your card as they scan through the stack of cards. Include a bold headline that concisely summarizes the major benefit of your software. Then, include a graphic that supports the headline. Once your card has been set aside for further consideration, the battle is half won.

The copy on your card must be clear and concise. With the limited space provided by a post card, every word counts. Get to the point quickly, state your proposition, and ask readers to take action.

It is important that you close the sale. You do this by telling buyers how to order or request additional information. Should they mail the card back to you or can they fax it? Do they get something, such as a discount, if they respond within a specified time period? Tell readers what you want them to do and what they will get in return.

Get a commitment. Leave room on the card for name, address, phone number, and credit card information. Take a look at some of the cards you receive. (If you do not receive any card decks, then you are not subscribing to business publications that can help you run your business. Take a look at the list of publications in chapter 17.) Notice that some ask you to tape your business card to the post card. This provides a way to identify your title and weed out non-business responses. Notice that some cards have you write your name and address in the space where a return address typically goes. This saves space and leaves more room for copy.

Do not forget to include your phone number (many people do). Also, include a fax number if you have one. Fax machines are increasingly used to order merchandise by "mail."

In looking through card decks, you might notice that many cards are business reply cards. The respondent does not need to put a stamp on it. Making your card a postage-paid, business reply card will help generate more responses. The easier you make it for someone to respond, the more responses you will get. However, providing a postage-paid card is not a necessity when selling a product that costs more than $10 or $20. Before buying into a card deck, you might want to look at a few past decks to see what others have done.

9
Trade shows and conventions

You can attend a trade show as an exhibitor or a spectator. First, I'll discuss attending trade shows at which you'll want to have a booth. Many trade shows and conventions other than COMDEX can help boost your business. Without some previous experience, COMDEX can be a difficult first step. Many chambers of commerce run local trade shows. You might try user-group meetings, industry-specific conventions, and government-sponsored trade shows that highlight local products. There are many meetings and conventions where you can put trade-show skills to work to promote your software.

Exhibiting

In general, trade shows aren't effective for directly generating sales, but that shouldn't be your objective. As with everything else I've discussed, you must first determine your objectives. General trade-show objectives might include the following.

- Getting sales leads
- Increasing name recognition in the marketplace
- Selling your software
- Meeting magazine editors
- Exposing your software to dealers

You also need to set specific objectives for a trade show. Specific objectives might be to contact 80 dealers, 5 distributors, or 10 magazine editors, or to meet 12 other shareware authors. After determining your objectives, you should determine how you're going to get the attention of your targeted group.

Notice that I used the word *or* in the listing of possible objectives. If you try to achieve all your objectives, you usually won't achieve any of them. You need to focus on one specific objective, although you might have some secondary objectives. Of course, if an opportunity presents itself, take advantage of it even if it isn't part of one of your original objectives. Conventions and trade shows are exciting, dynamic events. You might unexpectedly meet someone who can help you—which is how this book got published.

Overall, however, you need to maintain your focus on your identified objective. If you want to talk with distributors, you won't have time to sell software to individual users. If you want to generate leads, you'll be so busy collecting people's names and handing out copies of your shareware that you won't be able to meet distributors. If you want to sell software, you'll end up talking about its features and benefits with users or dealers and will have many potential leads pass by your booth.

Once you've identified your objectives, you next need to put together a plan for achieving them. What type of booth do you need? What equipment will you need to bring? Do you need to rent computers? Be sure to tell the show organizers that you need power if you'll be running a computer. How many people do you need to staff your booth? What handouts do you need? Are you going to give away copies of your shareware? All the details must be planned months before the show's date. Simply setting up a booth and standing around to see what happens will result in an unsuccessful exhibit.

Planning your booth

Before a show, call or send a mailing to the people you're targeting and have them meet or talk with you at the show. If you're trying to contact dealers, use a direct-mail campaign to let them know about your booth. If you're trying to sell to users, go through your mailing list and send invitations to anyone who has expressed interest in your software. When inviting users to a local trade show, you might limit the mailing to people who live within 200 miles of the show.

When sending out a mailing to announce your show booth, offer a special to get people to come to your booth or to make their first purchase at the show. If your objective is to get sales leads, you might offer a small, low-cost gift. If you're trying to make sales, offer a special show price or include a coupon with your invitation. Another incentive is to ask people to bring in problems that your software can solve. It's a great way to qualify prospective customers and it provides you with an opportunity to demonstrate your software. (To *qualify* a customer means that you determine whether or not that person has a need for your software, and whether or not that person has the authority or inclination to specify, purchase, or recommend your software.)

Most business people will have their time at a show fully scheduled in advance. If you want to meet with distributors or editors, call them before the show and make an appointment. You should have a good reason for wanting to talk with them. For example, you might want to meet with an editor if you have a new product that might particularly interest him. If you plan to talk with distributors or dealers, know what you want to talk about, and what you're willing to offer them, before you meet with them.

When sending out press releases before the show, include a cover letter that mentions your booth. If your objective is to get exposure with the press, prepare a press kit you can leave in the press room at the show. Here is what Marilyn Young, editor of *Shareware Magazine* has to say about press kits:

Include short press releases on the news you have. For instance, if you have a new product or an update, include that information. Answer the question "What is your product?" So many times, we get a press release and it sounds like a neat product, but we can't quite figure out what it is. It sounds fun. Is it a game, or is it a database, or a contact manager? You have to spell out clearly exactly what it is. Also, state the advantage your product has over other products. And include other basic information about your product's capabilities. Include the price, system requirements, and where we can go for additional information.

The press kit should also include information about your company background. Are you a new company? Have you had a name change or major staff change? Just a little background. Nothing in-depth, but enough to help the editor remember where they heard about your company before. You might include a longer press release as well, offering more in-depth information about your key product.

Photos are helpful. Usually, magazines can use black-and-white glossies or color slides. You might want to have a product shot as well as a screen shot. Include basic information about how to look you up. How can the editor contact you at the show? And don't forget to include your company's phone number and address.

In putting together your press kit for a trade show or convention, make it look professional. Use quality paper, a laser printer, and put it all in a nice binder. Don't make it too thick, because most people already have more stuff to carry around than they want. Unlike the media kit discussed in chapter 7, a press kit for a trade show should not include your software. If you want to give people a copy of your software, get their business card and send the software to their office.

In addition to everything else, you should also be sure to mention the show in any of your ads. You want to let as many people as possible know you'll be at the show. Meeting people face-to-face is one of the most effective ways to sell both your software and your company.

Assuming you can afford it, the size of your staff and the design of your booth must be tailored to the show and your objectives. For example, if you're trying to sell site licenses to corporate customers, design your booth to accommodate as many 10-minute "quickie" demonstrations as possible. Then set up a hotel room or suite for in-depth demonstrations to qualified prospects. You can also use this same approach for distributors, except that your presentation should be oriented around showing the benefits distributors would have in carrying your software.

At a large show, your booth should be staffed by people who can give a quick overview of your product. If customers are qualified and want more information, you can schedule a follow-up appointment or invite them to your hotel suite for a demonstration. The objective of the booth is to qualify customers and either schedule a follow-up meeting or give them a brochure and send them on their way. It is easy to get tied up with people that have lots of questions. But one person who ties up your time might cost you five others who walk by and find no one to help them. By the way, don't expect to meet more than four or five qualified customers per day.

For large booths, you'll need a staff of three or four people. They should pay attention to the people who walk by your booth, and talk to anyone who shows interest to determine whether or not that person is a qualified prospective customer. There will be a few times when someone who appears to be a casual browser actually turns out to be a corporate buyer interested in your software. These are the people you're looking for. If someone doesn't stop them and ask a few questions, they might pass by your booth and never realize you were offering the solution to all their problems.

For smaller companies the formula is the same, just on a smaller scale. If you're a one-person company, you might be the only person available to staff your booth, although you'll be much better off if you can get a second person. Don't try to operate a booth alone during a multiple-day trade show. There's too much to do and you'll become too tired to effectively demonstrate your software. Even with two people, a three-day show can be tough. My wife and I once tried manning a booth by ourselves for a three-day show. By the morning of the third day, we were exhausted. It took us a week to recover after the show.

How should you run your booth? If you're trying to sell site licenses or meet distributors, set it up for quick demonstrations. Invite qualified customers to dinner or to a demonstration in your hotel room. With two people, one can qualify people while the other can give more detailed demonstrations.

To build a list of names of people interested in your software, but with whom you don't get a chance to talk, set out a bowl for business cards. Run a contest giving away a copy of your software to a name drawn from the bowl. If you're the only person in your booth, having a bowl for business cards is a very important way to collect names.

What to say and do

In manning a booth, don't just stand around and wait for people to talk to you. Be a little aggressive. Stand up and look alert. If there isn't much traffic, move around so it doesn't look like you're guarding the entrance to the booth. Be aware of your body language. Don't stand around with your arms folded and a scowl on your face. Smile, keep your hands loose at your side, and move around.

When someone comes into your booth, be aware of his or her body language. For example, if a visitor glances at a watch, time is short. If the person leans toward you, totally engrossed in what you're saying, he or she is interested. By the way, don't spend all your time talking at prospective customers. Ask them questions. Find out what their needs and problems are and then tailor your discussion based on their needs.

What do you say to people who come by your booth? Try to avoid saying things like "May I help you?" and "Are you familiar with our software?" While "May I help you?" might be appropriate in a store, at a trade show it's too easily answered by a simple "No." Openings such as "How are you doing?" aren't good either because they don't move the conversation toward determining the visitor's qualifications or interest in your software. A good opening line might be "Thanks for stopping by. What made you interested in our software?" The objective is to get customers to talk with you and tell you about their needs. Then follow up with questions about their business or about problems your software can solve.

Another, less direct opening could be "How are you enjoying the show? What are you here to see?" The topic of conversation is directed toward what's happening at the show and the visitor's interests and needs. A more direct approach that I use frequently is "Welcome to my booth. May I give you an overview of what this software can do?"

Following up contacts

Follow up trade-show contacts fast, especially with potential customers. Send a letter that reminds them of the show, of the circumstances under which you met, and include your literature and possibly a copy of your shareware disk—even if you gave them one at the show. Important contacts should be followed up with a phone call. Figure 7-1 shows a sample follow-up letter.

Attending fall COMDEX

The most important trade show is COMDEX. You should attend COMDEX to meet people and build a network of contacts. At COMDEX, everything is secondary to making contacts and meeting people. You want to make contacts with the press, people in distribution companies, other shareware authors, and dealers. Talk with everyone. Several times, I've spent

HomeCraft Software
P.O. Box 974
Tualatin, OR 97062
(503)-692-3732

XYZ Stamp Company
555 Main Street
Anywhere, ST 99999

ATT: Mr. John Smith

April 25, 1991

Dear _____:

Thank you for attending our booth at the recent Portland
User Group Computer Trade Show. Enclosed is our catalog
describing the software we currently publish. Please note
that the dealer price for any of the software in this
catalog is 50% off list, plus shipping.

If you find that you have customers interested in software
for cataloging stamp collections, please give me a call.
We always have copies of *For Stamp Collectors* in stock
ready to ship to you or directly to your customer.

If I can be of any further help, or if you have any
questions, please feel free to call me.

Sincerely,

STEVEN C. HUDGIK
President
HCP Services, Inc.
HomeCraft Software

9-1 Always follow up the contacts you make at trade shows and conventions with a letter. Most people are so busy during the show that they need a reminder in order to remember you and any discussions you might have had.

time talking with people I thought weren't important to me only to have them call three or four months later to place a big order or hire me as a consultant.

How important are contacts? When I started my sales career, one of the managers who interviewed me described the company's sales strategy by telling me he would hire me and keep me employed as a salesman for possibly 10 years before I made my first sale. What was I supposed to be doing during those ten years? Making contacts! This company was willing to invest 10 years of an employee's time just to have the right contacts in place when the time came to make a big sale.

Unlike working in a booth, where you want to qualify the people you meet, when attending COMDEX, the people you meet don't have to be direct business contacts. Make as many contacts as you can. Maybe you won't meet the president of a company, but if you've gotten to know a product manager, you have a contact—a way in.

The importance of contacts

When I was first introducing my software for cataloging collections, I wanted to meet magazine editors and demonstrate my software. They're busy people and it can be tough for a small, part-time software publisher to get an appointment. What I did was to call the salesperson who handled my advertising at each magazine. This was the contact I needed to get in. In each case, the salesperson gave me the names of the right people to see and set up an appointment for me. Once, the salesperson bought me lunch after I spent all morning talking with the editors.

If someone does you a favor by arranging a meeting or making an introduction, be sure to thank them. At a minimum, send a thank-you note. If you can, include a small gift. In my case, I usually send a small package of dried northwest salmon. It symbolizes the region in which I'm located and it's something most people like.

COMDEX parties

Press contacts are important because the press reports on people they know personally or people they've heard of. At COMDEX, to meet and know the people of the press, you not only have to attend the show but you have to go to the parties. Calling them *parties*, however, isn't entirely accurate. They're more like informal meetings. You aren't going to meet any reporters walking around on the show floor. On the show floor, there often isn't enough time to talk to one particular person—especially when thousands of others want to talk to that same person.

When attending a COMDEX party, introduce yourself to people, particularly the press. In many cases, I've noticed people from the press standing around by themselves or talking with other members of the press. They're also there to meet people. If you don't know what to say to people from the press, come straight out and tell them so and ask them to tell you what they discuss with other software publishers. It's a way to get a conversation started and it works quite well.

Don't be disappointed if someone from the press isn't interested in talking with you. We all have our special areas of interest. If your software doesn't interest someone, don't be upset when that person wanders off. Remember, most press people attend conventions to find things they can write about. Some of them are looking for you, but finding you is difficult—there are too many people. So if someone isn't interested in talking with you, move on and find someone else. The next contact might be the one to get your software reviewed in a magazine.

Both vendors and magazines sponsor parties at COMDEX. The best way to find these parties is to ask about them. Ask the people manning booths about their company's or magazine's party. Join the ASP and you'll automatically get information about the ASP party. Once you're at the ASP party, ask other authors which parties they recommend you attend. Or try wandering near the ballrooms and meeting rooms of the hotels hosting COMDEX—you'll surely spot some parties. Most of them are open and you can walk right in. Once you're in a party, ask people where they're going next. You'll be able to build a schedule of four or five parties to attend each evening.

For shareware authors, magazine parties are the most useful. At the magazine parties you get to meet the press—it's their party and they have to be there. And you get to meet the people in the software industry who are interested in being visible. Recently, however, magazine parties have become invitation-only parties. But you can still get in. This is where the contacts you made earlier come in handy. When all else fails, my tactic for getting into invitation-only parties has been to wait outside the door, introduce myself to people leaving the party, and borrow their passes to get in.

Another method for getting into closed parties is to do what you normally should be doing—meeting people. For example, last November I wanted to go to the *PC Computing* party, but found I had arrived an hour early. While there, I met an interesting couple from England. We had a very enjoyable conversation, at the end of which they gave me their press pass for the *Computer Shopper* party. By the way, both are members of the press in the U.K., although I didn't know that when we started talking (they weren't wearing their press badges). Meeting people who can help you happens in the most unlikely places, so take a moment to say hello when you're standing in line or waiting for a cab.

There's one other way to get into closed magazine parties and that's to be invited. When I was buying advertising in computer magazines, I was invited to the closed COMDEX magazine parties. This, however, is an expensive way to get an invitation to a party.

You should also attend some of the smaller parties. At the bigger parties, you might get the opportunity to shake the hands of magazine editors. At smaller parties, you might have a chance to talk with them.

One objective in attending a party is to see how the press works. Watch how other people work with the press, how they answer questions. Listen to the types of questions being asked. Listen to how other people answer. Listening and paying attention will help you avoid being caught off guard when you're talking to the press.

Visiting booths

During the day, you can set up appointments at booths and spend a lot of time on the show floor. Exactly what you do depends on your objectives. One possible objective is to get to know the competition. Find out how people react to products similar to yours. Find out what other software publishers are doing so that you don't reinvent the wheel. Look for products from major publishers for which you might be able to make add-on utilities. Visit booths run by other shareware publishers and those run by shareware distributors. You might also take the opportunity to test your software on various machines. Most of the computer manufacturers are there. If you ask to try your software on their machine, they'll generally agree and schedule a convenient time.

Planning ahead

Get the COMDEX guide before the show so you can look at the floor plans and building locations. Find the booths you want to see and plan your schedule to get to them all. It's a big show. You can see only 20% to 30% of it. Seeing everything you want will take some planning.

Plan the logistics of going to COMDEX well in advance. If you're coming from an area with a lot of computer companies, make your airline reservations early. Call the visitor's bureau in the host city and get a map of hotels around the convention center. Most times, you'll be better off making your own hotel reservations instead of going through The Interface Group.

What to bring

It's a waste of time to give out software packages at COMDEX. Don't go loaded down with copies of your product and expect to hand them out to people in booths. They aren't interested in carrying stuff back to their office. Just take your literature and use it to show what your product can do. You might bring a supply of shareware disks, but don't bring the complete, registered version. If you do bring disks to hand out, expect people to lose them. You're better off mailing a disk to someone after the show.

Get business cards from the people you meet. You can also hand out your business cards, but again expect people to lose them. When you finish talking with someone, make a few notes about your discussion on the back of the business card. It's the only way to remember what you talked about. Follow up any important people you meet by sending them letters after the show. Include a copy of your software if you think it's appropriate.

What to wear

Wear business clothes. Dress as you would for a meeting with an important corporate client. Jeans and T-shirts are definitely not appropriate.

The best approach is to dress conservatively. You never know who you'll meet. And be sure to wear comfortable shoes or even black sneakers. You'll be doing a lot of walking on hard, concrete floors. In the footwear department, at COMDEX, comfort is important.

Listening

While at COMDEX, you should be a good listener. All the exhibitors want to talk and push their products. Be a good listener and you'll learn more. Get near the people you've seen quoted. See what they're like and listen to what they have to say.

The ASP

In the past, the day before fall COMDEX started, the ASP held its annual meeting at the COMDEX meeting site. In addition to a business meeting, speakers were invited to talk about various aspects of shareware. For example, at one ASP COMDEX meeting, Bill Machrone, editor of *PC Magazine*, spoke for two hours about registration incentives, how to get the attention of the press, GUIs, the home market, and strategies for increasing sales. In addition to Bill Machrone, several successful authors presented talks on techniques to improve documentation, how to handle viruses, and customer service.

If you can get to Las Vegas for fall COMDEX, the ASP meeting gives you the opportunity to meet and discuss shareware marketing with other authors in addition to learning from the various presentations.

Being a member of STAR

One of the benefits of being a STAR (Shareware Trade Association & Resources) member is that you can participate in the STAR reception at COMDEX. STAR rents a large room, provides food and drinks, invites the press, and provides space for about 20 booths. If you're a STAR member you can rent a booth to use in promoting your software. It's a great opportunity to show off your software and possibly make a contact that'll help your company grow.

Attending spring COMDEX

Up to this point, I've talked about attending fall COMDEX. Whether or not you should attend spring COMDEX depends on your market. Spring COMDEX is smaller and more oriented toward corporate buyers as opposed to dealers. If you're trying to sell to corporate buyers and you can afford a booth, spring COMDEX might be worth attending. If you live in the Southeast (or have frequent-flyer miles to spend) and can afford the time, spring COMDEX is worth attending just to make press contacts. For more information about COMDEX, and for an attendee preregistration form, write to:

The Interface Group
300 First Ave.
Needham, MA 02194

Summer Shareware Seminar

Throughout this book I recommend that you attend the Summer Shareware Seminar, held in June of each year. When you read the profiles of successful shareware companies in chapter 15, notice that every one of the three big shareware companies recommend going to the SSS. It's the one place you can go to meet nearly all the big-name successful shareware authors, and spend three days learning about what they did to become successful. It's also the place to meet shareware distributors from around the world, retail software publishers, magazine writers, and suppliers.

This is a three-day conference that's scheduled for a Friday, Saturday, and Sunday to make it easy for part-time shareware authors to attend. It features panel discussions on key topics of importance to people in the shareware industry. Subjects that have been covered in the past include: getting media attention, writing software for ease of use, packaging, customer support, legal aspects of shareware, registration incentives, tips from the pros, and the international marketplace.

The Summer Shareware Seminar also includes a trade show where disk vendors, software publishers, and suppliers set up booths and make themselves available to talk with you. There's even entertainment. This past year the Great Shareware Bowl Trivia Contest was held on Friday evening and the Shareware Industry Awards banquet was Saturday night.

I talked with a shareware author last week who was bemoaning the lack of business information for shareware authors. He told me that, other than this book, there was nothing available. I mentioned the Summer Shareware Seminar and he said had heard about it and had heard how good it was, but couldn't see spending the money to attend. A few minutes later he told me that to run a successful business he needed to have the right tools, and purchasing a $600 compiler was no problem. He understands the need to have the right programming tools, but he doesn't understand the need to have the right marketing tools. The Summer Shareware Seminar is the right marketing tool, and with discounted airfares it costs less than a $600 compiler. For information on the next Summer Shareware Seminar, write to:

Summer Shareware Seminar
c/o Public Brand Software
P.O. Box 51315
Indianapolis, IN 46251

The Summer Shareware Seminar brochure comes out in April of each year, so be patient, you might not hear from them before that time.

Finding meetings

How do you find out about shareware-related meetings and seminars? If you have a modem, check the SHARE forum on CompuServe. The library for Section 0 will normally contain information files announcing upcoming meetings (if any are scheduled). The best way to stay in touch is to join STAR or the ASP. The ASP newsletter, ASPects, includes announcements for upcoming meetings. You could also subscribe to shareware-related publications such as *Shareware Magazine*.

Other trade shows and conventions

The following provides a list of addresses you can write to for information about other trade shows and conventions that might be of interest:

PC Expo
P.O. Box 1026
Englewood Cliffs, NJ 07632

OS/2 Device Driver
   Conference
Chiswick Park
490 Boston Post Road
Sudbury, MA 01776

CD-ROM Expo
P.O. Box 4010
Dedham, MA 02027

Netucon
P.O. Box 23917
Pleasant Hill, CA 94523

Softworld
202-2871 Olafson Ave.
Richmond, B.C. V6X 2R4
CANADA

Multimedia International Conference
945 Front St., Suite 945
San Francisco, CA 94111

Lap & Palmtop Conference
   104 E. 40th St.
Suite 802
New York, NY 10016

MacWorld Exposition
P.O. Box 9107
Framingham, MA 01701-9107

MultiMedia Expo
600 Community Dr.
New York, NY 10012

VAR Conference
600 Cummunity Dr.
Manhasset, NY 11030

10
Running a business

The purpose of this chapter is not to make you an expert in running a business—that would take a whole shelf of books. I just want to make you aware of some of the basic tools and principles used by successful business people. The best way to learn about running a successful business is to get started and run a business. Then read as much as you can, take business courses (starting with marketing courses), and spend time with other people who have home businesses.

Running your own business is nice. You get to do what you want. You make the decisions and control what your business does. And you have to work only a half-day—you decide which 12 hours it will be. Unfortunately, in running your own business, finding enough time to do everything can be your biggest problem. Learning more about running a business is the first thing that's pushed aside when time is short. I've found audio cassettes helpful in allowing me to continue learning about business while using my time productively. An excellent source is the Tape Rental Library, Inc. You pay a yearly fee and borrow all the tapes you want. For the cost of buying one or two audio programs, you can listen to a dozen or more. Contact them for a free catalog. Their address is:

Tape Rental Library, Inc.
One Cassette Center
Covesville, VA 22931

Start with the How To Start and Succeed In Your Own Business tapes (number 25184) by Brian Tracy. They are excellent. A key point that Tracy makes in his first tape is the difference between winners and losers in business—winners learn from their mistakes, pick themselves up, and try again. You have a choice. You can either make the same mistake again or learn from your mistake. When you learn from your mistakes, you gain judgment.

"When I started with the first version of AutoMenu I didn't know much about running a business. I talked to friends of mine and they suggested I go to a business school where they had a small business assistance program. After we talked, they wrote three pages of notes on things I wasn't doing right."

— Marshall Magee, president of Magee Enterprises, Inc.

Don't expect to be successful without making a lot of mistakes. When you look at successful people, you tend to see the trappings of their success: the profitable business, nice cars, big house, etc. You don't see the hard work and mistakes littering the path to that success. Expect to make mistakes and learn from them. That is why starting a business is the first and most important step in learning how to run a business. Start as soon as possible. Make your mistakes when you and your business are as young as possible. That's when mistakes have the smallest impact and you can most easily recover from the results. Since you'll never be any younger than you are today, today is the day to begin.

"The one thing I think is more important than anything else is to be a self-starter. You have to know when to work and when not to work. Especially when working at home."

— Martin Schiff, a shareware author

Targets and goals

Once you decide to start a business, the first step is to determine your targets and goals. A target is where you want to go. Goals are the intermediate steps you use to reach your target. If you don't know where you want to be or what your target is, you won't know when you get there or if you're getting any closer.

Of course, your goals will change over time. Don't put off thinking about where you want to be in one year, two years, or five years from now just because you know you'll change direction as your business grows. Target where you want your business to be and then set goals to reach that target. If needed, you can modify them later.

Possible targets for your business include making a lot of money, gaining a market share, getting a 25% return on your investment, and establishing a market position. You should note that these are business goals. I discussed personal goals in a previous chapter. For example, you might have a personal goal of learning about running a business. Based on that personal goal, a target you might shoot for would be to stay in business for the first year and have a 5% profit at the end of the second year.

Targets and goals must have several characteristics to be effective. They must be specific, measurable, and have a set time limit. In the examples I just gave, both targets meet these requirements. They're specific (stay in business and make a 5% profit), they're measurable (you'll know if you're still in business, and a 5% profit can be measured), and they're time-based (the first target covers one specific year and the second target a second specific year).

Nebulous or indefinite targets are not effective in building a successful business. For example, you could say your targets are to stay in business and make a profit. Does that mean that, if you get a registration payment in the mail this afternoon and make a profit for the day, you've reached your target? You did stay in business until this afternoon and you did make a profit. Exactly what do you mean when you say you want to stay in business and make a profit? If I asked ten people, I would get a variety of answers. To be effective, your targets and goals must be specific, measurable, and time-based.

Once you've set your targets, then set the goals you need to achieve to reach each target. For example, to help achieve the target of having a 5% profit within two years, one of your goals could be to have 300 shareware dealers selling your shareware by the end of the first year. Now you have a direction and can focus your energy toward achieving your goals and reaching the target you've set.

Running your business

"If your primary motivation is service to people and providing a superior product, you will make more money than if your primary motivation is just making money."

— Bob Wallace, Quicksoft Inc. (maker of PC-Write:)

Here are 11 suggestions to help you run your business. When setting your targets and goals, keep these points in mind:

Be concerned about the customer at all times   That's what the quotation is about. Profits are the result of running a successful business, not the objective. If your objective is to make a lot of money, you'll fail. To be successful, you must be service-oriented. One of the most profitable and successful companies in the world, IBM, defines its business not as manufacturing computers, but as providing service. I recommend reading *Father Son & Co.* by Thomas J. Watson Jr. and Peter Petre (Bantam Books, 1990). This book tells the story of how IBM stayed closer to their customers than any other company. It's a story of what IBM did right. As we know, with a change in leadership IBM lost touch with its customers and, as a result, lost billions of dollars. So be concerned for the customer at all times. Be concerned about complaints and problems. Treat customers as if they were important, because they are. Love your customers.

Do more than you're paid to do   Put a little extra effort into anything you do for your customers. Give a little extra. If you promise two free updates, give your users three under some circumstances. If you promise a printed manual, include a free quick-reference card. This is how to get happy customers.

For example, when someone calls with a problem, I help them, even if it's a hardware problem or a problem with not understanding DOS. I promise help only for registered users and only for problems with my software, but I'll help anyone who calls with any problem. As a result, many of the people I've spent an hour with on the phone buy two, three, and sometimes four additional programs. They recommend my software to friends and write nice letters to magazines. The letter section in the Sept./Oct. 1990 issue of *Shareware Magazine* has a letter one of my customers wrote about my Home Money Manager IIa software praising my customer support of unregistered users.

Write a business plan   Yes, it's difficult to do, it's tedious, and it takes a lot of time, but it's one of the most important things you can do. Why? Because in learning how to put together a business plan, you'll learn a lot about running a business. The ability to put together a good business plan demonstrates competence in business. It requires skills and knowledge that you'll need to run your business. Having a business plan is the best way to show you're a competent manager. It tells the world you're ready to run a business.

Generate cash flow and conserve the cash you have   This means you must sell your software (get registrations) and have cash come into your business. Cash flow is the lifeblood of a business. You need cash flow to survive. Without a cash flow, you won't have the money to accomplish your other goals. If you have no cash flow, you either stop paying your bills or you go into debt.

There's more than one way for your business to go into debt. Bank loans or running up charges on a credit card come to mind immediately. But without a positive cash flow, you won't be able to get a loan. Banks lend money only to businesses that don't really need it. Any money you put into your business should be looked at as an investment and you should expect a return on that investment. In other words, plan for your business to pay back your investment with interest.

Shareware is unusual because you can start a shareware business with very little cash. However, this doesn't eliminate the need for cash flow; it just makes it easier for your business to survive on a lower sales volume.

It seems like a simple concept—you need to sell software to stay in business. It's so simple that many people forget how important it is. A lack of cash flow is one of the leading causes of business failure. How do you generate cash flow? Put most of your efforts into marketing. Marketing and sales are like a pump and water. If you stop pumping (marketing), the flow of water (sales) stops.

I also mentioned conserving cash. Many people starting a business go out and spend money on things they feel a business needs. They rent an office, hire a secretary, buy all the "necessary" office equipment, etc. The cash starts flowing out, but there's little coming in. The business quickly bleeds to death as the owner runs out of cash.

Make market share a prime objective   Get as many people as possible to use your program. Send out disks to as many dealers and user groups as you can afford to. Upload your program to CompuServe, GEnie, and the major BBSs. Give away copies to anyone who asks. Do everything you can to make your software the most widely used program of its type. Don't worry about registrations; work to get everyone using your software.

Market share gets your software noticed by the press. The quicker you build market share, the more difficult it is for your competition to get started. Once you have a significant market share, people and particularly large businesses will buy your software just because it's the program everyone else uses. Build a large user base and you can support your business just by selling goods and services to your user base.

Plan to work hard and be patient   If you're the only person running your business, expect to work long hours, seven days a week. Don't forget the "law of three"—for anything you want to do, take your most conservative estimate and multiply by three. Be patient, because things will take three times longer than you expect.

Join professional groups and associations   Join your local chamber of commerce. When I discussed COMDEX, I talked about meeting people and making contacts. Your local chamber of commerce is a source of contacts to help your business locally. For example, you can get to know bankers, who are essential to any business. You'll also meet people who can help you find employees (when you need them) or used equipment, and help you evaluate services such as legal and accounting services.

Keep in mind that "social" business meetings aren't really social gatherings. They're a means to meet and talk with people in a more relaxed atmosphere. Just as COMDEX parties are really ways to make industry contacts, Chamber of Commerce breakfasts (or whatever your local chamber sponsors) are a way to make contacts with people that might be able to help you. You aren't there to eat. You're there to listen and meet people.

You should also join the Shareware Trade Association & Resources (STAR) or the Association of Shareware Professionals, or both—they both have different approaches toward helping their members. As a member of either organization, you'll have an inside track to meeting other shareware authors and making useful contacts to help your shareware business. Both organizations are discussed in chapter 14. In addition, if there are any local or regional software associations in your area, join them. These groups are another important source of contacts.

"ASP has been a source of professional contacts I would not have otherwise had. It's been a great source of education. I've learned how to conduct myself in a professional manner. Since joining ASP my sales have gone up over 300%. Being an ASP member has done more than anything to increase my registrations."

— Shareware author telephone survey responses

Make a specific division of duties and responsibilities If two or more people are involved in your business, you can divide tasks according to skills. A software business can typically be separated into three areas:

- Programming, product development, documentation, and user support (Product Manager)
- Sales and marketing (Marketing Manager)
- Production, order processing and shipping, and finance (Operations Manager)

If you took my advice from chapter 2 and found someone who's good at marketing, the two of you can divide the functions handled by the operations manager.

Set aside a specific area exclusively for your at-home business Make it clear to your family that when you're in your business room, you aren't to be disturbed. One of the most difficult aspects of running a home business is to get family and friends to recognize that you're working.

Don't expect to use venture capital to get your company started To get venture capital, you must first have a track record showing previous successful experience starting another company. You also need an innovative product ready to be delivered to users and good experienced management.

Watch out for people who offer to make a lot of money for you I regularly get calls from people who want me to give them the right to use my software in one manner or another. They have "great" ideas that can't miss and will make me rich with little effort on my part. Look into these "opportunities," but be prepared to run. Ask callers to describe their proposal in writing. Never sign a contract until you get your lawyer's opinion or at least discuss it with other ASP authors.

These are just some basic guidelines. Running a business involves much more than I can include here. Please take the recommendation I made at the beginning of this chapter and read as much as you can and attend some courses in marketing and small-business management. Start today by going to your library or bookstore and look for books on running a home business.

Equipment and services

The purpose of this section is to describe some of the services and equipment you might need and explain why you might need them. Although I'm cheap and will pinch a penny until Lincoln screams, I've always found that it pays to have the right tools and to hire the right expert. I've also found that buying quality, not low price, is the best way to save money. I don't mean that when you're buying something you should evaluate only high-priced services and equipment. Many times you can find the quality you need and still not spend much.

Keep in mind that your time is valuable, but don't sacrifice your health or your family by running yourself into the ground so you can build a big cash balance in your bank account. Buy the equipment and services you need to run your business properly. For example, don't spend all day copying disks when an outside service can do it for a few cents more per disk. Or hire one of your neighbor's kids to do disk copying for you. Your time would be much more productively spent on marketing or improving your software. Evaluate expenses by asking yourself whether or not the money you spend will buy something that will bring in more profits. If buying a $10,000 desktop publishing setup will bring in an additional $12,000 in profit, then buy it. That is a 20% return on your investment.

Buying used equipment or buying from warehouse discount stores might allow you to get the equipment you need and still conserve cash. Among your contacts in local businesses, you might find people willing to give you equipment they no longer need—that's how I got my fax machine. Your contacts can also let you know about businesses that are closing or moving and selling off equipment. And don't forget warehouse discount stores such as Costco, Office Depot, Bizmart, and Office Club. Watch for sales and special prices on closeout items.

Now I'll discuss specific equipment useful to a business. I'm not going to discuss computer equipment. I assume that you have a computer that's capable of reading all the disk sizes and formats that your customers use.

Answering machines

An answering machine is essential for a small business. It will answer your phone while you run to the post office or are in the shower (the most likely times that people call). Be sure to get a machine with remote message retrieval capability. This way you can pick up your messages when you aren't at home. Expect to pay a minimum of $50 to $100.

Answering machines are becoming more accepted as a greater number of people use them. Although a few people still don't like to leave messages on machines, you'll get more orders if you have an answering machine. You can even have people leave their order on the message tape. I've tried several outgoing messages and the most effective has been:

Hello. This is HomeCraft Software. I'm very sorry, but I can't get to the phone just now. If you will leave your name and number I'll call you back as soon as I can. If you are calling to purchase one of my programs, please leave your name, address, phone number, the name of the program you are purchasing, and your Visa or MasterCard number. I will ship your software within 24 hours.

Notice that this message doesn't say whether I'm there or not. Because I work out of my home I don't want to tell people that I'm not there. The message is very generic, yet reassures callers that if they leave a message they'll get a response. If they order software, it will be shipped within one day.

What's better than an answering machine is to use your computer to run a voice-mail system. It provides a better image for your company and you'll sound like a larger, more prosperous company. It also provides the ability to switch incoming calls between you voice message system, fax, and data modem. A typical system costs about $259 and will run on any system that can run Windows. If you're working a regular daytime job while running your shareware business, a voice-mail system is a necessity.

Telephones

A telephone with a hold button is another vital piece of equipment. It allows you to put the caller on hold while you switch to another phone, look up an error message, or confer with another person. This is especially important if you have kids. There's nothing more unprofessional-sounding than the background noise of kids yelling and dogs barking when you set down the phone. With phones costing so little, it's worthwhile to get a phone with a hold button.

Should you have a separate business phone line? Yes, once you start exceeding $30,000 to $40,000 in sales, or sooner if you can afford it. I ran my software business for four years using one personal phone. This worked fine. My wife and I always answered the phone as if it were a business call and our family and friends quickly got used to it. However, having a line dedicated to your business has several advantages.

I converted my personal line to a business line when I started working on shareware full-time. The first day the number was listed under my business name I got two calls from people who got my number from directory assistance. Both became registered users. A few months later, *Business Week* magazine printed an article about my software, but didn't include my phone number or mailing address. Fortunately, their readers could get my number from information and my phone was ringing constantly for two weeks.

A separate business line lets you take time off. If you use your personal phone, you feel like you must answer every call. You never know when it might be a family member trying to get in touch or a neighbor with an emergency. If you have a separate business line, you can stop taking calls in the evening and spend more time with your family.

800 numbers

Do you need an 800 number? A basic fact of business is that the easier you make it for customers to buy from you, the more sales you'll have. An 800 number makes it easier for users to call and register your software. However, my telephone survey of shareware authors showed mixed feelings. Some authors said that 800 numbers made for larger phone bills, but no increase in sales. Others saw a dramatic increase in sales after installing an 800 number. Whether or not an 800 number will increase your profits depends on your circumstances. For example, an 800 number should be used only for customer orders, but this might require a separate line for the 800 number. A small business might not be able to justify paying for the second line. I'll discuss more about 800 numbers in the section on telephone services.

Laser printers

For printing manuals, press releases, and business correspondence, a laser printer has become a "must-have" item. You can get by if you have a daisywheel printer. This is a good way to get started without spending much money. However, sending out a press release printed on a dot-matrix printer hurts the image of your software. It looks unprofessional, and generally is a waste of time because it will be ignored. The same applies to writing business correspondence. Letters printed on a dot-matrix printer are taken as a sign of a lack of professionalism.

Photocopier

A photocopier was one of the first major office machines I purchased. Now I wouldn't give it up even if I closed down my software business. In many cases, having your own photocopier cannot be immediately cost-justified. However, it's a tremendous convenience and time-saver if you have a lot of small-quantity printing jobs such as duplicating press releases. Another use is for making brochures. When my company was smaller I'd buy $8^1/2 \times 11"$ glossy paper and make my own brochures in small quantities. This approach allowed me to include the latest quotes from magazine reviews and produce specialized brochures for each of the small niche markets I target.

Fax machine

A fax machine is another piece of equipment that comes to mind. If you need to quickly exchange documents with someone, a fax machine is the only way to do it. Fax machines are also starting to be increasingly used for placing orders. Customers like using a fax because they can place their order now and do it in writing.

A fax machine is essential if you publish business software or work on an international basis. If you get a voice-mail system as I recommended earlier in this chapter, you don't need a separate fax machine. The voice mail system works as both a fax machine and a data switch. If you don't have a voice mail system, get a line switch that allows you to have the fax machine and your voice phone on the same line. Fax machine prices are dropping rapidly and will be going down more. Currently you can expect to pay between $300 to $800 to get a fax machine, and about $100 to $200 for the line switch.

Fax boards for your computer are also available. You can get a combination 2400-baud modem and 9600-baud fax for under $150. There's a disadvantage to using a fax board, however. You can't send documents that are in paper form, for example, a contract your lawyer just wrote. There have also been times when I needed to fax a section of my user's manual. It's quicker and easier if you can photocopy a document and send it using a stand-alone fax machine.

Postage machine

A postage machine was one of the most important pieces of equipment I added to my business. Postage-machine manufacturers advertise their machines by telling about the money you save putting the correct postage on your mail. I didn't have that problem. I kept a box containing a wide variety of stamps and could always put the correct postage on my mail. What a postage machine did for me was save time, and that was more valuable than saving a few cents.

You can't buy a postage machine; you must rent one from a postage-machine company. Look in the Yellow Pages for a listing of the brands available in your area. Pitney-Bowes is the biggest supplier of postage machines and I've found its machines to be the best. However, it's also the most expensive, costing about $29 a month to rent. I've also found Pitney-Bowes' service to be terrible, but maybe the company can get away with that since it's the biggest.

Postalia is a brand that's cheaper to rent (about $24 a month), but its machine is technically not as good at a Pitney-Bowes. For example, to change the date on a Postalia, you need a flashlight. Even then, the numbers are still difficult to read. The Pitney-Bowes has easily accessible thumb wheels. The Pitney-Bowes includes a lock that prevents printing postage over $1 without pushing a second key. On the Postalia, you can easily enter $7.50 when you intend to enter $0.75 (I've done it). As a result, I recommend getting a Pitney-Bowes.

Office supplies

Some basic office supplies are also necessary if you want to be taken seriously as a business. The most important are business cards and letterhead. Both should be professionally typeset and printed on quality paper. If you have a laser printer and some good fonts, you can design your own letterhead and print it as a part of each letter. If you do this, be sure to use good quality bond paper. Plain white copy or laser printer paper does not convey a quality, business-like image. In general, I've found that creating my own letterhead isn't worth the savings. Your best bet is to get printed stationary.

Producing your manuals

When you're small it's best to keep, as much as possible, the production of your registered versions directly within your control. You can produce small quantities of just the manuals and other material you immediately need. This means you might want equipment such as bookbinding machines and shrink-wrapping machines. I list sources that supply this type of equipment in chapter 17. I've found a shrink-wrapping machine to be particularly useful. Shrink-wrapping your software makes it look more professional and helps your company appear more substantial and stable. The neat, professional look it gives to your package increases the value of your package significantly. You can purchase a shrink-wrapping machine for under $400.

Even as you grow, having your own shrink-wrap machine is handy. You can fix damaged packages, shrink-wrap media kits to make them look sharper, and use it for test runs of new products.

Services

Now let's look at services your business might need. There are three essential services: a good lawyer, a good accountant, and a good printer.

Finding someone who is "good" is a major problem. Unlike a product you can examine and for which you can get a feel for the quality, it's difficult to determine the quality of a service until you try it. My experiences with referral services for lawyers and accountants suggest they're really no better than looking in the phone book. You can also ask a friend to refer you to someone. Sometimes this will work out well; other times, your friend's needs will be different from yours and the person he or she hired might not be the best person for you.

Joining the Chamber of Commerce or a regional software association is one way to find the services you need. It gives you a chance to meet professional people whose services you might need in the future. You can evaluate them and determine how well you communicate and work with them before you actually need their services.

Another method is to call lawyers and accountants you pick out of the phone book. Tell them what you're looking for and ask what they can do for you. Make this a short, ten-minute conversation. Some will ask you to come to their office and will charge $100 or more for this visit. I pass those by. In my conversations, I look for someone I feel comfortable talking with. The most crucial elements in this type of relationship are communication and understanding. The person I feel comfortable with is the one I can communicate with.

You should also ask about rates. I can feel just as comfortable with $75-an-hour lawyers as with $200-an-hour lawyers if I can easily work with them and they have the required knowledge and skills. And I've found that the $200/hour attorneys usually know what they're doing and can get the job done in a quarter of the time a $75/per hour attorney takes—so they actually can cost you less (although this isn't always true).

When do you need to hire a lawyer or an accountant? When you have a problem that needs to be resolved. In starting a shareware business, you aren't in a position to hire a lawyer for every small question (remember, conserve cash). However, if you have a personal need, such as a will, use a lawyer who also can help with your business. Once you've hired a lawyer for one or two small jobs, you've established a relationship. It's then easier for you to call with small questions or for advice.

A lawyer

Your business will require a lawyer when you form a corporation or partnership, or need to review contract documents. Don't try to do these on your own unless you have some experience; even then you might want to consult an expert. For example, I have extensive experience as the team leader in negotiating multimillion-dollar contracts. Yet I wouldn't sign a partnership agreement, for example, until my lawyer reviewed it.

You can reduce your costs by using standard forms and learning the key points to look for in some types of contracts. However, be sure the standard forms you're using are applicable to a software business and that you aren't blindsided by a contract that has all your key provisions but has an additional clause you don't understand. For this reason, it's a good idea to hire an attorney who's familiar with shareware to review contracts involving software.

Finding a good attorney can be difficult. One of the best ways is to talk with other shareware authors in your area and find out who their attorneys are. There are thousands of shareware authors and it's likely there's someone near you who can provide some advice.

If there are any other software companies in your area (check the yellow pages), call them. If you're calling a large company, ask to speak to someone in the legal department. If they're a small company, ask for the owner. These people might be able to refer you to the appropriate law firm.

If there are no local resources you can use, then go to the SHARE forum on CompuServe and post a general message asking for the name of a good attorney.

An accountant

A good way to find an accountant is to hire one to do your personal income taxes. An accountant is usually worth the cost and, again, you establish a relationship that's handy when you need more important services. It also allows you to evaluate how well you work with this person and the quality of the work.

I found it very useful to have had an accountant doing my taxes for several years before I formed a corporation. Then I had some tax-related problems relating to my shareware business. My lawyer called my accountant, they worked it out, and I just came in to sign the papers on the correct day. And my accountant didn't even charge me! Because he was familiar with my financial situation, he could answer the questions in just a few minutes. If he were starting from scratch, it would have cost me $50 to $100 for the accounting advice.

A printing service

Why do print shops fit in the same category as lawyers and accountants? Having a good printer is essential to your business. You need a printer that will do quality work, will get it done right the first time, and can handle rush jobs. You can find printers that fit these requirements both in quick-print chains and local print shops. The only way to determine who is good and who isn't, however, is to try them.

Almost all printers have the equipment to do the type of work you'll need, although many quick-print shops can't handle color printing on glossy paper. (Make this one of your criteria for qualifying printers; it's a service you might need in the future.) The service and quality you get depends on the people you deal with. The first good printer I found was part of a national chain. Everything was fine until the manager of the store I was dealing with left the company. I then went through five or six printers until I found the one that currently does all my work.

I'm constantly approached by other printers offering lower prices and faster service, but there's no way I would change now. With my current printer, I know that I'll get my printing when it's promised and that I'll get quality work. Besides, they do exactly the type of graphic design I like.

When you find a good printer, treat them right. For example, when I exhibited at a local trade show recently, my exhibit included a poster of the front cover of my software package. This poster was made by the graphic artist at the print shop I use. I asked the artist to make up a little sign that stated the printer had designed the cover and that gave the printer's address and phone number. I put this sign next to the poster. The printer appreciated this and it cost me nothing.

Getting Visa/MasterCard merchant status

"We talked about Visa merchant status a month ago. You and a few others gave me some very good advice. I took it. I visited the branch manager of the bank I have had a checking account with for over 20 years and today I got my merchant account."

— Shareware author John Bauernschub

When you decide to start operating as a business, one of the first things to do is to get a separate checking account and use it only for your business. Deposit all your receipts into this account and write checks from this account to pay all your expenses. You'll immediately see whether or not you're making money and your bank statements will give you much of the information you need at tax time.

When you select a bank for your business checking account, you should also check to see whether or not they offer Visa/MasterCard merchant accounts. One of the biggest problems shareware authors have is obtaining Visa/MasterCard merchant status. Accepting credit cards brings you more business. It allows you to convert calls for help from unregistered users into immediate sales. If you don't accept credit cards, your business will appear smaller and less legitimate. In addition, the more home users you have, the more sales you'll get from credit card users (most businesses and institutions pay by check or purchase order). If you're going to sell your software internationally, credit cards are essential. They eliminate all the problems with currency conversion, making registration of your software easier for both you and the user.

Here's the bad news: it's harder to get merchant status than it is to get a loan. Banks must meet the guidelines set by the credit card companies. However, these are just guidelines and banks can request that Visa/MasterCard grant merchant status to companies that don't meet all of them.

It's your job to help your bank decide to grant you merchant status by getting them to ask Visa/MasterCard to waive some of the requirements. Banks are in the business of making money. One of the ways they make money is by issuing credit card merchant accounts. They want your business. You just need to give them what they need to feel comfortable.

The best situation is to work with a bank you've had personal accounts with for many years. If this isn't possible, get to know the bankers in your community better. For example, join the Chamber of Commerce—many bankers are members. Or go into a bank and ask to meet the manager. Tell him or her that you're starting a business and want to learn more about the services a bank can provide. Don't be in a rush to establish a merchant account. Banks don't like to rush into things that require them to bend the rules. Project an image of someone who is thoughtfully and carefully investigating the right way to run a business.

When you visit a bank, be sure to dress like a banker. People feel more comfortable talking with others who are similar to themselves. Men should wear a gray or blue suit, or a sport jacket with matching pants. Women should wear solid-color suits or dark dresses. If you aren't sure what to wear, pay attention to what the bank manager wears (not the tellers) the next time you visit your bank.

Applying for merchant status

The merchant status guideline that will cause you the most problems is the one requiring a store front. There is a good reason for this guideline. Credit card companies have often lost money to "boiler room" mail-order businesses that can quickly go out of business and leave town. To get around the store-front requirement, demonstrate your long-term stability. Have you lived in the same place for five or more years? Have you banked at the same bank, and do you have money in your account? Have you been in business for several years? Have you shown a commitment to the business—by advertising, for example? If so, you might be able to demonstrate your stability.

Document proof of your stability, and bring that proof along on your visit to the bank. Bring all the information you can put together that will make the bank feel comfortable with you. Be sure that any information you bring helps your cause. For example, leave out a personal balance sheet if it shows you're heavily in debt. The following is a list of possible documents you could bring with you to the bank.

- Your personal financial statements, including a balance sheet. These should show that you personally are financially stable and can back the financial obligations of your business.
- Your last two or three years' tax returns. These should show that you have already had a steady income over the past few years. Again, you are showing that you personally are financially stable. It is even better if you have been in business for a few years and your tax returns show that your business has made a profit.
- Copies of your registered version, if it looks like a quality package that could go on a retail shelf. In other words, "sell" your software to the banker. Also bring copies of any magazine reviews, promotional material, and letters from satisfied customers. The shareware marketing method might not appear to be a reliable source of income to many bankers, so be prepared to discuss shareware in general. Take along information, such as magazine articles, that discuss successful shareware authors. Bring a copy of Dr. File Finder's Guide To Shareware (available in most major book stores).
- A copy of your resume showing your work experience, educational background, and accomplishments—if you've worked for the same company for more than five years. Continuous employment shows that you're less likely to relocate and helps the bank feel more comfortable about your staying around.
- A copy of your business plan, if you have one. If you don't have one, put together a one-page description of your market, your estimate of

how much software you expect to sell and why you expect to sell that much, and a description of how you plan to market your software.

- A recent assessment of your home or, if one hasn't been done, a picture of your home and something that shows its value, such as property-tax bills. Also, bring a history of your previous addresses, if there have been few. This again is to show that you have assets and a commitment to staying in the community. Homeowners are less likely to relocate than renters.

The banker might tell you that none of this is needed; mine did—but he then took copies of it all and put it in my file.

Expect to get "no" for an answer. Some banks have a firm policy on accepting no mail-order businesses, while others will work with you. This can even vary from branch to branch for the same bank. I recently talked with four banks. Two said no way. The other two said no, but agreed to submit my package of information to the bank manager. If you're completely turned down, try again at another bank. Your first objective is to find a bank that will give you the application form. Once you have completed an application, your chances of being approved are much greater.

When you go to a bank to discuss merchant status, ask to talk to the manager. That is the only person who can waive the bank's rules and requirements. If you start at a lower level, it can be difficult to have your information forwarded to the manager. If you start with the manager, you're speaking with the decision maker. If the manager refers you to a lower level, the person at the lower level becomes aware that the manager is interested enough in what you have to say to ask another person to spend some time listening to you.

Rules for keeping merchant status

Once you gain merchant status, don't lose it. Be aware of the activities that can cause your business to lose its Visa/MasterCard merchant status. The following list describes the activities that will cause you to lose your merchant status:

- Entering a credit card transaction long before shipping the product.
- Not letting the customer cancel the purchase within three days.
- Chargebacks and credits totaling more than 10% of credit card transactions.
- Excessive complaints to the Better Business Bureau or your state's credit card consumer relations office.

Alternatives

You might find that you can't present a positive image to the bank if, for example, you work for a company that has relocated you several times or if you live in an apartment. Even then, however, you can sometimes still get a merchant account. There are banks that operate on a national basis and are familiar with the shareware industry. For example, the INB National Bank in Indianapolis is such a bank. They provide complete Visa/MasterCard merchant services, including an 800 number you can use to deposit transactions electronically. Although they don't just sign up anyone who asks for merchant status, they are familiar with shareware and shareware authors. You won't be turned away because you're a shareware mail-order business. For more information, contact the Visa/MasterCard Merchant Department at 317-266-6917. Or write to:

Card Services
INB National Bank
One Indiana Square, Suite 1370
Indianapolis, IN 46266-1370.

Ad response companies

Some answering services will take your calls, handle your orders, and process your charges with their bank. These services are actually 800-number ad response companies (thus, they're also a way for you to have an 800 number). The problem is that they know nothing about your software. They're good at handling orders for simple consumer products, but many software users ask questions before placing an order. To find an ad response company, check the Yellow Pages under answering services.

Having disk distributors handle your orders

Some shareware dealers will handle credit card sales for you. Falsoft, Inc. will handle registrations and credit card orders for you. They add a 3.5% credit card processing fee, which is probably what they pay to the bank. There's also a reasonable product shipment fee. You can contact Falsoft by calling 502-228-4492. Some of the larger shareware disk dealers also sell registered versions. This provides another alternative for users to order your software using a credit card (and access to an 800 number). Expect to sell your software to the shareware dealer at your distributor price of about 60% off list.

National Association of Credit Card Merchants

Another organization you can turn to is the National Association of Credit Card Merchants. This group is a for-profit organization operated by a company called the Credit Card Bureau. This company is in the business of publishing books and supplying information to merchants who need Visa and MasterCard merchant status. It can help you get and keep your merchant status.

A yearly fee of $250 provides you with a free copy of the book Getting

And Keeping Your Visa/MasterCard Merchant Status and provides access to help in getting merchant status. For example, the association maintains a list of over 200 banks located around the country that will work with home-based mail-order companies. The association claims that, with its help, nearly everyone who joins is able to get merchant status—if the member is a legitimate business. For more information about this company, call 407-737-7500 or write to:

The National Association of Credit Card Merchants
217 N. Seacrest Blvd.
Box 400
Boynton Beach, FL 33425

Discover card

The Discover card is a fast-growing card that some of your customers might prefer to use. The bad news is that when I last heard from them, Discover was not granting merchant status to mail-order businesses. They called me a couple of weeks ago to try to sell me on accepting the Discover card. As soon as they heard I was a mail-order business our conversation was just about over. I was told that they no longer give Discover merchant status to mail-order businesses.

American Express

If you're interested in accepting American Express, you can contact the company by calling 800-528-5200, or 800-528-4800 in Alaska and Hawaii. American Express doesn't have any problems with accepting mail-order businesses as merchants. They will, however, thoroughly check out your business, ask you to give them original copies of your advertising, ask for bank and commercial references, and require you to demonstrate that you're a real business.

And American Express's rates have recently become more competitive. They don't have a monthly fee, as do most banks that offer Visa/Master-Card merchant accounts, and the percentage of each transaction they take as their fee is lower than I'm now paying for Visa/MasterCard. Combined with computer-based electronic processing of transactions, American Express is a good deal and might cost you less than Visa/MasterCard.

The post office and UPS

Anyone running a mail-order business should know how the U.S. Postal System works. First, let's look at how mail is handled:

First-class mail First-class mail receives the highest priority for normal mail. It includes personal mail, mail that must move quickly, and mail that includes checks and money orders. In 1989, 53% of all mail was sent first class.

Priority and express mail   Priority mail costs $2.90 for the first two pounds and provides two-day service between major cities. Unlike UPS's two-day service, priority mail doesn't guarantee delivery in two days. However, I now ship all of my software using priority mail and have found it to be very reliable. The post office also offers a next-day express mail service that costs less than any of the overnight package delivery services such as Federal Express and DHL. If you need weekend delivery, express mail really shines—you can get your package delivered on Saturday or Sunday at no extra charge. The drawback to express mail is that at some post offices you need to get your package to the post office early in the morning in order to get next-day delivery. I've found that, if I'm bringing a package to the post office late in the day, I can get it delivered just as fast by using priority mail.

Second-class mail   This includes newspapers, magazines, and other periodicals. Second-class mail makes up 10.5% of all mail.

Third-class mail   Third-class mail includes advertising and promotional mail, and parcels weighing less than a pound. It's handled only after first- and second-class mail are delivered and only when carriers have room in trucks and bags for it. This accounts for 38% of all mail.

Since you can send mail weighing up to three ounces for $0.198, third-class mail can save you a lot of money. For example, you can mail update disks for $0.198 each instead of $0.52 each for first-class mail. Third-class mail is ideal for mailing newsletters and promotional material. However, if you're just mailing upgrade announcements, you're better off using form-feed postcards because they cost only $0.19 to mail.

Third-class mail requires at least 200 identical pieces to be sent at one time, and addresses must be sorted by zip code. Thus, a good mailing-list manager is important. The cost of using third-class mail is $60 per year for the permit, plus postage for each piece sent. The highest postage rate is $.198 per piece for the first three ounces. Some bulk-mailing situations (many pieces going to the same city, for example) lower the cost per piece. For more information on third-class mail, get publication #49, Third-Class Mail Preparation, from your local post office.

By the way, when the post office says that you must mail identical pieces, it means that pieces must be the same size and weight, and contain the same material. However, some people have found that the contents of each envelope can be different, as long as each envelope is the same size and weight.

Fourth-class mail   Fourth-class mail (parcel post) is used for packages and books. If you're mailing only your user's manual, book rate is the cheapest, and in many cases the fastest, way to send it. Material sent using book rate is delivered within five days, and would cost you only $1.48 for a two-pound package.

For international mail, send letters that weigh one ounce or less by letter air mail. Anything heavier (such as catalogs, disks, and registered versions of your software) should be sent via small-packet air mail. This includes packages to Canada and Mexico. The rates vary depending on the distance, but it's cheaper and just as fast as letter air mail. For more information on international postage rates, get a copy of publication #51, International Postal Rates and Fees, from your post office.

The United States Postal Service also publishes a free newsletter for mail-order businesses called Memo To Mailers. It contains information on changes in rules and regulations, plus tips on how to save on mailing costs. To get on the mailing list for this newsletter, write to:

U.S. Postal Service
P.O. Box 999
Springfield, VA 22150-0999

Depending on your circumstances, the post office might provide all the services you need. The disadvantage of the post office is that they don't automatically insure packages. I haven't found this to be a big problem. I've been using priority mail to ship my software for the past year and only one customer has not received his order. Since the material cost of my software is only about $7.00, losing one package over a year's time isn't bad, even taking into account that I used Federal Express to get a replacement copy of the software to my customer.

United Parcel Service   United Parcel Service (UPS) will pick up packages at your door daily. The advantage UPS has over the post office is that every package is automatically insured and the packages are still processed by people. This means that if the address isn't correct, the package will still, in many cases, be correctly delivered. I've had a package that both Airborne Express and the post office were unable to deliver using an address I verified with the customer three times. UPS delivered it with no problems. Another advantage of UPS is that it will accept copies of your logbook as proof that the package was sent.

Although it might take more time to ship by UPS because you need to fill out a logbook, having a readily accessible proof of shipment record can be worthwhile. Although I now ship all of my software using priority mail, I use UPS whenever I'm shipping something that's difficult to replace or is valuable. UPS bills you on a weekly basis for all packages you've shipped and you can pay the bills monthly. With UPS, there's also a weekly fee that covers all pickups for that week.

UPS second-day air delivery is an essential service that many customers will require. The cost is only slightly more than ground delivery, and many customers are willing to pay extra to get their software in two days. UPS also offers overnight delivery that includes Saturdays. If you have a daily UPS pickup, using their next-day service is easy and relatively inexpensive.

Next-day air services   I recommend that you sign up with an overnight air carrier such as Federal Express of Airborne Express. It costs nothing to open an account and an account makes it easy should you need to ship something that requires overnight delivery. In addition, some customers will ask for (and pay extra for) this service, which can be essential for business software. I've also found overnight delivery useful for these reasons:

- When you want to let people know they're important, for example a software reviewer, send the software by overnight express.
- When you have a big customer who needs a bug fixed yesterday.
- When a shareware disk dealer needs a new disk in time for a big computer show opening in two days.

You can find the phone numbers for all of the major overnight delivery services in the Yellow Pages of almost any phone book.

Using the telephone

How do you answer the phone? I'm not talking about the words you say—although if you want to sound professional, you should answer the phone using your company name. I'm talking about your attitude. What type of image do you project?

You want to convey the image of a cheerful, pleasant person who is eager to help. It's very easy to make your voice sound exactly the way it needs to sound to present this image—whether you're in a good or bad mood. Just smile. Smile when you answer the phone and you'll sound like a person with whom people want to talk. The image you create with your body will also be reflected in your voice.

I learned this technique as a morning disk jockey. How do morning DJs sound cheerful and pleasant every morning, even when they're sick and are having a bad day? They smile when they're talking. It works in the opposite way also. If you're having trouble with a supplier and you want them to know you're upset—but you don't want to say anything directly—clench your hands into a tight fist and your voice will take on an edge of anger and frustration.

Handling complaints

What happens when you pick up the phone and it's a user who has been struggling with a problem related to your software? The person is upset, maybe even angry with you. These can be some of the most difficult calls to handle. Most of us don't like complaints. They sound like personal attacks. We get caught up in the emotion of the personal attack on our competency or software. We might end up trying to prove the complainer wrong. We do everything except listen. If handled properly, complaints and problems can help your business grow. The most likely source of a registration is a person calling with a problem or complaint.

The best approach for handling an angry user is to stay silent and listen to the problem. Give the caller a chance to vent frustration, then go over the problem in a step-by-step manner. If you can, follow what the user is doing on your computer until you identify the problem. No matter how upset a user gets, remain calm and supportive.

The most difficult call I've had was from a user trying to install my hard-disk shell, YOUR MENU. Nothing was working the way he wanted and he wouldn't stop complaining long enough to let me ask some questions. He wouldn't try my suggestions, but insisted the software should work like WordStar. With a great deal of patience on my part, we worked through the problem and, at the end of the call, he gave me his credit card number so he could register as a user.

Most customers understand that software is occasionally faulty or has bugs. They'll give you a chance if you treat them fairly and with respect. Remember, the customer is always right. That doesn't mean they're technically right; it means that if you treat customers as if they're wrong, they won't be your customers.

Your company will be judged on your courtesy, the information you provide (give full explanations), and your responsiveness (avoid delays). Letters of complaint should be answered within 24 hours. If giving an answer takes longer, inform the user you're investigating and will be back in touch as soon as possible.

Phone services

Some phone services are beneficial and others aren't. For example, you should avoid call waiting. It's annoying to the person you're talking to, especially when that person is paying for a call to order your software. When you interrupt a call to answer your call waiting, you're telling the first person that he isn't important to you. If you have so many calls that you must have call waiting, then it's time to have a second phone line installed. An answering machine on the second line can take messages while you're talking on the first line.

Call forwarding, however, is very useful. This allows you to have your phone calls automatically sent to another phone. You can visit relatives or go away for a weekend and still get all your calls without the callers knowing that you're spending three days at the beach, for example.

800 numbers

Do you need an 800 number? This is a difficult question. The answer is yes, all mail-order businesses should have an 800 number for customers to use to place orders. It will bring additional sales from impulse buyers. However, the other side of this question is that many shareware authors don't feel they can afford the extra expense. If you aren't sure about 800 numbers, the following criteria might help with your decision.

The value of an 800 number can depend on your software. If you have a unique program, you have less of a need for an 800 number. If you sell the same product as six other publishers, and all six of you advertise in the same magazines, then an 800 number is essential to help differentiate you from or keep you equal with the competition. A general rule of business is that you should make it as easy as possible for your customers to do business with you. An 800 number makes it easier for your customers to call you.

If you have a complex product that requires a lot of telephone support, you should have an 800 number. Build the cost of the 800 number into your registration fee.

An 800 number helps show that you're in business for real; it makes you appear less of a fly-by-night outfit. It gives you credibility. An 800 number is also very useful if you travel. Instead of using a credit card to check your messages, call your 800 number. The cost of using the 800 number will be significantly less, and this use alone can sometimes justify it.

An 800 number is good for building a mailing list. If the call is free, even people with a casual interest will call for information. Once you get them on your mailing list, you can put together a direct-mail campaign to sell them on your software.

An 800 number can increase your contact with customers. People who have questions (or complaints) are more likely to call when they don't have to pay for it. If you can resolve the problems over the phone quickly, these people are more likely to be a repeat customers. (You want to keep people using your software so you can sell upgrades and enhancements.)

The most economical use of an 800 number is to restrict it to customers calling to place an order. A second, conventional number should be provided for users calling for information or help. However, if you want to expand your mailing list or improve customer service, allow everyone to use your 800 number.

Your existing phone can be set up to provide your customers with a toll-free number for reaching you. All the major long-distance companies have services that provide an 800 number that will ring on your existing phone. However, if you can afford a second line, it provides a way to tell whether the caller is using your 800 number or your regular number.

The biggest providers of 800 numbers are AT&T, MCI, and Sprint. Usually, several levels of service are available.

AT&T AT&T has four levels of service for 800 numbers. 800 Readyline delivers 800 service over regular lines and is compatible with local options such as call forwarding and call waiting. Intrastate and interstate calls are on the same line and require no new lines or hardware. The cost is $20 per month, plus $0.22 to $0.25 per minute—billed to the second. There is a $43.50 installation fee. A 5% discount is available if you spend more than $50 on long distance calls per month.

AT&T BASIC 800 service is similar, but uses dedicated lines. AT&T Megacom 800 delivers service over digital lines. AT&T 800 Masterline offers Canadian access in addition to intrastate and interstate access on a single dedicated line. Call 800-638-8326 or 201-658-2664 to talk with AT&T.

US Sprint US Sprint offers FONLINE 800. You can receive intrastate and interstate calls on a single line. The cost is $10 per month with a $50 installation fee. US Sprint also offers ULTRA 800 for heavier users. It features overflow control that sends calls to designated local business lines should the 800 line be overloaded during peak calling periods. Contact US Sprint by calling 913-541-6100.

MCI MCI does not have bundled packages but instead offers an "a la carte" selection of services. Basic service is $20 per month and between $0.19 and $0.25 per minute. MCI is just beginning to offer a new service for residential phone lines that provides 800 service for $2 per month. You can reach MCI by calling 800-888-0800 or 202-872-1600. Because competition is fierce in the phone business, things change rapidly; call each 800–service provider for current information.

Questions you should ask

Questions you should ask long-distance companies when comparing services include:

- What is the monthly service fee?
- Is there a minimum monthly charge?
- What is the cost per minute, and how does this vary depending on distance and time of day?
- Are there any volume discounts? (For example, AT&T offers a 5% discount if you use more than $50 per month.)
- Are there any installation fees?
- What is the timing increment for billing? Some services bill by the minute, so if you use 62 seconds, you pay for a two-minute call. It's better to use a service that bills in smaller increments. For example, some bill by the second or for every six seconds.

Be aware that the cost varies depending on your location because of local phone company charges.

Taxes and the IRS

If you're running your own business, you'll need to learn about local, county, state, federal, and possibly metropolitan tax laws. I can discuss only federal income tax here. You'll need to find out about your state and local laws.

People starting their first business seem to run into two problems when filing federal income-tax forms: They file the wrong forms, and they don't correctly account for inventory.

Tax forms

Once you start a business, you can no longer file form 1040EZ. You must complete forms 1040 and 1040 Schedule C. Form 1040 is for people who itemize deductions. 1040 Schedule C is used to determine the profit or loss from your business.

Inventory

When calculating the profit or loss from a business, many people like to look at how much money they've received and subtract what they spend during the year, resulting in a profit or loss. You can't do this. Any inventory you have must be accounted for.

Here's a simple example. If you're selling 386FX widgets and spent $1,000 to purchase 100 widgets last year, then your business expenses are $1,000. If you had no sales, you might expect your business had a loss of $1,000 for the year. That isn't true. You still have $1,000 of widgets in your possession. You haven't lost anything, unless the widgets have lost value or become unsalable. The way you calculate your profit or loss is:

gross sales – cost & expenses + inventory = profit (or loss)

If, in the example above, you had sold ten 386FX widgets for $50 each, your profit would be:

$500 (sales) –$1,000 (cost of goods) + $900 (inventory at $10 each) = $400 profit

Notice that although you made a profit, you have a negative cash flow. More cash has gone out ($1,000) than you took in ($500). That's why, in an earlier chapter, I highlighted cash flow as being important. You can make a profit, but if you have a negative cash flow, such as in this example, you'll soon be out of business.

Home-office deduction

You'll most likely be running your software business from your home and will be eligible to deduct depreciation on your home. While this might seem to be a nice way to reduce your taxes, keep in mind that home-office deductions might not provide the advantages you expect. For example, when you sell your house, you might not be able to defer the capital gains tax on all of your profits. Under normal circumstances, you can defer paying taxes if you purchase another house within two years. If you've taken a deduction for using part of your home for your business, you'll need to divide any gain on the sale of your house between personal use and business use. It doesn't matter how long you've had your business in your home. If you've deducted depreciation, you could save a few hundred dollars in taxes this year, but will have to pay several thousand dollars more in taxes if you sell your home next year.

Before taking a tax deduction for an office in your home, discuss your situation with your accountant. There are exceptions you can take advantage of to save money. For example, if you took home-office deductions in the past but don't take them in the year of sale, you might be able to defer paying capital gains tax on the entire gain.

Hobby or business?

Whether you operate your software company as a hobby or a business can make a big difference in your tax bill. We all want to call our software publishing efforts a business. If your software company is defined by the IRS as a hobby, your tax deductions will be limited to the amount of income your software company earns. You can't deduct losses from a hobby. But if you're publishing software as a business, all of your business expenses are deductible. (If the IRS defines it as a *sideline business*, your business expenses might be deductible only after they exceed 2% of your adjusted gross income.)

What can you do to protect your status as a business and prevent the IRS from reclassifying you as a hobbyist? As far as the IRS is concerned, a business is any activity that results in a profit. However, you don't actually have to make a profit; you only need to show that you intend to make a profit.

The easiest way to meet this requirement is to make a profit. Based on IRS guidelines, if you make a profit in three of any five consecutive years, you're running a real business. It doesn't matter how big your profit is in those three years, as long as you make a profit. If you have a business that's producing yearly losses, you need to prove that your intention is to make a profit.

Here is a list of things you can use to prove you're running a legitimate business:

- Operate in a businesslike manner and keep accurate financial records. For example, you should have a separate bank account that's used only for your business. You should, at a minimum, be using a spreadsheet to track your sales and expenses.
- Act in a professional manner. For example, joining professional associations such as the ASP and your state's software association help establish you as a legitimate business.
- If you can show you're making a serious effort to earn a profit, you've demonstrated you're trying to run a real business. For example,

sending copies of your shareware to five or six distributors is not a serious effort. Sending disks to 200 distributors helps demonstrate a serious effort toward generating sales. Other activities such as advertising, obtaining Visa/MasterCard merchant status, and printing a catalog or brochure help demonstrate that you're making a serious effort to run a profitable business.

- Run your business as a business is expected to be run. Have business cards and stationery printed. Get a business phone that includes a listing in the Yellow Pages. Rent a postage meter and buy a photocopier. These are things nearly every business requires and they're the types of things you wouldn't have unless you were seriously running a business.

You don't need to use everything listed, but if you're losing money you'll need all the evidence you can put together to show that you intend to earn a profit and have the potential to do so in the future. The IRS's typical approach is to try to show that you get personal pleasure from your business. If they can demonstrate this, it will count against you. A hobby is something you do for personal pleasure, even if it earns a profit. You need to prove that your motive is to earn a profit.

Employing your children

You can make your children's weekly allowance tax deductible by paying them to work in your business. Children with no other income can earn up to $3,000 without paying taxes. To do this, you'll need to keep good records showing the type of work they did, the hours they put in, and the hourly pay rate. The pay rate should be comparable with what you would pay someone hired from outside of your family to do the same type of work.

Getting tax help

Many community colleges offer evening courses on taxes for people in small business. If you aren't familiar with how businesses are taxed, I recommend that you take one of these courses. Although you might hire an accountant, you still need to provide correct information. For example, your accountant has no way of knowing the value of your inventory. If you mistakenly report a value of zero, that's the way it will appear on your tax forms.

I started this chapter by recommending that you learn more about running a small business, and that's how I'm ending it. I've discussed some key topics that should help you get your business started, but there's more to learn. In business, there's always more to learn. So read, take some courses, listen to audio tapes, and get involved in groups where you can discuss your business problems with others who have faced the same problems.

11
Legal considerations

There are no legal requirements for starting a business, no forms to fill out or papers to sign. Your business exists the moment you decide you have a business. However, what type of business you have and how you operate it might require some legal work.

I'll start with some of the simpler topics and save the complex ones for later. I'm assuming that you're running your business out of your home.

Local licenses

Many different local laws affect businesses. I won't even attempt to discuss local laws, permits, and regulations here. I will cover basic legal considerations in a broad fashion. You need to check local requirements and laws yourself.

Zoning is usually not a problem for a home-based software business. If you don't have any external sign of a business, you can usually operate in an area zoned as residential.

Your city, town, or county might require a license for your business. Sometimes, this license is solely a source of revenue for local government. If you have employees, a local license might be required to ensure that you have safe working conditions. Enforcement of local licenses is often minimal or nonexistent. However, check with your city, town, or county clerk to find out what licenses are required, if any. Government penalties for not following the rules can be substantial, especially if your business turns out to be successful.

Sales tax

In the 48 states that have a sales tax, you're generally required to get a re-seller's permit before you begin selling a product or service (specifics vary from state to state). In some states, computer software is not taxed. Contact your state's Department of Revenue for information. Also ask them for an application for a state tax-identification number.

Doing Business As (DBA) forms

In many states or counties, you must file a Doing Business As (DBA) form if you use a name other than your own name. You can do business using many different names. For example, you might use one company name for business software and another for educational software. However, you must file a DBA form for each name you use. This form allows the state to identify you should there be complaints or problems with your business. It prevents you from hiding behind a business name not linked to a person.

In many cases, you cannot open a business account at a bank without the proper DBA forms for the bank to put in their files. By the way, be sure to give the bank copies (not originals) of your DBA forms. I've run several businesses and, in every case, the banks have lost my DBA forms.

Where you file a DBA depends on your location. In some states, you file a DBA with the county clerk. In other states, a DBA is filed with that state's Department of Commerce. If you don't know where to file a DBA in your state, call one of the offices I mentioned. If you call the wrong one, they'll tell you.

Choosing a legal form for your business

The three forms your business can take are a sole proprietorship, a partnership, and a corporation. How you run your business will affect your personal liability, your taxes, how you handle any profits, and how decisions are made. The best form for your business will depend on your situation. Talk to your attorney and accountant for help in making this decision.

Sole proprietorship

If you're the only person involved in your business and you don't form a corporation, your business is a sole proprietorship as soon as you start its operation. The sole proprietorship is the most common way shareware businesses are organized. For legal and tax purposes, you and your business are one and the same. Your business operations and activities are treated as a part of your personal activities.

A sole proprietor is not a separate tax-paying entity, but you do need to keep separate business records for business income, deductions, inventories, capital acquisitions, and dispositions. Your tax-reporting year must be the same for you and your business. For tax purposes, the profit or loss from your business is calculated separately using IRS Form 1040, Schedule C, and then combined with your personal income.

Note that in a sole proprietorship, if your business makes a profit and you haven't already paid the maximum Social Security tax, you must pay a self-employment tax for Social Security. You might also have additional taxes to pay to your local or regional government.

Partnerships

If two or more people are involved as owners of the business, then the business is organized as a partnership. While you can form a partnership with a handshake, it's best to have a formal contract. Even if the partnership includes only family members, all of whom are on good terms with each other, put your agreement in writing and have an attorney write the contract. This isn't a matter of whether or not you trust the other people in the partnership (although if you don't trust them you shouldn't be going into business with them).

It's important because there's more to a partnership than agreeing to work together. For example, how will profits or losses be split? How is the work to be split? How are disputes to be resolved? What happens if one partner wants to leave the business or passes away? An important consideration is that one partner can bind the partnership in a contract. This means that either partner can be sued for the acts of one partner. So be careful. There are more issues than you might realize; having a specialist write the contract is the only way to be sure most possibilities are covered.

Forming a corporation

Whether you start as a sole proprietor or partnership, you might eventually want to form a corporation. One of the major reasons to incorporate a small business is to protect you from personal liability. Generally, sole proprietors and partnerships incur personal liability. If your business is incorporated, it becomes an entity separate from you. Many other reasons can affect your decision about forming a corporation. These range from marketing-based reasons to tax advantages. To make your choice, you and your legal adviser should look at your specific situation.

In most cases, if you want to incorporate, you should declare your corporation a Subchapter S corporation for tax purposes. This allows you to operate in a corporate form, but not pay tax as a separate entity. This eliminates a lot of paperwork and avoids the double tax on corporate operations. To qualify as a Subchapter S corporation, your corporation must meet certain stock and income tests. For example, trusts, partnerships, and other corporations cannot own stock in your corporation. On the income side, there are limits on the percentage of income that can come from rents, royalties, dividends, interest, annuities, securities sales, and foreign sources.

Whether to declare your corporation as a Subchapter S corporation might require that you talk to your attorney or accountant in order to be fully informed. For example, in a few states, although you're a Subchapter S corporation for federal tax purposes, the state might consider your company to be a regular corporation. This can result in extra accounting costs.

There are booklets that tell you how to form a corporation for $50. I've read them and I recommend that you hire an attorney instead. The cost of hiring an attorney to form a Subchapter S corporation might run from $400 to $1,000 (depending on your location), but it's well worth it. In addition to providing all the documents and filing the necessary forms, your attorney can advise you on how to conduct business as a corporation. For example, as a sole proprietor you can do what you want. Once you're incorporated, the powers of the corporation are described in its charter. If you want to do something not allowed by the charter, it needs to be amended.

Export licenses

No licenses are required to export your software to most countries. Software falls under the general provisions of export control regulations. You can mail it directly to the user via U.S. air mail. There are exceptions, though. For example, no exports are allowed to North Vietnam, Cuba, North Korea, or Iraq. These restrictions are not related to software, but are general export restrictions. If you receive an order from a user living in a country you suspect might be a problem, check with the U.S. Department of Commerce. Although the world situation is rapidly changing, question any order you receive from a communist country, a country not friendly with the U.S., or a country the U.S. has or has had a serious dispute with, such as Iraq.

One significant limit on exporting software is that you aren't allowed to send software that includes DES and other encryption standards outside the U.S. For example, copies of the hard-disk backup program Fastback cannot be shipped outside the U.S.

Copyrights

Copyright law is intended to protect your work from anyone copying, reproducing, or distributing it without your permission. It allows you to benefit from any financial rewards that are a result of your efforts. The 1980 amendments to the copyright law make it clear that software programs are protected. An exact definition of the extent of this protection is still being hammered out in the courts and Congress.

A copyright begins at the moment you start to create your program or documentation. To make the public aware that you protect your work, you just need to put a copyright notice on it. You don't need to file any forms with the copyright office. A copyright remains in effect for the life of the author, plus 50 years.

Copyright notice

A copyright notice consists of the name of the program followed by the word *copyright*. The word must be written out—putting the letter C in parentheses is not acceptable. The only acceptable abbreviations are COPR. and the letter C enclosed in a full circle. List the year the program was first publicly distributed and all years in which a revision was publicly distributed. You should also include the name of the person or company holding the copyright (you or your business). Be sure the complete copyright notice is on one line. For example:

BOOK MINDER Copyright 1988, 1989, 1990 Steven C. Hudgik

Include this notice as a part of a title screen that first appears when the software is booted and build it into your program code as a remark. According to the copyright office, the copyright notice does not need to be printed on your disk labels, but you might want to do this to help ensure that it's noticed. Your manual can be copyrighted separately with its own copyright notice or as a part of the software package. If you include your manual as a disk file, be sure to include the copyright notice for the manual as a part of that file. In addition, you can copyright data files that you create for use with your software and text files for adventure games separately. A separate copyright can be used in the case of a data file that's updated periodically, with the software remaining unchanged. If you think you might want to sell data files separately, it's a good idea to copyright them separately.

Copyright law doesn't specifically identify databases as copyrightable, but legal history shows that Congress considers computer databases as material that has copyright protection. However, the protection for databases is not as strong as it is for other "literary works." In many cases you can't copyright the information in a database; you can copyright only the compilation. This means that your database cannot be copied directly, but if someone rearranges the information and adds some additional work, he can republish your database. To fully protect your database you need to tightly control its use, and the rights of others to copy it, using a license agreement. If you're planning to publish a database, I recommend you hire an intellectual property rights attorney to write a license agreement that will protect your data. For more information about copyrights for databases, contact the copyright office and request a copy of Circular 65. Their phone number is 202-707-9100.

International considerations

Assume that copies of your shareware will find their way to other countries, even if you don't permit them to be distributed outside the U.S. The U.S. has officially subscribed to the Berne Convention, an international copyright agreement. Under this agreement, if you publish your work in the U.S., it automatically has copyright protection under the laws of other countries. The laws in other countries are different and provide different levels of protection, so don't assume you have the same protection as you get under U.S. copyright law. To make sure you have full protection, you need to include the additional line "All Rights Reserved." Be sure to include this statement just under your copyright notice.

Another suggestion for protecting your copyrights internationally came out of my discussions with the Department of Commerce. They recommend that the abbreviation GTDR be written on the outside of all packages containing copyrighted software shipped outside the U.S. This abbreviation stands for General Technical Data Restricted and helps protect your copyright in other countries.

Registering your copyright

Putting the copyright notice on your software and manuals provides only limited protection. You can stop someone else from copying your software, but you must do it at your expense, meaning that you must pay your own legal fees, and you can't collect damages. If you register your copyright before any infringement, however, you can then sue for infringement in a federal court and collect damages and attorney's fees.

The filing fee is $20. You can file for a copyright yourself or have an attorney do it for you. It's a simple procedure and thus shouldn't be expensive for a lawyer to do. To do it yourself, call the copyright office for information. Their number is 202-707-3000 (8:30 A.M. till 5:00 P.M. Eastern Standard Time).

The copyright office also has a forms hotline for callers who know what forms they need. The hotline number is 202-707-9100. This number is answered by a machine 24 hours a day, 7 days a week. Ask for Information Package 113. It includes the necessary forms and booklets that describe how to file for a copyright.

Most questions concerning registering a copyright have to do with deposit requirements, the nature of authorship (form TX, line 2), derivative work (form TX, line 6), or compilation information.

Deposit requirements

The deposit requirement states that "one copy of identifying portions of the program" be submitted with your application. This requirement is defined as the first 25 and last 25 pages of program code. If your program code is less than 50 pages, then the entire listing must be submitted. The only exception is if the code includes trade secrets. There are three alternative deposit procedures for protecting trade secrets. If you need to protect a trade secret, call the copyright office for more information. The intent of the deposit requirement is to have a sufficient amount of code on file with the copyright office to prove infringement. In addition, the copyright office will also accept deposits of your entire program, on disk, as evidence that can be used in an infringement lawsuit.

If you have a question concerning the deposit requirements, call the copyright office. Very helpful people answer the phones.

Nature of the material created

Line 2 on form TX asks for the "nature of the material created" for which a copyright is claimed. I recommend using all-inclusive language such as "entire computer program and manual." If you get too specific, you might unintentionally exclude something. If you're too vague, on the other hand, you'll be asked to clarify the information. Some things cannot be copyrighted. For example, don't include terms like "program design" or "look and feel." This will cause it to be rejected.

Identifying preexisting work

If your copyright notice contains more than one year, you'll need to fill out section 6 of form TX. This section is used to identify any preexisting work incorporated into your program. For example, if you use QuickBasic, the license granted you by Microsoft requires you to include their copyright notice. This should be included as a preexisting work and is described in section 6 of form TX. This also applies if you've written and modified your software over several years and have included all these years in your copyright notice.

The importance of correctly and completely filling in this section was brought to public attention in the Ashton-Tate vs. Fox lawsuit. In this court case, the judge initially ruled that Ashton-Tate's copyrights on dBASE were not valid because Ashton-Tate's copyright application did not reveal that dBASE was partly based on preexisting public-domain program code.

If you aren't sure whether or not to include some items in section 6 of form TX, attach a letter that discloses everything imaginable. (Add "see attached letter" to section 6 of form TX.) The letter can be used to disclose the compiler used (which inserts some code), any toolboxes used, and any minor parts of the code written by someone else.

Why you should register your copyright

Registering a copyright is a legal formality that generally isn't required for protection. If your work was first published before March 1, 1989, and the copyright notice was not included or the name or year date was omitted or had an error, you should see a copyright attorney. However, there are several advantages to registering your copyright. These include:

- If you register your copyright within five years of publication, registration establishes prima facie evidence in court of the validity of the copyright and the facts stated in the certificate. *Prima facie* means that, just by having the registration, it's assumed that your copyright is valid. It's up to any parties challenging your copyright to show that it isn't valid.

- If registration is made within three months after publication of the work or prior to an infringement of the work, you'll be able to collect the minimum statutory damages plus attorney's fees. Otherwise, you can collect only actual damages and loss of profits.
- Registration provides a public record of your copyrighted material. Putting your work in an envelope and mailing it to yourself so that it's postmarked does not establish a record of your ownership of published material. Registering it with the copyright office will accomplish this.
- If your work is of U.S. origin and is infringed by a foreign work originating in a country that is not a Berne Union country, registering is required for you to file suit.

Copyright summary

Laws that protect software are changing. For example, there have been some moves to allow certain aspects of software to be patented. Another example is that in the past you couldn't copyright screen displays. An interesting development is the June 28, 1990, decision by Judge Robert E. Keeton in the Lotus vs. Paperback Software copyright infringement lawsuit. This decision extends copyright protection beyond literal code to non-literal elements of a program, for example, the menu command structure of Lotus' 1-2-3 spreadsheet.

Although it isn't yet settled, Lotus' suit against Borland, accusing Borland of copying the Lotus 1-2-3 menu bar in the Quattro Pro software, appears to be going in favor of Lotus. On the other hand, Apple hasn't been successful in its claim that Microsoft infringed on Apple's copyright when creating Windows. None of these cases are simple issues and there's a lot of background information needed to fully understand what has happened in each case. However, the end result is that your rights to borrow user-interface elements from existing products have been legally reduced.

As you can see, the issue of copyrighting user interfaces is not clear. Hopefully congress will further clarify copyright law as it pertains to software, although it might take several years to resolve all the issues.

Copyrights and shareware

Shareware is copyrighted software with full protection under copyright law. In distributing your software as shareware, you grant a license that allows others limited rights. You should specifically describe those rights in a shareware license included in your documentation, introduction files, and possibly the opening copyright screen. Some of the rights you might want to grant others include:

- The right to distribute copies of your software, provided that no fees are charged for the disks.
- The right for ASP vendors to distribute copies of your software without getting permission from you.
- The right to review your software within a certain time period. At the end of that time period, registration is required.

You might also want to specifically identify actions you don't allow, such as distribution of your shareware outside the U.S., distribution on retail racks, or placing your shareware on CD-ROM disks.

By waiving some of your rights, you haven't eliminated your copyrights. Except for the rights you specifically identify, no other rights are waived. This type of selective waiver is enforceable. Shareware copyrights were upheld in the Datastorm, Inc. vs. Software-To-go, Inc. court decision several years ago. Here is an example of a shareware vendor distribution license:

Without regard to how you obtained it, you may not sell copies of this software, even if the purchase price is just to cover duplication costs; you may not include this shareware on a CD-ROM or other type of package produced by any user group, commercial library, or any for-profit or nonprofit organization; and you may not distribute it with any other product or as an incentive to purchase any other product without the express written permission of H.C.P. Services, Inc.

This software may not be sold on retail racks or CD-ROM disks, by either ASP or nonASP vendors, without specific written permission from the author.

User groups (except for user group BBSs) must have written permission prior to distributing this software.

BBSs may distribute this software provided that the date on the OYC.EXE file is no more than 24 months old.

The files on each disk may not be modified or adapted in any way. All of the files provided on the disk must be distributed together.

Individual files or groups of files may not be sold separately. Additional files may be added to disks containing this software, but this software may not be integrated into or included as a part of any other software.

Individual copies of this software may not be sold for more than $10.

This software may not be represented as anything other than shareware and the shareware concept must be explained in any ad or catalog that quotes a price and on any packaging used to display the disk. The explanation of the shareware concept must make it clear that with shareware an addition registration fee is required if users continue to use the software.

You must stop selling/distributing copies of this version of this software upon notice from the author or HCP Services, Inc.

The terms of this distribution license are subject to change with the release of new versions of this software.

In this license, I feel the first paragraph is key. It requires that everyone have written permission before distributing the software. If they don't and they charge a fee for distributing the software, they are violating copyright law. Notice, however, that this paragraph applies only to people/organizations charging a fee. This license still allows individuals to freely copy and share your software.

Some authors prefer not to require vendors to get written permission before their disks are distributed. They like to release their disks and get as wide a distribution as possible by allowing everyone to distribute them. By doing this, however, you give up a lot of control over your software. I've spoken with several authors who took this approach; a few years later when they had become more successful and released improved versions of their software, they were unable to stop the distribution of older versions. The older versions were poor quality and were hurting the authors' image, but the old license agreement didn't give them the ability to easily stop distribution.

If you want to get wide distribution, with as little effort as possible on your part, include a statement in this first paragraph that says ASP vendors may distribute the software without getting written permission. The ASP requires vendors who are ASP members to meet certain minimum requirements. They must properly explain shareware. They must also stop distributing a program at the author's request.

The second paragraph is optional, depending on how you feel about retail rack and CD-ROM distribution of your shareware. I like having my shareware on CD-ROMs and retail racks, and will give permission to anyone who wants to distribute it this way, as long as they're properly identifying my software as shareware. I've provided a separate paragraph covering retail racks and CD-ROM distribution in this example because some authors prefer to handle these forms of distribution differently. This paragraph might say that the sale of this shareware on retail racks is not allowed (leaving CD-ROM distribution to be covered by the first paragraph). Or it could specify that a royalty must be paid, should the program be distributed on retail racks.

I've found that requiring vendors, at least all nonASP vendors, to have written permission does several things for me. It allows me to place additional requirements on vendors on a case-by-case basis. For example, if I'm not familiar with a vendor I might require that he send me a copy of his catalog, CD-ROM, or retail packaging, so I see whether it properly explains shareware. It also lets me know who is distributing my shareware so I can send them updates and new software.

The drawback of requiring written permission is that you must respond to every vendor who writes to you. It's not good business to require that vendors write to you for permission to distribute your software, and then not respond to those requests. What I do is to have a standard letter with several check boxes. The letter gives the vendor permission to distribute my software and then I check off items I require from that vendor. For example, there's a box to check if I want to see a copy of the vendor's catalog.

The third paragraph specifically tells user groups that they must also have written permission. Although paragraph one includes user groups,

I've found that user groups sometimes feel they're a special case and the rules don't apply to them. This paragraph makes it very clear that the rules do apply to user groups.

Since most BBSs are run on a nonprofit basis by individuals, I give blanket permission for my software to be placed on BBSs. The only problem I've had with BBSs is that some of them have refused to remove old versions. They add the new versions, but I've had BBS sysops tell me that they don't care what I want. As a service to their callers they want to provide all the old versions of my software. I don't understand how the distribution of old, out-of-date software is a service, but as a result of this attitude by a few BBS sysops, I've added the 24-month time limit specified in the fourth paragraph covering BBS distribution. This gives me some legal leverage I can use to get older versions of my software off of a BBS.

The fifth paragraph is very important. Without this paragraph, someone could modify your software, distribute only part of it (leaving off files that contain information about registering), or add different messages. Paragraph six is important for the same reasons. However, many vendors like to add their own startup files to shareware disks. This helps them to reduce their technical support since they can then supply a standard set of "getting started" instructions. For this reason I let vendors add additional files to disks containing my software.

Paragraph seven sets a limit on what a vendor can charge for your shareware. This is important. Without this limit they could charge whatever they wanted. Earlier this year I found out about a disk vendor in Montana who was including my Play 'n' Learn software as a part of a package of educational shareware. The package included six disks and he was selling it for $149.00. After paying $149.00 to get the shareware version I don't think anyone would be interested in sending me the $10.00 registration fee for my software.

The eighth paragraph requires that vendors, and anyone else distributing this software, not misrepresent the program as anything other than shareware. Paragraph nine gives you the right to stop a vendor, BBS, or anyone else from distributing your software for any reason, or without a reason. And the final paragraph notifies everyone that you might change your distribution license in the future.

By the time you read this, it might be several years after I've written it. Before finalizing the wording in your distribution license, find out if there have been any changes in the industry that would affect the this license. Check some of the top-selling programs, Apogee games for example, and see what they've included in their distribution license.

The copyright office's Shareware Registry

As a part of the 1990 Software Antipiracy Bill, the copyright office was required to create a Shareware Registry. The Shareware Registry is a place for shareware authors to file their distribution licenses. This places your distribution license into the public record in an official way that applies to the entire country. Once your license is recorded in the Shareware Registry, no one can complain of not knowing about your distribution license. The cost to have your license recorded in the shareware registry is $20.00 for one program and an additional $10.00 for each group of 10 programs.

This can be very important. For example, the distribution license is usually placed in a separate VENDOR.DOC file. What happens if you find someone who is infringing on your copyright, but claims there was no VENDOR.DOC file with your program? Who knows, maybe whoever had it previously erased the VENDOR.DOC file. Although legally it doesn't matter whether your VENDOR.DOC file was still included with your program or not, such a claim will muddy the waters and slow up the process of reaching a settlement.

Once your distribution license is on file with the Shareware Registry, you're in a much stronger position. Courts will defer to what the copyright office has done and will be more inclined to see things your way. It gives you a much more powerful position.

The Shareware Registry is not related to the copyright on your software. You still need to copyright it, and registering the copyright on your software is the one most important things you can do to protect your software. The Shareware Registry is separate from the copyright on your software. It is used only to officially record the terms of your distribution license.

At this time there is no official form for submitting your distribution license to the Shareware Registry and it appears that the copyright office won't be creating a form. A recommended form may be released by the ASP in the future, but at this time there's nothing available. This means you need to be somewhat careful when submitting your distribution license to the Shareware Registry. For example, if you include the registration price of your software, be sure to indicate that it's subject to change in the future. Otherwise the registration price you give will be set in official documents as being the registration price. (I don't recommend including the registration price in your distribution license.)

For more information about the Shareware Registry, you can contact the copyright office by calling 202-707-3000. Ask for a copy of announcement number ML-460.

Taking action to protect your software

If you find someone who is violating your distribution license and distributing your software in a way you don't like, you can take legal action to both stop them and recover damages. It's not complex or expensive to do, provided you have properly protected your software by registering your copyright. I have a three-step approach I use when I discover someone distributing my shareware in violation of my distribution license agreement.

Step 1: make a friendly phone call I first call the company/person with whom I have a problem. I identify myself as the author of the shareware and tell him about the problem I have with what he's doing. I do this in a friendly, open manner. If you're angry and aggressive in this first phone call, you probably won't be able to accomplish anything constructive. In 95% of the cases, I'm able to resolve the problem on the phone. Most vendors recognize the author's right to control distribution of their software, and are either willing to accommodate the author's wishes or stop distributing the author's programs. The important thing about this phone call is to give the vendor a chance to correct the problem. All people deserve a chance to correct their problems.

If the problem I had with the vendor had to do with packaging, labeling, or how my software is described in the catalog, I'll generally ask him to send me a copy of the revised packaging or catalog. This way I can see whether the change to eliminate the problem has been made. None of the vendors who have agreed to fix this type of a problem have ever had a problem with sending this type of material to me.

Step 2: send a letter If I'm not satisfied with the response I got from the company or person I talked with on the phone, I then send a letter. Some of the reactions to the phone call I make in step one have been hard to believe. Some people have told me that, since my software is shareware, they can do whatever they want with it. Others have said "We don't care what you want," knowing that most authors will take no further action. With these types of responses, I move to step two in which I send them a letter.

The letter I send identifies the program they're infringing, identifies me as the author, describes what the problem is, and tells them what I'd like them to do. In most cases, at this point I want them to stop distributing my software. The letter gives them 30 days to respond, after which I'll turn the matter over to my attorney.

In most cases the person I sent the letter to will call and apologize for the problem and agree to either correct the problem or stop distributing my software. However, once or twice a year there is someone who ignores my letter and I have to go to step three.

Step 3: take it to a lawyer At this point I turn everything over to my attorney for him to handle. If you reach this point, you'll need an intellectual property attorney who's familiar with software copyrights. Don't ask your family attorney to handle copyright infringement.

There are two crucial characteristics your copyright infringement claim will need to have before you can take it to an attorney. The person infringing your copyright needs to have the assets to pay a settlement and they need to have infringed your copyright in your state. Let's talk about each of these.

It's important that the person have assets because you'll want the attorney to be paid on a contingency basis. This means the attorney gets paid a percentage of the settlement. If the person infringing your copyright doesn't have the assets to pay a settlement, then the attorney cannot be paid. In that case you might find yourself giving the attorney an $8,000 to $10,000 retainer fee—and it'll be money you never see again. It's unfortunate, but if the person infringing your copyright has no assets, then there's very little you can do to stop him.

You need the infringement of your copyright to take place in your state so you can bring suit (or threaten to bring suit) in a federal court that's local for you. This means that to defend himself, the person will need to hire an attorney in your state and handle everything from a long distance—something that's very expensive to do.

It's easy for you to be sure infringement has taken place in your state. If he publishes a catalog or advertise in a magazine that's distributed or sold in your state, that means infringement has taken place in your state. The best way, however, is to get him to sell you a copy of your software through the mail. This not only means he's sold it in your state, it gives you a copy of the infringing material that can be used as evidence.

Once someone who is infringing your copyright has heard from your attorney and has brought the problem to his attorney, the attorney will generally tell him that it's cheaper to settle with you than to try and defend himself in court. If he goes to court, he'll be faced with the possibility of statutory damages that can be as high as $100,000, plus not only his own attorney's fees, but yours as well.

Don't try this on your own

You've probably heard the saying "A little knowledge is dangerous." The review of copyrights I've just provided gives you just a little knowledge. I've tried to provide enough information so you can protect your rights. However, copyright law is complex. If you're in a situation where you've found someone infringing your copyrights, talk to your attorney. Beyond the first, friendly phone call and letter, don't try to handle it yourself.

Trademarks

A trademark protects your right to use a word, name, symbol, or device to identify and distinguish your product from those produced by others. If you start distributing your program without a trademark (TM) notice, you might lose the rights to your trademark. Under trademark law, you own the word, name, symbol, or device that identifies your software as soon as you use it in commerce. You don't need to register a trademark to own it. The purpose of using the (TM) notice is to make it clear to others this is your trademark. Without the (TM) notice, others might inadvertently start using your mark, and as a small publisher you wouldn't have the financial ability to defend it in court. The (TM) notice is used prior to registration of a trademark to show that you intend to defend your mark against infringement. Once registered, an R in a circle is used to indicate the mark is a registered trademark.

What registering a trademark does for you is to provide notice nationally that this is your trademark. It also puts your trademark on the federal database so that when other people do a trademark search, they will find it and know that the trademark is already in use. Once a trademark has been registered for five years, it becomes incontestable, with just a few exceptions, making it much easier to defend your mark. For information about registering a trademark, write to:

U.S. Department of Commerce
Patent and Trademark Office
Washington, D.C. 20231

Request the information package called Basic Facts About Trademarks. You can also call 703-557-3158 to order this package.

Unlike a copyright, which can be registered regardless of whether or not the work is published, a trademark must be used in interstate commerce at the time the application is filed. Or you must have a bona fide intention to use the mark.

An application consists of a written application form, a drawing showing the mark (the mark can be typed if your trademark is a word), three examples showing actual use of the mark, and the required filing fee, which is currently $175.

Once you register a trademark, you'll need to file a Section 8 Affidavit of Continued Use between the fifth and sixth year after registration. The fee for this is $100. A notice of this requirement is attached to the registration certificate that you receive when your mark is registered.

Trademarks remain in effect for 20 years. You may renew your trademark for an unlimited number of 20-year periods. Currently, the renewal fee is $300.

Registering a trademark

As with a copyright, you can register a trademark yourself or have an attorney do it for you. I have registered several trademarks and have had problems filling out the forms and providing the necessary backup information. The application process is specific and you need to follow procedures exactly. When you file to register a trademark, your application is assigned an attorney in the trademark office. I have found these attorneys to be very helpful and understanding of people who don't have a legal background. They will guide you in putting together a proper application, if you have done most of the work correctly. They won't put together an application for you. An application with a lot of problems will be rejected and you'll lose your application fee.

Some of the things that will cause a trademark application to be rejected include:

- If the mark consists of immoral, deceptive, or scandalous matter, or matter that might disparage or suggest a connection with persons living or dead, institutions, beliefs, or national symbols.
- If the mark uses the flag or coat of arms or other insignia of the United States, of any state or municipality, or of any foreign nation.
- If the mark uses the name, portrait, or signature identifying a particular living person without that person's written permission, or if it uses the name, signature, or portrait of a deceased president of the United States during the life of his widow, except by written consent of the widow.
- If the mark resembles a mark registered already, or a mark or trade name previously used by another that is likely to cause confusion or be deceptive.
- If the mark is descriptive or generic. For example, I publish a program for cataloging stamp collections. I wouldn't be able to register Stamp Database as a trademark.

You can also register your trademark in some states. The process is much faster and cheaper. However, because of their limited jurisdiction, state trademarks are weaker than federal ones. The major benefit of a state trademark is that it can be used to strengthen your case against trademark infringements. Applications are usually available from the State Corporation Counsel office or the office of the Secretary of State.

For both copyrights and trademarks, it's your responsibility to protect them. No one else will do it for you. Some trademarks, such as aspirin, have been lost over time because they became synonyms for products. A trademark is very specific and you must reproduce it correctly when you use it. Don't be sloppy or careless when you use your trademark as you can weaken your own rights to your trademark.

Trade dress

An area that is similar to trademarks is that of trade dress. Trade dress protection protects the image and overall impression created by your products, packaging, and advertising. In other words, no one else can create a package that so closely resembles your software package that the two could be confused. For example, in 1960 the Coca-Cola company registered the shape of the Coca-Cola bottle. A trade dress registration is obtained in the same manner as a trademark registration.

Warranties and liability

Nearly all software publishers offer no warranty on the software. You might want to provide a warranty that states that the disks and manuals are free from defects of manufacturing, but that you don't warranty the software or content of the manuals. If you want to reassure your customers that they're buying a quality product, offer a no-questions-asked, money-back guarantee.

It's important that you not warranty the software and manuals because you have no control over how they will be used. A warranty can provide the basis for a lawsuit. If you provide a warranty on your software, you could end up in lengthy and expensive court battles. In addition, damage awards can be high. Bugs in software have caused losses of many years of work, crucial data, and miscalculations resulting in significant monetary losses. As a small publisher, the first warranty lawsuit would probably put you out of business. Offer a money-back guarantee and you've limited your liability to refunding the purchase price of the software if a user is not satisfied.

Place a warranty statement in the front of your manual or on the disk envelope that states:

> This software is provided as is.
> There are no warranties, expressed or implied.

However, there's more to include in your warranty statement. Just because you say that you don't provide a warranty doesn't mean you've avoided all warranty liability. The Uniform Commercial Code (UCC) creates implied warranties for all sales of goods and provides that you cannot disclaim these unless you conspicuously use specific words.

These specific words are called a *warranty disclaimer*. To be conspicuous, the warranty disclaimer should be printed in capital letters. Using all capital letters is not a legal requirement. The UCC does not define what is meant by conspicuous. Using all caps has become the accepted standard for meeting this requirement. In addition, you cannot use fine print. In most states, the warranty disclaimer must be a minimum of 6-point type.

You also want to be sure that your warranty disclaimer is in a location where most people can be expected to see it. The best spot is to put it in the first page or two of your documentation. If you want to see an example of the type of wording you should include, look at any of the software packages put out by the major publishers. Highly paid legal staffs protect these companies by being sure the wording in the warranty is the best possible. It's interesting to note that the wording used by the various publishers is relatively uniform. Here is the warranty disclaimer that I use:

HCP SERVICES INC. DISCLAIMS ALL WARRANTIES RELATING TO THIS SOFTWARE, WHETHER EXPRESS OR IMPLIED, INCLUDING BUT NOT LIMITED TO ANY IMPLIED WARRANTIES OF MERCHANTABILITY AND FITNESS FOR A PARTICULAR PURPOSE, AND ALL SUCH WARRANTIES ARE EXPRESSLY AND SPECIFICALLY DISCLAIMED. NEITHER HCP SERVICES, INC. NOR ANYONE ELSE WHO HAS BEEN INVOLVED IN THE CREATION, PRODUCTION, OR DELIVERY OF THIS SOFTWARE SHALL BE LIABLE FOR ANY INDIRECT, CONSEQUENTIAL, OR INCIDENTAL DAMAGES ARISING OUT OF THE USE OR INABILITY TO USE SUCH SOFTWARE EVEN IF HCP SERVICES, INC. HAS BEEN ADVISED OF THE POSSIBILITY OF SUCH DAMAGES OR CLAIMS. IN NO EVENT SHALL HCP SERVICES, INC.'S LIABILITY FOR ANY DAMAGES EVER EX-

CEED THE PRICE PAID FOR THE LICENSE TO USE THE SOFTWARE, REGARDLESS OF THE FORM OF CLAIM. THE PERSON USING THE SOFTWARE BEARS ALL RISK AS TO THE QUALITY AND PERFORMANCE OF THE SOFTWARE.

SOME STATES DO NOT ALLOW THE EXCLUSION OF THE LIMIT OF LIABILITY FOR CONSEQUENTIAL OR INCIDENTAL DAMAGES, SO THE ABOVE LIMITATION MAY NOT APPLY TO YOU.

THIS AGREEMENT SHALL BE GOVERNED BY THE LAWS OF THE STATE OF OREGON AND SHALL INURE TO THE BENEFIT OF HCP SERVICES, INC. AND ANY SUCCESSORS, ADMINISTRATORS, HEIRS, AND ASSIGNS. ANY ACTION OR PRO-CEEDING BROUGHT BY EITHER PARTY AGAINST THE OTHER ARISING OUT OF OR RELATED TO THIS AGREEMENT SHALL BE BROUGHT ONLY IN A STATE OR FED-ERAL COURT OF COMPETENT JURISDICTION LOCATED IN MULTNOMAH COUNTY, OREGON. THE PARTIES HEREBY CONSENT TO IN PERSONAM JURIS-DICTION OF SAID COURTS.

The last paragraph is important because it requires that any legal action be made in a court that's local to you. Without this statement, you could be sued in a remote state. The cost of defending a lawsuit in a remote state is so high that you would be forced to settle without going to court.

The warranty statement protects you from not only warranty claims, but also claims for any other damages someone thinks might be caused by your software. However, keep in mind that you don't have ironclad protection from being sued. Anyone can sue anyone else for any reason. This wording just makes a suit against you much less likely to succeed and therefore makes bringing suit against you not worth the effort.

In addition to warranties and limiting your liability, you also need to protect your copyright. Your documentation should include the terms under which other people can use your software. The most important term is that your software can be used on only one computer (unless you've granted a site license). Check other software packages for typical wording. Here is what I use:

This software and the disks on which it is contained are licensed to you, for your own use. This is copyrighted software. You are not obtaining title to the software or any copyright rights. You may not sublicense, rent, lease, convey, modify, translate, con-vert to another programming language, decompile, or disassemble the software for any purpose.

You may make as many copies of this software as you need for back-up pur-poses. You may use this software on more than one computer, provided there is no chance it will be used simultaneously on more than one computer. If you need to use the software on more than one computer simultaneously, please contact us for infor-mation about site licenses.

Site-license agreements

A site license is a legal contract in which you and a registered user agree on the terms under which the user can install your software on more than one computer. These terms generally allow the user to install the software on a specified number of computers in return for payment of a specific site-license fee.

When you sell a registered copy of your software, the registered copy is no different than retail software. It is copyrighted and the user cannot give copies to other people or install it on more than one machine without your permission. As the copyright holder, you can set the specific conditions under which the registered version of your software can be copied. Most shareware authors treat their registered versions exactly like retail software; the software can be copied for backup purposes only. Some authors allow the registered copy to be shared with other users, but use of the software on multiple computers within one organization or on a network requires a site license.

Following are some typical questions and answers relating to copyrights and site licenses. For these examples, I'll be using a fictional program called FastWrite.

Question: We have 100 computers in our company, but only 25 people are trained to use the FastWrite program. We want to install FastWrite on all of our computers so that the most convenient machine can be used at any time. How many copies of FastWrite do we need?

Answer: This user must purchase 100 copies of FastWrite. According to copyright law, an application that is installed on a hard disk is a copy regardless of how often it is used. If you have copies of a program installed on 100 hard disks, you must own 100 copies.

Question: We have purchased a registered copy of FastWrite and installed it on one computer. Can we use the shareware version on the other computers in our office?

Answer: No. Purchasing one registered version of a program means the software can be installed on only one computer. It doesn't change the licensing conditions under which the shareware version is used. These conditions usually state that if a shareware program is used for more than a reasonable test period, it must be registered. Thus, every computer on which a shareware version is installed must have the shareware version replaced by a registered version or the shareware version must be removed.

Question: What happens when I receive an upgrade to FastWrite? Can I use the old version on another machine?

Answer: No. Upgrades and updates are improvements on the original software, not a new copy. Legally, they are the same program and you haven't purchased the right to use it on additional computers.

Question: Can nonprofit groups and schools register one copy of a program and use it on multiple machines?

Answer: No. The copyright laws apply to nonprofit organizations and schools in the same way as they do to individuals and corporations. As the owner of the copyright, you can make a marketing decision to allow certain groups to use your software on more than one computer. Should you do this, you are essentially granting a site license to that group and not charging for it.

Question: We've installed FastWrite on our network, which has 50 terminals. Only one person is trained and authorized to use FastWrite. How many copies do we need to purchase?

Answer: There is no one answer to this question. Legally, the user needs to purchase only one copy of FastWrite because, in this case, it is installed on only one hard disk. However, as a part of the terms of your user license agreement, you can require the user to purchase additional copies if the software is used on a network. The number of additional copies he must purchase is a marketing decision you must make.

In addressing the use of shareware on a network, some people reason that it would be possible to have a user at every terminal, all using the FastWrite software. Thus, the publishers should require network users to buy a site license that covers the total number of terminals. This approach simplifies the site license accounting because, if additional terminals are added, an additional site-license fee is required.

Another approach is to require a site license for the average number of people who might use FastWrite simultaneously on the network. With this method, you're dependent on the customer to provide an accurate estimate of this average.

A simple approach is to charge a one-time site-license fee for unlimited use of the software on a network. The unlimited-use license grants the user the right to put the software on as many computers within the organization as they want.

Some publishers license their software for use on a network by a specified maximum number of people. A counter is built into the software that tracks the number of simultaneous users. If the maximum number covered by the site license is exceeded, the software is designed to prevent additional users from accessing it. Other programs in these circumstances just flash a warning message on the screen.

How you approach network licenses might be different than these examples and depends on your marketing goals and the terms of your site license. In my survey of shareware authors, the most common response to the questions about site licenses stated that they're negotiated on a case-by-case basis. There is no one right answer. Every site license can be different, with varying terms based on the needs of your customer and on what you feel is a fair price.

The following provides a sample site-license agreement. I recommend that you include a copy in each registered version of your software. This will make users aware that a site license is required to use the software on more than one computer and provides an easy way for them to request and pay for a site license. Keep in mind that all contracts are negotiable. In some cases, this sample would serve only as a starting point that could be modified to fit the situation.

HCP Services, Inc.
HomeCraft Software
Site-License Agreement

If you want to use this software on more than one computer, a site license is required. A site license is also required to use this software on a network. A site license allows you to copy and use this software within your organization on as many computers as contracted for. An unlimited site license allows unlimited copying of the software for internal use only. This is copyrighted software and any distribution or reselling of the software to third parties is prohibited.

HCP Services, Inc., grants _____ a site license for the use of the following software program(s):

This is a perpetual license for the use of the software within your organization, and is not transferable. This site license allows internal use and copying of the software for use by/on _____ users/computers.

This license is distinct from shareware use. It does not authorize the continued use of shareware. If, in addition to the software used under this license, shareware is in use, that shareware must be registered with HCP Services, Inc.

HCP Services, Inc., will provide technical support for one year from the date of this agreement to one person, designated as the key contact within your company or organization.

HCP Services, Inc., warrants that it is the sole owner of the software and has full power and authority to grant the site license without the consent of any other party.

HCP Services, Inc., disclaims all warranties relating to this software, whether express or implied, including but not limited to any implied warranties of merchantability and fitness for a particular purpose, and all such warranties are expressly and specifically disclaimed. Neither HCP Services, Inc., nor anyone else who has been involved in the creation, production, or delivery of this software shall be liable for any direct, indirect, consequential, or incidental damages arising out of the use or inability to use such software even if HCP Services, Inc., has been advised of the possibility of such damages or claims. In no event shall HCP Services, Inc.'s liability for any damages ever exceed the price paid for the license to use the software, regardless of the form of claim. The person using the software bears all risk as to the quality and performance of the software. (Some states do not allow the exclusion of the limit of liability for consequential or incidental damages, so this limitation might not apply to you.)

This agreement shall be governed by the laws of the State of Oregon and shall inure to the benefit of HCP Services, Inc., and any successors, administrators, heirs, and assigns. Any action or proceeding brought by either party against the other arising out of or related to this agreement shall be brought only in a state or federal court of competent jurisdiction located in Multnomah County, Oregon. The parties hereby consent to in personam jurisdiction of said courts.

Company _____
Address _____
City _____ State/Prov _____ Zip _____
Country_____ Phone _____

_____   _____
Authorized Signature   Authorized Signature

Steven C. Hudgik
_____
Print or Type Name

President, HCP Services, Inc.
_____
Title

_____
Date   Date

On the back side of this agreement form, I provide my proposed site-license fee schedule. In some cases, your customer might want different contract terms that will affect your licenses fees. For example, the customer might ask you to provide printed manuals or support for each user. These can be included in the contract, but be sure to modify your fee schedule to include them.

Software rentals

Although not directly related to shareware, before finishing this chapter I would like to include an interesting legal note about renting software. After five years of intensive lobbying by the software industry, the 101st Congress approved the Software Rental Amendments Act. This legislation prohibits "the rental, leasing, or lending of commercial software without the express permission of the copyright holder." It is now against the law to rent, lease, or loan software without the publisher's permission. This means that the only legal method to try software before you buy it is shareware.

12
Business skills

This chapter will help you with some essential business skills: writing a business plan, selling, communication, and writing a proposal. These are all things you can learn to do. They're also skills that continually need refreshing. Most of us don't use these skills every day. As with anything else, if they aren't used, they become rusty and are eventually lost. Keeping your skills shiny and ready to use requires regular maintenance. Take the time to read a book about one of these areas or listen to an audio cassette. You might even reread this chapter once in a while.

At the 1992 Summer Shareware Seminar, I was surprised when a panelist asked all the people who had a business plan to raise their hands, and only four or five (out of 200) did so. How can you know what you need to do if you don't know where you want to be in a year or two? A business plan is an important tool to help focus your efforts in the direction needed for your company to grow.

Writing a business plan

I'm going to take a different approach to business plans than what you'll see in any other book or publication. Most books that discuss the writing of business plans are directed toward larger businesses—typically with a million or so dollars in sales every year. I feel that for a small, one- or two-person company, this approach is overkill and leads to nothing being done about planning because a business plan looks so big and overwhelming. The approach I'll describe is a two-step one. The first step provides a very simple business plan that's perfect for internal use by one- or two-person companies. The second step involves writing the more traditional detailed business plan that can be used externally. (Internal documents are those that are seen only by people within your company. They're never given to anyone who doesn't work for your company. An external document is one that can be given to people outside your company such as bankers or insurance agents.)

Before I start, there's a key element I need to address: why you need a business plan. There is a long list of reasons; here are the six most important:

- To better know your business and yourself.
- To get to know your software better.
- To get to know your customers and understand your market.
- To learn the business skills you'll need to run a business.
- To get the resources your company needs from outside sources such as banks.
- Provide a "blueprint" for what you want your company to do and where you want it to go in the future.

Notice that the first four items are things that help you directly. A business plan is usually thought of as a document that a "big" (meaning bigger than a one- or two-person home business) company uses to attract investors or other people interested in the company. The typical opinion has been "If I'm not trying to attract investors, why do I need to bother with writing a business plan?" In reality, for the small business, having a business plan is important more because of what you learn in writing it than how it's used. Writing a business plan is a good way to learn many of the skills you'll need to run a professional and successful business. Think of it as a learning plan. As you work through each section, you'll learn business skills, more about your business, and more about yourself.

This doesn't mean that a business plan has no value once it's complete. For example, a business plan can be a key ingredient in getting your Visa/MasterCard merchant status. It goes a long way toward showing a bank that you're a serious, professional business because it demonstrates that you have the skills needed to run a business.

The sixth item in the previous list, providing a blueprint, is also a key point for a small business. What does this mean? Having a business plan will bring focus to your business. This helps in making decisions and in determining how you approach your product and customers. There was a discussion on CompuServe several months ago concerning the amount of time a user should be allowed to use a shareware program before registering. Most people were saying thirty to sixty days was a good time period. My opinion was that users should be able to take as long as they want. I based this on the following objectives I have in my business plan:

- Get my shareware into the hands of as many users as possible.
- Make my shareware interesting and good enough that users will try it.
- Make my shareware good enough that they will continue to use it and not switch to another program.

I feel that these three objectives are the most important things I need to accomplish with my shareware. If I'm unable to accomplish them, I won't have many sales. For me, how long users test my software before registering is not important—as long as they keep using it. If they switch to another program, then I've lost those users and there's no longer a possibility they'll register.

Your business plan is a blueprint for your business. It provides guidance and keeps you on track with what you want to do. It's easy to be distracted and go in the wrong direction. Your business plan serves as a reminder of where you want to go and helps to keep you heading in that direction. Studies done by Dun & Bradstreet have found that lack of direction is the major cause of business failure. The root cause of this is that most people don't understand the importance of planning.

If you're determined to succeed and make shareware more than a part-time hobby, planning is important.

The mini business plan

Just as you'll find a quick-start section in many software manuals, here is a quick-start section on writing business plans. You'll end up with a "mini plan" that will help you understand your business, your product, your market, and your customers better. It also serves as an excellent foundation for a full-blown business plan.

As a software consultant, I've helped people start software companies and launch new software products. I've almost always found that they have a product or idea they're excited about and are anxious to get started selling it. But if they were to immediately start selling software, the chances are they would join the 80% of businesses that fail within their first five years. The problem is that they don't have the answers to some very basic questions.

I've already talked about knowing your product and your market, but there's more. When someone hires me as a consultant, I first ask that he fill out a questionnaire. I think of the answers to this questionnaire as providing a mini business plan for small companies that don't need external financial help. It's also a good place to start for getting your thoughts together to write a full-blown business plan.

The following ten items will help bring focus to your business. As you go through them, don't just answer them in your head. Put your answers in writing. If you expect to benefit from these items, you must answer them in writing. Then periodically review your answers to help maintain your focus and direction.

Background information What is your company name and your name? What is your background? What are your qualifications for writing this software?

Purpose Why did you write this software?

Short description   Describe your software in one sentence. It's surprising how many people can't do this. This should be a short, concise statement describing your software. Imagine you have a 10-second sound bite on the CBS evening news. What would you say?

Why do you need to be able to describe your software in one sentence? The average person can't hold an image of more than one relationship in his head. A description that's longer than one sentence becomes too complex for most people to understand and remember. You need to be able to describe your software in a concise manner. If you can't describe your software in one sentence, don't expect users to remember it.

Long description   In one or two short paragraphs, describe your software, its purpose, its scope, the problem it solves and how it solves that problem, and the benefits users of your software will see.

Expand on the one-sentence description you wrote for the third question. Include more details, but don't write a long-winded description. If the answer to question 3 was a 10-second sound bite, answer this question as if you were writing an ad for your software but can afford to buy only two column inches of space. Keep it short and to the point.

Features   List ten features of your software that would be of special interest to users. Explain why users should be interested in these features. How will these features benefit users?

This can be a tough item. It's usually easy to come up with three or four features. However, if your software doesn't have at least ten features that users will find attractive, you're going to have a tough time selling it. Be honest with yourself. List only features that you feel are truly of special interest to users. If you can't come up with ten, then work to improve your software until it has at least ten features that are easily identifiable as being of special interest to users. To verify your answer to this question, send a survey to some of your users and ask them to list features they particularly like. Most users will list only four or five features. The reason you need ten on your list is that various features are of interest to different people.

Uniqueness   Describe at least one feature that's unique to your software. Why have you included this feature? How does this feature benefit users? To be successful, you must be able to differentiate your software from the competition. It must have at least one unique feature you can point to and say "You should buy my software because . . ."

Your users   Describe the typical user of your software. What background knowledge, experience, and skill will the user need to use your software? Why will this person be interested in your software? Why would this user use your software instead of another program?

Marketing plan   What is your marketing plan for this software? Are you promoting it using shareware only, or do you also plan to advertise, send out press releases, go to trade shows, or engage in other promotional activities? What are your yearly sales objectives? What is the registration price? What do users get when they register? How are you planning to package the registered version? What type of support will you provide?

The competition   Is there existing software (both shareware and commercial software) that is similar to your software? If so, list each program with a brief description. For each competing program, describe how your software is different or better.

Beating the competition   List any characteristic weaknesses and omissions in competing software. Does your software have the same weaknesses? If so, describe what you've done in your software to eliminate these weaknesses and omissions. Are these important to your customers? Why are they important?

Write out your answers in the form of a report. Put a nice cover on it and keep it handy. Just going through the process of answering these questions will help you know more about software, your market, and what you need to do to reach your targets. Keep a copy of this document handy and mark it up as you think of new things or as your situation changes. It should be a living, changing document that grows as your company grows.

The mini plan's purpose

The mini plan forces you to think about what you're doing and why you're doing it. It forces you to think about your software, your prospective customers, and whether or not there is a match. Over 85,000 shareware programs have been released, but software libraries carry only two to three thousand at the most. Why? Because many authors have released software that no one is interested in. There's no match between potential customers and the software.

The mini plan forces you to think about the competition. If you've written a DOS shell, you might get writer's cramp before you finish listing all of the competing software. This should help you realize that the DOS-shell market is not a good market to be in if you want to make some money.

Writing out a mini plan forces you to think about a marketing plan and to commit to that plan in writing. No, it isn't a contract requiring you to market your software in a certain way. But by writing out your marketing plan, you better focus your thoughts about how you want to approach marketing your software.

Writing a full business plan

If you're going to use your business plan as part of a loan application or in order to attract investors, you'll need to put together a full business plan using the standard format. You can get by with using the mini plan to help organize your business and get your Visa/MasterCard merchant status, but for almost anything else you'll need to put together a full business plan.

Before we get started, I'd like you to keep several things in mind. You can't be casual about putting a business plan together. A business plan must use correct spelling, grammar, and punctuation. It must be well thought-out and organized. Your plan needs to be focused, clear, and specific. Don't say you'll do something without describing how you plan to do it. Don't use superlatives. If you say that your product is the best in the market, explain why and back up your explanation with facts. As you complete each section, take the time to have your plan proofread by at least three other people.

If you're getting the impression that a business plan is an important document that can't be thrown together over a weekend, you're right. Expect to take several months, at best, to complete it. A business plan involves not only writing, but also a lot of research, forethought, and careful consideration of what you want your company to do and where you want it to go.

The major sections of a business plan

Following is a brief outline of a business plan. Each item provides a summary of what needs to be included in each section.

Section 1: mission statement This is a short statement explaining why you're in business and what you want to accomplish.

Section 2: company description In this section you should provide a brief history of your company and the products you make.

Section 3: product descriptions Each product you make should be described here in detail. What does it do? What are the outstanding features? And what makes your software different from the competition?

Section 4: marketing plan This section identifies who your potential customers are, what your objectives are, and how you plan to achieve these objectives.

Section 5: competitive analysis This section is used to describe your competition and how they approach the market.

Section 6: management This is where you describe your background and experience as well as the backgrounds of any other key individuals in your company.

Section 7: financial plan This final section lays out the financial condition of your company, provides your financial plan, and includes your financial statements.

When complete, a typical business plan runs 30 to 60 pages. This might seem to be an overwhelming writing job, but you don't have to do it all at once. It's good to get started when you don't need to have a business plan other than for your own use. Then as your company grows, you gain experience, and you learn about your market, you can add to your plan and build it a piece at a time. It's a less formidable task that way.

Now let's go ahead and take a detailed look at what goes on in each section. I'll be discussing writing a business plan from the perspective of a one- or two-person home-based business.

Mission statement

In a handout called "Tips for Software (and other) Companies," Bob Wallace, founder of Quicksoft, Inc., gives Quicksoft's mission statement as "We help people create documents."

This is one of the shortest mission statements I've seen, but it includes all the key ingredients. It states why Quicksoft is in business and what its overall goal is.

Although most mission statements are longer, you should try to keep it as short as possible and still express the basic concept of your business. Use the mission statement to explain the nature of your business in one sentence (two at the most).

Your mission statement is the foundation of your business and all else flows from it. Keep it short. I've seen some that run four or five pages and they become meaningless.

Here's the mission statement for my company, HomeCraft Software: "To build a business based on high-quality customer service and honesty that supplies products and services to meet the cataloging needs of collectors."

When working on a mission statement, focus on writing something that you can refer to any time you have to make a major decision. Are you looking at adding a new product? How does it fit with your stated mission? Are you looking for new ways to do business? Are they in tune with your mission statement?

Of course, over time circumstances will change and you'll want to adapt your mission statement for a new situation, but always give it a lot of thought before you change your mission statement. Don't change it quickly or on a whim.

Company description

Here is where you describe the past history of your company, why you started it, and what you're doing now. Start with an introductory section.

Who founded your company and when was it founded? Why was it founded? Have there been any name changes since your company was founded? If so, why did you change the name? How many people are there in your company now?

What markets has your company served in the past? Are you creating a new market or responding to an existing market? Who buys your products?

Next, provide a brief description of your products. What type of software do you publish? What benefits does your software provide users? Do you have any technological or innovative advantages? You don't need to go into a lot of detail here because there's a later section that deals specifically with describing your products.

Briefly describe shareware and how it works. (A more detailed description should be included in the marketing section, so be brief here.)

Describe any awards your software has received and include quotes from positive reviews.

Summarize your objectives for your company. What are the crucial factors affecting your potential for success or failure? What risks and opportunities does your company face? What are your company's strengths and weaknesses? What barriers are there to achieving your objectives? How are you going to overcome these risks, weaknesses, and barriers? What contingency plans do you have if you can't fully overcome them?

By the way, don't try to do a snow job by describing only your strengths. If you ever have to present your business plan to a bank manager, for example, it will immediately be recognized as a fraud and you'll lose the respect of the manager. Bank managers might look at 10 to 15 business plans a week, in some cases, and they know what to expect. All businesses have weaknesses and risks they have to face. If you don't include them in your business plan, it shows that either you're hiding something or you don't know what you're doing. Neither circumstances are good. There's no reason to emphasize the negative aspects of your business, but you should be honest.

What is the business environment your company faces? Briefly describe your market. Who is your competition?

Many of these questions will be answered in detail in later sections of your business plan. In this section, use only a sentence or two to answer most questions and answer only those that are relevant to your company's history or current status.

Product descriptions

This section provides a detailed description of each of your existing products and describes any plans you have for future products or services. If you have multiple products or services, each should be described separately.

If you've already done the mini plan I described earlier, use the sections from that document that describe your software as your starting point for this section. Include the description of your software that describes its purpose, scope, the problem it solves, and its approach to solving that problem. List the ten features in your software that are of special interest to users and explain why. Describe at least one feature that is unique to your software. Why have you included this feature? How does it benefit the user?

Describe any weaknesses your software might have and your plans to correct or overcome them. Don't try to hide weaknesses. All products have weaknesses. By showing that you're aware of your software's weaknesses and have a plan to address them, you show you know how to run a business.

Describe the features of your software that others would say were excellent. Excellence is an important characteristic of any product. To be successful, all software has to offer some form of excellence in an area of interest to potential users. If your software isn't excellent in some form or manner, you have to ask yourself two questions: "Should I get out of this product area?" and "What can I do to develop this product and keep it in its current market?

Is your software ready to ship or is it in development? If it's in development, show a development plan and schedule. How long will it be until it's ready to ship to customers? How are you planning to handle beta testing and bug fixes? A development plan is a detailed schedule showing the various stages in the development of your software and when they're scheduled to be started and complete. Figure 12-1 shows a simple development schedule.

Do you have any patents or licenses that affect this software?

How are your products different from the competition? A good way to present this information is to use a comparison table similar to those used by magazine reviewers. List your software and the competition's software across the top. Show the key features down the left side of the chart. Then fill in the boxes. Table 12-1 provides an example using three competing products. Assume that we're comparing mailing-list managers and your product is called ZipBase (this is one of mine).

Do you anticipate any changes to your existing software? Are you planning any new software or other products? How often do you plan to issue updates or upgrades? What is your policy for discontinuing software? This is an important question. All products have life cycles. How will you know when it's time to discontinue or divest yourself of a product?

Marketing plan

Most businesses skimp on this section. This happens because marketing information can sometimes be difficult to get or, in many cases, you might have to estimate. Put some extra effort into this section. Go looking for information about your market and your competition. Any time you make a statement about your market or the competition, be prepared to back it up with facts.

Target market Start this section by describing your target market. What are you selling? Who will buy it and why? What is your typical user like? If your target is a niche market, you must identify the niche. What are the characteristics of the niche? Why is this niche market right for your software? If you make a profit in this niche, will larger competitors enter it?

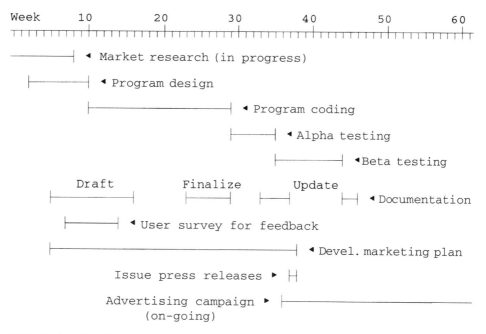

Week   10   20   30   40   50   60

◄ Market research (in progress)

◄ Program design

◄ Program coding

◄ Alpha testing

◄ Beta testing

Draft   Finalize   Update

◄ Documentation

◄ User survey for feedback

◄ Devel. marketing plan

Issue press releases ▶

Advertising campaign ▶
(on-going)

12-1 A simplified fictional development schedule. Horizontal bars are used to indicate the duration of each phase of developing a new software product.

What happens if larger competitors enter this market? Is this market ignored by the competition or not properly served by the competition?

What is the current economic environment affecting your target market and what are the economic trends for the future?

What is the market size? What has the size been in the past? What is the projected market size in 5 to 10 years? What are customers in this market buying (what benefits are they buying)? Why are they buying these benefits?

Provide a market-share analysis. What products are currently available? How many other suppliers provide this type of software? What percent of the market does each of these suppliers get? Based on the past, what are the market-share trends?

How do you get this type of information? All you have to do is ask. To find out about commercial software, request a copy of a publisher's annual report. Also, send for your competitors' brochures. Check with local software stores and ask about the comparative sales of competing software. Purchase a report on your competition from Dun & Bradstreet. Look for references to your competitors' software in magazines and newspapers.

To find out about shareware, talk with a few disk distributors and ask them about the sales of competitive software. They might not provide exact numbers, but you should be able to get a good idea of how one program compares with others.

Table 12-1 This is a typical chart that can be used in a business plan to compare the features of several competing programs.

	ZipBase	FastBase	QuickMailer	MailMgr
Capacity	10,000,000	32,000	32,000	5,000
Sort by zip code	Yes	Yes	Yes	No
Drop-down menus	Yes	No	No	No
# of fields	21	8	4	2
# searchable fields	21	8	4	2
Types label printed	3 built-in + user defined	Standard Avery labels	User-defined	Two standard
Supported printers	All	All	Epson	Epson & HP
Memory requirements	256K	512K	256K	640K

Objectives Next, talk about your objectives, starting with your *strategic objectives*, which are the objectives you set in order to reach a specified target. Supporting strategic objectives are *tactical objectives*, which are the things you need to do to accomplish the strategic objectives. A strategic objective states what you're going to do to reach a target you've defined. Your tactical objective describes the specific activities you'll do to accomplish your strategic objective.

As an example, let's say you're targeting to have your software in the top five programs of its type within 24 months. To do this, you need to reach annual sales of $250,000. One of your strategic objectives would be to inform the market that your software is available and that you're ready to ship it. A tactical objective to support this strategic objective would be to send disks to disk distributors, start advertising, print brochures, and send out press releases.

Another strategic objective would be to arrange for the supplies needed to run your business. The tactical objective that supports this would be to identify suppliers and establish a business relationship with them.

Always list strategic and tactical objectives in the order of importance. Set your priorities so that the most important things are done first.

Crucial success factors What are the crucial success factors in your business? In other words, what do you need to do to be successful? In this section, provide a break-even analysis that shows how much software you must sell on a monthly basis in order to cover your expenses for the first year. Also, show the same information on a yearly basis for the next three to five years.

Market analysis This section should be a detailed analysis of the market in which your software will compete. Your understanding of the market will be demonstrated in this section. Bankers and investors know you won't be successful unless you have a complete and thorough understanding of the market.

One of the most frequent questions I'm asked concerns how to find market information. Where do you look and what do you do to get the facts? Sources of information are everywhere.

You can talk with existing suppliers of similar software and get their brochures. Meet with competitors at trade shows or use information services such as GEnie or CompuServe. It might take some nerve to ask your competitors about their business, but you might be surprised at how much they'll tell you. They are one of your best sources of information.

Read trade publications. For example, computer magazines are good sources of comparative reviews of mass-market software and software that serves large markets. Industry-specific publications can provide details about niche markets. For example, if you make software that car dealers use to track inventories and customer preferences, you should be subscribing to *Automotive News.* How do you find publications? Go to your library and look in the Standard Periodical Directory published by Oxbridge Communications, Inc.

Talk with users of existing products. This includes the users of your products and your competition's. Attend user group meetings or post a survey on CompuServe or GEnie. Visit some of your potential customers. For example, if you make software that businesses use, stop in and visit the purchasing people in several corporations or use personal contacts to arrange appointments with people in the industry you serve.

You should also talk with potential users. This is a key area. You should have as many discussions as possible with users before and after you introduce your software. Their feedback should be incorporated into both your software and your plans. Find out what magazines they read. What are their tastes and preferences in software—for example, do they prefer GUIs or command-line-driven software? How much software do they buy? What type of computers do they have?

The marketing section of your business plan should also include an analysis of market opportunities. How is the market segmented? Is it segmented by industry? Is there a difference between volume buyers and single-unit buyers? What are the growth prospects for each segment? Is this a mature market (no growth) or a new market with a high growth potential? What are the trends in each segment and why? Are there government regulations affecting your market?

Promotion and distribution Promotion and distribution are an important part of marketing. How are you planning to promote and distribute your software? The answer might be obvious to you—you're using shareware to promote your software and you'll handle all sales directly, via mail order. To someone outside your company, however, it won't be obvious; in most cases, they won't eveb know what shareware is. Describe how shareware works in detail and, if you're just starting, provide examples of successful companies that use shareware to market their software. Describe the role shareware disk distributors play and your plans for sending disks to distributors, BBSs, and user groups.

Also, describe any other methods you plan to use to promote and distribute your software, such as advertising, disk distributors to handle credit-card sales, or even sales through retail stores (if you can arrange it). If you're planning to advertise, list the publications you plan to advertise in and explain why. Are you planning to send out press releases? If so, specify to what type of media, how many, and on what schedule. Do you have any experience working with software distributors or dealers? Will you be selling your software internationally or limiting distribution to the domestic market? If you're limiting your market, explain why and the circumstances that would cause you to drop this limitation.

Are you planning to hire anyone to help with marketing or sales? If so, what are you planning to pay? Be realistic in your estimates. For example, don't state that one of your objectives is to hire an experienced marketing manager, and then state that you've budgeted $15,000 as the salary. It isn't realistic and only shows that you're out of touch with the cost of doing business. Of course, if you can hire an experienced person at a low rate of pay, for example a retired family member, provide a complete explanation.

How do you plan to ship your software? Will you charge extra for shipping and handling? What level of inventory do you plan to maintain? How often do you plan to turn over your inventory?

Sales objectives   Another part of the marketing section of your business plan is discussing your sales objectives. What are the sales targets you are shooting for? What levels of sales do you expect your company to have in one year, two years, and five years? How much income do you expect to be earning in one year, two years, and five years? At what point do you expect to be profitable? Do you want your shareware business to be your full-time job? If so, by what date? What are you going to do to reach these targets? What happens if you don't reach these targets?

Having a backup plan that comes into play when your first plan runs into problems is important and is the sign a of a good manager. The future holds too many unknowns. There's no way you can establish a single business plan to achieve your objectives. Expect problems and have plans in place to deal with the unexpected.

What sales tactics do you plan to use? For example, one strategy would be to have a low registration fee in order to try to make a profit on selling upgrades. Another approach is to have a higher price and sell software based on the value it provides to the user. A third approach, focusing on customer service, might be appropriate if your market consists largely of novice users.

What type of product image does your software have? Low price? Outstanding customer support? Advanced features? Are you planning to change this image? What type of warranties and guarantees do you offer? How are you going to package your software?

Answer all of these questions and explain the reasons why you're taking the approach you describe. Back up your explanations with solid facts.

Pricing Next, talk about your pricing. Relative to the market, is your software priced high, medium, or low? Explain. What is your billing policy? C.O.D.? Net 20, 30, 60, 90 days? Do you accept purchase orders and, if so, under what conditions? Do you accept credit cards? If not, is it important to you to accept credit cards? If so, what are you doing to get merchant status and how are you planning to handle credit-card orders until you can get merchant status?

Do you accept foreign checks and under what circumstances do you accept them? Do you offer dealer discounts? What are they? What is your exchange/return policy?

Competitive analysis

You had better know your competition. Who are they? How do they approach the market? What are their strengths and weaknesses? What is their reputation in the market? What niches are they in?

What do you do better than the competition? People almost always buy because they feel a product is superior to its competition. Explain why your software is better and back up your explanation with facts and comparisons.

What type of history and experience does your competition have? Have they been in business a long time or are they new? You might think that it's best to show your competition as weak and in a poor position to compete against you. If you're creating a new market, this approach is good as long as you have the only viable product in this new market. However, if you're entering an existing market, showing that the competition is weak might mean that this isn't a viable market. Showing that you have strong, successful competition can be important. It shows that you are in, or plan to enter, a good market.

Management

The first part of this section should identify the key people in your company. If you're a one-person company, this is where you get to talk about yourself. If other people are involved in your company, you should discuss why they're involved and what their backgrounds are. For each of the key people in your business, answer the following questions:

- Who are the people involved in your business?
- What are their backgrounds, experiences, and qualifications?
- What are their achievements and how successful have they been?

Will your company need to hire additional people in order to achieve the goals described in the previous section? Where are you going to get them? What are you going to pay them? (Remember, pay must match the skills required.) Will these employees need training? Will you purchase the outside services of consultants, contract programmers, etc.? If you have three or more people in your company, include an organizational chart.

In addition to people, your company needs material resources. Describe how you produce the registered versions of your software. What equipment and facilities do you need to produce your software? Where are you going to get your supplies? Will you be hiring outside services or producing your software completely in-house? What type of quality control program will you have?

Financial plan

This is one of the first sections most bankers will look at. It summarizes, in numbers, the current health of your company and your company's potential for the future.

Start by describing the financial history of your company. How was its start-up financed? Most shareware publishers are financed by the author. Did you write checks drawn on your personal account to pay the bills when you first started your company? How much money have you put into your company? What types of gross margins do you expect to have and what is the industry average? This is a tough question. Essentially, all shareware companies are owned by individuals and none publicly publish their financial statements. (I'll be using future author surveys to try to get an answer to this question.) For most industries, a minimum of a 40% gross margin is typical.

What is your philosophy concerning debt? What debt does your company currently have? What is the source of that debt? What type of credit arrangements do you have with suppliers? What other business-related liabilities do you have?

Provide the following financial statements: projected revenue, projected cash flow, and a pro forma (projected) profit & loss statement. What assumptions did you use as the basis of these financial projections? For example, did you anticipate deferring your own salary? What was the basis for depreciation? What was the assumed interest rate?

As a part of these statements, include the number of copies of your software you expect to sell and the estimated gross revenue for a given time period, for example, for the next year. Show what you expect your cash reserves will be, what the cost of goods sold (COGS) will be, what your operating expenses will be, and what your net income or loss will be (negative numbers—losses—are shown in parentheses).

Another financial statement that you will need to provide is a pro forma balance sheet. Describe how you plan to monitor and control funds.

How will you handle accounting? How will sales be recorded? How will expenses be tracked? A shoe-box accounting system won't impress your banker. At a minimum, you should be using a spreadsheet to track your daily (or at least weekly) sales and expenses.

How do you plan to finance your business? In almost all cases, a shareware business will be financed internally—meaning you provide cash as it's needed. What do you expect the financial requirements of your business to be and what personal resources do you have available for meeting these requirements? Are you going to need financing from external sources? If so, what do you plan to use for collateral and how do you plan to get that financing?

That's it—everything you need to put in your business plan. Now let's look at how to put it all together.

Producing your business plan

I've described the seven major sections of a business plan. Once you have those completed, there are a few other short sections you'll need to add.

There should be a cover page that includes the title, the name of your company, and the date your plan was last updated. Even if your business plan is only for your own use, you should include a cover page to tell which version (based on the date) you're looking at. If you'll be distributing copies outside your company, the cover page should also include a control number. This number is used to track which copy was given to whom and whether it was returned or is being held in someone else's files. You could think of the control number as part version number and part ID number. This number should be recorded in a log book and include information about who this specific copy of your business plan was issued to. If you're concerned about the confidentiality of the information in your business plan, include a nondisclosure statement on the cover page. A typical nondisclosure statement could be:

The HomeCraft Software Business Plan is confidential and contains proprietary information. Neither this plan nor any of the information in the plan or appendices may be reproduced or disclosed to any other person under any circumstances without the express written permission of HomeCraft Software.

In the first section inside the front cover, before anything else, include an executive summary of the plan. This is the most important part of your business plan. If you're applying for a loan, for example, your banker will first glance at the executive summary and then turn to the financial section to study your pro formas. Only after he had looked at these two sections will he look through the rest of your business plan. If you have a poor executive summary, your business plan and your chances for a loan might be dismissed without anyone having read the details of your plan.

The executive summary should be as short as possible, and under no circumstances should it exceed three pages. It needs to be a concise and clear summary of what your company is about and it must give readers some sound reasons that explain why they should read your plan. It should include the following information:

Your company A brief description of your company, your mission statement, when the company was formed, and how you market your software.

Your products What products do you sell and what are the distinguishing features? Is your software ready for the market or under development? Does your software have any unique features?

Your market What is the current size of your market and is it growing? What is your estimated market share? Do you sell your software domestically or internationally?

Financial summary What are your five-year projections for sales and revenues? Are you looking for financing and why? How long will you need financing? When will your company be profitable?

The management team Provide a brief description of your background and experience. If other people are involved in your company, include a description of their background and experience.

Following the executive summary, include a table of contents. Then include the body of your business plan based on the outline and questions I've presented. At the end of your business plan, include appendices that have information such as:

- Resumes of key people.
- Schedule of events.
- List of major customers/users.
- Supporting financial information, including detailed information about assumptions, receivable policies, payment policies, depreciation utilized, and any other information used to put together your financial statements.
- List of principle suppliers.
- Description of any insurance coverage you have for your company.
- Expense budgets.
- Any other documents or data that supports what you've written in your business plan.

When you are finished, put your business plan in a good binder or bind it using a GBC machine. Do not just staple the pages together.

Now that your business plan is complete, do not put it on a shelf and forget it. Read through it every couple of months. Reading your business plan helps keep you on track with what you want to do and it allows you to pencil in changes. As you gain experience and your company grows, your business plan will need to change. It will also need to be adapted to changes in your market and in economic conditions.

Selling skills

When I asked other shareware authors about the selling skills they needed, I was surprised at the number who said they didn't need to know how to sell. They felt shareware didn't require selling. Once they had sent out their disks to distributors, they could just sit at home and wait for the orders to come in. That is how they felt shareware worked. Many felt that you didn't have to sell software in a face-to-face meeting with customers. You just needed to send shareware to disk distributors and wait for the orders. Who needs selling skills? Well, selling skills are important and I'ill tell you why in a moment.

Mention the word *selling* or *salesperson* and right away you have a problem. Selling and salespeople have a very bad image. When most people think of a salesperson, they call up an image of a pushy guy trying to sell then something they don't want. The words *selling* and *salesperson* are both seen as negative words. Yet, these are two of the most important words for someone running his own business. And the images they bring up are wrong!

Then there's the question concerning whether salespeople are born or if selling is a skill you can learn. People think of a salesperson as someone with a permanent smile—a back-slapping, glad-handing person with an aggressive attitude—telling jokes and being the center of conversation. These are things you're born with, right? Right! But they aren't the skills that make someone a good salesperson.

Take me as an example. I'm basically a quiet and shy person. I don't particularly like social functions, and I'm terrible at making conversation. I prefer to read a good book and enjoy time by myself. This isn't the description of a typical salesperson. Yet in 1989 I was the top salesperson for Combustion Engineering Power Services, Inc. I've made individual sales with values over 10 million dollars and, in 1989, I made a million-dollar-plus sale to a customer who no one else in the history of the company had been able to sell anything to. In the ten years I was responsible for the Pacific Northwest, I helped build a 75% market share for my company while facing four other major competitors. Overall, that isn't a bad sales record for a quiet, shy person.

Sales skills are something anyone can learn, and some of the best salespeople are the quiet, wallflower type of people. Although there might be more books written on how to be a good salesperson than any other type of business book, the basics you need to learn are very simple and easy. I can list everything you need to know in two paragraphs. But first, let me answer some of the other questions I've raised.

Why you need sales skills

When you're talking to your banker, trying to get a Visa/MasterCard merchant account, you're selling yourself, your honesty, and your ability to run a business. When someone using your shareware calls for help with a technical question, you're selling the quality of your technical support and the ability of your software to do what the user requires. When you talk with a magazine editor, you're selling your software as something the magazine's readers will be interested in. When you talk with a supplier about purchasing disks, you're selling your image as a strong, stable company that can buy supplies on terms instead of C.O.D.

Selling is an integral part of any business and all people, if they're good at what they do, need selling skills. If you work for a big multinational corporation that has 100,000 employees, each of those employees serves a customer and each needs some level of selling skills. For someone in an entry-level position in the mailroom, that person's customers are the people he delivers mail to. The mailroom clerk is selling his ability to deliver the mail, and thus keep his job. He's selling his ability to do his job and thus get a promotion. He's selling the mailroom's ability to deliver the mail, and thus keep the mailroom from being replaced by an outside contract service.

What are you selling?

In the software business, you're selling software. That was the easy answer, but what else are you selling? Not everything you sell has a price attached to it. Before you can sell your software, you must "sell" a lot of other things—things like your:

- Image
- Belief that your software will be beneficial to your users
- Reputation
- Trustworthiness
- Technical-support capabilities
- Programming skills
- Ability to write good documentation
- Background and knowledge in the field in which your software is marketed

I have deliberately picked eight items that are abstract—things that aren't physical. Generally, before people buy a copy of your software, you have to sell them on all eight of these abstract items. Sometimes it's easy—your shareware package sells itself. Sometimes you're selling and might not be aware of it, such as when a user calls for technical support. Other times, when a user asks you to explain why your software is better than anyone else's, it's obvious you need to be wearing your sales hat.

What is selling?

Selling is providing a service to a potential customer by matching that customer with a product or service that will benefit the customer. Notice that I didn't say that selling is getting people to buy something. Getting people to buy something they don't need isn't selling; it's fraud. I also didn't say that selling is fast talking and a lot of hype. That is one of the images we have of salespeople, and it's wrong.

The best salespeople are those who are themselves, who are honest, and who have a sincere desire to help customers. Do you have to be a joke-teller and socialite? No. Be honest and be yourself. But, as with anything else, there are some skills you can learn that will help you do a better job. The following is a list of skills that should make you a better salesperson:

Be a good listener Most salespeople talk too much. Good salespeople not only listen, but they pay attention to what the customer says and does. In many cases, while another person is talking, we're thinking about what we're going to say next. We're only half paying attention to what the other person is saying. If you're going to provide people with the best possible level of service, you need to pay attention to what they say, how they say it, and what they do.

Help the customer A good salesperson's main motivation is a desire to help customers. Good salespeople are service-oriented. Making money and the satisfaction that comes from closing a sale should make you feel good, but if these come before your desire to serve the customer you won't be closing the sale nor making money.

Be honest The only thing a salesperson can directly offer a customer is trustworthiness. If a salesperson loses a customer's confidence in his or her trustworthiness, that customer will never again buy from that sales-person. Yes, you can make a sale by lying. It might even be the easiest sale you ever make. It's easy to offer the best product if you can make up features and benefits. But after that first sale, the customer will find out the truth and you'll never sell anything else to that customer. (We all would like to sell upgrades, right?) Even worse, your bad reputation will spread and soon you'll have no customers.

Understand your customers' needs Good salespeople are able to put themselves in their customer's shoes. Being able to understand the customer's problems and needs is important. It's the best way to truly understand how you can serve customers and match them with the software that's best for them. In many cases, when a good salesperson's products aren't appropriate for what a customer needs, that salesperson will refer the customer to a product made by another company.

Be positive No one likes to talk or do business with a grump or someone who always sees the negative side of things. That's why a positive attitude is important when you sell your software. A good salesperson looks for the good in people and for the positive aspects of any situation. The worst thing that can happen to a salesperson is to lose a sale. But when that happens, a good salesperson doesn't start blaming the loss on unfair tactics by the competition or stupidity on the part of the customer. A good salesperson takes a positive approach, getting feedback from the customer to find out what he did right and what areas should be improved.

When I was working in sales, I did something few, if any, other salespeople did. About once a year, I would visit with my customers and ask them to tell me what I was doing right and what I could improve. I would have my customers evaluate my performance and that's how I learned to do a better job for my customers.

That doesn't sound too bad, does it? In fact, for most people being a salesperson means being the person you are, not some fake image. Is there anything wrong with being someone who listens to other people? A person who cares about and wants to help other people? A person who is honest and can understand another person's point of view? A person with a positive attitude? Sounds like a really nice person to me. Somebody I would want to know.

These are only some of the skills you'll need when you talk with customers, suppliers, editors, and many other people. Although sales training courses teach a variety of skills, such as how to ask open-ended questions, I feel there are two basic skills every salesperson needs. Things such as open-ended questions will develop from the characteristics I previously listed. For example, if you're honestly interested in a customer's welfare, you'll automatically ask open-ended questions because you're interested in learning more about that customer.

Two key things that I feel a salesperson must do are follow up on a sale and ask for the order.

You should always follow up—whether you win or lose a sale—to find out why. With shareware, many times you won't know you've lost a sale because users will simply delete your software. So how do you follow up when you're using shareware to market your software? I have five suggestions:

- Call disk distributors and ask if they've gotten any feedback on your shareware. Find out whether your shareware sells a lot or just a few copies. Remember, however, that several hundred people might buy your software for each person who registers. All you're trying to find out from the disk distributor is whether or not your software catches people's interest.
- Do a presentation about your software for a user group. During the presentation, pay attention to how the group reacts to your software. Are they interested or are they drifting off to look at something else? Following the presentation, hand out a questionnaire.
- Beta test your software and get feedback from your testers. Ask them whether or not they continue to use your software when they're done testing and find out why (or why not).
- Send questionnaires to people on your mailing list who've asked

about your software but have never purchased it. Find out why they asked but then didn't purchased it.

- When an unregistered user calls with a question but doesn't register during the phone call, ask if there is anything you could change in the software that would make it better fit his or her needs.

One of the most difficult things you should do is ask people to buy your software. It's called *asking for the order*. It's very hard to do and most salespeople don't do it. I once attended a seminar in which 15 other experienced salesmen were participating. Some had more than 20 years of experience in sales. We were all asked to sell a fictional product to the person running the seminar. Out of 15 salespeople, only one person—me—asked for the order. The others made their presentation, talked about the features and benefits of their product, gave the price, and that was it. They left the customer wondering about what to do next and, like most people, the customer put off making a decision.

When talking with unregistered users on the phone, I have several approaches for asking for the order. The one I use most frequently is "If you'd like to order a registered copy now, I do accept credit cards and can take your order on the phone." Another way to ask for the order is to say "I just started shipping the current version. I'd be happy to take your order now and ship it to you right away."

If you aren't able to accept credit cards, you're at somewhat of a disadvantage, but there are still ways you can try to close a sale on the phone. For example, you could offer a free copy of another shareware program: "I have a special offer I'd like to let you know about. If I receive your registration check within the next week, I'll include a free copy of the 1991 Shareware Almanac with your order." You could also offer a reduced price on your software and include additional utilities at no charge.

The two-paragraph summary

I said earlier that I could list everything you need to know about selling in two paragraphs. Well, here they are:

Be yourself and have a positive attitude. Be honest and concerned about the customer. Try to see things from the customer's viewpoint.

Whenever you can, get feedback on why the customer bought or didn't buy your software. Don't forget to ask for the order.

That's it—two rather short paragraphs at that.

Communication skills

Another important skill that will help you make your software successful is the ability to communicate. We all envy those people who have the gift of gab. They can meet a complete stranger and be in a deep conversation a few seconds later. That isn't the type of person I'm talking about. I'm talking about you and me, ordinary people who have learned a few communication skills.

"Shareware authors need to be able to talk to people. I've met a lot of authors who when you get into a conversation it's like talking to a brick wall. They may talk up a storm on CompuServe, but you get them one-on-one and they don't say anything."

— Marshall Magee, president of Magee Enterprises (AutoMenu)

The ability to talk with people is a useful skill that can be learned. As a business person, it's important that you have the ability to talk with people and communicate your message. I mentioned talking and communication separately because they're two different things. You can be talking, but if the other person isn't listening and paying attention, there's no communication. What's the best way to encourage communication? Talk louder? Talk faster? Kick the other person in the shin to get his attention? No, but here is a list of suggestions:

Ask and be asked questions If you want to communicate with someone, you should find a way to not only ask questions but get people to ask you questions. The point is that you want to tell them something, not have them tell you things.

Asking questions makes sense. Before you can deliver your message, you first must get the other person's attention. Then you must learn enough about that person so you can deliver your message in a way that interests him. How do you do that? You ask questions. Use your questions to learn about the other person's interests. It makes starting a conversation easy because all people's favorite subject is themselves. Once you learn a little about what the other person likes and dislikes, you can deliver your message in a way that will interest him.

Make eye contact If you are talking with somebody, look at him. That doesn't mean to stare at him continuously, because that makes people uncomfortable. However, if you're looking around the room or looking at other people, that tells the person you're talking with that you aren't interested in what he's saying.

Be aware of your body language Some studies have shown that up to 85% of what is communicated is nonverbal. For example, if you're trying to have an open and friendly conversation with someone but your arms are folded, your body is delivering a message that says you're upset about something. When you first meet someone, try to have a relaxed, easy posture. By the way, a simple way to learn about body language is to watch TV. Actors are aware of their body language and use it to help express the emotions of the character they're playing. In many cases, especially in sitcoms, they'll use exaggerated body language. Key in on one character, identify the emotion he's expressing, and then notice what he does with his body.

Promote your software   As a software business person, you should "talk up" your software with anyone who will listen. It's an important aspect of promoting your software. "Oh, but I never know what to say!" That's how I feel. My natural inclination is to be a wallflower and avoid conversations. I'm perfectly happy being a wallflower, just watching other people have a good time. But if I'm going to make my business successful, I have to step away from the wall and introduce myself.

That's all there is to it; that's how you start a conversation. Just introduce yourself. After that, ask the other person a few questions about himself. What type of business is he in? What does he do? If you're at a meeting or convention, ask him if he's enjoying the meeting. If you're at a bus stop, ask him if he takes that bus often. Mention the major news events of the day and ask him his opinion.

To be able to carry on a conversation, you need to know what you're talking about. Knowing your subject builds your confidence and makes it easier to talk with individuals and in front of groups. If you want to talk about your software, you need to have an in-depth knowledge of it and of the people who use it. Because you wrote it, you might think you know it all. That isn't true, and I'll talk about that in a moment.

Knowing your subject also means having a wider breadth of experience than just knowing about your software. For example, you can't talk about the day's news unless you read the newspaper. You can't talk about the state of the computer industry unless you read a few computer publications. So do a little outside reading and be aware of what's going on in the world around you.

To be able to tell people about your software, you must know everything there is to know about it. Don't assume that, because you wrote your software, you know all about it. Knowing all about it means knowing who uses it, why they use it, how they use it, and everything else you need to learn in order to write a business plan. As I said in the section on business plans, that is one of the main reasons for writing a business plan.

Sometimes it takes a lot of research, but knowing your subject gives you confidence. Knowing a one-sentence description of your software, and having thought about that one sentence in detail, allows you to intelligently answer when someone asks you "What type of software do you publish?"

Writing a proposal

Proposal writing is another area in which the initial responses I got from authors indicated they didn't feel they needed to know about it. If you ever plan on your business being more than part-time, you need to know how to write a proposal. For example, would you like to sell a 5000-copy site license to United Airlines? If so, you'll need to know how to write a proposal. Would you be interested in a purchase order from the New York City school district for 1000 copies of your educational game? If so, be prepared to write a proposal.

A proposal doesn't need to be a 50-page document, written in response to a formal request for proposal (RFP). Some proposals are single-page letters or, in some cases, nothing more than a photocopied price list. If you have a catalog, at times that might be considered your proposal. The form a proposal takes will depend on the situation. In this section, I'll describe a formal type of proposal you'd use in making a fairly large sale. However, except for the title page and executive summary, even a two-page letter proposal would still be based on the same format I describe here.

Why is it important that you know how to write a proposal? If you're planning to sell your software to a business, you have to present a professional image in order to be taken seriously. Here is what Marshall Magee, president of Magee Enterprises, Inc. (AutoMenu), had to say about selling to corporations:

"Corporations like to deal with a stable, established company. You need to assure them that you are going to continue to exist. What is the best way to help corporate customers feel secure in doing business with you? Show them you know how to present a professional-looking proposal."

Types of proposals

There are two types of proposals. The first type is a proposal sent on an unsolicited basis, meaning the customer didn't ask for your proposal. In most cases, this type of proposal is designed to persuade people that they need your product or service.

The second type of proposal is one that's sent to potential customers who have an identifiable need and your proposal, and you must convince them that your product or service will best fill that need. This is the type of proposal most shareware authors are likely to use. For example, this is the type of proposal you would send to a corporation interested in purchasing a site license for your software.

Before you start to write a proposal, you need to have your approach well organized. Most proposals are written to present a solution to a problem. For example, if you sell a DOS shell, the problem might be that the average user in an organization is having problems accessing various programs on a hard disk.

Use your proposal to describe your understanding of the customer's problems or needs. Then present a solution and explain why your solution is a good approach. That's all there is to it, so let's get started.

As with so many other things, the first step is to define your objectives.

Before you start to write a proposal, you must have a clear understanding of what your objectives are and what strategy you want to use in your proposal. To define your objectives, first ask yourself the following questions: "What are the main reasons this corporation should buy your software?" "Why is your software better than the competition's?" "What features of your software provide a unique benefit to customers that will help solve their problems?" "Is your software the most efficient, easiest to use, least costly, and most capable?" "Do you offer the best support, outstanding training, and most complete documentation?" Out of these, or possibly others your software offers, pick one or two overriding advantages and base your selling strategy on them. Your proposal needs to focus on the customer's needs. Don't try to be everything anyone could want. Your message will be diffused and the result will be a weak proposal.

Before you start to write your proposal, talk to customers and find out what they need. Look for the root cause of problems. In asking for your proposal, a customer might have defined only the symptoms. To be successful, you need to dig to find the causes of the problem. Ask your customer to describe the problems and then ask him to tell you what he think the cause is. Keep asking questions until you feel satisfied that you've found out why the problem exists.

With the problem defined and the key benefits of your software identified, you now have a focus for your proposal. Focus on the key benefits (assuming, of course, these benefits are what your customer needs to solve his problem). Carry this focus throughout the proposal. Emphasize it in your cover letter, in the executive summary, and even in the headings you use for each section of the proposal.

Proposal guidelines

Every proposal should have a title page as the front cover. This page includes the name of the organization to which you're submitting the proposal, the date of submission, the customer's RFP number or other reference number, your proposal number, and, if the proposal contains confidential material, a confidentiality statement. Many times, a proposal will be rewritten two or three times. Put a proposal number on each so you can easily identify which version you're working with. A typical proposal number might be 91-003-02. This means the proposal was written in 1991 and was the third proposal you did that year. The 02 indicates this is revision 2.

First, always keep in mind that your proposal, whether it's a price list, a catalog, or a 50-page site-license proposal, should always look neat and professional. Appearance counts. The appearance of your proposal provides a strong first impression about the quality of your company and how you do business. Don't submit proposals printed on a dot-matrix printer. Don't send copies that are smudged or streaked.

If the proposal is longer than 8 to 10 pages, you should include a table of contents. Use the table of contents to provide a detailed outline of the key information in your proposal. This will help the reader find information and serve to jog his memory about the contents of your proposal.

If your proposal includes exhibits, client lists, or screen shots, include a page listing these. Also list any extra material, such as brochures, so the reader can tell if something is missing.

The first section of a proposal is generally an executive summary. Use this section to summarize the key details. Describe the important benefits your software provides and describe the facts that support your claims. If the schedule is important, highlight it and your ability to meet that schedule. Assume that the only section the decision maker will read is this section. You need to mention all the essentials, but don't clutter this section with details. Just highlight the one or two key reasons why the customer should do business with you.

Description of requirements Use this section to summarize your understanding of the customer's problem. Include an analysis of the problem based on the conversations you have had with the customer. If you feel there are several problems, describe them and tell the customer why you feel this way. By doing this, you're laying the groundwork for the alternative solutions you'll be describing in the next section.

If you've made any assumptions, list them here. Also list any customer requirements such as the number of users, type of material to be delivered (for example, printed manuals), and the schedule.

Proposal This is the section in which you describe the software and services you're offering. Discuss your proposed solution to the customer's problem in full detail, focusing on the customer's goals and the results he can expect. List the advantages of your solution and tell the customer how to measure or evaluate the results of using your software.

Cover all the details. Don't let the reader make assumptions because they might be the wrong assumptions. Discuss every benefit, even if it appears to be an obvious benefit. It might not be obvious to the reader. Help the reader focus on the key benefits you want to emphasize. For example, if the key benefit is that your software is easy to use, use a chart to show how quickly users can learn your software compared with other programs. If cost is a key issue, show a per-unit cost breakdown. Evaluators might not always think to break things down or might be distracted by someone else's proposal.

Make sure the proposal answers the key questions. Put yourself in the customer's place and visualize the questions you would have. But be careful; some proposals try to have all the answers before they have the questions. Be sure you understand your customer's concerns, problems, and needs before you start writing your proposal. If you show that you understand the customer, the customer will feel more confident that your solution is the correct one.

Should you be concerned about giving too much information? No. Be open, honest, and give the customer the full details. Your proposal must be specific enough to show that you clearly know what you're talking about. Don't be vague. Vagueness is usually used to hide a lack of knowledge.

Don't include extravagant claims that you can't back up with facts. Avoid words and phrases such as *best* or *undisputed leader* unless you can provide proof. Unless your competition agrees that you're the leader, you cannot be the undisputed leader. A good way to support your claim is to include copies of reviews and quotes from letters from users. You should always get permission from the magazine that did the review before you copy it. I've found that, in most cases, magazines don't charge for this as long as you give them proper credit for the review and have their permission in writing.

Also, be careful not to use hedging language or vague qualifiers. For example, never say "Our software should perform to the specification requirements." Either it will perform as required or it won't. Any time you use the word *should*, you're telling your readers you aren't sure your software is right for them.

Never knock the competition. Knocking the competition just shows a negative attitude on your part. Let the qualities and benefits of your software speak for themselves. Yes, you can compare products if you have facts. But never bad-mouth the competition.

Options You might find that the customer is asking for something that won't solve the problem. In all cases, always propose what the customer asks for. If you then have a better solution you'd like to offer, offer it as an alternative. In the option section of your proposal, describe each option in the same detail as you did for your base proposal.

Other options you might want to include in a proposal for a site license include:

- If the base proposal doesn't include printed manuals, you can offer an option to supply printed manuals. Or, if they're included in the base proposal, offer an option that reduces the price if the customer duplicates the manuals.
- Offer an option to provide user support based on an hourly rate.
- Offer an option to provide on-site training.
- Offer an option for other software you publish that the customer might find useful. Many times you can put together a package price that's more attractive should the customer buy two site licenses.
- Offer an option for customized screens, customized programming, or customized user manuals.

References and experience list If you've sold similar site licenses to other companies, include a list of references. The best references include the specific names and phone numbers of people who can be contacted. If this isn't possible, include only a list of previous customers if it's substantial. This means the list must have some recognizable names on it and it must be at least 10 to 15 names long. It's best, however, to have enough names to fill a page—even if you have to use large print.

If you or other employees in your company have any specialized experience that applies to the situation, describe that experience in this section.

Pricing   Include a separate section that lists the prices for your base offering and for any options you've proposed.

Terms and conditions   This section should contain a copy of the site-license contract you're proposing. (See chapter 9 for a sample site-license agreement.)

Miscellaneous exhibits   The final section of your proposal contains any brochures, copies of reviews, magazine articles about your company or software, your resume, and anything else that supports your proposal and demonstrates your track record.

The cover letter   Whenever you send out a proposal, always include a cover letter. If it does nothing else, the cover letter says "Here it is." It documents that you sent your proposal and to whom it was sent.

But a cover letter can also do more! Include a few brief sentences that summarize what you're proposing. Emphasize the key benefits of doing business with you. Also use the cover letter to answer any anticipated questions about the proposal in general. If you're unable to propose exactly what the customer asked for, explain why. Also explain any omissions or changes in your proposal. Put yourself in the reader's place. After you've examined the proposal, what questions would you have? At the end of your cover letter, thank the customer for asking you to submit a proposal.

13
Writing and testing software

Software users, in general, want ease of use, good documentation, and technical support. In some respects, these three are the same. They mean that users want software that has a short learning curve and that can be quickly put to use for its intended purpose. By the way, that's the number one item on the list—software must provide a solution to a problem. It must be useful and nontrivial. Otherwise, there's no reason to purchase the software.

What users want

The following comments are from users, and they basically repeat what I said, above, about what users want:

- I like well-written documentation.
- I want to see four things in the software I purchase: 1) good documentation, 2) ease of use, 3) good support, and 4) cost, but only if the above three are equal or the price difference is substantial.
- I definitely go with the program that is easier to use.
- I think wide use of the program is important. If it is not widely used, your ability to get support is limited to the technical support department of the company.

Once users decide they need to purchase new software, they want true ease of use. This means that most users in your target market can intuitively use existing software, that the documentation is easy to read and complete, and that quality support is readily available. The problem with the phrase "easy to use" is that people have various definitions of what it means. When I asked other shareware authors how they defined it, these are some of the answers they gave:

"I like to think 'easy to use' is when I start the program up and can do something useful with it without having to resort to using the manual. I don't mind using the manual for advanced features, but I want the startup and basic use to be obvious."

— Tom Simondi, author of TUTOR.COM

"Easy to use is when the computer novice does not have to wade through 300 pages of text and make 10 calls for assistance. An author needs to listen to the calls and letters he gets and ask 'What can I do to prevent the user from having this problem?' In designing a program and its documentation, you have to apply KISS—that means Keep It Simple Stupid. Even complicated programs such as a payroll system can be easy to use. I am thrilled when users of my ZPAY 3 program call and tell me how easy to use the program is."

— Paul Mayer, author of GRAB Plus and ZPAY3

"I don't think it is easily defined. Perhaps something along the lines of intuitive enough such that the average user can figure out how it works based on what appears on the screen."

— Bob Falk, author of EasyFormat and ProPak 2.0

Finding out whether or not your software is easy to use

There are no specific step-by-step instructions you can follow to make your software easy to use. The definition of is different depending on the experience and background of the end user. A program that is easy to use for a business user might not be easy for a home user. What is intuitive for one person is unintelligible to another. The only way you can know whether or not your software is easy to use is to test it. Find someone with no computer experience. This might be your spouse, a friend, or even students in a computer or business class at your local high school. (My thanks to Paul Mayer for this suggestion.) Get their comments. Pay attention to what makes them frustrated. What questions do they ask? Note the areas they have problems with. Then change your software so that the next user does not have the same questions or problems.

Another approach to finding out how easy to use your software is would be to release it to a few distributors and get feedback as people start to use it. Then once you've confirmed that your program is easy to use or after you have improved it, release it to a larger number of distributors. Keep in mind that you might be imposing on these early users. Be prepared to put extra effort into providing them super service. If they make suggestions, make changes in your software and send out free updates as quickly as possible. By the way, don't use this type of testing to debug your software. Releasing buggy software just frustrates users and results in a bad reputation for you. The purpose of this type of testing is to find out if your software is easy to install, easy to use, and whether or not it has all the functions users need. To encourage feedback, include a special offer such as a reduced or free registration fee, and be sure to properly identify the software as a prerelease version.

"If they have a problem or can't understand something, see what you can do to make it easier. If you can modify the user interface and change program actions to minimize technical support calls, then you have a winner."

— Paul Mayer

Making a program intuitive and easy to use is especially important with shareware. People will put your disk in their computer, give it a quick try, and if they can get it started without reading the documentation, they're more likely to use it. The way most people learn a new program is by first trying to use it. They read the manual later to learn about the more advanced functions.

Getting feedback

Remember, what's easy for you might not be easy for most users. Test, test, test, and listen to the feedback. Try different approaches in designing your software and test them. When talking to users or testers, remember what I said in the section on handling complaints. Don't get upset. Users will find a lot of problems and they'll have some complaints and suggestions that aren't justified. Always stay calm and keep in mind that different people see things differently.

It's often easy for users and testers to identify problems, but you need to find solutions. This isn't easy. Sometimes the solution to one problem creates difficulties in another area. Once you've released the final fully tested version, keep listening to users and continue looking for ways to improve your software and make it easier to use. The feedback and improvement never stops.

This chapter provides some guidelines to help you make your software easy to use. I'm not going to try to show you how to write program code or discuss the specifics about programming languages. After all, this is a marketing book, not a programming book. However, the principles covered here can be applied using any programming language.

Benefits of good software design

The benefits of writing good software are that you can more easily get people to pay the registration fee and avoid spending all your time on the phone providing support. I've talked with people who have written a program and don't want to release it because they don't want to answer questions on the phone all the time. Or they release the program and specify that all questions must be mailed to the author; no phone number is given in the documentation. This is fine if you run your business as a hobby. However, if you're serious about publishing software and making money doing it, you need to include your phone number. If you have any intention of selling your software to businesses, you must include your phone number.

The solution to the telephone support problem is to listen to the questions users ask and then change either your documentation or your program to eliminate the questions. It takes some time, but you'll have a better program. And when the phone rings, it will be a call from a user wanting to register, not someone with a question.

Getting started

The first rule of writing good software is not to rush. Take the time to write a good program. Find other people to test it or, if you're on your own, put it aside for a few weeks before you test it. Anytime you get an uncomfortable feeling in the back of your head telling you that some part of the program doesn't work right, change the software. Don't ignore feelings that make you uneasy about parts of your software. Take the time to listen to your inner voice.

Keep in mind that because you designed and wrote the program, it will all seem intuitive to you. An outside opinion, possibly that of your spouse, is useful in determining whether or not the software really is intuitive. Try to have people who aren't familiar with the program use it without looking at the manual. What problems and questions do they have?

Software installation

The first thing users do with a new program is install it. They're anxious to get started, so reading the documentation generally takes a back seat to getting the program installed and running. There are four key points concerning installation that you need to pay attention to:

1. Make installation as easy as possible.
2. Make the installation instructions easy to find.
3. Assume the user has no knowledge of DOS or DOS commands.
4. Make as much of the installation process as possible automatic. For example, your software should automatically detect a computer's video card type.

Making installation easy

The simplest programs to install are contained on a single floppy disk that can be immediately run directly from that floppy disk. All you need to do is tell users to make a backup copy and then give them the command that starts the software. I've found that over 80% of the software I've looked at falls into this category.

Although most people have hard disks, don't assume that users will want to install your software on their hard disk. Many users like to try the software before installing it on their hard disk, especially if it's shareware. If your software is a TSR (terminate and stay resident) program that should be installed as a part of the AUTOEXEC.BAT file, give them a way to try the program before they install it.

If your program can be copied directly to a hard disk using the DOS COPY command, let the user know this. Many experienced users prefer to copy a program directly instead of going through the installation process. However, no matter how simple your program is, always include a way for the software to be automatically installed. Use a filename that's intuitive for starting the installation. In the past it was common to use the first letter of the program's name and the word INSTALL. For example, for my Play 'n' Learn software, the installation file used to be called PINSTALL. I no longer recommend doing this. Users have come to expect that the command to install a program will be INSTALL, and that should be the name you use for your installation utility. I also recommend having only one installation utility. If there's a difference between the hard-disk and floppy-disk installation procedures, have the first question be "Are you installing this software on a hard disk or a floppy disk (H/F)?"

The installation process should provide a series of questions that prompt users to enter the information needed to install your software. With each question, a default setting should be provided and explained on the screen. For defaults, use the most common response. For example, when you ask users to enter the letter designating their hard disk, the default should be C.

When a user has responded to all of the installation questions, put a summary of the user's responses on the screen. Give the user the opportunity to change any of the responses or accept them all as correct.

During the installation of your software, especially if it's a time-consuming process, put something on the screen to tell the user what is happening. Watching a blank screen while your disk drive churns away can be disconcerting. Include short status statements such as "Copying files . . ." or "Checking for CONFIG.SYS file . . . ." These let the user know that the installation is proceeding and, most likely, functioning properly.

If you don't want to write your own installation utility, there are a lot of good programs available that will create one for you. Most of them are available as shareware. Look for programs such as Quik-Install, First Impression, and EDI Install. Most shareware catalogs don't carry software installation utilities, so you'll need to look on Compuserve, GEnie, or some of the major BBSs.

Making the installation instructions easy to find

Your installation instructions should be the first section in your manual. If you feel the user needs to have an understanding of DOS before installing your software, put a DOS tutorial in an appendix at the back of the manual.

The installation instructions can then refer inexperienced users to the appendix. If you want to explain shareware and talk about the ASP, and if it's more than a one-page summary, put that information in an appendix.

For shareware disks, I also recommend including a brief description of how to install and start your software in a READ.ME file. Give users the word they need to enter to start the installation process. If there's something they should know before installing your software, refer them to a specific page in your manual. Also, tell users how to start your software and use it directly from a floppy disk, if possible.

DOS and DOS commands

Using the DOS DIR command might appear to be simple to you and me, but many people don't know what it is. Since the release of DOS version 4 and Windows version 3, many people buying their first computer never see the DOS prompt. They don't know what it is and might not know to get one on their screen.

Even users who have earlier versions of DOS might not be familiar with DOS commands. In the past, they might have installed other software by following the instructions in a cookbook-like way. If you ask users to type a DOS command, be extremely detailed in providing step-by-step instructions. Describe each keystroke and provide an illustration of what the screen should look like.

Be careful when asking users to do something with the CONFIG.SYS or AUTOEXEC.BAT files. For example, my database software requires the CONFIG.SYS file to have a FILES=20 statement. I explain this in my documentation and tell users how to create or modify their CONFIG.SYS files. My software will also automatically create the necessary CONFIG.SYS file during the installation process if the user requests it. What could go wrong?

I get calls from users who get error messages telling them to add a FILES=20 statement to their CONFIG.SYS file. They tell me, yes, they do have a CONFIG.SYS file. When I have them use the DOS TYPE command to list the contents, it shows a FILES=20 in the CONFIG.SYS file. After I've asked a few more questions, I find that they're running my software on a floppy disk and have put the CONFIG.SYS file on that floppy disk instead of on the DOS disk.

You have to write your installation instructions just as if you were writing a cookbook. Don't leave out anything. Have a complete novice test your instructions to ensure that you haven't left out something that's obvious to you but not to a beginner.

Making installation as automatic as possible

If your software needs to know specifics about the hardware being used, have the installation software automatically detect as much of the hardware configuration as possible. For example, your installation software should be able to determine the type of video card installed.

If your software uses a COM port, give the user the option of entering the COM port number or having the software find the right COM port. For example, if you publish telecommunications software, have your software automatically check each COM port for a dial tone.

If your software can use EMS memory, it should automatically check for EMS memory. Don't assume that the user knows what EMS memory is or what a COM port is. Use your installation software to automatically detect as much of the configuration information as you can.

There will be some external peripherals that your software cannot identify, such as a printer or a modem. For these types of peripherals, provide a list of brands and model numbers and allow users to select the one they have.

For example, if your software needs to use special features provided by some printers, display a list of printers that your software supports. Printers that use the same drivers should be listed separately. For example, most Panasonic printers are Epson-compatible. However, you should list each Epson and Panasonic printer model separately. Many users will look for their specific brand and model number. If they don't find it, they'll assume their printer is not supported by your software. I once helped a friend who could not get WordPerfect to print. He had an Epson RX-80 and that printer was not listed among the printers that WordPerfect supported. WordPerfect did list the Epson MX-80, but he didn't know that an RX-80 and an MX-80 were the same. By the way, this person was trying to print a draft of his doctoral thesis, so he was not unintelligent.

I've seen a lot of shareware that requires users to enter printer control codes during the installation process. This is a poor choice and I don't recommend doing it. You might allow printer control codes to be entered to accommodate people with oddball printers, but you should provide drivers for all of the common printers such as Epson and Hewlett-Packard.

Be sure to test your print drivers before releasing your software. I've had people purchase my software because they couldn't get someone else's software to work with their printer, although it was supposed to. Most printer manufacturers have developer-support programs that will loan printers to software publishers for the purpose of testing print drivers. You can contact Hewlett-Packard by writing to:

HP ISV/IHV Program
16399 W. Bernardo Dr.
San Diego, CA 92127

and you can contact Epson by writing to:

Epson America, Inc.
Developer Relations
2780 Lomita Blvd.
Torrance, CA 90505

In most cases, printer manufacturers that don't have a developer support program will be willing to send you a copy of their user manuals. This will allow you to write drivers and then, hopefully, find a friend or a beta tester with a printer on which you can test your drivers. Another way to test print drivers is to visit a computer store when they aren't busy. If you have a program that will automatically test your driver in a few minutes—in other words, you don't have to sit there and manually test the printer driver—the store will often let you run a test.

An approach I use is to send only standard ASCII characters to the printer. No fonts, no bold, just ASCII characters and form feeds. This works fine for applications that require only information to be listed. If you do this, keep in mind that dot-matrix printers use 66 lines per page while laser printers use 60 lines per page. You might want to let users indicate whether or not they have a laser printer; otherwise, all printed reports should be limited to no more than 60 lines per page.

AUTOEXEC.BAT and CONFIG.SYS files

Never modify a user's AUTOEXEC.BAT or CONFIG.SYS file without first getting permission. If the user tells the installation software that it's okay to modify these files, always make backup copies of the original files. Indicate the filenames used for the backup copies so the user can recover them if necessary.

Never change users' PATH statements without telling them. For example, I've tried software that was divided among several directories on the original floppy disk. During the installation, the PATH was reset to accommodate the directories on the floppy disk. After installing the software, I found my computer no longer worked as it should, and I eventually discovered this was caused by a change in the PATH setting. Rebooting the computer restored my old PATH, but finding the problem was very frustrating and should not have been necessary.

Verifying the configuration

Once the configuration of the user's computer has been determined, display the configuration settings on the screen. Give the user the opportunity to change any of the settings before they're installed.

Program design

The best summary I've seen of practical suggestions for writing an easy-to-use program was written by Rosemary West. Rosemary is the author of 17 shareware programs, including one called Book of Changes. When I was looking at shareware to see what other authors included on their disks, her programs impressed me as being very easy to install and use. Here is what she has to say:

"I'm not sure what 'easy-to-use' really means since I get a lot of different opinions from users. Most seem to like menus with simple descriptive words. The kind of menu that puts a short explanatory message at the bottom of the screen as you scroll through the choices is popular.

People don't like to go more than a couple of layers deep into menus. Very few people use F1 for help. Most users seem to feel a program with a pretty screen is better even though it performs exactly the same as one with an unpretty screen.

Cluttered screens seem to confuse people. Screens that use color or highlighting to draw attention to important items are a big help.

Documentation that includes extremely simple explanations about how to copy disks, how to get the software onto the hard disk, how to start the program, etc., are very much in demand."

Making your software intuitive

"Today, people won't put up with lack of menus, with command-line-operated programs, and with simplistic stick-men graphics."

— Roger Jones, president of Shareware To-Go

For shareware, designing intuitive software is particularly important. People get to try your software before they pay for it. If they can't quickly get it running, they're likely to move on to the next program.

Two types of people will look at your program: those who read every word of the documentation before starting, and those who try to use the program without reading any of the documentation. I've found that there are a surprising number of the first type of person, people who read manuals. But the majority of people are of the second type. Most people want to put your shareware disk in their computer and give it a quick try to see if they like it before they commit to spending a lot of time with it. That is the advantage shareware offers users, the no-risk trial. But it makes your job harder.

Your program must be easy to use. If you want users to try your shareware, they must be able to get started without reading the manual. They must be able to use enough of the basic features of your software to get a good feel for how it works. They must be able to use the software well enough that they become interested in spending more time learning how to use it. Most importantly, they must not become frustrated and stop using your software.

Keep in mind that users want to spend as little time as possible learning new programs. They'll stay with their existing software, even though it has fewer functions and is less powerful, to avoid the hassle of learning a new program. If you have a program that's unique and has no competition, you might be able to get away with it being difficult to learn—but don't count on it.

What does it take to design intuitive software? For most programs, the user must be able to figure out how to use the basic functions with only a minimal amount of reading the manual. The best way to accomplish this is to provide a series of menus or prompts on the screen that identify the functions available. Pull-down menus are becoming very popular as a user interface, but be careful. Be sure to let the user know how to pull down a menu.

Do help screens make your software easier to use? I agree with Rosemary West when she says that very few people actually use help screens. They seem to be important in helping your software get a good review in a magazine, but they don't seem to be used. The problem with help screens is that they can display only a limited amount of information and it usually doesn't apply directly to what you're trying to do. Most users find it easier to use the reference section of the manual to find the information they need. I dropped help screens from my software almost four years ago and haven't had one user ask for them to be put back in, although users have asked for a lot of other changes in my software during the past four years.

Instead of relying on help screens, you're much better off making the user interface easy to understand and intuitive. The one place where help information is useful, however, is in your error messages. I'll talk about error messages shortly.

To make software intuitive, be sure to follow established standards for user interfaces. This is easy for some software. For example, if your software is designed to be used with Microsoft Windows or a Macintosh, Microsoft and Apple have published standards describing how the user interface must look and operate. Unfortunately, few standards exist for IBM DOS programs. Some authors follow the "WordStar standard," although this standard seems to be in decline. Others follow the "WordPerfect standard," but WordPerfect doesn't follow some of the traditional function-key assignments, such as using F1 for help. No one follows a "Lotus standard," because Lotus Corporation likes to sue people over user-interface standards.

To determine what standard your software should follow, review other software in the same category as yours and see how it handles the user interface. Also, look at the interfaces used by the best-selling retail programs. These will be the programs that a large number of people have. Thus, more people will be familiar with the standards used by these programs.

One standard that you should never violate is that the Esc key is used only to escape (or exit) the current function. Never use the Esc key to select or start a program function, or as a toggle key. Esc should be used only to exit from or stop the current function, or to exit from the program.

Whatever you do, be consistent. Function keys should activate the same function throughout the program. For example, don't use F5 to select a filename in one case and then F2 to select a filename in another part of the program. Maintain the same style and arrangement of information on all your screens. Don't change things around so that the user has to hunt for information with each new screen.

To help users know what they're supposed to do, always list the possible alternatives on the screen and provide a default based on the most likely choice. For example, if the user wants to select a new filename, list all the filenames in the selected directory and show the current filename as the default.

Intuitive software should appear to be simple. Don't clutter the screen with prompts for numerous functions. Include prompts only for the basic functions and allow the user to access menus or screens for more complex functions by using Alt-key combinations or pull-down menus. In designing your software, work to keep it simple. Some magazine reviewers like to compare software based on the number of functions each program offers. This has led developers to focus on adding features instead of designing software that solves problems. First design your software to solve users' problems in as easy a manner as possible. Once you've done that, then you can add features for reviewers to count.

Another important part of designing intuitive software is to make the program run in a way that matches how people think. For example, when most people make a typographical error, they want to fix it right away. They don't want to wait until they get to the end of a document and then go back to fix it. Always allow users to correct errors at any time, allow them to back up and correct mistakes on previous screens, and provide a way for them to change their mind. For example, it's very frustrating to start a large database sort and then realize there was something else you wanted to do, but you cannot stop the sorting process. Users should always be able to exit from whatever the computer is doing by pushing Esc. The best programs allow users to exit or shell to DOS, use another application, then return and continue the original function, picking up where it left off.

Also keep in mind that everyone thinks differently and that each of us is comfortable with different ways of doing things. Build some flexibility into your program. Allow users to select the screen colors they prefer. If your software includes sound effects, allow users to turn them off.

Handling errors

Error trapping and handling is one area many shareware authors have a problem with. There are just so many things a user can do to screw up your software. Plus, I've found that different versions of DOS report the same error in different ways, making it more difficult to identify a specific cause.

Error trapping is an important part of software design. When users try your software and run into an error, they need to know what caused the error and how to avoid it in the future. If they get an error message and can't get out of it, the most likely thing they'll try is rebooting the computer. If that doesn't fix the error, they'll probably delete your shareware program and move on to the next one.

The first step is to design the software to avoid errors. The fewer error messages the user sees, the better. Do this by designing your software so that it doesn't accept incorrect keystrokes or keystrokes that take it beyond a boundary condition. For example, in my database software, when someone tries to type beyond the end of a field, the software beeps and no longer accepts keystrokes.

Another way to avoid errors is to design software that includes features users expect in your type of software. For example, if you've written a word-processing program that doesn't provide word wrapping, users will continue to type beyond the right edge of the screen, possibly creating an error condition.

Even when you've done everything you can to prevent errors from happening, users will still find ways to get into error conditions. For example, they might try to access a function that isn't appropriate for what they're doing at the time. Or they might not have installed the software correctly. That is why you have to trap errors.

Trapping errors is easy; the hard part is explaining to the user why the error occurred and how to avoid it in the future. Every error should display an error message that provides the user with some help. In some cases, the explanation will be easy: the user was trying to print something and the printer was off. Other times, you might have to refer the user to the manual for a discussion of possible causes. Whatever you do, don't just display an error code and expect the user to figure it out.

Compilation

With compilers available at under a hundred dollars, it's surprising that anyone writes software that isn't compiled. However, a lot of GW-BASIC code is still released as shareware. Here is what the president of one of the largest shareware disk distribution companies had to say about compiling programs:

"People won't put up with GW-BASIC. We had an author, who is well known now, who submitted a program to us about a year ago. It was a wonderful program. It was in the area of financial planning. A great program, but it was in BASIC.

I called him and said 'You're telling users they should plan on an income of $100,000 a year and you don't even have your program compiled! You can't expect a person who is fairly well heeled and in the upper middle class, and who you want to use this disk, to first load BASIC. They're not going to fool with it."

That author compiled his program and now has seven successful shareware programs. His income from shareware now exceeds what he makes as a financial planner."

— Roger Jones, president of Shareware To-Go

Always compile your programs so they run as stand-alone .EXE files. Compiled programs also offer you many advantages because you can use some of the many programmer's libraries that are available. Libraries such as Crescent Software's QuickPak can add pull-down menus, error trapping, math functions, and access to DOS functions with little programming effort on your part. They'll make your program look professional and help it run faster.

Cleaning up

Sometimes, I concentrate so hard on getting something done that I forget about some of the final details. For example, you might design the greatest software that has ever existed for printing financial reports. It uses special fonts for titles and automatically carries totals from one report to the next. But if you don't send a form feed to the printer at the end of the last page, you'll have frustrated users. Yes, it's the little things that can bring down the best software.

You have to clean up after your software. Always return the computer's settings and the settings of any peripheral equipment to their default condition. For example, never leave a printer set to print in a special font or graphics mode. After all, that is what the master reset printer control code is for, to reset the printer back to its default settings. Use it!

When the user exits your software, close all files and return the video display to its default mode. Erase any temporary files your software might have created and clean up the computer's memory. If your software has done anything that affects the PATH statement or other internal settings of the computer, return them to their original condition. When your software is done running, the user should find no evidence that your software was used (other than the data or document files it might have created).

Finally, remember to keep things simple and thoroughly test your software!

Testing software

If you're a software author, you know that it typically takes 20–30% of your time to write the program code and 70–80% to test and debug it. Testing and debugging software is, by far, the most time-consuming and frustrating part of writing software. However, if approached logically and in an organized manner, the time can be minimized.

The best approach to testing software is to get someone else to help. Generally, you're too close to your software to do a good job of testing it. However, if you're like me, you'll probably do some of the initial testing yourself as you work with the program. The following are some guidelines to follow when testing software.

Be organized

Always write down what you do and what happens when you conduct a test run. Don't plan on remembering what happens. I find that using a spiral-bound notebook is very helpful. It keeps all of my notes about bugs, new features I want to add, user comments, etc., together in one place. If I run into a bug that I remember fixing previously, I can quickly look through my notebook to find the notes describing what I did the first time I "fixed" that bug.

Try each function, feature, and capability individually. This might seem obvious, but I've seen many authors plunge ahead, testing a variety of features all at one time. It might seem faster to try to do more than one thing at a time, but in the end it takes more time. Trying each function one at a time—in a methodical, orderly manner—helps you isolate and identify the cause of problems more quickly.

Test boundary conditions

A boundary condition is a point at which any movement, beyond that point, takes your software outside of normal operating conditions, while movement in the other direction easily falls within the operating conditions that your program can handle. For example, let's assume that you've written an accounting program and this program is designed to handle only positive numbers. A boundary condition occurs at the numbers −1, 0, and +1. Although your manual tells users to never enter a negative number, what happens if they do? What happens when zero is entered? What happens if a user enters the numbers 243,837,878,8287,888? This is a number that's far larger than your software can handle and it goes beyond the upper boundary.

Another boundary condition might distinguish among numbers, letters, and other keyboard characters. How does your software handle receiving a letter as the input when a number is expected? What happens when you enter punctuation? What happens when Ctrl-or Alt-key combinations are pushed?

Look for boundary conditions throughout your software. What happens when the user attempts to move the cursor off the top or bottom of the screen? Can the cursor be moved beyond the left and right boundaries? Be sure to check all the keys that are used to position the cursor. While the cursor movement might be fine when using the arrow keys, the Tab, PgUp, or PgDn keys might move it beyond a boundary or produce an unexpected response.

The first use of a program or function is a boundary condition. A function might work fine the first time, but produce odd characters, wrong calculations, out-of-memory messages, or invalid filename errors the second time it's used. Exiting a program is another boundary condition. Does your software allow users to exit without saving the file or document they were working on?

The largest and smallest amount of memory the software can cope with is another boundary condition. I test the memory limits of my software by first installing a small RAM disk. I increase the size of the RAM disk until my software runs out of memory and no longer runs. This tells me exactly how much memory my software requires. Keep in mind that as you use a program, it might open more files or require additional memory. Don't just boot your program and check for the opening menu. Use it a while to ensure that all of its functions work with the available memory.

Look for boundaries of time. How does the software handle the 30th and 31st at the end of a month? Can it handle the 28 days of February, and what happens in a leap year? What happens at noontime and midnight? How does your software handle the end of a year? Plus, keep in mind that we're only a few years away from the new century. Will your software be able to handle the 21st century?

Look for boundaries within data and document files. Can your software read the first record in a database correctly? The last record? How does the program mark the end of a record or the beginning of the next? What happens when the software tries to read data or a document that isn't in the correct format?

Test output

Try all of the printed reports offered by your software to be sure that they all print correctly. Are all the page breaks correctly skipped? What happens if the printer is turned off or disconnected? What happens when the printer runs out of paper? Keep in mind that when a computer sends something to a printer, it opens a file. If the CONFIG.SYS file doesn't have a high enough number in the FILES= statement, you'll get an error when trying to print a report. How is this error handled?

If your software uses a serial port, test to see what happens when the wrong serial port is specified. Does the software confirm that the specified port exists and that the information being sent actually was sent and received?

When storing information on a disk, can your software handle nine-character filenames or four-character filename extensions? If the user types an invalid filename, you want to be sure that the information doesn't end up in a file with an unrecognizable filename. What happens when the user tries to save a new file using an existing filename? Does the software provide a warning that the old file is about to be erased?

Never make assumptions when testing software. Never think that because you wrote the code, and that it was a simple piece of code, that it will function fine. Test everything. Make no assumptions. If you make a code change, test the function you modified and all related functions. Often, a change in one section of code can result in problems that will show up in another area.

Types of software errors

It's impossible to list every error a user might make. In fact, that list could be infinite. Every time I've seen someone announce that all possibilities were covered, a user manages to come up with something that wasn't anticipated. Being aware of the general types and categories of errors will help you do a better job when testing your software.

User interface errors   As you test your program, be aware of how it feels. To do this, you might need to put it aside for a while; otherwise, its operation will always feel natural. If there are areas in the program in which something feels awkward or confusing, then you need to make some changes. If you have someone else who can test your software, ask him to watch out for areas he doesn't feel comfortable with or in which he feels something is missing.

When testing software, pay attention to how the software keeps the user informed about what's going on. Are the error messages clear or are they insulting? I've seen software that intentionally insults users in an effort to "help" them remember how to avoid making certain errors. Don't do this—it will make users feel negative about you and your software.

How do people learn to use the program? The best way to test this is to give your program to a novice and watch as he tries to install and use it. Is the documentation complete? Does each screen provide a simple explanation of the functions available from that screen? Is it easy to get lost in the program? Are some commands easy to confuse with others? Are there places you can reduce the number of keystrokes required? Under what circumstances does the user make mistakes?

Error-handling errors   It sounds strange to say, but there can be errors in your error-handling routines. Try to intentionally cause errors and see how your software responds. Do you get the right error message? Are you able to correct the error or do you end up in an endless loop of error messages? Be sure to test all of the error-recovery routines. Do they properly recover from the error? Does recovering from an error result in the user possibly losing several hours of work?

Calculation errors   On my old CP/M computer, I used to have a terrible time dealing with the computer's rounding errors. I had spent $3,000 for a computer that couldn't even do arithmetic correctly. You should be aware that computers can lose precision as they perform calculations. This happens as a result of rounding off and truncation errors—even if the program code is correct. Look for these errors and change your code to avoid them.

Errors in handling data If you load a document into your word processor and then just let it sit for a few days, you might come back to find some things changed. No, the cat didn't walk across the keyboard and no one touched your computer. It's possible for parts of the computer's memory to change randomly for no visible reason. Possibly there was a spike in the line voltage. Maybe some radio interference caused a change. I've even seen computers that have been left on stop functioning for no apparent reason and then work fine when rebooted.

As your program handles data, watch for errors. When reading data from a file, be sure it's valid data. If, for example, the file has been erased, your program could read the remnants of old files and interpret this as valid data.

Version control

Version control is something many shareware authors ignore, but it's important. Here's where the good documentation of past problems and how you fixed them can be invaluable. For example, a bug you thought you had fixed can reappear if an old version of one subroutine is linked with the latest version of the rest of your program.

Also, check your opening screens to be sure the program has the right copyright message and version numbers. Make sure these match those in the documentation. Use version numbers to help you track changes, bug fixes, and updates. Some authors include a file on their shareware disk that lists all the versions and the changes made in each version. Even if you don't put this file on your disk, it's a valuable record you should have.

Making a shareware distribution disk

It's obvious that your shareware distribution disk will contain your program and documentation. But other information should be on your disk and you need to pay careful attention to what you name the files.

"In shareware, the naming of some of the programs is absolutely terrible. I can't tell you how many times a great disk has been submitted to us with the most archaic, technical, totally oblique name. A name that wouldn't begin to make it on Madison Avenue. Let's face it. Shareware, like anything else, has to be merchandised. You can't merchandise it with a name that turns people off or leaves them totally blank as to what the program does."

— Roger Jones, president of Shareware To-Go

"There is value in maintaining consistent file-naming conventions for your software. I've also seen a lot of software succeed because people have used a unique and descriptive name."

— Bob Mahoney, president of Exec-PC BBS

Naming files

When naming your files, you should use a name that helps describe what your software does. Then use that name as a part of naming all of the related files on your disk. I'll use my Play 'n' Learn software to provide some examples. The files on my Play 'n' Learn disk include:

```
PLAY.EXE
PLAYPGM.EXE
PLAY.DOC
PLAYREAD.ME
```

Notice that they all start with the word PLAY. By making the filenames similar, I ensure that they will stay together in a directory listing and it makes it easier for a user to identify them as belonging together. Why is this important? Because your files might be combined with other programs on a compilation disk or the user might dump a bunch of programs together in a directory on a hard disk.

The word PLAY also helps to identify these files as something fun to use. Instead of using PLAY, I could have used the initials of the program name, PNL. This would have resulted in the following filenames:

```
PNL.EXE
PNLPGM.EXE
PNL.DOC
PNLREAD.ME
```

Which set of filenames more clearly conveys a fun and interesting image? For me, at least, PNL doesn't create any type of image. The word PLAY does a much better job of describing the software and attracting attention.

Notice that I called the documentation file PLAY.DOC instead of MANUAL.DOC. I do this because it keeps the manual close to the program files in a directory listing. Another reason is that a lot of authors have already used MANUAL.DOC and your manual file could easily be erased and replaced by someone else's file when programs are combined in the same directory of a hard disk.

If you feel you must include an AUTOEXEC.BAT file or CONFIG.SYS file on your disk, be very careful. In testing software, one of the tests I run is to have a computer novice install and use the software. A couple of days ago, I got a call from one of my testers. His computer had stopped functioning. It booted okay, but the DOS prompt looked different and all of his software had disappeared. After having just paid $300 for WordPerfect, he was rather upset that it was no longer on his hard disk. He was also very angry with me for giving him a program that wiped out his hard disk.

I took a look at his computer and it was immediately obvious what had caused the problem. The program he was testing told him to copy the files from the floppy disk to his hard disk, which he did. He copied them directly to the root directory on his hard disk. This shareware disk also contained an AUTOEXEC.BAT and CONFIG.SYS file. They replaced the files in his root directory, his PATH setting was gone, and his computer could no longer find the files he normally ran, even though they were still there.

If you want to supply an AUTOEXEC.BAT or CONFIG.SYS file, give them other names and provide an installation file that renames them. For example, for my Play 'n' Learn software I could use PLAYAUTO.BAT and PLAYCON.FIG. This would help keep them grouped with the other Play 'n' Learn files and identify their function.

Documentation

Providing on-disk documentation brings up some special concerns. For example, be sure that your documentation is in straight ASCII, with no formatting commands or control characters included. You should be able to use the DOS TYPE command or Mac TeachText program to list it on the screen with no unusual characters, colors, or sounds appearing. To ensure that your documentation contains no control codes other than the control code for a formfeed, send the manual to your printer by typing:

```
COPY FILENAME.DOC LPT1:
```

replacing FILENAME.DOC with the name of your documentation file. I recommend using a formfeed at the bottom of each page. Because of the different number of lines printed by dot-matrix and laser printers, this is the only way to ensure that the printing is correctly positioned on each page.

Don't count on users knowing how to copy your manual to the printer using the method I've just described. Include a batch file or program on your disk that will automatically print the documentation. A batch file with a single line containing COPY FILENAME.DOC LPT1: is adequate.

The manual you provide on your shareware disk should be the same as what's supplied with the registered version of your software. The first page should be a title/cover page that also includes your copyright notice. Even the shortest manuals should have a table of contents that comes just after the title page. The next page or two should identify the software as shareware, provide a brief description of shareware and how it works, include your terms for distributing your shareware, and have a warranty and disclaimer as was discussed in chapter 9. Include any further details about shareware, the ASP, site licenses, and other programs that you publish in appendices at the end of your manual.

Each page of your manual should be numbered. Place page numbers in either the upper right or lower right corners of the page or centered at the bottom of the page. This is where most people expect to find page numbers. If your manual is more than 12 to 15 pages long, include an index.

Other files

Several other files should be included on your disks. These are files that aren't related to the operation of your software, but they provide more information about your software and the conditions under which it may be distributed. Two files you should include on every disk are:

VENDOR.DOC
FILE_ID.DIZ

In addition, you might want to include files such as:

PACKING.LST
README.1ST
ORDER.DOC (or ORDER.FRM)
SYSOP.DOC
GO.BAT
HISTORY.DOC

VENDOR.DOC provides the terms and conditions under which vendors may distribute copies of your software. These were discussed in chapter 11 and a sample distribution license was shown there. The VENDOR.DOC file also contains information that will help the vendor understand your program requirements and do a better job of promoting your software. This includes information such as a short and long description of your program, the system requirements, the registration price, whether you're a member of a professional organization, what users get when they register, and your address.

Try to keep this file short, preferably no more than 80 or 90 lines. VENDOR.DOC files that are too long become ineffective because disk distributors can't find the information they need. Put the important marketing information at the top of the page. This includes the program name, the recommended BBS filename, the short and long descriptions, and how to contact you. The terms and conditions covering distribution of your software should be on the lower half of the page. Keep the terms for distributing your software short and to the point. You want to provide legal protection for your software, but also keep in mind that when vendors are faced with a choice of two programs to carry, they will usually carry the one with the least restrictions. The following is infomation you might find in a VENDOR.DOC file (using my Play 'n' Learn as an example):

Program name   Play 'n' Learn

Version   2.15

Publisher   HomeCraft Software, P.O. Box 974, Tualatin, OR 97062

Numbers   (503) 692-3732 / CIS 71450,254 / Fax (503) 692-0382

Preferred BBS filename   PLAYNL.ZIP (or ARC)

System requirements   IBM PC, XT, AT, PS/2 or compatible with 256K of memory, CGA video (or better), and DOS 2.10 or later.

Short description   A set of eight educational games for children 18 months to 3 years old.

Description A program designed to introduce very young children, 18 months to 3 years old, to the computer and to help them learn about the alphabet, numbers, colors, and shapes. Games include simple keyboard response activities, color matching, shape matching, an "etch a sketch" type painting game, a lottery game based on the alphabet, plus an arcade-type game called Underground Alphabet. Reviewers have called Play 'n' Learn "one of the best available programs for very young children."

Keywords Educational, Children, Alphabet, Preschool, Kids.

Conditions under which this software may be copied and distributed Individual users may freely copy this disk and share it with friends and family.

Nonprofit groups (including user groups and BBSs) may distribute copies of this disk. A fee of no more than $5 may be charged to cover disk copying costs. If the files on this disk have dates more than a year old, we request that you contact us for a free upgrade to the current version.

Disk distributors and dealers must have written permission before selling copies of this disk. When you contact us, you will receive a free copy of the latest version and you will be placed on our mailing list to receive updates as they are released. Disk distributors may charge no more than $10 per disk for copies of this software. If, as a distributor, you supply copies to other resellers, the end price to the user may not exceed $10.

Anyone distributing copies of this software, whether for profit or as a nonprofit organization, must conform to the following:

The files on each disk may not be modified or adapted in any way. All of the files provided on the disk must be distributed together. Individual files or groups of files may not be sold separately. Additional files may be added and this software may be combined on a disk with other programs.

This software may not be represented as anything other than shareware and the shareware concept must be explained in any ad or catalog that includes this software and on any packaging used to display the disk.

You must immediately stop selling/distributing copies of this disk upon notice from the author or HCP Services, Inc.

Registration $15.00 (includes shipping)

Registered users get You can use check boxes for each of these and check off as many or as few as you want:

- Current version
- Biannual newsletter
- 1 year free updates
- Free phone support
- Free hard disk shell
- Printed manual
- Discounts on other software
- Tech support via fax

One of the best ways to stay up to date on the type of information included in VENDOR.DOC files is to be a member of either STAR or the ASP. For example, the June 1993 issue of STARgazer (STAR's newsletter) has an excellent article on VENDOR.DOC files. STARgazer is distributed as a shareware file and this issue is available in the UKSHARE forum on Compuserve and on many BBSs. Another way to stay up to date is to get copies of some of leading shareware programs and check the VENDOR.DOC files included with them.

The FILE_ID.DIZ file

Bulletin board software has become automated to the point where someone can upload a program and the BBS software will virus check it, extract a description of the program, and make it available for downloading—all without any action on the part of the sysop. For MS-DOS software, the BBS gets the description of the program from a file called FILE_ID.DIZ.

The FILE_ID.DIZ file is an ASCII text file. It can have up to eight lines of text, and each line can be no longer than 40 characters. The first line should contain the name of the program and the version number. Most BBSs provide users with the option of getting a one-line description of the available programs. The first line in the FILE_ID.DIZ file will be what they see.

The second line is also very important. Some BBS systems will display only the first two lines from the FILE_ID.DIZ file. So the second line should contain a concise description of what your software does. The remaining six lines can then be used to further describe the software and the benefits of trying it. Because of the need to fit a lot of information into a limited space, there is a tendency to ignore rules of grammar and punctuation in the descriptions in FILE_ID.DIZ files. This is okay, but be careful that you don't make it unreadable. Here is an example of a FILE_ID.DIZ file:

```
ORGANIZE! Your CDs, Albums & Tapes v5.60
Softw'r for cataloging music collections
Designed specifically for cataloging CDs
records, tapes, and video disks, the OYC
software makes keeping track of what you
have easy. Rated as THE BEST music cata-
loging software by numerous magazines.If
you want the best, give this one a try.
```

The PACKING.LST file contains a listing of the files you put on your disk and a short description on each file. You can also include the dates and size of each file. The PACKING.LST file accomplishes two things. It allows users to determine whether or not they have a complete copy of your software and identify any additional files added to the disk by someone else.

The SYSOP.DOC file provides distribution information for BBSs. In many cases, this file is nearly a duplicate of the VENDOR.DOC file with the references to distributors taken out. If that is the case, a SYSOP.DOC file only adds to building clutter on your disk and shouldn't be included.

For software that's primarily distributed by BBSs, such as communications software or file-compression software, it's very important to include the SYSOP.DOC file. For example, some authors feel it's very important that BBSs have only the latest version of their program. They'll personally call several hundred BBSs and upload the current version to each. In cases such as this, the author might not want to have BBSs distributing software without permission and a SYSOP.DOC file becomes the method for notifying sysops of the distribution conditions.

The ORDER.DOC file, or the ORDER.FRM file as it's sometimes called, is the order form customers can use to order the registered version of your software. It's an ASCII text file that needs to contain everything the user needs to know to register your software. This includes your name and address, your phone number, and whether or not you accept telephone orders. It should list the incentives and benefits of registering the software, the cost to register, and the shipping and handling charges. There needs to be a place where users can fill in their name, address, and phone number. And there needs to be a place for users to indicate how they're going to pay the registration fee, as well as place for a credit card number and expiration date. If you don't want to have to ship both $5^1/_4$-inch and $3^1/_2$-inch disks to everybody, provide some check boxes that can be used to specify the disk size needed.

A HISTORY.DOC file provides a list of the changes made in each version of the software. I never included a HISTORY.DOC file until I spoke with Marsha Meier, one of the disk reviewers at Public Brand Software. She pointed out that this is important information for disk vendors. When they receive an updated disk, the HISTORY.DOC file allows them to just check the features that have changed or been upgraded since the previous version. This greatly speeds up the evaluation process.

I use a README.1ST file to give the user information on how to install the software and read the documentation. I provide a GO.BAT file that prints the README.1ST file on the computer's screen. This combination of files gives you a way to help novice users understand what they need to do to get started.

I recommend that there be no more than 24 lines of information in a README.1ST file. Otherwise some of the information will scroll off the screen leaving some users confused.

As with anything else, there are no hard-and-fast rules, only general guidelines. We all approach our businesses differently and have different objectives, different products, and different markets. The key is to know your objectives and your market and adjust your distribution strategy to support your objectives.

Distributor identification

In the past, I used to put the distributor's name on every disk mailed out. My software was designed to read this name from the disk and print it on the registration form, thus allowing me to identify which distributor, BBS, or user group provided the disk that resulted in a registration. I could tell which ones generated a lot of registrations and which ones generated few or none. Because I had already put the name on the disk, I also could do the distributor a favor by displaying their name on the copyright screen each time the software was booted. Figure 13-1 shows the copyright screen for my software For Record Collectors.

It's sometimes very useful and interesting to notice where disks come from. For example, I just received a disk a user obtained from a distributor on the East Coast. The distributor was registered with me and I had provided them with update disks on a regular basis. But the disk contained a three-year-old version of my software and the name of a distributor in Texas. A quick call to the distributor helped get the correct version back into their library.

Having the distributor's name on my disks has also helped me identify distributors who might have a bad master disk. There have been several

```
        F O R   G U N   C O L L E C T O R S
           PC / MS-DOS   Version 1.00

      Copyright 1988, 1989, 1990 - Steven C. Hudgik

      This software is published as shareware by:

 HOMECRAFT COMPUTER PRODUCTS - P.O. Box 974 - Tualatin, OR
```

```
 SHAREWARE DISTRIBUTED BY: C.A.R.R.S.
                           219 Potomac Avenue
                           Buffalo, NY 14213
```

13-1 The opening screen for all my software gives the name and address of the distributor. When the user prints the registration order form, the distributor's name is automatically printed on it, allowing me to track which distributors sell disks that result in users registering.

occasions when users sent me bad disks for replacement and I've been able to identify them as all coming from one distributor.

Why do users send me their bad shareware disks? Because I guarantee that they have a good copy of my program or I'll replace their disk at no charge. It doesn't matter where they got the disk or who they got it from. If they're having a problem, I'll replace the disk. I do this because if users cannot try my program, they generally won't register. Plus, it's a good way to identify people who are interested in my software and get their names on my mailing list.

When I discontinued the For Record Collectors software in 1990, I replaced it with a new program called ORGANIZE! Your CDs, Albums, & Tapes, which used a different method for tracking the source of registrations. I generally have the disks I send to vendors duplicated by an outside service. Before I put them in an envelope so they can be mailed, I run them through my computer and use a little BASIC program to put a serial number on the order form. This allows me to tell which distributors are generating registrations for my software, and it's much quicker than putting the vendor's name on the disk, as I did in the past.

Compressing files

If you've created a large program, you might be thinking about putting it into a zipped or stuffed file. (A zipped file is a compressed archive created by the PKZip software. StuffIt does the same thing on a Mac.) For copies you're sending to BBSs, this is a must-do requirement. Many BBSes won't accept files unless they're zipped and contain a FILE_ID.DIZ file within the zipped file. A zipped file can be automatically posted on the BBS, saving the sysop a substantial amount of time.

However, for disks that are going to catalog vendors, I recommend that you don't zip your files. Many users, in particular users who have purchased shareware from a retail rack, don't know how to unzip files. Even if you provide PKUNZIP (the unzipping utility) and instructions in a README file, they still won't understand how to unzip a file, or they'll try to unzip onto the original floppy disk, or they'll try to read the README file by typing README at the DOS prompt.

If you need to compress your files, I recommend putting them in a self-extracting archive. This makes it easier for the user to get the files out of the compressed archive. Both PKZip and the LHA software can be used to create self-extracting archives.

Another approach you can take is to use the LZEXE utility. This utility compresses an EXE file by about the same amount as PKZip, and puts the EXE file in a self-extracting compressed file that has the same name as the original file. When the user runs the program, the EXE file self-extracts into the computer's memory. I use LZEXE with some of my software and find that a 210K .EXE file is compressed down to 95K. As far as the user knows, it's a 95K file, because the amount of time it takes for the file to decompress and load into memory isn't noticeable.

LZEXE provides another advantage. Viruses can't be spread by a file compressed with LZEXE. If a virus should infect an LZEXE compressed file, that file won't be able to decompress into the computer's memory. It can't execute and the virus spreads no further.

LZEXE is a small utility that you can find on CompuServe, GEnie, and most major BBSs. The documentation is in French, but most versions include an English language summary.

For additional information about what to put on your distribution disk, see chapter 14, which discusses the Association of Shareware Professionals. The ASP has minimum standards concerning information that must be on a distribution disk.

14
Professional associations

In chapter 9, I talked about how important it is to make contacts, to get to know people, and for people to get to know you. That is one of the main reasons for attending conventions and trade shows such as COMDEX. The best way to get to know people within the software industry, make contacts, meet people with similar interests, and get help with business questions is to join a professional association. There are three professional associations for shareware authors. I'll cover the two largest in this chapter. Both are international organizations with members around the world.

The Association of Shareware Professionals

If you want to learn more about how to be a successful shareware author, find the answers to questions about marketing your software as shareware, help promote the shareware concept, and help improve shareware's image of quality and professionalism—then join the Association of Shareware Professionals (ASP).

The Association of Shareware Professionals was formed by a group of shareware authors in 1987. It's now a group of about 300 authors (and growing) who believe in the shareware concept and who have agreed to abide by a professional code of ethics.

ASP objectives

The ASP has four purposes:

- To set standards for shareware authors and vendors.
- To educate users and, in particular, deal with misleading advertising

put out by some disk vendors and misleading information published in the press.

- To pool information and serve as a resource for shareware authors.
- To protect the shareware concept so it remains a viable and growing method of marketing software.

The most important thing about the ASP is that its members are professionals who act in a professional manner. Members must meet a minimum code of ethics and standards to maintain their membership. Applicants for membership are reviewed to ensure that they meet the requirements and standards.

The ASP works to educate users by publishing information in various files posted on BBSs and through discussions on CompuServe, exhibits at trade shows, and a vendor program that has gotten many vendors to stop listing shareware in the same category as freeware, demos, and public-domain software.

Through continuing discussions on CompuServe and via the ASP newsletter (ASPects), members help each other, answer questions, support each other, and help solve problems. Even if you aren't a member, you can ask questions and "listen" to conversations by going to the shareware forum (GO SHARE) on CompuServe. You'll find plenty of good advice and interesting discussions.

The ASP has taken significant steps to protect shareware. For example, as a result of ASP's efforts, the wording of a bill recently passed by Congress was changed. Without the change in wording, shareware would have lost copyright protection and would have been lumped in with public-domain software. This could have had a significant negative impact on shareware and, essentially, eliminated shareware as an effective means of distributing software.

Why you should join the ASP

Throughout this book, I've mentioned the ASP and recommended that all shareware authors be members. I've also mentioned benefits such as professional contacts. The following is a summary of why you should be an ASP member:

Learn how to be successful   As I've already mentioned, the ASP is the place to learn how to be a successful shareware author. This is the benefit mentioned by every ASP member I interviewed and, in most cases, the only reason given. In my interviews, there were many success stories about how registrations doubled or tripled after an author joined the ASP and started to apply new methods.

Exposure   The ASP sponsors events that give you the opportunity to gain exposure to the press and the public. They've had booths at both COMDEX and PC Expo. Authors can use the booth to help promote shareware and to promote their own products. The ASP also sponsors a party at COMDEX that gives authors the opportunity to meet the press and other authors.

Protect the shareware concept   One of the more important benefits is that the ASP has been fighting to keep the word *shareware* in the public domain. ASP has filed protests on three different continents to prevent people from using it as a trademarked word.

If a magazine publishes an article that misrepresents shareware, the ASP will respond with a letter that, in many cases, gets published in the magazine's letter section. It helps the author of the article to better understand shareware and, through publication in the letters section, hopefully, clears up the misinformation.

Meet professional standards   Another benefit is that by agreeing to the ASP standards, you tell potential customers that you're meeting standards of professionalism and quality. Your users know they won't get crippled software. They know they can get support. They know you operate in an ethical manner. Although today the ASP label on software has limited effect, as users become better educated and more aware of what the ASP stands for, the value of being able to identify yourself as an ASP author will grow.

Why join if you're already successful?

In talking to some highly successful authors who aren't members of the ASP, they told me that they didn't need to be members of the ASP because they had "already made it." There was nothing further they could learn or gain from ASP membership. Unfortunately, this isn't true. The ASP continuously provides you with benefits, even if you've achieved great success. The ASP's efforts in Congress, in protecting shareware, and in working to get shareware recognized as a professional way of marketing software benefit all shareware authors and publishers. So even if you've made it and know all there is to know, your membership in the ASP helps support shareware and ultimately helps you.

Disk distributors and BBSs

The ASP also offers membership to disk distributors and BBSs. One of the reasons vendors and BBSs join the ASP is because many ASP members automatically send their disks to all ASP-member vendors and BBSs. Authors do this because they know an ASP vendor or BBS won't misrepresent their software. The need for the vendor or BBS to contact the author for permission to distribute the software is eliminated. It's a great way to reduce paper and I'm all for anything that reduces paperwork!

How to join the ASP

The following is a letter that's included in the ASP application package. It provides an excellent summary of the ASP and being a shareware author.

This letter serves as an introduction to the disk that the ASP sends out to prospective members. The files described in the letter are available by writing to the ASP, at the address at the end of the letter, and requesting an application (specify either DOS or Macintosh disk). You can also download them from the shareware forum on CompuServe.

Dear Author,

Thank you for your interest in becoming a member of the Association of Shareware Professionals (ASP). We are a group of shareware authors who are working to improve the image of shareware as an alternative way of purchasing high-quality software.

Many of us operate by ourselves and have a "regular daytime" job and operate our software businesses during the evenings and weekends. Others of us, through hard work and "the right product," are running our shareware business full time, and a few even have a dozen or so employees. The term "right product" means that the author has developed a product that is highly needed, has wide appeal, is highly acclaimed, and that the author worked hard at marketing and became highly successful. Not all of us (myself included) are in that category.

Many of us target our software to a niche in the software market. We realize that our expertise is in that niche and are willing to write to that limited market. We can't all write good word processing, database, communications, or spreadsheet software. We have discovered that we can be compensated for our efforts through registrations, without the HIGH cost of advertising and distribution associated with the "traditional" methods of software distribution. Most of us really enjoy the direct contact with our customers. This allows our shareware to live and grow in ways that are just not possible with the "traditional" methods of distribution.

I have placed several files on this disk to help you prepare your software and documentation for ASP membership.

APPLIC.FRM READ THIS FILE!!! This is the full file that describes in detail what is expected of the ASP author's software and documentation. One of the MOST important sections contains ASP's No Crippling policy. This is the sticking point on many applications. All of us FIRMLY believe that the potential registrant MUST be able to make an accurate "buy" decision based on a freely distributed shareware disk.

Some shareware has created a bad name for our industry by being highly crippled as a registration incentive. If your shareware does not meet the No Crippling policy, you should either meet the requirements or withdraw your application.

Speaking for myself, when I revised my software to fully document and include ALL features on the shareware disk, my registration rate went up significantly!

APPLIC.TXT This is the last few pages of APPLIC.FRM and is the application form itself. Fill this out and CompuServe mail or U.S. mail (on disk) this file to our Executive Director after you have filled it out. In accordance with the instructions in APPLIC.FRM, sign a paper copy of APPLIC.TXT and mail with the disk containing the filled-out APPLIC.TXT file. BE SURE to either mail the disk or e-mail the filled-out APPLIC.TXT file or your application will be delayed until you do send the file. Myself and the reviewers are all volunteers and having this ASCII file will save us a lot of time {many thanks!}.

Please COMPLETELY describe your shareware in the section titled Major Features. Take as much room at this point in the file as you wish. If you just say "see attached" and include a paper write-up, I will return the disk to you to complete. I have a tough time stuffing brochures into my A: drive {grin}.

Please COMPLETELY describe ANY differences between your freely distributed shareware disk and what is sent to registrants. If you leave this blank, the application will come right back to you.

SHAREW.PRN Your documentation should contain a description of the shareware concept. You may wish to include a warranty and you must include something that lets the registrant know what he/she will get for registering. Paul Mayer developed the text in this file as an example of this type of text wording. Feel free to include portions or all of this file in your documentation.

GUIDE.EXE This self-extracting file contains a WEALTH of information put together by Nelson Ford. Just type GUIDE (enter) and this file will self-uncompress into a set of text files. It will give you a lot of ideas for preparing and marketing your shareware.

REASONS.TXT A collection of messages from the ASP's open forum on CompuServe that give many good reasons to join the ASP.

The address of our Executive Director is:

Executive Director
Association of Shareware Professionals
545 Grover Rd.
Muskegon, MI 49442
CompuServe PPN: 72050,1433

Thank you,

George Abbott
ASP Author Membership Coordinator

ASP membership application

Statement of purpose of the ASP   The ASP is an association for shareware authors with the general goals of educating shareware authors, distributors, and the public; setting standards; and sharing resources and information among members.

Definition of shareware   For the ASP's purposes, *shareware* is software that meets the following general criteria:

- It's a complete program, i.e., it performs all of the major functions normally expected of a program of its type, unlike a commercial demo, which usually has a major function disabled. (The distinction is sometimes a judgment call, and the ASP has a procedure for arriving at such a judgment if necessary.)
- It's copyrighted (as opposed to uncopyrighted software, which is termed *public-domain*).
- It can be copied for others to try out, subject to copying restrictions that the author might choose to require.
- Registration fees can be required from the user as a condition of continued use of the program beyond a trial-usage period. Not requiring such a fee or requiring fees only from specific types of users,

such as businesses and government but not individuals, does not disqualify a program from being considered shareware.

- Compliance with specified standards can be required from anyone copying the program for a fee or in conjunction with any business enterprise.

Membership criteria   Membership is open to programmers who are authors of at least one "nontrivial" program (in the judgment of a membership committee) that's currently marketed and supported as shareware, who agree to abide by standards adopted by the association and whose membership, in the judgment of the membership committee, will not be detrimental to the goals or reputation of the ASP.

Access to CompuServe is not required, but it's anticipated that this is where much of the decision-making process will take place because of relative ease of access. I encourage those who don't want to use CompuServe or can't get access to it to join the ASP anyway. Communication will also be accomplished via newsletters and possibly by other means.

ASP membership requirements   These requirements are followed by all members of the ASP. When accepted as a member, you'll be required to abide by them.

These requirements apply to all programs you produce that are distributed as shareware (even if the ASP name or the word *shareware* are not used). By applying, you're confirming that all your shareware programs meet these requirements. The one program you submit is evaluated for the nontriviality test (which applies only to that program) and standards of professionalism (which apply to all programs).

The following sections contain the general standards that all ASP authors (full members) have agreed to follow. Each was passed by at least a ²/₃ vote of those members voting and is binding on all authors. They consist of a support policy, a policy on payments, a policy on noncrippled software, an ombudsman policy, and some miscellaneous items.

ASP software support policy

All ASP members' shareware products must provide support (included in the purchase price) for a minimum of three months from the date of registration. If the support is by telephone, there may be a limitation on both the total connect time and the period after purchase during which it's available without additional cost, so long as the connect time is at least 30 minutes during the required three months. Support may be provided for a fee after this initial period has elapsed. The support policy must be clearly stated in the shareware documentation. Support during the initial period can be one or more of the following:

- Mail support.
- Telephone support (if this is the only support provided, at a mini-

mum an answering machine must be available for four hours per day; this support may be limited to thirty minutes of connect time at the option of the author).

- For communications products, or ones associated with a communications product by a BBS or major communications service.
- By any alternate method approved by the ASP Board of Directors by a $^2/_3$ vote (of those directors voting).

The minimum level of support required by this policy involves answering questions and fixing serious bugs during the minimum three-month period. For problems involving a specific hardware or software environment or feature, the author may choose not to modify the program. In that case, if the report is within three months after purchase, then the author shall offer to refund the user's purchase price.

Any money sent to an author to register an unsupported product shall be promptly returned with an explanation that the product in question is no longer supported.

Known incompatibility with other software or hardware and major or unusual program limitations must be noted in the documentation that comes with the shareware (evaluation) program.

ASP registration payment policy

The documentation must clearly describe how to register the product and what goods and/or services the user will receive for registering.

Fees must be expressed in fixed monetary amounts. Voluntary payments or contributions may not be solicited, although phrasing such as "if you use and like this product, please register" is allowed.

Multiple levels of registration may be set, as long as each level individually satisfies the above two requirements.

The ASP policy is on no crippling. The principle behind shareware is "try before you buy." ASP believes that users have a right to try a fully functioning shareware program in their computing environment. Accordingly, ASP authors agree that:

- The executable files (and/or items linked in with executables) in their shareware and registered versions will be the same (with the exceptions noted below).
- All the program's features will be fully documented.
- Registration encouragement procedures that, in the judgment of the board, are either unreasonable or unprofessional are not allowed.

Exceptions to a strict interpretation of this policy are as follows:

- To save disk space, tutorial and additional explanatory material may be left out of the shareware documentation.

- The shareware version may have registration encouragement procedures absent from the registered version (or they can be disabled with a code provided only to registered users). The term *registration encouragement procedure* means a method for alerting users of their duty to register the program. Permitting registration encouragement procedures is not to be construed as a means of avoiding the anti-crippling requirements.

Registration reminder screens should:

- Be displayed no more than twice each time the program runs (or twice per day for long-running programs such as TSRs).
- Not require more than two keystrokes to bypass.
- Not have a forced minimum display time of more than three seconds. In other words, the screem shouldn't take control of the computer away from the user for more than three seconds.

Practices such as creating undocumented hidden files or printing a registration form without the user's knowledge or consent are prohibited. It is not necessary to have any of these procedures—a simple "strike any key to continue" is the least objectionable to the user.

The registered version may include sample files not included in the shareware version.

If source code is offered with the registered version, it may be withheld from the shareware version.

The author may provide two shareware versions: a small version that the author designates as the distributed version in normal circumstances (e.g., language tools in C available only in one model) and the full shareware version, available from some public source (possibly for a small distribution fee), which may be copied for trial purposes. The small version's documentation must clearly describe how users can obtain the full shareware version.

The author may provide an enhanced retail version of the program so long as it is not (in the opinion of 60% of the Board of Directors) merely an attempt to circumvent the nocrippling policy.

The author may provide registered users with bonus utilities unrelated to (and that don't change) the basic functionality of the program.

Registered users may be given utilities that provide a convenience but that aren't essential.

Exceptions are approved by the ASP Board of Directors by a 60% vote (of those voting).

ASP Ombudsman policy

The board shall set up the Office of Ombudsman and appoint someone to that position. The Ombudsman's sole role shall be to mediate disputes between ASP members and their customers. The Ombudsman shall report to the board situations where he feels board action or knowledge is appropriate. All ASP members and vendor associate members are required to cooperate with the Ombudsman when approached.

The shareware version of any program produced by an ASP member must contain the following text as part of some file on the disk (the shareware version means the one intended for trial use):

This program is produced by a member of the Association of Shareware Professionals (ASP). ASP wants to make sure that the shareware principle works for you. If you are unable to resolve a shareware-related problem with an ASP member by contacting the member directly, ASP may be able to help. The ASP Ombudsman can help you resolve a dispute or problem with an ASP member, but does not provide technical support for members' products. Please write to the ASP Ombudsman at 545 Grover Road, Muskegon, MI 49442 or send a CompuServe message via CompuServe Mail to ASP Ombudsman 70007,3536.

This statement must be included in the shareware version of any program. Versions of ASP shareware sent to users when they register with the author or his direct agent shall also have the Ombudsman statement, but it may be in a written form included in the registration package. Packages of the registered version (essentially identical to those sent to registered shareware users) intended for sale in retail establishments or primarily retail mail-order firms need not have an Ombudsman statement included. However, if the version contains any reference to shareware, it must also contain the Ombudsman statement. Members are free to include the Ombudsman statement in printed documentation, ads, and other mailings.

The first sentence of the statement may be replaced by "(member's name) is a member of the Association of Shareware Professionals (ASP)." If a member's company qualifies under the company name policy, the company name may be used instead of (member's name).

ASP-approved vendors must include the following statement with their catalogs and newsletters, and are encouraged to include it with all disks sold:

Company X is an approved vendor and associate member of the Association of Shareware Professionals (ASP). ASP wants to make sure that the shareware principle works for you. If you are unable to resolve a shareware-related problem with an ASP member by contacting the member directly, ASP may be able to help. The ASP Ombudsman can help you resolve a dispute or problem with an ASP member, but does not provide technical support for members' products. Please write to the ASP Ombudsman at 545 Grover Road, Muskegon, MI 49442 or send a CompuServe message via CompuServe Mail to ASP Ombudsman 70007,3536.

The Ombudsman statement may not be hidden in a file, which 60% of the Board of Directors regard as obscure.

ASP miscellaneous standards

A program should be thoroughly tested by the author and should not be harmful to other files or hardware if used properly. Any discussion of the shareware concept and of registration requirements is done in a professional and positive manner.

The program's author will respond to people who send registration payments, as promised in the program's documentation. At a minimum, the author will acknowledge receipt of all payments.

The author will keep the ASP apprised of changes in his mailing address and of any changes in the status of his programs.

Membership dues The ASP has annual membership dues. First-year dues are currently $50 per year, prorated from the quarter the applicant is accepted for membership. Subsequent yearly dues are currently $75. The $50 dues check must be sent in with your application.

Mailing-list option The ASP provides mailing lists to outsiders. The mailing list, provided as labels and not in electronic form, is provided by whomever keeps the official ASP membership list (currently the Secretary). The list consists solely of names and addresses and not phone numbers. Members have the option of being included in the mailing list or not, as follows:

Your name will be included on this list unless you indicate that you don't want it included by checking the box on the application. At any time, any member may change his include/exclude status by notifying the keeper of the list in writing or via Easyplex.

Applying for membership The three easy steps to apply for membership in the ASP are as follows:

1. Write to the ASP and request a membership application. The address is:
   Association of Shareware Professionals
   545 Grover Rd.
   Muskegon, MI 49442-9427
2. Read and understand the guidelines. If you're in compliance with the guidelines, then you may apply for membership. All of your shareware programs must comply with the ASP requirements, not just the submitted program.
3. Fill out the application and mail it together with a copy of the program you elect to use as your submission for review.

Shareware Trade Association and Resources (STAR)

STAR is a newly formed group and has just started to become organized. A meeting was held at the 1992 Summer Shareware Seminar at which the basic foundations of STAR were established. By the time the 1993 SSS came around, they were ready to hold their first membership meeting. However, they're still working on and developing ideas for various activities that they want to sponsor or support. STAR also publishes a newsletter called STARgazer, on an irregular schedule, that is an excellent source of information about shareware.

STAR's approach is very different from that of the ASP. Membership in STAR is open to anyone who is interested in shareware, including authors, vendors, BBSs, and users of shareware. Similar to the ASP, STAR sponsors various events and meetings for its members.

For more information about STAR write to:

STAR
P.O. Box 13408
Las Vegas, NV 89112
702-735-1980

The Association of Shareware Authors and Distributors (ASAD)

The ASAD is the third professional association in the industry. It was established in August 1992 to help promote the shareware concept and to assist members in reaching their professional goals. Anyone interested in making the shareware concept work can join.

ASAD is establishing a network of BBS nodes that authors can use for distributing their shareware, plus a free 800 number members can use to upload shareware to the ASAD Headquarters BBS. ASAD also provides a disk-mailing service for its members. If you would like information on the ASAD, write to:

ASAD
2425 N. Limestone Street
Springfield, OH 45503-1109

Other software associations

I also recommend that you join other associations that might help you make useful business contacts or learn more about software publishing. If there is a software association in your state, you'll find it very helpful to join that group. Only a few states have software associations at this time. They are:

Software Entrepreneur's Forum
P.O. Box 61031
Palo Alto, CA 94306
415-854-7219

Southeastern Software Assoc.
P.O. Box 467190
Atlanta, GA 30346
404-458-3835

Illinois Software Assoc.
c/o Richard A. Reck, President
KPMG Peat Marwick
303 E. Wacker Dr.
Chicago, IL 60601
312-938-5052
312-938-0449 (fax)

Massachusetts Computer Software Council
581 Boylston St.
Boston, MA 02116
617-437-0600
617-437-6297 (fax)

Minnesota Software Assoc.
c/o Tom Kolbo, President
P.O. Box 14965
Minneapolis, MN 55414
612-331-8844

Software Entrepreneurs and Developers Assoc.
c/o Karl Smith, President
3825 Academy Pkwy. South, NE
Albuquerque, NM 87109
505-344-8891

Software Asso.of Oregon
Ken Maddox, Executive Director
1600 NW Compton Dr., Suite 345
Beaverton, OR 97006
503-690-1395

Washington Software Assoc.
18804 North Creek Pkwy., Suite 112
Bothell, WA 98011
206-483-3323
206-485-8475 (fax)

15
Profiles of success

In this chapter I'm going to tell you about five successful shareware companies and describe how they got started and what they did to achieve their success. I picked the companies for these profiles by calling some of the larger disk vendors and asking them which programs they thought were particularly outstanding. Of the five I selected, three were published by full-time shareware companies and two were published by part-time authors. This way you can see how both kinds of authors handle their business.

Before I begin, let me give you my definition of a financially successful shareware company. In my opinion, a financially successful shareware company has over $75,000 in sales for a full-time author and over $25,000 in sales for a part-time author. In the profiles in this chapter, all three of the full-time shareware companies each have well over $100,000 in annual sales. The part-time companies each have over $25,000 in annual sales.

As you read these profiles, keep in mind that the advice given comes from very specific points of view. The information in the profiles was provided by representatives of each company and represents their opinion. For each company, I interviewed either the founder of the company or one of the first employees. As the companies have expanded, each has had to face different problems and situations. As a result, each company has different ideas about what is important. Keep in mind that, other than the fundamental business principles, there are no standard rules that are right for everyone.

What are fundamental business principles? The full-time shareware companies all had several important characteristics in common:

- The underlying secret of their success is that they all produced quality software that people needed and wanted to buy.

- They all did extensive market research to find out what users needed, what users liked and disliked about existing software, and what the competing software's strengths and weaknesses were.
- The shareware they produce positively identifies itself as shareware in multiple ways. It explains how shareware works and it provides an easy, convenient way for users to register.
- The people profiled have an attitude I call "make something happen." They didn't sit around and wait for something to happen; they actively went out and made it happen. They weren't always successful, but when they failed they learned from their mistakes and went on to try another approach.

These four key characteristics are fundamental business principles. There are others, such as being aware that starting a full-time software company generally requires the involvement of more than one person, and, as you'll see in the first profile, it requires one person to be dedicated to marketing. But I feel that these four key characteristics are the underlying foundation of success in shareware.

I encourage you to get the shareware versions of the software published by the companies described here. See how they present their shareware and encourage users to register. I also encourage you to use and register the software made by each of these companies. They are all quality programs and an excellent value.

Profile #1

Contact Plus Corporation
P.O. Box 372577
Satellite Beach, FL 32937
407-779-4900

Ed Trujillo, President
Roger Arias, Marketing Director

Contact Plus Corporation publishes business software to automate offices and enhance productivity. Products include:

- Contact Plus Personal (contact management system)
- Contact Plus Professional (not available as shareware)
- Contact Plus LAN (not available as shareware)
- VMSYS (vehicle management system)
- Hours, Expenses, Miles (HEM) (tracking business expenses)
- ZeppeLAN (utilities for Novell networks)
- Quotes & Invoices (quotes and billing system; not available as shareware)
- A variety of add-on products for use with Contact Plus

The story of the beginnings of Contact Plus Corporation is a typical example of how many shareware authors get their start: they write a small program they need for themselves, offer it as shareware to see what will happen, and listen to user feedback to improve the software. As a result, Contact Plus Corporation has grown become a substantial company. Here's the story of how Contact Plus Corporation became one of shareware's success stories.

Success doesn't come on the first try

In 1985, Ed Trujillo left his job at Hewlett-Packard and formed a partnership with a friend to start a company called Dalton Software. They created a $4000 vertical market software package that they were soon selling directly to a variety of businesses. The first year was rough, but by the beginning of the second year they started to make some money. Unfortunately, as happens many times in partnerships, there were some disagreements and, a 1 1/2 years after Dalton Software was formed, the partnership came to a bitter and sour end.

Ed lost everything. The only thing he had left was his sports car, and he sold that to purchase a 286 computer and a car that could be called only "$500 worth of basic transportation." He was determined not to go back to Hewlett-Packard and try to get his old job back. So, to pay the bills, he started working as a consultant. He was able to get a contract with the Air Force and several other small clients. But he felt he needed a project of his own to work on. Ed had time available—he was a bachelor and didn't have a television set. He also needed a completed application that he could show to prospective clients. He needed to write some software.

At about the same time, someone told Ed about CompuServe. So he bought a modem and started looking through the software available on CompuServe. He needed software to help him keep track of his phone calls, but he couldn't find any good software of this type on CompuServe. So he decided to write it himself. That was the start of Contact Plus.

At the time he didn't plan to start a company based on his software. He just wanted to write a program and get more experience. He posted his program on CompuServe and started to get a lot of feedback. People were suggesting new features, such as adding a dialer and a notepad. These were things he didn't need himself, so he hadn't put them in the software. But as people asked for new features, Ed changed the software and uploaded improved versions to CompuServe.

He started trying to earn a little bit of money with his software by asking people to donate money if they used the software. He didn't receive one donation. However, his software did receive some nice compliments. When the next version was released, Ed required a $30 registration fee from people who used his software.

Ed's first break can early in 1988 when the *PsL Newsletter* ran a short but positive review of his software—and, as a result, he got a couple of registrations. He continued to work on and improve the software. He listened to what users where telling him and continued to add the features they wanted. He released another new version later that year and increased the price to $79. Then in September 1988 *InfoWorld* published a good review and sales began to pick up. Although his software was now being reviewed in a mainstream computer publication, it was still packaged in baggies and came with a primitive manual and hand-written invoice. Ed had a start, but there was still a long way to go.

The success of Contact Plus is based on quality, and that quality started to pay off when, in January 1989, *Business Marketing Magazine* ran a review that called it the "best buy of the year." As a result of that review, Ed sold a hundred copies, and decided that pumping out products was easier than consulting.

First employee

Ed started by hiring his sister to help with the phones. This was an important step in the growth of Contact Plus Corporation. Having someone else answer the phone made Ed's small software company look a little bigger. When you're selling software to other businesses, it doesn't make a good impression to have the president answering every single phone call. Corporations like to feel that they're buying from a substantial company, not someone working out of a closet in his home.

Ed's first full-time employee was Roger Arias. Roger had just left the military and was looking for the opportunity to get into upper management. A small, growing company such as Contact Plus Corporation could offer that opportunity. If Roger had gone to work for a large corporation, he would have had to start at the bottom and, by the time he reached retirement age, might have been able to work himself up into the middle level. However, Contact Plus Corporation could offer him the opportunity to start at both the bottom and top simultaneously. He was emptying the office trash cans at night, but talking to corporate presidents during the day. The idea was that if the company did well, everyone would prosper.

At the time Roger was hired, the orders were still sporadic. The company was averaging three to four hundred dollars per day (about $100,000 per year), but Ed knew that it takes more than one person to make a company grow. If he was to increase his sales, he was going to need help. One person has a limited scope of vision and not enough time to do everything that needs to be done.

Focus on what you do best

After hiring Roger, Ed was able to focus on programming. He kept a check list of user suggestions, and continued to incorporate those suggestions into his software. There was now someone else who could pay attention to marketing, someone who could look at the commercial products that were available and see what was needed to improve Contact Plus in order to make it competitive with retail software.

In order to get copies of their competition's software with the limited budget they had at the time, they obtained copies of the competition's demo disks. They looked at every competitive product they could find, learning about their weaknesses and how to improve Contact Plus at the same time.

Publicity

While Ed worked on improving the software, Roger's goal was to get publicity for it. He didn't know what he was supposed to do or how "the system" worked; he just started calling magazines. He made a lot of mistakes. He embarrassed himself in front of editors. But he was persistent, and he eventually did get to know the key people at the magazines. Roger now offers these suggestions for people who are trying to get publicity for their products:

"When contacting the press don't assume everyone wants to look at your product. At companies like *PC Magazine* the average editor may get 100–200 packages per week. Only a very few of those get looked at at all. And if it looks like Bob's product—a white box wrapped in saran wrap or something—it has a real low chance of getting looked at. So it has to look real professional if you want to get in there. Professional packaging is expensive and difficult for shareware authors to do, but it does help.

Having a professional-looking package is tough for a shareware author just getting started, but there are ways around this problem—we did it with phone calls. The key was to get the software package off the editor's shelf and on the editor's desk. At *PC Magazine*, at the end of the week they throw all the software on the shelf away.

What I did was to call them and ask some questions. Remember, your product needs to have some unique aspect to it in order to get it there in the first place. If there is nothing unique about it that you can talk about, then you don't have much of a chance.

When you call, don't ask 'Have you seen my product?' The answer will be 'No.' Instead, ask 'What aspects of the program did you find intriguing?' In our case, I would ask 'Did you find the WordPerfect interface to be particularly useful?' And then I'd try to bring some statistics in such as 'Did you know that 80% of all DOS-based word processors are WordPerfect? And those people are looking for a product like this.'

It also serves to embarrass them somewhat if you end up the conversation by saying 'Well, I'll check back with you in a few days.' If your software is unique and of interest to their readers, they will then try to look at your software before you call back in order to prevent you from embarrassing them twice."

Registration incentives

At Contact Plus Corporation, they feel that success is not just a matter of registration incentives, it's how the product is presented. If you look at a lot of products in shareware, you'll find that most don't do a good job of promoting themselves. In many cases you can't even tell they're shareware. At Contact Plus Corporation, they've taken an approach that clearly identifies their software as shareware.

This isn't something that can be done with a README file. End users don't know about README files and they don't read them. The first screen in Contact Plus identifies it as shareware. It's not a "nag" screen; it just clearly and concisely identifies the software as shareware.

After the software has been used 50 times, a new screen comes up that says "Congratulations! You've used this software 50 or more times . . ." and gently reminds users that, if they plan to continue to use the software, then they must register it.

On the main menu screen, there is a large box with menu choices. Below that is the prompt ALT–O to Order (see FIG. 15-1). When the user pushes Alt–O, the software prints an order form and explains about shareware and Contact Plus.

The user also has the option of pushing Alt–S for a "slide show," which demonstrates what the program does.

Make a copy for a friend

A unique feature in the registered version of Contact Plus is that users can push Alt–C to make a copy for a friend. Pushing Alt–C takes the registered version and creates a shareware version that users can give to friends. When people like the software they're using, they tend to like to pass it on to other people. It's easy to copy disks, so many people tend to copy the registered version. The Alt–C option makes it easier to make a shareware version, and users tend to do that instead of copying the registered version.

The only difference between the shareware and registered versions is that the shareware program doesn't include a manual. The manual isn't available for the shareware version, but with the detailed help screens provided as a part of Contact Plus, including help that's immediately available on the first screen (FIG. 15-2), most people can easily use the software without the manual.

The Alt–C feature puts the registration reminder screens back into the software and removes the bonus utilities that are available only in the registered version. Removing these utilities doesn't cripple the software—they aren't required for using the program—but they can make using it more convenient.

For example, the shareware version supports only ports COM1 and COM2; the registered version supports COM ports 1 through 4. When using the shareware version, people can switch their COM ports around, but

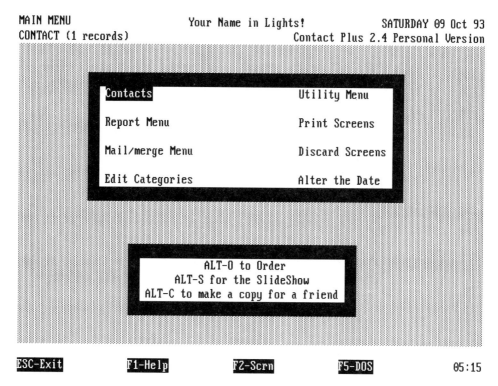

Contacts   Utility Menu

Report Menu   Print Screens

Mail/merge Menu   Discard Screens

Edit Categories   Alter the Date

ALT-O to Order
ALT-S for the SlideShow
ALT-C to make a copy for a friend

ESC-Exit   F1-Help   F2-Scrn   F5-DOS   05:15

15-1 The main menu screen of Contact Plus provides an Alt–O option to print an order form and an Alt–C option to create a shareware copy for a friend.

it's more convenient to have support for all four COM ports. Another feature of the bonus utilities is that they allow the user to transfer records from one database to another within Contact Plus. The utilities also provide for importing data from other programs.

Contact Plus's strategy

The company's main strategy is to apply Apogee's trilogy philosophy to business software. Apogee's approach of using a trilogy of games to get people to register has become one of the most well-known examples of how to be successful in shareware. What Apogee does is to release the first game of a series of three games as shareware. If you want to get the second and third games in the series, you have to register the software.

Contact Plus is like that in that there's a series of different versions of increasing power. There's no heavy sales push to get people to buy the more advanced versions, but when they do they get 100% credit for their previous purchases. This means that users don't have to pay for what they've already bought. They can upgrade to a more advanced version at any time at a reasonable price without losing what they paid for the previous version. And, over time, most people do purchase the more advanced version.

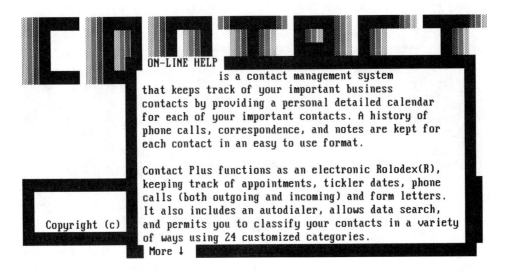

15-2 Starting with the opening copyright screen, Contact Plus provides detailed help information when you press the F1 key.

Technical support

Contact Plus Corporation is very focused on their customers. Starting from the days when Ed, working in his closet at home, kept a check list of user suggestions, they've continued to make customer service a top priority. Technical support is available to anyone who calls. And if someone is trying to use an old shareware version, they'll send them the current version for free.

Business planning

Business planning is important at Contact Plus Corporation. People like Roger regularly attend small-business conferences to help them keep their business planning skills sharp. They feel that they need to have a plan in order to know where they're heading.

In creating a business plan, they try to look ahead and then develop products they know will sell. What does Contact Plus Corporation see in the future? Windows software is where sales will be coming from. People are buying more Windows-based products and are no longer buying DOS programs. As a result, their current plan is to expand into Windows software.

The most important source of information

Just as it is for many other major shareware companies, the Summer Shareware Seminar is the single most important event of the year for Contact Plus Corporation. This is where they get to meet other people, network, pick up new ideas, and make important contacts. For example, Roger told me that they've been able to cut their packaging costs by $2/3$, just from what they learned at the SSS.

They feel that the SSS is more valuable for shareware authors than events such as COMDEX, because at the SSS you meet people who are doing things on a small scale. You get to talk with people who are thinking on the same scale that you are.

Advice for other authors

There are three areas in which Roger offers advice for other authors:

First, as a shareware author you need to talk with other shareware authors. Keep a list of questions you need answered; put yourself into situations where you can meet and talk with other authors, and ask other authors questions—about packaging, how to market, what registration incentives work, etc. You'll find the answers more quickly by asking than you will by trying to find out for yourself.

Go to small business meetings. Go to Chamber of Commerce meetings. Go to the Summer Shareware Seminar. Talk with people and get to know them. You don't know who you're going to meet or how they might be able to help you. And do your best to help others, even if you don't think they can help you; you never know when it will pay off.

If you aren't good at networking, make sure the first person you hire (or the person you form a partnership with) is a good talker and listener. If you want your company to grow, you need someone who is very good at networking, someone who can talk with other people. Making contacts is important and you never know when a contact will help.

Even if you aren't good at conversation, listen to people. Listening is a special skill that involves more than just hearing the words. You need to understand what the other person is saying. If you don't, then ask questions.

Second, a lot of authors are too close to their software and therefore get very defensive when people tell them it can be improved. Their software often looks like a first-generation program from the 1980s, but they're unwilling to accept that it needs to be improved. Be open to advice and criticism. Take suggestions seriously. Try to be objective about your software.

Third, presenting your software in a professional manner is important. I try to avoid words like *slick*, But a slick look is important because people see it. They can't see technical expertise. They can't see the thousands of hours you've put into your software. Roger admits that having a slick-looking package seems like a silly thing, but it's important.

Quality packaging is important. The package has to be solid and it shouldn't feel like it can be crushed. It's got to feel like it has value. It must not feel cheap. This is important in direct marketing because many of your sales will be referrals. Your customers will show your package to other people. For example, the at the Fresh Water Game Commission in Florida, one person bought a copy of Contact Plus. He showed it to some other people and, as a result, the entire Fresh Water Game Commission now uses Contact Plus.

Profile #2

Thunder Byte
P.O. Box 175
Madisonville, TN 37354

Jeff Cook, Owner

Product: Thunder Byte Anti-Virus

Thunder Byte was recommended to me by Jim Horowitz, the software librarian at The Software Labs. I had asked Jim which programs were the highest-quality, best-selling products in their catalog. One of the names he gave me was Thunder Byte. If you haven't heard of this program, it's because it's getting only very limited distribution. The author has sent it only to The Software Labs and a handful of BBSs. In spite of that, it's generating many times more registrations than most shareware authors ever see and, combined with the author's direct-sales efforts, has resulted in first-year sales of over $25,000.

Like most shareware authors, Jeff Cook started his business as hobby. He's now been a shareware author for over a year, and, at the time of this writing, was still employed full-time as an electronic repair technician. Unlike many authors who start by writing software they need for themselves, Jeff started with the intention to write a program he could sell to make a few dollars. However, he never expected that it could lead to a full-time software company—something that now seems like a possibility.

Jeff started by playing around with data compression, but soon found that field to be boring. He then moved on to the more exciting, constantly changing field of virus protection. He likes working with virus protection software because something new is happening all the time. He's always learning new things and creating new versions of his software to keep up with the changes in viruses.

Version 1.0

The first version of Thunder Byte Anti-Virus took a couple of months to write. It first entered shareware distribution in 1992. However, the first couple of versions drew very little response and few registrations. Jeff didn't start to get a significant number of registrations until March 1993.

Jeff feels that people won't register anti-virus software until they feel confident that the publisher is stable and will be around for a long time. There isn't much difference between each version of the software; the updates are primarily to add coverage for new viruses—although each new version also increases in speed. What people want to know is that, if they buy today, updated versions of the software will still be available next month.

One common characteristic I've found among successful shareware authors is that they *make something happen*. Jeff is this type of person. Most of his sales come not from shareware registrations, but from his efforts to sell his software directly to corporations and institutions.

Direct sales

His approach is to get in touch with the Chamber of Commerce for a specific area and obtain a list of businesses. He then targets several businesses or universities and finds out who the MIS director is. He sends that person a shareware copy of his program, along with some promotional literature, gives them a week—and then calls to try and set up a meeting.

Jim has the advantage of having a full-time job that involves rotating shifts. This leaves gives him some days when he's free during the daytime to meet with his potential customers. It takes a good bit of time to sell software this way, but Jim feels that it's the best method to convert his hobby to a full-time business.

Competing against the "big guys"

Virus protection software has become a big market, and there are a lot of big-name publishers involved. Both Central Point Software (PC Tools) and Symantec (Norton Utilities) have anti-virus products—and big marketing dollars to promote their products. In shareware, there are already several big names, with McAfee's Scan software leading the list. How can one small, part-time shareware author compete with these big names? The answer is to build a better, high-quality product that meets user needs. Jeff Cook feels he has done this.

Thunder Byte does everything the other anti-virus programs do, but it does it faster—seven to eight times faster. Speed has been one of the biggest problems with anti-virus software in the past. It has always taken a long time to scan a disk and check for viruses. By creating software that works faster—and by providing regular updates—Jeff has created a unique product that provides the user with a good reason to buy.

In addition, Thunder Byte also provides several utilities that other programs don't have. Jeff has decided that it's best not to rely on a scanner's ability to detect specific viruses. He concentrates on detecting the activity of a virus and preventing any destructive activity. For example, one of Thunder Byte's memory-resident utilities watches for any program trying to become memory-resident that isn't supposed to. Another utility detects direct disk access—any software trying to modify executable files. These are activities that viruses (but not general applications) typically do.

Registration incentives

Both the shareware version and the registered version of Thunder Byte are the same except for a few additional features that are useful to network users. For example, if you have the scanner check each computer on a network when it's booted, Thunder Byte runs so that virus scanning cannot be aborted. This is important because many people in a business environment might not be familiar with viruses and the importance of scanning for them. In their rush to get started in the morning, they'll abort the anti-virus software before it finishes scanning.

Another difference is that the registered version can extract virus signatures from any file. The signature is the pattern of program code that a virus puts in an infected file. If your computer comes up with an unknown virus, you can have Thunder Byte extract its signature. Then, when Thunder Byte Anti-Virus scans in the future, it will look for and detect that virus in any file.

One of the key registration incentives for Thunder Byte Anti-Virus is that updates are provided free via the company's BBS at any time, and users can call the BBS for technical support at any time.

Technical support

Handling technical support while working a regular full-time job can be difficult. When Jeff is at home during the day, he can handle technical support calls directly. When his schedule puts him on the day shift, his wife takes the calls. Jeff's wife isn't a virus expert, so he has provided her with written information that answers the most common questions people have. Although there are thousands of different viruses, only a few are commonly encountered. If she can't answer the customer's question, she can fax the information sheet Jeff has prepared. If it's a particularly difficult question, Jeff carries a beeper so his wife can reach him and have him call the customer.

Major problems

Jeff's biggest problem is time. There isn't enough time to do everything that needs to be done. In particular, Jeff feels he could do better if he had more time available for sales and marketing. Making direct sales to customers takes a lot of time, and he could make more sales if he had more time. When he gets into a position where he can hire someone to help him, the first person he'll hire is a salesperson.

Distribution

Jeff feels that BBSs are the best way to distribute Thunder Byte Anti-Virus. His primary method of distribution is the SDN (Shareware Distribution Network), which gets it to several hundred BBSs. He also sends it directly to about 30 BBSs, and one copy goes to The Software Labs. In addition, other disk vendors have been picking this program up from BBSs and placing it in their catalogs.

Advice for other authors

Jeff's advice for other authors is that they need to develop a product that everybody needs. Create a quality product. Measure it against the competition. Make yours better. Do everything they do and then do things they don't do.

Analysis

Thunder Byte is profiled here because I feel Jeff has created an excellent product, and, in spite of the limited distribution, he's getting a significant number of registrations. However, I believe that one of the things people should try to do in business is to find ways to multiply their efforts. If you spend ten hours putting together and mailing shareware disks to 100 disk vendors, and they each spend one hour promoting your software, you've multiplied your time by a factor of ten. You're getting one hundred hours of promotional effort for 10 hours of your time.

By sending disks to a hundred or so distributors, Jeff could probably increase his sales dramatically without having to spend more time making direct sales calls. This doesn't mean that Jeff is taking the wrong approach. He might enjoy calling on customers, or have other reasons for taking the direct sales approach. And whatever his reasons, he has created a successful shareware product.

Profile #3

Software Vision Corporation
P.O. Box 1734
Pinellas Park, FL 34664-1734
813-545-4354

Julian Achim, President

Product: EnVision Publisher

I hope you've heard of EnVision Publisher. The success of EnVision is the most remarkable story in shareware. It was released at the end of September 1992, and, by the end of June 1993, it had received three of the Shareware Industry Awards presented at the 1993 Summer Shareware Seminar.

It also achieved over $600,000 in sales in just its first ten months—solely from shareware registrations. During those first ten months there were no retail versions, license deals, or royalty contracts—100% of that $600,000 was received as shareware registrations.

The EnVision story

"EnVision exceeded all expectations; I wasn't ready for this."
— Julian Achim, President, Software Vision Corporation

Julian Achim got into the software business in 1983 with a tax preparation program he had written for the IBM PC. It was sold through direct mail and was a successful product that was recognized as one of the best in its field. In 1989 he sold his business to a much larger competitor and started looking for something else to do.

Market research

Julian was familiar with shareware, having previously released several programs as shareware—including a pop-up spreadsheet. These hadn't done well, and this time he knew he needed something unique—a product that was not available in shareware. Here's how Julian tells the story of how EnVision began:

"We noticed that there weren't any DTP (desktop publishing) programs in shareware. That's why we chose desktop publishing. There were good spreadsheets, good word processing, good database software. But there wasn't a desktop publishing program. We looked at the retail market and saw that low-end DTP software was selling very well. We decided that a DTP program was something that was needed in shareware.

When picking a product to develop you have to make something people really want. Something they can use. For example, I was running a tax software business. There wasn't an awful lot of products I was using to run my business; there was a spreadsheet, a database, and I had a DTP program for doing my flyers and mailers. These are the products people use and would want to buy.

We looked at First Publisher and realized that that was what we didn't want to look like. We looked at high-end programs and some Mac programs and thought that these were programs we should try to emulate in quality."

It took three years for Julian, with some help from his wife, to write EnVision. Its design evolved during that time, and it turned out to be important that he had used high-end commercial DTP software as his model. As a result, EnVision was created as a low-cost DTP program with high-end features.

Doubts about shareware

Even though he originally started with the idea of putting EnVision into shareware, the further along Julian got with its development, the more unsure about shareware he became. He stated feeling like we all feel sometimes, that putting his program out as shareware would be like giving it away—everyone could use it, but few people would register.

So when EnVision was finished, he first tried to sell it to some of the retail software publishers. He had experience with retail software and knew how to approach them, but they weren't interested. They wouldn't even talk to him unless he had a Windows program to offer.

In June 1992, Julian went to the Summer Shareware Seminar (SSS) in Indianapolis, and what he learned there convinced him that shareware was the way to market his software. Here's what Julian said about his 1992 SSS experience:

"I'd recommend that everyone involved with shareware go to the SSS. The 1992 SSS made us decide that shareware was the way to go. At the SSS you see that there is a real industry out there; people are really making money. Otherwise, with the nature of shareware, you don't know whether it is a joke or whatever. Prior to the 1992 SSS I wasn't sure about shareware, but afterward I was.

If you are an outsider to shareware you can easily think that it's impossible to be successful. Because of the nature of shareware you can't easily see how well the shareware principle works. And it seems unnatural for people to send you money for something they already have. But, if you talk to the right people, those who know what is going on, they will tell you otherwise. To find the right people, get on CompuServe and go to the SSS."

Getting into distribution

In September 1992, Julian and his company sent shareware copies of EnVision to all the vendors on the ASP vendor mailing list and to every nonASP vendor they could find—about 1000 vendors altogether. It was also uploaded to CompuServe. The registrations started coming in almost immediately—within a couple of hours of uploading it to Compuserve. By the end of the first month, they had received a $1,000 in registrations. During the next month they sold nearly another $9,000, and sales have been increasing steadily since.

It still takes marketing

It sounds like all Julian had to do was release EnVision and sit back while the money rolled in. It doesn't work that way, even for a record-setting program such as EnVision. Part of the reason for EnVision's incredible sales record is that distributors in other countries quickly became interested in carrying EnVision. This helped because the distributors handled the foreign registrations, increasing EnVision's sales volume while reducing the effort required. This was important because Software Vision is a small company. Even now, in August 1993, it is still only a four-person company. Attempting to expand fast enough to directly handle a large volume of orders would have been impossible.

The four employees are Julian's wife, who handles billing and most of the technical support; his father, who helps with packing and shipping; a recently hired programmer, who is working on a new program; and Julian, who does marketing and is writing the next version of EnVision—a job that typically takes fifteen hours a day. And when a large order comes in, the work day for all four might start at 9 A.M. and end sometime during the afternoon of the next day.

The international market

Selling internationally has been a very significant source of sales for Software Vision. Their experience has been that the international market works much faster than markets in the United States. It took about five months before EnVision started to generate large numbers of orders from U.S. customers. However, distributors in the U.K., Australia, Germany, Denmark, Scandinavia, The Netherlands, and Belgium were able to get the program into distribution quickly and to start generating registrations. They were able to get new shareware disks out to users more quickly, get publicity for the product, and, as a result, start generating registrations sooner than the U.S. distribution system does.

A special shareware version of EnVision is made for each international distributor. It includes the distributor's name, address, and phone number so that the user can register it with the local distributor.

Software Vision uses an excellent method of handling international sales. Distributors sign a contract in which they commit to selling a minimum quantity over a one-year period, and they get a discount based on that quantity. During the year, they can still order 50 or 100 copies at a time, as long as by the end of the year they have purchased at least the minimum number they agreed to buy.

After the contract is signed, Software Vision ships all the required user manuals by ocean freight, and the distributor pays only the actual printing costs of the manuals. The normal way to ship software overseas is to ship the complete package by air. The cost of freight can be as much as 20% to 30% of the cost of the software. By using surface freight, Software Vision is able to dramatically cut the distributor's costs.

When the distributor places an order for software, Software Vision ships disk labels and user licenses by air. The distributor duplicates and labels the disks, and then combines the disk, license, and manuals into the package the user receives.

As is the case with every shareware company I've talked with, the international distributors came to Vision Software and asked to carry the EnVision Publisher software. Julian also found that the Summer Shareware Seminar was a good place to meet distributors and to get to know people from other countries who are involved in shareware.

Registration incentives

The main registration incentive in EnVision Publisher is that registered users get additional fonts. The shareware version comes with three fonts. The registered version has 17 fonts and includes half a megabyte of clip art.

When you first boot up EnVision Publisher, it displays a screen that explains shareware, identifies it as a shareware program, and provides ordering information. This information stays on the screen until the user pushes a key. The software then goes to the main EnVision screen and displays an About box that once again identifies it as being a shareware program. The user needs to press a key to make the box go away. On the main screen, "unregistered shareware" appears in the upper left corner in small print.

However, it might be that the quality of EnVision is the real reason people register. When they call to register, people say they're registering because they've been stunned by the quality of the program.

The registered version also includes a 300-page printed manual, a new set of disks, technical support, and a quarterly newsletter with news about updates.

Technical support

Anyone who calls, whether they're registered or not, can get technical support. At Software Vision they've found that most people call with legitimate questions. There has been only one case in which they've had to tell the user that it was time to print the manual and read it for himself.

The people in shareware

Julian has been involved in nearly every method of selling software. What he has found is that the quality of the people he deals with in the shareware industry is totally different than what he experienced in the retail market. In shareware, you know you're probably talking to honest people. In retail, when distributors or buyers from big retail chains call, you know they're probably trying to get the most they can out of you. They want to make the best deal for their company and they don't care what happens to you.

In shareware it's a win-win market—everybody wins. The user wins because he gets to try software before buying it, the distributor wins because he gets software to sell, and the author wins if he has created a quality program that people find useful. In retail software it can also be a win-win situation, but you need to put a lot more effort into watching out for yourself.

Advice for other authors

Julian's advice for other shareware authors is that they need to make software that meets and maintains the highest quality standards in the software industry. You aren't only competing against other shareware programs, you're competing against the retail software. The retail market is constantly changing; new products are constantly being developed that provide better software at lower prices. Things don't stay the same.

Do your market research prior to starting to develop a new product. Find out what products are out there, how well they're selling, what users like and dislike about them, and how they can be improved.

Keep in mind that you need a product that is not only different, but is something people need.

Also, take advantage of opportunities to put yourself into a position to meet people. Go to the Summer Shareware Seminar. Talk with people on CompuServe.

And finally, remember that as your company grows, you won't have time to do everything. So find some way to get help in your weakest business area. If you're a good programmer, find someone who knows marketing and likes to talk with people. If you're a good marketer, find a good programmer.

Profile #4

OSCS Software Development, Inc.
354 NE Greenwood Avenue, Suite 108
Bend, OR 97701-4631

Glen Tippetts, President
Dave Riley, CEO

Products available from OSCS Software Development are:

- QuikMenu
- QuikMenu III (not available as shareware)
- NeoPaint
- The Pro Pack (not available as shareware)
- NeoShow
- NeoShow Pro
- Phantom Screen

For years, one of the fundamental pieces of advice given to prospective shareware authors has been not to make "yet another menu program." There are so many menu programs on the market that it just doesn't seem worthwhile to make another one. Glen Tippetts and Dave Riley ignored that advice and created a shareware corporation with over a $1,000,000 in sales during the past year.

OSCS's main product is QuikMenu. They also publish Neopaint and several other graphics-based programs. However, the program that shouldn't have been successful—QuikMenu—is still their top-selling program. And those sales are generated primarily from shareware registrations. Over 60% of the sales are direct shareware sales, with another 10% of sales derived from shareware.

Getting started

OSCS was started in February 1990. Both Glen and Dave were working for a retail computer store in Bend, a small city in central Oregon. There were both working in sales, but wanted to be doing something else. Dave is more of a programmer and therefore preferred working with computers to doing sales and marketing. He asked Glen to join him in forming their own software company, and Glen agreed.

To support themselves while their software company was getting started, they formed a consulting company called On-Site Computer Services. That's where the name OSCS comes from, although now that they're no longer in the consulting business it has no real meaning.

Dave had written a small menu program for the computer store, and that became the basis for their first program. While Dave spent most of his time writing code, Glen did outside consulting and market research for their new software.

Market research

How do you figure out how to make yet another menu program, one that will sell? Glen started by downloading most of the major menu programs and looking at them. He had also talked with users about menu programs while he was working in the computer store. He continued to do this while working as a consultant. He found out what people liked and didn't like about existing menu programs. What he found was that the existing programs lacked usability. He then looked at the menu programs available commercially and found they were typically designed from the programmer's point of view and not the end user's point of view. Glen and Dave knew that they could create a menu program that was both easier to use and the type of program people wanted.

In August 1990, the first version of QuikMenu was released. It was followed a week later by version 1.01b, and by the end of the month they had eliminated all of the bugs and released version 1.03. As you can see in FIG. 15-3, QuikMenu doesn't look like a conventional menu program. It features high-quality graphics and push-buttons for each menu choice. This is what makes QuikMenu unique and a program people want to buy.

When they first released QuikMenu, Glen and Dave knew very little about the shareware industry. They had originally heard about shareware through a users group sponsored by the store in which they worked. They were aware of what shareware was and how it worked, but only vaguely. Since they didn't have much money, they were left with shareware as the only option for marketing their software.

They started by uploading it to Compuserve and sending it to The Software Labs and Public Brand Software. It found its way to several corporate BBS systems operated by major computer companies, and this gave it a big boost in distribution, which led to rapid success. By November, they were getting so many calls that they had to stop doing consulting. There was no time. They had two phone lines and both lines were ringing constantly.

As is typical with shareware, they got a lot of feedback from users, and they used this feedback to make QuikMenu better. Their policy was that, if they could implement a user suggestion without making the software more difficult to use, they would do it.

QuikMenu sales have continued to grow since then. In January 1991, OSCS released a commercial version that was designed for retail stores.

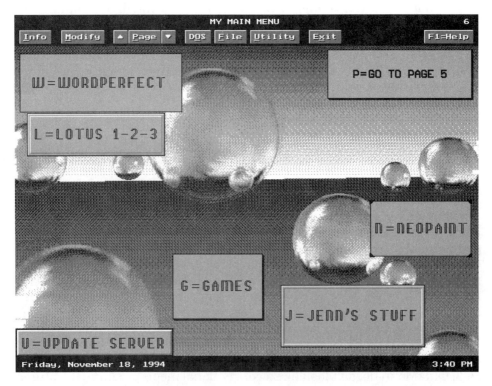

15-3 The QuikMenu screen doesn't look like a traditional menu program. Its uniqueness and quality make this program a best-seller.

The difference between the two versions is that the commercial version supports icons and can translate Windows icons into QuikMenu.

Selling retail versions

One of the problems some shareware authors have encountered when moving into the retail channel is that retail stores are often reluctant to carry programs they feel users can get for free as shareware. But, in the case of QuikMenu, OSCS has not had any problems. Glen Tippetts explained it this way:

"They see this as two different things. They see the shareware market as being so small as to be insignificant to them that they just blow it off.

We'll be doing a licensing agreement with Neopaint, which will be out this fall as a commercial program. We asked them whether they were concerned about the shareware version and the response was that 'you can have the shareware market; it has no effect on us whatsoever.'"

As many authors do, the version of Neopaint that OSCS is licensing for retail distribution is version one. Version two, which is the current shareware version, is a better program. Therefore, the lower-cost retail version shouldn't reduce the sales of the shareware version.

Glen and Dave originally got into the retail channel because they decided that they needed to actively pursue the retail market. They felt that, if they wanted their company to grow at an accelerated rate with multiple product lines, they needed to get more exposure for their products. To accomplish that, they felt that they needed to get into retail stores.

The retail channel works entirely differently from shareware and requires different skills. To help them get their products into stores, OSCS hired a salesperson. First they evaluated the cost of hiring a sales person vs. the financial return of getting into retail. It looked viable, so they gave it a try.

They started by trying to sell their software to large chains such as Egghead Software. Egghead's response was "How many hundreds of thousands of dollars per year do you spend on advertising?" OSCS was too small to support the type of marketing effort Egghead required.

The other response they got from Egghead was that QuikMenu was just another menu program. They had heard that before and knew that it didn't matter—QuikMenu had already proven itself in shareware.

Creating a market pull

Another approach to the retail channel was needed. OSCS wouldn't be able to break into big-time distribution right away. The big-name distributors and chain stores didn't know who they were, and OSCS's products were general-market products that already had a lot of competitors who were backed by much larger marketing budgets. So instead of going through the front door, Glen and Dave decided to go the other way around and get dealers to start carrying their software. They felt that when they got enough dealers selling it, the big-name distributors would notice the consumer demand. It worked.

Their approach was to start calling dealers in a particular part of the country, and then follow up by sending the dealers a demo version of the commercial software. The demo version could be used only 100 times before it deleted all the icons and you had to start over again. The demo program was created, with these features, specifically for the purpose of selling QuikMenu.

Over time, OSCS has been able to build up their retail sales. It now accounts for about 40% of their business.

Registration incentives

Why do people register OSCS products? To start with, they're good programs; all of the programs are quality software, software that people find useful and enjoy using. Beyond that, OSCS uses two different approaches to encourage people to register QuikMenu and NeoPaint.

When you start QuikMenu it comes up and tells you that it's shareware and explains how shareware works. At that point the user can press a key to print the registration form. QuikMenu makes it extremely simple for anyone to order a copy.

Glen feels that having the registration information on the opening screen is a key point in QuikMenu's success. Some programs use the last screen for registration information. But, if the user has a menu program or is using Windows, the last screen will never be seen. The user might see that screen for only a tenth of a second. Even an honest person wouldn't get a chance to find out that the program is shareware and see how to register it. It's important that the end user knows how to order the software and that the ordering information is presented to them in a way they can't miss.

The registration information screen for QuikMenu comes on only when the program is first started, not while it's being used. There is, however, a little reminder window that will pop up for a second or less while the program is being used. It says "Please remember to register." QuikMenu gets registered because the reminder is in front of them all the time, but it's not annoying. It's just there. It's a program that's used every day and the reminder about registration is seen every day.

Neopaint is different. A menu program is used each time the computer is turned on, but a paint program is only used now and then. You don't use your paint program every time you use your computer. So a paint program needs stronger registration reminders to let people know they need to pay for it.

When NeoPaint is first started, an opening screen similar to the one in

QuikMenu is displayed. It explains about shareware and gives you a chance to register. But Neopaint is different from QuikMenu in that when you exit from Neopaint, there's a little man who walks across the screen. You need to wait until he gets across the screen before you can go to the next screen. It takes four or five seconds for the man to cross the screen.

The only time the little man walks across the screen is when you exit from the program, or when the program changes video modes. Glen knew that putting a delay into the program might be annoying for some people and is generally not an effective registration incentive. He wanted to make the delay more interesting and give the user something to look at. That's the reason for the little man. He adds a touch of humor, and makes waiting for the delay a little easier.

Another registration reminder method used in NeoPaint is a series of "please register" messages displayed in the upper right-hand corner. There are several different messages and the software cycles through them using various colors so as to catch the user's eye. However, the messages are there only part of the time. This part of the screen (the upper right-hand corner) is also used to display the mouse position, so any time the mouse is moved the mouse-position display returns.

However, as with the other programs profiled here, the main reason people register NeoPaint is because it's a useful, quality program. Figure 15-4 shows the main NeoPaint screen. This screen shot was provided by OSCS and is typical of the screen shots they use to promote NeoPaint. The screen shots always include graphics that evoke images of quality.

Meeting customer needs

It's crucial to provide network support for applications that might be used on networks. That's where the sales are. If I sell a copy of QuikMenu, with shipping I get $40 for a copy. If I sell a copy to 500 users on some university network, I get $2000 for the same cost of materials. As long as I address the network situation—multiple users can use the software and whatever other enhancements they need—it's that much better and worth the invested time.

"If it is a program that can be used by business, it should be network compatible. All our programs are network compatible, although QuikMenu is the one most likely to be used on a network."
— Glen Tippetts

Free updates

Something OSCS did that is hurting them now is to include free upgrades as one of the benefits they offered registered users. Users can call the OSCS BBS at any time and get the latest version. OSCS won't mail disks for free, but the updates are available free on the BBS. Unlike anti-virus

15-4 Whenever OSCS provides a promotional screen shot for NeoPaint, it includes pictures that evoke images of quality.

software where updates are essential for keeping your computer protected, with a menu program, updates provide the user with an improved version of the software. Since an update increases the value of the software, users should pay something for an update. By not charging for updates, OSCS has given up a significant source of revenue.

Glen has found that the effectiveness of offering free updates as a registration incentive depends upon who he's offering them to. Both the low-end (typically home users) and the high-end (typically large corporations) purchasers find free updates to be a positive incentive to register, but the users in the middle don't.

On the low end, free updates can be important because people are registering the software because it's a good, inexpensive program that works. But they don't want version 2 to come out next week and then have to pay an additional fee to get that update. They feel more comfortable with a program they can update at no cost.

On the other end are the network customers who might have 5,000 or 10,0000 systems. They don't want to pay another $5,000 to upgrade all their users. However, in the corporate world the standard practice is to charge for updates. Corporate buyers expect to pay for updates. A free update is like getting a free bonus! OSCS could probably start charging for updates and, if they did, they wouldn't be hurting themselves or their customers. They would only be conforming to standard industry practices.

OSCS has changed their site license policy. They now allow only up to a ten-user license for the basic version. Anything above that goes to the professional version. The pricing for the license is the same as it has been for the basic version, but they've now moved some of the larger corporate customers into a position where OSCS can charge them for upgrades. The low-end users, who have the basic version, still get their updates free.

What about the group of people in the middle for whom free updates don't make any difference? These are usually middle-sized bureaucratic companies. They have rules and procedures to follow, and the price they pay for something doesn't seem to make any difference. When someone within one of these companies wants to get an update, the proper paperwork must be processed, purchase orders issued, and the system works its way through a process that doesn't care whether the update is free. The people in the system don't notice whether the update is free or whether it must be purchased.

International sales

OSCS's software has been very popular internationally. Just like the other major shareware publishers, OSCS has distributors who represent them in various countries.

In almost every case, international distributors came to OSCS and asked to carry the software. When this happened, OSCS asked the distributors to send information about their companies, including financial information and a list of the shareware programs they were already carrying. For the large companies, OSCS often got a Dun & Bradstreet report on them. They also called some of the authors the distributor was representing and got feedback on how they were doing. It's the same thing when software customers want to check out an author. Nobody wants to be doing business with a small, fly-by-night company.

Business planning

OSCS uses a five-year business plan. It's difficult to forecast a five-year plan, especially in the software industry. But they do it because it includes their two-and three-year plans, which are more accurate. It also gives them a general long-term target to look at for employee growth, dollar growth, where they'd like to be, and how they're going to get there.

They start by setting their goals for where they'd like to be in five years. Then they work backward through each year, setting goals for those years. The whole process provides a roadmap for arriving where they want to be in five years.

License agreements

OSCS has found that license agreements can be one of the biggest problem areas a shareware author faces. You need to be very careful how license agreements are worded. If you aren't careful, you can lose control of your product.

OSCS became involved in a license agreement in which they did lose control of their software, fortunately without any great damage to the company. They thought they were licensing their software to be bundled on one specific brand of computer. It was a substantial brand-name computer manufacturer who had the ability to pay the bills, so it seemed as if there could be few problems. However, when that manufacturer decided to get out of the computer business, they found that the license for their software had been sold to another, less financially sound computer manufacturer. This new company put QuikMenu on thousands of computers, but didn't have the money to pay the license fee. OSCS found themselves supporting a large number of users without having been paid for the software by the manufacturer.

When dealing with license agreements, it's very important that you have them reviewed by an attorney, and not just any attorney. They should be reviewed by an intellectual property attorney who understands software licensing.

Here's what Glen had to say about how licensing works in the software industry:

"What typically happens in the shareware industry is that you have an author who is new to the software industry and not really up to speed on how the whole system works. You then have people who license products on a normal basis. They've been doing it for years and years. They know exactly what they want and exactly what wording to use. They also know there is a wide range of things they don't want to do versus things they could or can't do. They realize you are a novice author, and they say 'Here's what we want,' making it as lopsided as they can and knowing that you don't know what options are available. And so they take advantage of the situation. In their mind it is just business—they got the best deal they could for their company. But what happens in a lot of cases is that in a year or two the author realizes that the contract doesn't mean 'Gee we'll be good to you;' what it means is 'we'll take advantage of you, if we can.'"

Credit card merchant status

One of the most important tools you need as an author is the ability to accept Visa and MasterCard. 60% of OSCS's business comes from customers who charge their purchases using a credit card. But in the beginning, Glen and Dave faced the same problem we all face; it's difficult for a mail-order business to get a Visa/MasterCard merchant account. However, they took a unique approach to solving this problem.

Glen had an account with a bank in Bend for a long time, but that bank was unwilling to give him a merchant account for his mail-order software business. But Glen had another approach he could take. OSCS was a computer-consulting firm that had an office in Bend and which was doing business locally in town. As a local, nonmail-order consulting firm, OSCS qualified for a Visa/MasterCard merchant account. So OSCS got their merchant account and continued to use it as they grew from a consulting company to a mail-order software business.

OSCS has since switched banks and, now that they're an established business, had no trouble getting merchant status with their current bank.

Handling purchase orders

If someone wants to purchase software using a purchase order, OSCS will fax them a credit application before they accept the purchase order. However, this doesn't always work. For example, if someone needs to order just a single copy of a program, it's not worth the time and effort for the customer to complete a credit application or for OSCS to do a credit check. In that case, OSCS will return the purchase order to the customer and request it be sent back with a check. The only situation where this doesn't work is for schools and government agencies. And since schools and government agencies do pay their bills, although sometimes very slowly, OSCS will accept purchase orders from them.

However, Glen warns us to be aware that some companies use purchase order forms that look exactly like government purchase orders. They have government-sounding names, and in some cases names that are almost exactly the same as the name of a government agency. If you get a P.O. that looks like it's from a government agency, check it closely to see whether it includes the words *Company*, *Inc.*, or *Ltd.* as a part of the agency's name. If it does, then the purchase order is not from a government agency.

Profile #5

InfoTek

Patrick Cook, President

InfoTek's products are:

- Inside Secrets to Credit Repair
- Love Your Life
- Credit Pro

InfoTek publishes software that is designed to help people help themselves. And with a program that has been in the shareware top ten for the past eight months, the company is off to a good start.

Patrick Cook learned about the need for credit repair the hard way. He got involved in a business that failed back in 1987/88 and lost his shirt, almost lost his home, and did a lot of damage to his personal life and marriage. He still lives under a huge amount of debt. Patrick made a lot of costly financial mistakes and fell into many financial traps. But he also learned a lot. When he started InfoTek, his goal was to use what he had learned in order to help other people avoid the problems he had gotten himself into. InfoTek has a mission to help people. It does this by using the media of software and shareware.

The idea for Inside Secrets to Credit Repair had its start in 1989 when Patrick ran across a book called The First Book of Credit Repair. He read it and thought it was a good book, so good that he decided to put together a printed manual about credit repair and sell it through mail-order. That business didn't work out very well and he lost about $3,000. His credit-repair manual ended up in a file drawer and he forgot about it.

A year later he was cleaning out the drawer and was about to throw the manual out, when he realized that there might be a better way to market the secrets of credit repair. By that time he had become familiar with shareware; he thought his credit-repair system might be worth a try in shareware.

Getting started

Patrick's first step was to look for information on how to start a shareware business. At first he thought that nothing was available. Then, he found the first, self-published release of this book, which at the time was called *Writing & Marketing Shareware*. He bought the book, read it, and knew that shareware was the way to go.

It took about four months to find the programming tools he needed and to design and write the code for the program. He released the first version in October 1990. Like many new shareware authors, he didn't have much experience with shareware at the time. He sent out 100 disks to the top shareware vendors. By March of the next year a few registrations started coming in, but they didn't become significant until big catalogs such as The Software Labs and Public Brand Software started carrying the software a few months later.

Distribution and publicity

Patrick found that distribution and publicity are important. When he released version 3 at the end of 1992, he sent it to 280 vendors and then sent out about 400 press releases. That's when things started to happen. Here's how Patrick describes it:

"Version 3 went to 280 vendors and about 400 press releases went out. Before that it was, oh, this is neat. I didn't really wake up until I was browsing through Shareware Magazine and saw Inside Secrets was in the top 10. It dawned on me that I either was going to play around with this or I had to take it seriously."

InfoTek is a serious business that Patrick is working to expand. Often he gets home from his day job, has supper, and starts working on his shareware business at about 7:30 P.M., keeping it up until one or two in the morning. He also believes that if you're serious about being in business, you must have the right tools. So he has invested the money he's received from registrations in programming tools, new computers, and accessories, which include a state-of-the-art voice-mail system that makes his business sound as if he has hundreds of employees in a shining glass office tower.

Registration incentives

The shareware version of The Inside Secrets to Credit Repair is the same as the registered version. The shareware version is fully functional with no crippling. One aspect of the shareware version does show that Patrick is focused on his customers and is working hard to find out what they want and need. He has included a questionnaire as a part of his registration form. It asks users questions about why they're registering and whether they will recommend the software to other people. From the results of this questionnaire, Patrick has found that people register the software because they want to know about updates, and they want access to technical support when they need help.

There are some people who are using The Inside Secrets to Credit Repair without registering, and a recent phone call from one of these people illustrates one of the registration incentives. The call was from someone who was using a form letter that isn't supposed to be used until the software is registered. The software includes a complete set of form letters that can be used for credit repair. However, the shareware version is supposed to be used only to get credit reports; shareware users are not licensed to use the software for active credit repair.

The reason behind this requirement wasn't to put a registration incentive in the software. The software was designed this way because of liability concerns. Laws affecting what needs to be done to repair your credit are constantly changing. When people register, they get the most recent version with current information. If they're using a shareware version, it's possible that it could be an old, out-of-date version that no longer applies. If people use the out-of-date version to try to repair their credit, they could run into problems or even hurt their credit rating. Thus, it's important that Patrick know who his users are so he can get updates to them, and he can do that only if they're registered.

Patrick helped the unregistered user who was calling with a question about one of the form letters he wasn't supposed to use. Patrick also sent him a copy of the latest shareware version of his software. This is the way Patrick explains his attitude about unregistered users:

"There are so many registration stealers that I don't worry about them. If I'm going to play games and cripple my program, the people who would normally have registered it will not register because they won't be able to do a full evaluation. I can't worry about those people who are using it and not paying; they are on their own.

From the very beginning I decided to put out a high-quality program. It didn't go out until it was right. It was fully tested and not crippled. If someone doesn't want to register, I don't want to deal with them anyway.

I've found that people who do register want to stay with the program and learn about upgrades. When I put version three out, I did a mailing to all registered users, and 72% ordered the upgrade. Those are the kind of people I want to have as users because you get repeat business from them."

As with the other successful authors profiled here, Patrick uses an opening screen that identifies his program as shareware. In addition, as the software is used, a nonobtrusive message about shareware occasionally appears. For example, if users try to print a form letter they aren't supposed to use, they get a message that tells them they aren't supposed to use that form letter until they register. However, the software does let them print the letter.

The shareware version also randomly displays nonobtrusive messages describing the benefits of registering.

Other ways to make money

What Patrick has found is that shareware has provided not only a good way to promote his software, but to develop other business opportunities as well. Currently about 55% of his income comes from shareware registrations, but 45% has come from other deals with people who have noticed his shareware program. For example, a publishing company will be including his program with a book on credit repair. And he's creating a modified version of his software that includes another company's credit information. He is selling the modified software to the other company so they can use it to provide better service to their customers.

LCR racks

Patrick is finding that he gets five or six letters each week from people who want to put together some sort of deal involving his software. In particular, there have been quite a few LCR rack vendors who have wanted to place his software on their racks. Patrick doesn't allow any of the LCR racks to carry his software. He feels that it's unfair to people who've paid $40 to register the shareware to have the program available to others for $7 to $10. He feels that selling the shareware version on retail racks is okay and he has no problem with it being carried on CD-ROMs.

Not enough time

As with most part-time shareware authors, Patrick's biggest problem is that he doesn't have enough time to do everything he wants to do. And like most highly successful people, he focuses on only the project he's working on until it's complete. He has dozens of ideas for new self-help type programs and he plans to write and publish them, one at a time.

Advice for other authors

Patrick's advice for other authors is to learn all you can about shareware before you put your program out. And then don't release a program until it's absolutely the highest quality you can get. No bugs. No glitches. No problems. And a complete program. Expect to put a tremendous amount of time into creating a quality program.

And once you have your program out, don't get greedy and don't worry about registrations. The beauty of shareware is that you don't need to try to pay the bills from the income from your shareware business. It's a nice kind of business because you can build it on a bootstrap. You can let the business feed on itself and expand on its own money.

Patrick looks at shareware as a medium for communicating educational material. He's not in it for the money and he doesn't think anyone can be in it for the money at the beginning. If you focus on making money, you'll cripple yourself and the growth of your company.

The best advice I think Patrick offers for shareware authors is the following: "I went into shareware giving the user everything that I'd want as a user. That was my golden rule." Give the user what you like to get from the software you buy, and you'll build a good foundation for your business.

16

Shareware industry survey results

During the spring of each year I conduct a series of surveys of the shareware industry. In 1993 I surveyed the industry for a third time. I sent questionnaires to shareware authors, disk vendors, and BBSs. The objective of these surveys is to determine the current state of the shareware industry, to learn how shareware authors do business, to identify the differences between successful and unsuccessful authors, and to track any changes in how shareware is distributed.

This chapter summarizes the answers received in response to the 1993 surveys. However, these surveys cover many more areas than can be discussed in the space available here. For example, the 1992 survey results, which were published as an ASCII text file, resulted in a file that was over 200K in size. Each chapter in this book is about 50K. I will, however, cover all the key points and provide a general overall summary of each survey. The complete results will be included on the 1994 mailing list update disk (see chapter 17).

Shareware author survey

This section provides the results of the 1993 survey of shareware authors. For the previous two surveys, I used an author mailing list compiled from a list given to me by a vendor in 1990. I updated it as I found the addresses of new authors. But I started to wonder if the results were consistent from year to year because I was surveying the same authors year after year. I needed information from a new group of authors in order to feel that I was getting valid results. In 1993 I started over with a fresh, new mailing list that was based on a CD-ROM publisher's mailing list of over 2,000 authors. This list was combined with the ASP author mailing list. As a result, the survey forms were mailed to all ASP authors plus 800 nonASP authors. The change in the mailing list had no effect on the results of the surveys. The results from the 1993 surveys remained consistent with those from past years.

At the time the data for the 1993 survey was tabulated, I had received 225 completed survey forms. This is about the same number of responses I've received in the past. There are 27 questions, but some authors didn't answer all questions. I have divided the results into five groups based on authors' annual sales (see TABLE 16-1). The distribution of authors among the various sales levels was about the same as in past years with the exception of groups three and four. In past surveys, groups three and four had about equal numbers of authors, with group three being slightly larger. For example, in the 1990 survey, group three had 75 authors and group four 62 authors. In this year's survey, group four is about 30% larger and group three about 30% smaller than they've typically been in the past. I believe the reason for the higher number of authors in group four is that a large number of the surveys returned by ASP members were from authors who had just started their shareware business in 1992. Because of the change in the mailing list, ASP members were more heavily represented in the 1993 author survey.

Table 16-1   Authors broken down by 1992 annual sales.

	Sales level	1993 Number of authors	1990 Number of authors
Group 1	Over $50,000	20	20
Group 2	$10,000 to $50,000	36	32
Group 3	$2,000 to $10,000	50	85
Group 4	$0 to $2,000	102	63
Group 5	Not available	17	27
Total number of surveys returned		225	210

I would expect that a mailing list provided by any shareware disk vendor or CD-ROM publisher would be missing many of the authors who had recently started their shareware businesses. One of the most difficult problems a new author faces is to get the names and addresses of disk vendors, CD-ROM publishers, BBSs, and others who sell and distribute shareware disks (that's why there is a vendor/BBS mailing list on the disk included with this book). As a result of not being able to easily get a complete mailing list of disk vendors, it usually takes a year or so for a new program to get into wide distribution, and thus new shareware authors wouldn't immediately show up on a vendor's mailing list.

Background information

The first part of the survey asked authors to provide background information about themselves and their companies. This information is summarized in TABLE 16-2. The average annual sales figures for each group are showing some growth since last year. For example, the average sales figure for group one has increased by 10% in the past year and that for group two has increased by 7%.

Table 16-2   Background information on authors and publishers.

	Group 1	**Group 2**	**Group 3**	**Group 4**	**Group 5**
1993 average annual sales	$465,465	$24,759	$3,964	$588	n/a
1990 average annual sales	$423,150	$23,134	$3,802	$318	n/a
1993 average number of years in business	4.2	3.6	2.6	1.7	4.7
1990 average number of years in business	4.5	3.6	2.9	2.1	4.5
1993 range of years in business	.3–9	1.2–9	.25–8	.25–7	.5–9
1993 average number of programs published	11.5	4.9	2.0	2.2	6.5
Range of programs published	1–64	1–30	1–6	1–15	1–9

It's interesting to note that the authors in group one have been in business about the same number of years as the authors in group one had been in 1990. You'd think that this number would increase over time. What happened is that the authors responding to the 1993 survey were nearly a totally different group than those who had responded to the previous two surveys. You can also see that the 1.7 average number of years in business for group one is significantly lower than it was in 1990. This reflects the larger number of new authors who responded to the 1993 survey.

The shareware industry is different

The numbers for the overall average annual sales and median sales for all shareware authors show an interesting and unique characteristic of the shareware industry. The 1993 survey shows the average sales to be $46,500 per author. The median (half of the authors are above this level of sales and half are below it) is $2,400. These numbers are consistent with past years, although the median has dropped each year, reflecting the increased number of new shareware authors who have released their first programs. What the difference between these two numbers means is that a few authors are selling a lot of software and pulling the average up, while there are a large number of authors who sell very little software.

The shareware industry is unique because it's an industry in which you can have essentially no sales and still stay in business. It costs very little to stay in business as a shareware author. For example, many of the author surveys show authors who have been in business for several years but have not received more than 20 or 25 registrations. There's no other industry in which you can keep your business running with sales of only $200 per year. In other industries, you either make it and are financially successful, or you go out of business within two or three years.

It could be that many of these authors are running their business as a hobby, and they don't care how much money they make. But, from the messages I see on Compuserve, there are a significant number of authors who want to be financially successful and who aren't achieving that goal. What would happen to these authors in any other industry? They'd either find a way to be successful—by changing their product, by improving their marketing, by increasing their distribution, etc.—or they'd go out of business. Most new businesses don't survive. Over 80% go out of business after a couple of years. In shareware that isn't true. What happens is that unsuccessful authors hang on forever; they blame their lack of success on the "fact" that shareware doesn't work anymore, and they do very little to find out the real reasons for their lack of success.

One of the characteristics of owning your own business is that you'll fail. Most successful business owners have a string of failures behind them. Don't get caught in the "shareware trap" of blaming your lack of registrations on users. If you aren't selling as much software as you want to be selling, then find out why and do something to change your situation.

Survey questions and answers

Following are the answers to some of the key questions on the 1993 author survey.

The first question on the survey asked "For your top three selling programs, provide the registration price, whether or not the program is a Windows program, the year the program was first released, and the type of software." (Because of the low number of responses for some categories of software, the pricing information might not truly reflect the market.)

Tables 16-3 and 16-4 summarize the answers to this question. Two interesting trends are that the average registration price authors charge has been becoming more and more similar among groups two, three, and four, and it has dropped significantly since 1990. In 1990 the authors in group four were charging over $21.00 less for their software than those in group two. As you can see in TABLE 16-3, there is now less than a $6.00 difference.

Table 16-3   Summary of shareware registration fees in 1993.

	Group 1	Group 2	Group 3	Group 4	Group 5
Number of programs for which information was reported	49	80	90	183	36
1993 average registration	$60.53	$36.14	$32.67	$30.40	$33.44
1990 average registration	$58.50	$57.50	$40.50	$26.20	$59.40
Range of registration fees	$15–$250	$5–$149	$10–$300	$5–$495	$10–$250
# of Windows programs	9	9	16	37	3
% of Windows programs	18%	11%	18%	20%	1%

In 1990 the average registration fee for groups two, three, and four was $38.93. In the 1993 survey that has dropped to $32.28. Group-one authors show very little change in the average registration price they charge. In the 1990 survey, group-one authors charged an average of $58.50 for their software. In the 1993 survey, that had increased to $60.53.

During this same time period, there has been a strong downward pressure on business software prices. In particular, introductory prices for retail software and the availability of competitive upgrades have pushed the consumer's perception of what software should cost downward. For example, when Microsoft introduced Access (a database), they made it available for an introductory price of $99.00. It is a product that has a list price of $495 that would normally have sold in the range of $250 to $300. Many software publishers offer competitive upgrades that let you buy a $300 product for $79 if you provide proof that you already own a competing product. In most cases, software publishers are very liberal in allowing almost anyone to get the competitive upgrade price.

Table 16-4 provides a breakdown, by type of software and by group, of the registration prices authors are charging. It shows that programming tools and business software tend to be the higher-priced types of software. Business software, however, is a much larger market and publishers of business software sell a lot more software than publishers of programming tools. Business software, however, is the one category that has shown the

Table 16-4 Summary of shareware registration fees in 1993, by type of software.

	Group 1	Group 2	Group 3	Group 4	Group 5	1993 Average	1990 Average
Number of programs for which information was reported	49	80	90	183	36		
# of business programs	23	16	17	6	1		
Avg. regist.	$44.17	$32.44	$53.41	$98.66	$34.00	$48.71	$72.53
# of utility programs	25	13	12	12	10		
Avg. regist.	$22.37	$34.30	$32.25	$41.00	$19.90	$28.82	$31.83
# game programs	13	12	7	3	3		
Avg. regist.	$19.85	$21.83	$19.00	$38.33	$21.67	$29.75	$21.36
# communication programs	3	4	2	1	2		
Avg. regist.	$31.67	$92.50	$29.50	$24.00	$31.00	$50.83	$64.77
# programming programs	16	5	1	4	0		
Avg. regist.	$62.87	$27.60	$90.00	$50.00		$55.15	$40.37
# w.p. programs	6	4	1	3	1		
Avg. regist.	$39.00	$22.50	$80.00	$91.00	$25.00	$46.80	$39.92
# spreadsheet programs	0	0	0	1	0		
Avg. regist.				$39.00		$39.00	$35.00
# database programs	5	9	4	1	2		
Avg. regist.	$30.00	$45.00	$74.00	$49.00	$54.50	$48.05	$32.61
# graphics programs	0	1	7	2	2		
Avg. regist.		$30.00	$25.00	$35.00	$137.50	$45.83	$38.00
# educational programs	23	3	10	1	3		
Avg. regist.	$23.43	$28.50	$20.20	$49.00	$33.33	$25.01	$19.85
# home programs	14	11	3	5	4		
Avg. regist.	$24.14	$25.00	$33.33	$36.80	$25.00	$25.56	$34.17
# other programs	7	4	1	0	4		
Avg. regist.	$27.85	$25.00	$20.00		$52.50	$32.81	$48.22
# Windows utility programs	12	5	4	5	2		
Avg. regist.	$45.25	$19.00	$15.00	$44.00	$12.50	$33.67	n/a

Table 16-4   Continued.

	Group 1	Group 2	Group 3	Group 4	Group 5	1993 Average	1990 Average
# Windows utility programs	12	5	4	5	2		
Avg. regist.	$45.25	$19.00	$15.00	$44.00	$12.50	$33.67	n/a
# Windows business programs	4	2	1	3	0		
Avg. regist.	$51.00	$27.00	$80.00	$73.00		$55.70	n/a
# Windows home programs	4	0	3	0	1		
Avg. regist.	$24.45		$22.00		$5.00	$21.11	n/a

most dramatic decline in registration prices. In the 1990 survey, the average registration price for business software was $72.53. In the 1993 survey it was $48.71.

The games category shows a trend that has continued from year to year; typically the least successful game authors charge more for their software.

Registration incentives

The next question on the survey asked "Which of the following do you provide to registered users?" This question then listed the items shown in the left column of TABLE 16-5.

Overall, the responses to this question show that printed manuals, a current version of the software, and user support are by far the most common benefits offered to registered users. Be careful in how you interpret this information, however. There is more to registration incentives than just offering the things listed in TABLE 16-5. I've noticed a trend among shareware authors to look for the "magic" registration incentive that will make lots of users send them money. There is no such registration incentive, and if you focus all of your attention on registration incentives, you're looking in the wrong direction.

Remember what users said in chapter 4. They want a quality program that's useful to them. That's not something an author survey can measure—I think all authors would say they were producing a quality program that people need. Although they are important, the incentives listed in TABLE 16-5 are secondary to producing a quality program that people need. What that means is that most people do not register shareware to get the printed manual and technical support; these have become things that are expected in the software industry. In other words, these things don't

Table 16-5 Summary of registration incentives offered by most authors.

	Group 1	Group 2	Group 3	Group 4	Group 5
Current version	16	27	44	44	15
Printed manual	17	23	25	16	8
Free phone support	18	20	31	18	8
Photocopied manual	9	2	6	12	2
Newsletter	8	4	3	3	7
Other	7	5	12	15	5
Free updates	5	13	13	25	6
Copies of other shareware programs	5	4	7	11	5
Free copies of other software	3	7	11	10	3
Quick reference card	1	1	4	3	2
Source code	1	3	1	6	1
Commissions	0	2	3	2	0

specifically encourage users to register. Users won't buy software that doesn't offer a manual and technical support.

Technical support

To find out how authors handle technical support, the survey presented a list of options that could be checked off. These are shown in the left-hand column of TABLE 16-6. The second item on the list, Registered Users Only, indicates the number of authors who provide support only to registered users. The statistics show a trend that has been true in all past surveys. The more successful authors tend to provide support for anyone who calls. Successful authors have found that technical support calls from unregistered users can be turned into registrations. The key to this approach, however, is that you need to be able to accept credit cards. Often you can take callers' orders while they're talking to you and feeling good about all the help you've provided. If you have to ask them to send a check, they generally won't do it. Many authors who aren't set up to accept credit cards have found it to be worthwhile to send the software and include a bill. They have found that almost everyone will pay money that's due.

The answers in the Other category in TABLE 16-6 were mostly from authors who used CompuServe, a BBS, or Internet to provide support.

Table 16-6 Summary of methods used to provide technical support.

	Group 1	Group 2	Group 3	Group 4	Group 5
Supports anyone who calls	14	23	39	37	7
Supports registered users only	4	5	6	15	7
Support available by phone	19	28	35	35	12
Support by mail only	0	2	5	10	1
Provides 800 number	1	5	1	0	1
Support one 900 number	0	1	0	0	0
Other support methods	5	4	13	18	5

Advertising

Advertising continues to get low marks from shareware authors (see TABLE 16-7). Although the authors in group one find advertising to be somewhat effective, the authors in all other groups give it a very low rating. When you look at the numbers behind the average rating for the value of advertising, you'll see something interesting. In each group a few authors rated advertising very high, giving it nines and tens, as you can see on the range line of TABLE 16-7. The other authors generally gave it very low marks. What this tells me is that the authors who gave it high ratings have either learned how to use advertising effectively or they've hired someone who knows how to create good advertising, such as an advertising agency.

Table 16-7 Summary of how authors rate the value of advertising. The lower the number, the less effective authors felt advertising to be.

	Group 1	Group 2	Group 3	Group 4	Group 5
# of authors who have advertised	16	17	16	12	7
Value of advertising (on scale of 1-10)	5.0	2.7	2.6	1.8	2.3
Range of answers given	3–10	1–7	1–5	1–4	1–7

Creating effective advertising is an art that, in many cases, requires a lot of trial and error. Many of the authors wrote comments on their survey form that said something like "I tried running an ad in *PC Magazine* and didn't sell anything." Successful advertising requires more than running one ad in one magazine. In most cases, a computer magazine is the wrong place for a small software publisher to advertise anyway. Typically, specialty magazines are the most cost-effective. Also, keep in mind that not all software products can be effectively sold using magazine advertising. For some products, shareware is the most effective marketing tool available, while other products sales can be increased by using advertising, direct mail, catalogs, or even direct sales. This is one area for which there are no clear-cut answers until you've tried various means to promote your software, and have seen which work the best.

Press releases

The best form of advertising is free advertising. Many authors tell me that their first big break came when one of the big computer magazines reviewed their software. Yet the surveys continue to show, year after year, that relatively few shareware authors send out press releases. Table 16-8 shows that only 68 authors (28% of the authors surveyed) have sent out a press release. The survey also asked those who had sent out press releases whether they had seen an increase in sales as a result. On the average, less than half the authors had seen an increase in sales they could attribute to a press release. What does this say?

First, keep in mind that the only way you'll get free publicity is by letting the press know about your software. Just having your software distributed as shareware won't result in the press noticing it. The best way to tell them about your software is to send them a press release.

But, from TABLE 16-8, it appears that half of the shareware authors feel that press releases haven't resulted in any additional sales. That sounds about right. About half the time I send out press releases, nothing happens. That's why I continue to send out press releases. There are many situations in which your press release will be ignored by the entire industry, and then, six months later, when you announce a new upgrade, everyone

Table 16-8 Summary showing the number of authors who send out press releases and the number who felt their press releases resulted in additional sales.

	Group 1	Group 2	Group 3	Group 4	Group 5
Sent out press releases	11	18	5	13	6
Get additional sales as a result of a press release	8	7	7	2	4

is interested. (This is assuming, of course, that you write quality press releases that look good and are readable, concise, and complete.) For example, if you send out a press release at the same time that Microsoft makes a big announcement, it will be completely ignored. Two months later, however, the same press release might get a lot of attention. What this means is that you need to be persistent.

Distribution

One of the keys to success in shareware is getting your shareware into the hands of as many users as possible. Do this by sending your disks to distributors and BBSs. In 1990 my survey showed that one of the biggest problems authors had was that they weren't sending their disks to enough distributors. While the group-one authors were sending disks to an average of 268 distributors, the authors in the other groups were sending disks to an average of only 60 distributors. In the 1992 survey the numbers for groups two through four increased. In 1993, authors across the board for all groups sent disks to an average of 300 vendors.

One of the changes that has contributed to this increase is that the ASP now offers a disk distribution service. ASP author members can send one copy of their program to the monthly ASP disk distribution service and it will be sent to every ASP disk vendor and BBS. The costs are then divided among the authors who participated in that month's mailing. While the other shareware professional associations, such as STAR, don't offer this type of service, it appears that they will in the future.

An area that has been changing is the speed with which a shareware disk gets into distribution and starts generating registrations. In the 1990 survey (covering the previous year, 1989), authors were reporting that it was taking up to 36 weeks from the time they sent disks to distributors to the time they started receiving registrations. In 1993, that number dropped to 4–5 weeks. Table 16-9 provides a comparison, by group, between 1989 and 1993.

One of the reasons for this decrease is that BBSs are generating more registrations than they have in the recent past, although catalog vendors

Table 16-9   Comparison between 1989 and 1993, showing how long it took to start receiving registrations.

	Group 1	Group 2	Group 3	Group 4	Group 5
1989 average time (weeks)	9	34	36	26	24
1993 average time (weeks)	4.3	5.1	4.7	6.1	5.3
1993 range (weeks)	1–12	0–18	1–12	1–24	1–12

still dominate as the best channel for generating registrations. As more users get modems with speeds of 9600 baud and higher, it has become easier for them to get software from BBSs. Programs that used to take 30 minutes to download at 2400 baud can be downloaded in under 10 minutes at 9600 baud. As the cost of high-speed modems continues to come down I expect that the importance of BBSs will increase.

The survey asked authors to rate how effective various methods of shareware distribution are at generating registrations. The results are shown in TABLE 16-10. As you can see, catalog vendors get high marks and retail racks are rated as the worst source of registrations. Keep in mind, however, that retail racks have been around for only a very short time. I think the retail rack rating will improve in the future as consumers gain a better understanding of how shareware works.

Table 16-10 Authors' ratings of how effective various methods of distribution are at generating registrations.

	Group 1	Group 2	Group 3	Group 4	Group 5
Catalogs	7.0	7.5	6.2	n/a	n/a
Direct to users	6.4	2.2	3.2	n/a	n/a
BBSs	5.6	5.7	4.5	n/a	n/a
CIS/GEnie	5.4	4.6	4.9	n/a	n/a
Included in magazines & books	4.6	3.1	3.4	n/a	n/a
CD-ROM	4.1	2.6	2.6	n/a	n/a
Vendors with disk-based catalogs	3.6	3.2	3.2	n/a	n/a
Retail racks	2.7	2.4	2.3	n/a	n/a

Permission required

Some authors require that vendors receive written permission from them before they can distribute the authors' shareware. This requirement has become more widely used since the introduction of shareware on retail racks. Some authors don't want their software distributed on retail racks at all and others like to closely monitor how various rack vendors are presenting shareware. Table 16-11 shows the number of authors in each group who require various types of vendors to obtain written permission from them before the vendors can distribute the authors' shareware.

The top line of TABLE 16-11 shows that 35% of shareware authors don't require anyone to have written permission. Anyone may distribute their

Table 16-11   Number of authors who require various types of vendors to have written permission before distributing the authors' programs.

	Group 1	Group 2	Group 3	Group 4	Group 5	% of total
All vendors can freely distribute	9	12	23	22	8	35%
All rack vendors must have permission	8	18	14	15	5	27%
All CD-ROM catalogs must have permission	2	8	11	15	3	17%
Only nonASP rack vendors must have permission	4	10	9	12	2	17%
Only nonASP CD-ROM publishers must have permission	2	8	11	14	2	16%
User groups must have permission	2	5	7	10	2	11%
Noncommercial groups must have permission	2	6	6	10	2	11%
BBSs must have permission	1	3	3	5	2	6%
All ASP vendors must have permission	1	1	2	2	1	3%
Other must have permission	1	3	3	4	3	6.2%

shareware, as long as they meet the requirements given in the author's distribution license.

Table 16-11 also shows that 27% of shareware authors require that rack vendors have written permission, and 24% require that CD-ROM publishers receive permission before including the authors' programs on a CD-ROM. NonASP rack and nonASP CD-ROM publishers are listed separately because some authors allow ASP vendors to distribute their software without written permission, but require all others to get written permission. This can be done because the ASP has a set of requirements that vendor members must comply with. Most authors find that vendors who meet these requirements are acceptable and won't cause problems for the author.

One of the reasons some authors want rack vendors and CD-ROM publishers to get written permission is that these authors charge a royalty when their software is distributed by either of these methods. Most of the rack vendors who pay royalties just started paying royalties in 1993, so it's too early to get much in the way of hard figures on the impact rack vendor royalties are having on the industry.

Useful software

Authors were asked to list the programs they found most useful in their businesses. The following is a list of the programs most frequently mentioned. The number to the right of each program shows the number of times that a program was mentioned.

WordPerfect	20
Quicken	16
Word for Windows	15
MS Word	13
Excel	14
TAPCIS	9
Borland C++	8
PKZip	8
QEdit	8
PC-File	7
PC-Write:	7
CopyQM	6
Windows 3.1	6
Access	5
Filemaker (Mac)	5
Label Pro	5

Useful publications and books

The survey also asked each author to list the magazines or books they've found most useful to helping them run their businesses. The following is a list of the most frequently mentioned magazines and books. The number to the right of each publication shows how many times it was mentioned.

Writing & Marketing Shareware (early version of this book) by Steve Hudgik	15
The Shareware Book by Bob Schenot	11
ASPects (ASP monthly newsletter)	8
Computer Shopper (magazine)	5
PC Magazine	5
Shareware Magazine	5
PC Week (magazine)	4
$hareware Marketing $ystem (on-disk newsletter)	3
Promoting High Tech Products by Dan Janel	3

Advice for authors

The final question on each survey asked the authors to provide some general advice for other shareware authors. The answers authors have given in response to this question haven't changed much over the years. Here are a few samples from the 1993 survey:

"Do a program that people really need."
— Author with $212,000 in sales for 1992

"Develop applications used every day! Windows. Not utilities."
— Author with $62,000 in sales for 1992

"Talk to experienced authors."
— Author with $75,000 in sales for 1992

"Distribute your programs far and wide."
— Author with $250,000 in sales for 1992

"Join ASP, find a niche, work like hell."
— Author with $112,000 in sales for 1992

"The usual advice."
— Author with $118,000 in sales for 1992

"Make the program easy to use, easy to edit, and provide support to anyone who asks."
— Author with $55,000 in sales for 1992

"Be able to provide support, and lots of it."
— Author with $165,000 in sales for 1992

"Find a niche, constantly improve your product."
— Author with $155,000 in sales for 1992

"Produce commercial quality work."
— Author with $38,000 in sales for 1992

"Three things: Marketing, Quality, and Distribution."
— Author with well over $1,000,000 in sales for 1992

Shareware disk distributor survey

This survey was sent to 400 shareware disk distributors. A total of 60 survey forms were returned. This is about the same number that were returned in previous years.

Background

Table 16-12 provides background information on the disk vendors who responded to the survey. It shows that all 60 vendors carry software for IBM-compatible computers and six of them also carry Macintosh software. This ratio has remained unchanged since 1989. Types of computers that fall into the Other category are Atari, Apple II, and Commodore. In 1989, ten distributors were carrying software for one of these three types of computers. In 1993 only three were, and Atari software represented nearly all their sales.

In 1992, distributors were carrying an average of 2,292 MS-DOS titles in their library, a number that has been steadily increasing every year. The average distributor sold 5,023 MS-DOS disks per month in 1992.

There is one major component that is missing from this survey, however. None of the major vendors who are selling shareware on retail racks responded to the survey. Some of the vendors who responded to the survey (shown in TABLE 16-12) reported that they also sold disks in their own store-front operations, so there is a small retail component shown in TABLE 16-12. However, the rumors about shareware rack vendors who sell hundreds of thousands of disks every month are neither confirmed nor disproved by this survey. And the impact of the retail marketing channel is not included in the results of this survey.

Table 16-12 Background information on the disk vendors who responded to the 1993 Shareware Industry Survey.

#/type of vendors	# of retail vendors	# who pay royalties on racks	CD-ROM Publ.	Avg. # of titles	Avg. # of disks sold
IBM, 60	15	4	8	2,292	5,023
Mac, 6	2	1	1	264	847
Other, 3	0	0	0	233	105

One interesting bit of background information concerns vendors who sell shareware disks at flea markets and computer shows. These vendors report that they sell an average of 9,300 disks per month, almost twice the industry average.

Best-selling shareware

The survey asked vendors to rank how well various types of shareware disks sell. This ranking shows the type of software shareware users are buying and thus which types of programs most people are interested in purchasing. Table 16-13 shows the rankings, with the best-selling software listed at the top of the list. The number to the right of each category shows

Table 16-13 Best-selling types of shareware disks.

Type of program	Rating
Games	1.64
Education	3.42
Business	4.26
Home	5.07
Utilities	5.44
Graphics	5.72
Clip art	5.90
Windows utilities	6.27
Word processing	6.33
Windows home	6.68
Windows business	7.28
Database	7.32
Spreadsheets	7.57
Communications	7.74
Programming	7.80

the average rating given to each type of software by vendors, based on a scale of 1 to 10.

This ranking shows one possible problem area in shareware. Educational shareware is ranked as the second-best selling type of software. However, in the author survey, authors who make educational software generally report getting few registrations. People are using this type of software, but they aren't registering it. At this point, all I can say is that it will require further study to determine the reasons why there is this problem with educational software. However, you shouldn't conclude absolutely that people simply don't register educational shareware. Perhaps people don't register educational shareware because of the way it's currently being presented to them. This means that there's an opportunity for someone who takes the time to understand the educational market and solve the problem to make a lot of money.

Getting your software distributed

As more authors release greater numbers of shareware programs, it's becoming more difficult to get software into a vendor's catalog. As TABLE 16-12 showed, vendors carry an average of 2,292 DOS programs in their catalogs, and they report receiving an average of 57 new disks every month. Table 16-14 shows the percentage of programs that make it into various forms of distribution and the reasons why some shareware programs are rejected by vendors. The number shown on the For Sale in Stores line is based on information from the vendors in the survey who also have a

Table 16-14 Percentage of programs that vendors accept for distribution and reasons why vendors don't accept some software for their catalogs.

Type of distribution	Percentage of programs accepted
CD-ROM	55%
Mail order catalog	52%
BBS	51%
For sale in stores	24%
Shareware racks	1%
Percentage of programs evaluated	
Not good enough to distribute	27%
Software duplicates what's already in the library and is thus not needed	24%
Outstanding software	12%
Crippled software	7%

store-front operation. They typically report that about half the disks they accept into their catalog are put out in the retail store part of their operation. However, if a customer requests a disk that is in the catalog but not in the store, the vendor is usually able to sell a copy.

In general, only about half the programs vendors receive are placed in their catalogs. However, this number varies greater from vendor to vendor. There are some vendors who report that everything they receive goes in their catalog. Others, usually the larger vendors, report that as few as 10% of the disks they receive each month are acceptable.

Table 16-15 shows the average amount of time it takes for vendors to get a new program into their catalogs. A couple of vendors also reported that they have retail racks. They reported selling only an average of 45 disks a month from the retail racks, however, so racks aren't a significant

Table 16-15 Average time (in weeks) that it takes to get various types of software into distribution.

	Catalogs	Retail racks
Great program	4.1 weeks	6.8 weeks
Average program	4.5 weeks	7.7 weeks
Update	3.2 weeks	5.4 weeks

factor in the results of this survey. (As I mentioned, none of the big-name retail-rack vendors responded to the survey.) I included all the retail rack figures in TABLE 16-15 because it shows that it takes longer to get a program onto a retail rack than it does to get it into a catalog.

What is interesting about the information vendors reported concerning the time it takes to get new disks into distribution is that a couple of vendors reported that it took longer to get an update into distribution than it did to get a new program into distribution. One vendor reported that it took only 8 weeks to get a new program into the catalog, but 24 weeks to get an update into it. This bothers me. There is usually a very good reason that an update has been issued. Many times the update fixes a bug or other problem. Vendors who take three times longer to get an update into distribution than it takes for the original program are hurting both their customers and shareware authors. This delay is generally the symptom of a vendor who is not customer-focused, but has instead a "take the money and run" focus. I generally don't let this kind of vendor distribute my software, and you won't find them on the vendor mailing list included with this book.

Shareware distribution on BBSs

BBSs were part of the early days of shareware and were crucial to the early success of the shareware industry. However, as catalog vendors started selling larger numbers of disks, BBSs lost their importance for some types of software. Authors began saying that only small programs that could be downloaded quickly would do well on BBSs. This is changing. As more users get faster modems and as more new computers come with modems installed at the factory, users are starting to get more and more shareware from BBSs. The 1993 survey of BBSs showed that the largest increase in the distribution of shareware was through BBSs. BBS sysops reported a 70% increase in download activity over what it had been the previous year.

Table 16-16 shows the number of programs carried by the 123 BBS sysops who responded to the 1993 survey. Several sysops reported having over 200,000 DOS programs available, and two reported having over 300,000. Although these numbers include public-domain software and freeware, and also tiny special-purpose programs, I find it difficult to believe that all these programs are still supported by their authors. One of the biggest problems I've had with BBSs is that some of them refuse to remove old versions of my software. My guess is that the sysops reporting such large numbers of programs have either a lot of old versions, or a lot of duplicate software.

Table 16-17 shows the download activity reported by 118 sysops. The difference between the average and the median numbers show that there are a few very large BBSs and a large number of smaller systems.

To determine what kinds of software users are getting from BBSs, the survey asked sysops to rate various types of software based on the download

Table 16-16   Number of titles available on BBSs.

	MD-DOS	Macintosh	Other
Number of BBSs carrying this type software	123	34	29
Highest number of programs available for downloading	386,000	13,000	23,000
Lowest number of programs available for downloading	39	5	4
Average number of programs available for downloading	26,685	1,590	2,799

Table 16-17   Number of downloads per month.

	MS-DOS	Macintosh	Other
Number of BBSs answered this question	118	28	25
Highest number of downloads per month	160,000	4000	6000
Lowest number of downloads per month	30	0	2
Average number of downloads per month	10,784	491	808
Median number of downloads per month	1,200	100	100

volume for each. The results are shown in TABLE 16-18. As with disk vendors, games top the list and programming tools are at the bottom. The middle for both vendor and BBS lists show some similarity in the typical major commercial applications; spreadsheets, word processing, and databases rank low. One interesting difference is that Windows software is much more popular on BBSs than it is in shareware disk catalogs.

Educational software was not included as a separate category on the BBS survey but was included with home-use software. I cannot, therefore, draw any conclusions concerning educational software from the BBS survey.

Table 16-18   Types of software most frequently downloaded, based on a scale of 1 to 10. One represent the most frequently downloaded software, and 10 represents software that never gets downloaded.

Type of software	Rating based on download volume
Games	2.1
Utilities	3.7
Windows business software	4.2
Graphics	4.9
Windows home software	5.3
Communications	5.5
Other*	5.8
Home	5.9
Business	6.2
Windows, utilities	6.9
Word processing	7.1
Data base	7.2
Programming tools	7.7
Spreadsheet	8.3

*Adult software and OS/2 software was identified as being equally popular in the Other category.

17
Resource directory

This chapter is divided into two sections. The first lists resources you can use to learn more about running your shareware business. I've had several authors tell me they were unable to find anything, other than this book, to help them learn what they need to know to make their business grow. Throughout this book I've mentioned available resources. But there are many other resources available I haven't discussed. Many of them are listed here. One of the best resources that isn't listed is your local library. It's just like shareware! You can try a book before going to the book store to buy it.

The second section provides an alphabetical listing of suppliers for the material, equipment, and services you might need to help you produce and market your software. Although I've used many of these vendors, I'm not endorsing any of them. I'm only providing a list you can use when looking for suppliers. I can say that I know of no problems or of anyone who has had a problem with the companies listed here. However, you should contact these suppliers and make your own decisions concerning quality, service, and value. For more information, contact each supplier and ask for a copy of their catalog.

Educational resources

This section lists books, audio tapes, and other publications and resources for information about the shareware industry and how to be successful as a shareware author. All of the material listed here is available through mail order. Prices are listed when they were available. If there is no price listed, contact the supplier/publisher for more information.

Summer Shareware Seminar

If I had to recommend one event for shareware authors to attend, it would be the Summer Shareware Seminar (SSS). The SSS is more than a seminar; it's a three-day shareware event. It's the one most valuable source of information about all aspects of the shareware industry. The Summer Shareware Seminar is held on a Friday, Saturday, and Sunday in June of each year. For more information, write to:

Summer Shareware Seminar
c/o Public Brand Software
P.O. Box 51315
Indianapolis, IN 46251

The Summer Shareware Seminar brochure isn't available until April, so you might not receive anything until then.

Summer Shareware Seminar audio tapes

If you're unable to attend the SSS, you can still hear every word from every session. The entire SSS is recorded each year and made available on audio cassette tapes. If you'd like to catch up on what you've missed in past years, tapes are still available for both the 1992 and 1993 SSSs.

The SSS tapes provide high-quality audio that has been recorded directly from the sound system in each room using professional equipment. Microphones were used for each panelist, and were also placed in the audience, so you'll be able to clearly hear the questions and comments made by nearly everyone.

The 1992 SSS had excellent sessions on registration incentives, copyrights, producing quality software, how to work with the press, and a really great session called "Hints From The Pros," in which some of the big names in shareware explain what they did to become successful.

The 1993 SSS covered the hot topic of rack distribution, how to get your software noticed, the legal aspects of shareware, and international sales. There was even a panel of retail software publishers who talked about what they look for when they license software from shareware authors.

Both the 1992 and 1993 sets of SSS tapes consist of 11 two-hour tapes. The cost of each set of tapes is $79.95, including shipping. Add $12.00 for air-mail shipment outside North America. You can order them from:

HomeCraft
P.O. Box 974
Tualatin, OR 97062
CIS ID: 71450,254

Summer Shareware Seminar transcripts

If you don't want to purchase the complete set of SSS tapes, a written transcript of eight of the key sessions from the 1992 SSS is available as an ASCII text file. (Please note that these transcripts are on the disk included with this book.) The cost is $12.00 and the transcripts are available from:

HomeCraft
P.O. Box 974
Tualatin, OR 97062
CIS ID: 71450,254

At this time there are no plans to transcribe the 1993 or future SSS sessions, due to the high cost of creating transcripts.

$hareware Marketing $ystem

Jim Hood puts out an excellent quarterly publication called the $hareware Marketing $ystem ($M$). It's published on two floppy disks and is available as shareware.

The first floppy disk contains a newsletter with marketing news, tips, ideas, commentary, and general information for shareware authors. The second floppy disk provides a mailing list of over 4,600 shareware disk vendors, computer clubs, magazine editors, and BBS systems. Shareware evaluation copies are available on CompuServe and most major BBS. The cost to register is $49.95 for one issue, or $175 for a one-year subscription. For more information, or to purchase a registered copy, contact:

Jim Hood
P.O. Box 1506
Mercer Island, WA 98040
206-236-0470
CIS ID: 72020,2176

The Shareware Book

This 192-page guide to being a shareware author is available as a shareware disk, giving you a chance to read it before you buy it (sounds like a great idea). It looks at how to be a successful shareware author from a different perspective than this book, and a different perspective can be helpful in clearing up questions in some areas. I recommend trying the shareware version. The cost to register is $19.95 plus shipping and handling. The shareware version can be read only on your computer screen. When you register, you receive a 192-page perfect bound book and a 1.44Mb "author's kit" with tools and data that shareware authors will find useful. For more information, or to order your copy, contact:

Robert Schenot
P.O. Box 117
Portsmouth, NH 03802-0117
603-431-8030

The Proper Care & Feeding of Your News Media

This 80-page book, written by Jerry Olsen, gets to the heart of publicity and media issues for shareware authors. It's a practical, how-to handbook filled to the brim with useful information. It explains how, compared to submissions from most retail product publishers, those from shareware authors are usually woefully inadequate. It then goes on to show you how you can change this for your software and create a media package the press will notice.

The Proper Care & Feeding of Your News Media is available from The Advocate Press for $20 plus $4.50 for shipping and handling in the U.S. (actual shipping costs elsewhere). Copies can be ordered from:

The Advocate Press
1130 S. Michigan Ave., Suite 1816
Chicago, IL 60605
Fax: 312-939-3300

Credit card orders and orders from outside the U.S. and Canada:

Shareable Software International
P.O. Box 59102
Schauburg, IL 60159 USA
800-622-2793
708-397-1221

Books from the Graphic Artists Guild

Graphic artists face many of the same problems faced by shareware authors. They also publish creative work and have to deal with the same legal issues we face. There are two books that might be of particular interest to shareware authors.

A very valuable book is *Making It Legal* by Lee Wilson. The first half of this 272-page book deals with copyrights and trademarks. The second half covers topics such as libel, false advertising, and privacy issues—topics that anyone running a mail order business will find useful. This book costs $18.95.

I also recommend *Licensing Art & Design* by Caryn Leland. This book covers licensing issues, an important topic if you hope to sit back and collect royalties after getting your software onto LCR displays in retail stores.

The cost is $12.95. To order either of these books, or to request a catalog, contact:

The Graphic Artists Guild
11 West 20th St., 8th Floor
New York, NY 10011
212-463-7730

More excellent books

Nolo Press publishes a book that can help you better understand copyrights and other legal matters related to copyrights. The book is called *How to Copyright Software*. For more information and a free catalog, contact:

Nolo Press
950 Parker St.
Berkeley, CA 94710
415-549-1976

There are two other books that I recommend. The first is *How To Publicize High Tech Products and Services* by Dan Janal. Everyone I've talked to who has read this book says that it's excellent. For more information, or to order a copy, call: 800-933-3612. The second book is *How To Price Your Products and Services*, published by the Harvard University Press. Check you local bookstore for this book.

Magazines and periodicals

I assume that you're aware of the computer magazines available, thus they aren't included in this listing. The following magazines are ones you might not know about. They're all related to either shareware, marketing, mail-order businesses, and the use of technology in business. Write and ask for a sample issue of any that you're interested in.

Shareware Magazine
1030D East Duane Ave.
Sunnyvale, CA 94086

Office Systems 94
Box 4097
Woburn, MA 01908
Includes advice for small-and medium-sized businesses and articles about office use of computers and software, in addition to other office-automation equipment.

Software Development Magazine
600 Harrison St.
San Francisco, CA 94107
415-905-2200

Inbound/Outbound
12 West 21 St.
New York, NY 10010
A magazine for people who use technology to build sales and deliver customer service.

Midnight Engineering
1700 Washington Ave.
Rocky Ford, CO 81067
719-254-4558
Information for software entrepreneurs.

Telecomputing
2625 Pennsylvania NE
Albuquerque, NM 87110
505-881-6988
BBS use, products, and services.

PC Techniques
7721 E. Gray Rd., Suite 204
Scottsdale, AZ 85260
602-483-0192
A magazine for software programmers.

Upside
1159B Triton Dr.
Foster City, CA 94404
619-745-2809
A business news magazine for high-tech people and businesses.

C Gazette
1341 Ocean Ave. #257
Santa Monica, CA 90401
213-473-7414
213-479-5472 (fax)

Supplies and services directory

This directory provides addresses for mail-order companies. I also feel it's a good idea to have local sources for some of the materials you need. Should you be in a bind and need something fast, there's nothing better than being able to drive to a supplier and pick up what you need.

This directory isn't intended to be complete. There are many more vendors who supply these services, equipment, and materials. A good place to look for supplies is in *Computer Shopper* magazine. The purpose of this directory is to help you get started when you need to find the suppliers and services you need to run your business. If you have experience with any companies not listed here, please let me know about them so I can add them to this directory.

I have divided this directory into types of materials, equipment, and services, and the categories are listed in alphabetical order.

Advertising and brochure services

Hice & Associates
8586 Monticello Dr.
West Chester, OH 45069

The John F. Swift Co.
17 North Loomis St.
Chicago, IL 60607
312-666-7020

BBS upload service

Andrew M. Saucci, Jr.
641 Koelbel Court
Baldwin, NY 11510-3915
800-538-8461

Bookbinding

See Manual printing.

Bookbinding supplies

Three-ring binders, folders, GBC binding machines, and covers are available from the following two companies:

Vulcan Binder & Cover
P.O. Box 29
Vincent, AL 35178
800-633-4526
205-672-7159 (fax)

American Thermoplastic Co.
622 Second Ave.
Pittsburgh, PA 15219
412-261-6657

Bulk diskettes

Blank and preformatted diskettes, and disk sleeves are available from:

Midwestern Diskette
509 W. Taylor
Creston, IA 50801
800-221-6332

Bulk-mailing service

These are vendors who will handle your bulk mailing for you. For example, you can send them your shareware disk, a set of mailing labels for distributors, and any inserts you want to have included and they'll duplicate, label, package, and bulk mail your disks.

Sunshine Software Services
4255 S. Channel 10 Dr. #38
Las Vegas, NV 89119

AP-JP Enterprises
P.O. Box 399
Islip, NY 11751-0399

Diversified Systems Group
P.O. Box 1114
361 NE Gilman Blvd.
Issaquah, WA 98027
206-392-0900

The following supply bulk-mailing services to other countries:

G-Plex
194 Morris Ave. #7
Holtsville, NY 11742
516-447-9500

Johnson & Hayward
516 West 19th St.
New York, NY 10011
800-521-0800

Business cards

See Stationery.

Catalog printing/production

These companies specialize in printing catalogs. If you have a small manual, they can saddle-stitch it.

Dinner Klein
600 S. Spokane St.
Seattle, WA 98134
206-682-2494

Catalogs America
1840 Michael Faraday Dr.
Reston, VA 22090
703-689-4680

Color printing

This is a company specializing in printing color brochures and flyers.

American Color Printing
1731 N.W. 97th Ave.
Plantation, FL 33322
305-473-4392

Computer supplies

These are suppliers of general computer supplies and equipment.

Inmac
2465 Augustine Dr.
P.O. Box 58031
Santa Clara, CA 95952-8031
800-547-5444

QC Distributors
6011 Westline Dr.
Houston, TX 77036
800-888-2290

Lyben Computer Systems
1150 E. Maplelawn
Troy, MI 48084
313-649-4500

Disk duplication and labeling

These companies supply disk-duplication and labeling services.

FailSafe Media Co.
236 Egidi Dr.
Wheeling, IL 60090
800-537-1919

Ultimate Data Technology
7751 Hickory Ln.
Findlay, OH 45840

Monogram Media, Inc.
206 Parallel St.
Beaver Dam, WI 53916
800-527-2389

Diversified Systems
P.O. Box 1114
361 NE Gilman Blvd.
Issaquah, WA 98027
206-392-0900

Gean & Company
1930 Junction Ave.
San Jose, CA 95131
800-879-9536

Disk-duplication equipment

If you want to do your own duplication, this is where you can buy disk-duplication equipment:

Micro-Technology Concepts, Inc.
258 Johnson Ave.
Brooklyn, NY 11206
718-456-9100

Disk mailers

Flat- and folding-carton disk mailers are available from:

Calumet Carton Co.
P.O. Box 405
16920 State St.
South Holland, IL 60473
708-333-6521
708-333-8540 (fax)

DiskSavers
14023 N. 57th Place
Scottsdale, AZ 85254
800-528-2361

Mail Safe
4340 W. 47th St.
Chicago, IL 60632
800-527-0754

GRA
3800 Monroe Ave.
Pittsford, NY 14534
716-385-2060

Legal services

Help with copyright and trademark problems is available from the following companies:

Herb Kraft
Law Offices of Robert E. Gibson
Suite 210
1020 E. Lafayette St.
Tallahassee, FL 32301

Mark J. Welch
Turner & Beeler, PC
Centerpoint Building
18 Crow Canyon Court, Suite 110
San Ramon, CA 94583
510-837-5656

Mailing lists

Research Projects Corp.
Pomperaug Ave.
Woodbury, CT 06798
800-243-4360

Sunshine Software Services
4255 S. Channel 10 Dr., #38
Las Vegas, NV 89119
Author/shareware user lists.

Apogee Software
4206 Mayflower
Garland, TX 75043
Provides a mailing list of over 800 shareware distributors.

Mailing services

The following companies will handle the distribution of your shareware
disks to vendors and BBSs. At the time of this writing, these companies
were just getting started and I don't know whether they will be successful
or even still in business.

Public Media Services
P.O. Box 2764
Huntsville, AL 35804-2764
800-845-5807
205-757-8664 (fax)

Shareware Distribution Services
P.O. Box 52
El Paso, IL 61738-0052
309-527-8579

Manual printing and binding

Whitehall Printing Co.
1200 S. Willis Ave.
Wheeling, IL 60090
708-541-9290

BookMasters, Inc.
638 Jefferson St.
P.O. Box 159
Ashland, OH 44805
800-537-6727

Camelot Book Factory
39-B Coolidge Ave.
Ormond Beach, FL 32174
904-672-5672

Mailing, international services

Alternative service for overseas bulk shipping are available from:

TNT Mailfast
12560 N.E. Marx
Pacific Business Center, Bldg. 4
Portland, OR 97230
800-558-5555

Office supplies

This category includes folders, binders, paper, and general office supplies.

Visible
3626 Stern Ave.
St. Charles, IL 60174
800-323-0628

RTJ Associates
1601 Paterson Plank Rd.
Secaucus, NJ 07094

Packaging products

Tape, boxes, shrink-wrap machines and supplies, poly bags, and shipping supplies available from:

Chiswick Trading, Inc.
33 Union Ave.
Sudbury, MA 01776-2246
800-225-8708
508-443-8091 (fax)

Data Envelope
490 Division St.
Campbell, CA 95008
408-374-4336

Premiums and incentive gifts

These companies sell custom-imprinted promotional merchandise such as coffee mugs, jackets, pens, and hats. (Also look in your local phone book under Novelties.)

Nelson Marketing
210 Commerce St.
P.O. Box 320
Oshkosh, WI 54902-0320
800-722-5203

Sales Guides, Inc.
10510 N. Port Washington Rd.
Mequon, WI 53092-5500
414-241-3313

Best Impressions
P.O. Box 800
LaSalle, IL 61301
815-223-6263

Printed disk sleeves

Data Envelope
490 Division St.
Campbell, CA 95008
408-374-9720

Printer ribbons (color)

Ramco Computer Supplies
P.O. Box 475
455 Grove
Manteno, IL 60950
800-522-6922

Proofreading

Discover Software
P.O. Box 818
Castroville, TX 78009

Rubber stamps

The following company can provide you with preinked custom and standard stamps:

Shachihata, Inc.
23705 Crenshaw Blvd.
Torrance, CA 90505
213-530-4445

Screen shot conversions to film

Galaxy Graphics, Inc.
P.O. Box 220538
Chantilly, VA 22022
703-802-1111

Desktop Technologies, Inc.
Box 41, County Line Rd.
Boyertown, PA 19512
215-367-7599

Shareware programs

Shareware Tracker
BlueCollar Software
1321 South Route 68
Urbana, OH 43078
For tracking users, registrations, site licenses, shipping, submissions,
expenses, profits, and more. Includes the ASP vendor mailing list.

Super Shareware System
PractiComp
6490 Dubois Rd.
Delaware, OH 43015-8931
614-548-5043
A system for tracking customers, prospects, distributors, contacts,
products, sales, and expenses.

Shipping boxes

Iroquois Products
2220 W. 56th St.
Chicago, IL 60636
800-453-3355

Shrink-wrap machines

Chiswick
33 Union Ave.
Sudbury, MA 01776
800-225-8708

AJM, Inc.
1600 Wyatt Dr. #12
Santa Clara, CA 95054
800-858-4131

Software packaging services

Leahy Press, Inc.
79 River St.
Montpelier, VT 05602
800-639-6011
802-229-5149 (fax)

PakStar USA
2909 Langford Rd., Suite A400
Norcross, GA 30071-1506

Software Packaging Associates
4650 Lake Forest Dr., Suite 580
Cincinnati, OH 45242
513-733-8800

PolyWest Corporation
16018 Adelante Street, Unit C
Irwindale, CA 91702
818-969-8555

Stationery

Letterhead, business cards, envelopes, and mailing labels are available from the following company:

Stationery House
1000 Florida Ave.
Hagerstown, MD 21741
800-638-3033

Index

Order Form for Readers
Requiring a Single 5.25" Disk

This Windcrest/McGraw-Hill software product is also available on a 5.25"/ 1.2MB disk. If you need the software in 5.25" format, simply follow these instructions:

- Complete the order form below. Be sure to include the exact title of the Windcrest/McGraw-Hill book for which you are requesting a replacement disk.

- Make check or money order made payable to *Glossbrenner's Choice.* The cost is $5.00 ($8.00 for shipments outside the U.S.) to cover media, postage, and handling. Pennsylvania residents, please add 6% sales tax.

- Foreign orders: please send an international money order or a check drawn on a bank with a U.S. clearing branch. We cannot accept foreign checks.

- Mail order form and payment to:

    Glossbrenner's Choice
    Attn: Windcrest/McGraw-Hill Disk Replacement
    699 River Road
    Yardley, PA 19067-1965

Your disk will be shipped via First Class Mail. Please allow one to two weeks for delivery.

Windcrest/McGraw-Hill Disk Replacement

Please send me a replacement disk in 5.25"/1.2MB format for the following Windcrest/McGraw-Hill book:

Book Title_____

Name _____

Address_____

City/State/ZIP _____

DISK WARRANTY

This software is protected by both United States copyright law and international copyright treaty provision. You must treat this software just like a book, except that you may copy it into a computer in order to be used and you may make archival copies of the software for the sole purpose of backing up our software and protecting your investment from loss.

By saying "just like a book," McGraw-Hill means, for example, that this software may be used by any number of people and may be freely moved from one computer location to another, so long as there is no possibility of its being used at one location or on one computer while italso is being used at another. Just as a book cannot be read by two different people in two different places at the same time, neither can the software be used by two different people in two different places at the same time (unless, of course, McGraw-Hill's copyright is being violated).

LIMITED WARRANTY

Windcrest/McGraw-Hill takes great care to provide you with top-quality software, thoroughly checked to prevent virus infections. McGraw-Hill warrants the physical diskette(s) contained herein to be free of defects in materials and workmanship for a period of sixty days from the purchase date. If McGraw-Hill receives written notification within the warranty period of defects in materials or workmanship, and such notification is determined by McGraw-Hill to be correct, McGraw-Hill will replace the defective diskette(s). Send requests to:

Customer Service
Windcrest/McGraw-Hill
13311 Monterey Lane
Blue Ridge Summit, PA 17294-0850

The entire and exclusive liability and remedy for breach of this Limited Warranty shall be limited to replacement of defective diskette(s) and shall not include or extend to any claim for or right to cover any other damages, including but not limited to, loss of profit, data, or use of the software, or special, incidental, or consequential damages or other similar claims, even if McGraw-Hill has been specifically advised of the possibility of such damages. In no event will McGraw-Hill's liability for any damages to you or any other person ever exceed the lower of suggested list price or actual price paid for the license to use the software, regardless of any form of the claim.

McGRAW-HILL, INC. SPECIFICALLY DISCLAIMS ALL OTHER WARRANTIES, EXPRESS OR IMPLIED, INCLUDING, BUT NOT LIMITED TO, ANY IMPLIED WARRANTY OF MERCHANTABILITY OR FITNESS FOR A PARTICULAR PURPOSE.

Specifically, McGraw-Hill makes no representation or warranty that the software is fit for any particular purpose and any implied warranty of merchantability is limited to the sixty-day duration of the Limited Warranty covering the physical diskette(s) only (and not the software) and is otherwise expressly and specifically disclaimed.

This limited warranty gives you specific legal rights; you may have others which may vary from state to state. Some states do not allow the exclusion of incidental or consequential damages, or the limitation on how long an implied warranty lasts, so some of the above may not apply to you.

Information about this disk is included in both the appendix of this book and in a file, README.TXT, included on the disk. The appendix describes the different files on the disk and the README.TXT file gives instructions for extracting and installing the files onto your hard disk.

IMPORTANT

Read the Disk Warranty terms on the previous page before opening the disk envelope. Opening the envelope constitutes acceptance of these terms and renders this entire book-disk package nonreturnable except for replacement in kind due to material defect.